0 0 4313

D1341954

WITHDRAWN

Shuttleworth

100759

SHUTTLEWORTH COLLEGE
LIBRARY

Frohne/Pfänder
Poisonous Plants

A Colour Atlas of
Poisonous Plants

A Handbook for Pharmacists, Doctors, Toxicologists, and Biologists

Dietrich Frohne and Hans Jürgen Pfänder, Kiel
With a foreword by Otmar Wassermann, Kiel
Translated from the second German edition by
Norman Grainger Bisset, London

A Wolfe Science Book

Copyright © D. Frohne and H. J. Pfänder, 1983
Published by Wolfe Publishing Ltd, 1984
From the German edition of 'Giftpflanzen – Ein Handbuch für
Apotheker, Ärzte, Toxikologen und Biologen'
© 1983 Wissenschaftliche Verlagsgesellschaft mbH, Stuttgart
Printed in Germany
Separations: time scan, Leinfelden-Echterdingen
Printed by: Passavia AG, 8390 Passau 2
© English text translation, Wolfe Publishing Ltd, 1984
ISBN 0 7234 0839 4

This book is one of the titles in the series of
Wolfe Atlases, containing probably the
world's largest systematic published collection
of diagnostic colour photographs.
For a full list of Atlases in the series, plus
forthcoming titles, please write to
Wolfe Publishing Ltd, Wolfe House,
3 Conway Street, London W1P 6HE.

All rights reserved. The contents of this book, both
photographic and textual, may not be reproduced in any form,
by print, photoprint, phototransparency, microfilm,
microfiche, or any other means, nor may it be included in any
computer retrieval system, without written permission from the
publisher.

Foreword

Since remote antiquity the use of medicinal and poisonous plants has been surrounded by myths – and it still is, even in our own supposedly enlightened era. In scarcely any other field has superstition proved to be so resistant. Through uncritical copying of printed half-truths and misinterpretation of inadequately documented, supposed cases of poisoning, a burden of obsolete and/or nonsensical information has continued to be handed down.

Sensational reporting is of little help to the public, as ill-informed journalists seek to 'enliven their paper with the dead' when they ought instead to inform and explain things objectively. The blessing of the medieval Church procured the widest circulation for herbals which unscrupulously and irresponsibly suggested a cure for every ailment. But paradoxically, the same Church in its fanaticism condemned women – healers and herbalists, who were also often experienced in the use of poisonous and narcotic plants – to be burnt at the stake in their millions.

Great uncertainty in the diagnosis and treatment of plant poisoning is the result not only of incomplete and unclear information about the circumstances of the poisoning, but also, as far as toxic plants are concerned, of the inadequate pharmacological and toxicological training of doctors. But pharmacists as well suffer to an increasingly alarming degree from a lack of knowledge of plants, to say nothing of poisonous plants.

So, there is clearly a need for a comprehensive source of information, embodying the latest knowledge, and including all the essential plant-morphological, pharmacological, toxicological, and therapeutic details in possible cases of poisoning by plants from our surroundings. The authors have many years' experience in giving advice on cases of plant poisoning, and they have even experimented on themselves in order to clear up doubtful assertions. The splendid presentation of this book is worthy of their efforts. This book is sure to be a major aid in the diagnosis and evaluation of poisoning by plants and in putting treatment on a rational basis.

Prof. Otmar Wassermann
Department of Toxicology
Clinical Centre of the
Christian Albrecht University, Kiel

Preface

Next to medicines and household chemicals, plants or parts of plants occupy third place in the statistics of the Poison Information Centres relating to children. Admittedly, serious cases of poisoning – and this is also true for adults – are relatively rare, but with each case the question of the treatment necessary arises anew. Not until the plant involved has been identified with certainty and its toxicity correctly estimated, is it possible to take effective measures or to avoid superfluous therapeutic treatment which may be a considerable burden to the body of the often young patient.

In dealing with such cases of ingestion, during our advisory work we found repeatedly that essential information – concerning both the identification and toxicity of the various plants – is widely dispersed in the literature and is not immediately available to the doctor in charge or to the pharmacist who may be called upon for advice.

Moreover, in the newer books on 'poisonous plants', for the identification the reader is seldom offered more than a simple description of the plant, occasionally supplemented by a more or less adequate photograph of the plant *in situ*. Since in practice usually only parts of the plant (leafy twigs, ripe or unripe fruits, etc.), together with a layman's description of additional characters, are presented, in this book we have chosen a different path.

Characteristic parts of plants that are known as – supposedly or genuinely – poisonous plants are illustrated in colour, and also those whose fruits are harmless but which often give rise to enquiries. Further aids to identification, besides descriptions of the plants, are an identification key for fruits and a compilation of leaf characters illustrated in black and white. Finally, for the first time, microscopical characters, especially those of the epidermis of the fruit wall (pericarp), are here also utilised as a possible means of recognition and differentiation.

To assess how dangerous the plants discussed in the book are, the older literature has been critically evaluated and newer investigations and reports reviewed; and this has led to the inclusion of an extensive bibliography. In some cases, our own re-examination of contradictory assertions has been able to clarify the point, but. other problems are requiring more extensive study.

Along with those plants which are indigenous or naturalised in central (and mostly also western) Europe, we have dealt with the most commonly encountered (cultivated) decorative plants in gardens and parks and the more important house plants.

We are particularly indebted to Prof. O. Wassermann, Department of Toxicology, Centre for Theoretical Clinical Medicine II, Christian Albrecht University, Kiel, for critically reading the manuscript, especially with regard to the toxicological aspects.

We thank Mrs U. Laatzen for help in producing the bibliography and structural formulae and, along with Mr Sommer, pharmacist, in reading the proofs; Mrs I. Pfänder for the fair copy of the manuscript; and Mr D. Christiansen and the late Mr G. Schlue for horticultural assistance.

Thanks are due to the publisher, in particular Dr W. Wessinger and Mr W. Studer, for their pleasant co-operation and ready understanding and acceptance of our wishes and suggestions. The authors would appreciate having their attention drawn to errors, which inevitably must have crept in during the writing of a book for which no comparable models exist, and they would welcome suggestions and improvements.

June 1982   D. Frohne, H. J. Pfänder
Institute for Pharmaceutical Biology
Christian Albrecht University, Kiel

Translator's note

A note on the United Kingdom National Poisons Information Service (N.P.I.S.) has been inserted on p.16. A number of general references in English dealing with poisonous plants in Britain and elsewhere has been added to the list on pp.22 and 23.

Where possible, for those plants occurring wild in the British Isles the English names in the list of recommended names published by the Botanical Society of the British Isles have been given preference [D28]. These names are distinguished in the index by means of an asterisk. The Botanical Society list of names has been adopted by the Ministry of Agriculture and others in the agricultural industry, so that the use of such standard names should in the long run help to lessen possible confusion.

Some plants encountered in veterinary work in Britain and not otherwise mentioned in the book are discussed briefly on p. 232. It is a pleasure to thank Dr D. J. Humphreys, Royal Veterinary College, University of London, for advice on veterinary matters.

N. G. Bisset
Department of Pharmacy, Chelsea College
University of London

Contents

1. Problems arising from poisoning by plants

What in fact are poisonous plants?

Many plants produce chemical compounds that interfere in the metabolism of living organisms, in other words: they can exert – directly or indirectly – toxic actions (see also p.25). A listing of these naturally occurring poisonous substances yields the impressive total of 750, found in more than 1000 plant species (Duke, cited from [K28]). However, the number of actual 'poisonous plants' is very much less, if by this one means those that lead, or have led, to poisoning in man and animals.

It is only a small group of plants that, even after the ingestion of a limited amount of material, gives rise to serious poisoning. The other plants that because of their constituents must be considered toxic are, as a rule, much less dangerous; and they only cause poisoning under certain circumstances that may not always obtain. Finally, there is a third group of poisonous plants which is usually accepted as such but whose members do not contain a well-defined toxic substance or are not the subject of unequivocally documented cases of serious poïsoning.

However, the long-known principle 'Dosis sola facit venenum' is as true for 'poisonous plants' as it is for 'poisons'; but it also has to be realised that the content of active compounds – and hence the toxicity – in individual plants of a particular species can be subject to qualitative and quantitative fluctuations. These are in part determined genetically (chemical races) or are dependent on the locality, other environmental conditions, or the age of the plant or particular organ, i.e. the degree of maturity.

Preconditions for poisoning are that in the first instance there be the opportunity for contact with the given plant, that there be a sufficiently high dose of toxic constituents to exert their activity in or on the body, and lastly that the defence mechanisms or detoxification processes of the body be overcome. Many plants have only become a 'poisonous plant' in a given region after they have taken their place as a garden or ornamental plant in the human environment, e.g. *Primula obconica, Dieffenbachia.*

To what extent does poisoning with plants occur?

As poisoning in man is the main theme of this book, for the moment we exclude poisoning in animals and will return to this point later.

In the poisoning statistics of the Poison Information and Control Centres the proportion of cases due to plants or plant materials is of the order of 3–10%, and serious cases are very rare. Von Clarmann indicates that with 30000–60000 cases of poisoning per year in children alone, the proportion is about 3.5%. This amounts to 1000–2000 cases per year or '3 cases of poisoning by plants every day' [P42]. Plant materials are more frequently ingested in late summer and autumn, and the average number of cases during this part of the year is higher than the yearly average. With children, next to drugs and household chemicals, plants take third place in the statistics,* together with tobacco, which, although also a plant product, should be considered separately (chewing of cigarettes or tobacco left-overs) [M61].

The following survey reproduces part of the poison statistics (number of enquiries) for the year 1977 of the

---

* The order appears to be the same in the United States [F5] and the United Kingdom [V11], as well.

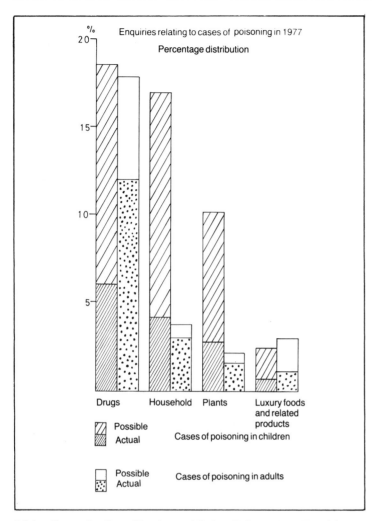

Mainz Centre for Detoxification and Poison Information. Enquiries in 1977.

Mainz Centre for Detoxification and Poison Information [O9]. It also shows the relationship between 'possible' (cases of ingestion) and 'actual' (cases of intoxication) poisonings. Generally, this distinction is not made sufficiently clearly in the statistical data relating to plant poisoning.

How does poisoning with plants happen?

Children, especially younger ones, in learning about their environment are inquisitive about plants and like to try bits of them. They are thus the first to be involved. Conspicuous and attractive organs, like the often-quoted 'brightly coloured berries', are the ones preferred, but none of the other parts of a plant are exempt from a child's curiosity. Often, not even a horrible taste frightens a child off. Fortunately, most of these efforts do not have any serious consequences. It is pertinent here to point out yet again the distinction between cases of ingestion and cases of poisoning [H8]:

Ingestion: The taking of plant material without the occurrence of symptoms of poisoning (at most a feeling of being unwell and vomiting once).

Poisoning: The occurrence of symptoms of poisoning, which may be of a mild or serious nature and which definitely require medical attention.

Usually, the consumption of plant materials by children results in nothing more than cases of ingestion; on the other hand, it must be remembered that the toxic dose of a highly active substance in a child is smaller, so that in principle poisoning is more likely to occur than with adults.

Poisoning by plants in adults is relatively rare. It can come about by eating unknown or incorrectly identified plant material,* e.g. in the search for alternative sources of food [R29], by self-medication with plants or the misuse of herbal teas [A8; E3; S56], by confusion with or falsification of plant foodstuffs [M65], and in suicide attempts. And in the younger generation, trying so-called 'drugs that expand the consciousness' is also a cause of poisoning. Not long ago, such a case attracted attention throughout Western Germany: *'Poison tea already sent to 300 clients in Germany!'* Many young people had got hold of *'drugs for mobilising the spirit'* from a dubious mail-order business in Hamburg and after taking the tea had *'dropped like flies'* [P49]. Two people had to be hospitalised. The drug, offered under the name *'Traumkraut'* (dream weed), consisted of various parts of a henbane species.

---

* Such a case of plant poisoning is clearly described in the Old Testament (2 Kings, chap. 4, verses 39 and 40 (Authorised Version)):[39] And one went out into the field to gather herbs, and found a wild vine, and gathered thereof wild gourds his lap full, and came and shred them into the pot of pottage: for they knew them not. [40] So they poured out for the men to eat. And it came to pass, as they were eating of the pottage, that they cried out and said, O thou man of God, there is death in the pot. And they could not eat thereof.

Which plant parts and which plants are especially important?

Plant organs. As already mentioned, cases of ingestion of 'brightly coloured berries', a lay designation that can refer to very different kinds of fruits as well as seeds together with aril, e.g. yew, head the statistics.

der Marderosian [M17] cites data of O'Leary according to which, of 1051 cases of ingestion in the course of a single year 454 concerned 'berries', 60 involved 'nuts', and 81 related to 'seeds and beans', i.e. pods of various kinds. With 288 cases of mushroom ingestion included in the total, the remaining 168 cases involved flowers, leaves, stems, and roots. Korninger and Lenz [K38] report that over a two-year period in Vienna 74% of plant poisonings concerned fruits, 10% flowers, 12% leaves, 3% bulbs, and 1% conifer needles.

As indicated above, the content of toxic constituents can be very different in the various organs and fluctuates according to the time of year and the age of the particular organ, e.g. the roots of perennials are often more dangerous in winter and spring than in summer *(Cicuta, Oenanthe, Aconitum)*, while with fruits often the content of toxic principles decreases during the ripening process.

Contradictory statements regarding the toxicity of fruits are in part explicable by the fact that no distinction is made between seed and pericarp. Mezereon and cherry laurel contain poisonous substances in the seed which are largely absent from the pulp. In contrast, the alkaloids of the opium poppy are found in the wall of the capsule, while the seeds are harmless.

Plants ingested. Tables 1 and 2 summarise data from the Berlin Poison Control Centre [K46; K47] and the Swiss Toxicological Information Centre in Zürich [S38], respectively. They show that plants with conspicuous fruits are the most important, but they also include fruits which have proved to be harmless, e.g. Oregon-grape. The majority of the plants are park or garden ornamentals – cotoneaster, firethorn, laburnum – but house plants are also represented – christmas cherry, philodendron, dieffenbachia. In spite of certain differences, which may be due to regional causes, e.g. the greater proportion of cherry laurel cases in Switzerland, the two tables are remarkably similar. The last two lines of Table 2 also point to the difficulties involved in poison information work: besides the 'usual cases', almost any other plant in the human environment can on occasion be ingested. Naturally, the problems of identification and estimating the dangers are then greater; see also Fawcett [F5].

Table 1. Berlin Poison Control Centre: Frequent enquiries and cases of poisoning (data covering a period of 15 years [K47]).

Plant name		No. of enquiries
Laburnum	*Laburnum*	553
Rowan	*Sorbus aucuparia*	368
Oregon-grape	*Mahonia*	326
Cotoneaster	*Cotoneaster*	284
Honeysuckle	*Lonicera*	244
Firethorn	*Pyracantha*	241
Yew	*Taxus*	166
Christmas Cherry	*Solanum pseudocapsicum*	163
Sweet Pea	*Lathyrus*	150
Lily-of-the-valley	*Convallaria*	144
Snowberry	*Symphoricarpos*	141
Privet	*Ligustrum*	133
Cherry Laurel	*Prunus laurocerasus*	108
Beans	*Phaseolus*	104
Mezereon	*Daphne*	96
Cape-gooseberry	*Physalis*	91
Philodendron	*Philodendron* or *Monstera*	71
Holly	*Ilex*	64
Poinsettia	*Euphorbia pulcherrima*	62
Mistletoe	*Viscum*	57
Barberry	*Berberis*	53
Dumb Cane	*Dieffenbachia*	50
Elder	*Sambucus*	48
Deadly Nightshade	*Atropa*	47
Black Nightshade + Bittersweet	*Solanum nigrum* + *S. dulcamara*	45
Guelder-rose	*Viburnum*	43
Potato	*Solanum tuberosum*	42
Lords-and-Ladies	*Arum*	41
Horse-chestnut	*Aesculus*	34
Spindle	*Euonymus*	27

For the United States the statistical details relating to poisoning by plants can be obtained from the reports of the National Clearinghouse for Poison Control Centers.

According to Oehme [O6], for example, in 1975 plants such as *Ilex* (333 cases = 5.8%), *Pyracantha* (306 = 5.3%), *Solanum* species (232 = 4.1%), or *Sambucus*

Table 2. Swiss Toxicological Information Centre, Zürich: Frequent enquiries and cases of poisoning (covering 1973–1979 [S38]).

Plant name		No. of enquiries
Cotoneaster	*Cotoneaster*	381
Oregon-grape	*Mahonia*	318
Firethorn	*Pyracantha*	241
Cherry Laurel	*Prunus laurocerasus*	230
Rowan	*Sorbus aucuparia*	227
Honeysuckle	*Lonicera*	175
Cape-gooseberry	*Physalis*	170
Nightshades (including Christmas Cherry)	*Solanum*	163
Yew	*Taxus*	159
Lily-of-the-valley	*Convallaria*	146
Laburnum	*Laburnum*	109
Mistletoe	*Viscum*	108
Mezereon	*Daphne*	97
Lords-and-Ladies	*Arum*	97
Deadly Nightshade	*Atropa*	92
Barberry	*Berberis*	89
Holly	*Ilex*	88
Spurge	*Euphorbia*	71
Elder	*Sambucus*	66
Dumb Cane	*Dieffenbachia*	63
Dogwood	*Cornus*	58
Tulip	*Tulipa*	57
Snowberry	*Symphoricarpos*	57
Philodendron	*Philodendron* or *Monstera*	56
Guelder-rose	*Viburnum*	50
Privet	*Ligustrum*	50
Daffodil	*Narcissus*	32
Horse-chestnut	*Aesculus*	30
Spindle	*Euonymus*	25
Unidentified plants		235
Miscellaneous plants		1108

Table 3. Plants commonly ingested in the United Kingdom (from [V11]).

Common name	Latin name	Part ingested
Berberis	*Berberis*	Berries
Bittersweet	*Solanum dulcamara*	Berries
Black Bryony*	*Tamus communis*	Berries
Black Nightshade	*Solanum nigrum*	Berries
Broom*	*Cytisus*	Seeds, pods
Bulbs	Many species	Bulbs
Cotoneaster	*Cotoneaster*	Berries
Cowbane*	*Cicuta virosa*	Roots
Deadly Nightshade	*Atropa bella-donna*	Berries
Firethorn	*Pyracantha*	Berries
Hawthorn*	*Crataegus*	Berries
Hemlock*	*Conium maculatum*	Leaves, seeds
Hemlock Water-Dropwort*	*Oenanthe crocata*	Roots
Holly	*Ilex aquifolium*	Seeds
Honeysuckle	*Lonicera*	Berries
Laburnum	*Laburnum anagyroides*	Seeds, pods
Lords-and-Ladies	*Arum maculatum*	Berries
Lupin*	*Lupinus*	Seeds
Mistletoe	*Viscum album*	Berries
	Phoradendron flavescens	Berries
Mezereon	*Daphne mezereum*	Berries
Monk's-hood*	*Aconitum napellus*	Leaves, flowers, seeds
Oak*	*Quercus*	Acorns
Rowan	*Sorbus aucuparia*	Berries
Spurge-laurel	*Daphne laureola*	Berries
Thorn-apple*	*Datura stramonium*	Seeds
White Bryony*	*Bryonia dioica*	Berries
Winter Cherry	*Solanum pseudocapsicum*	Berries
Yew	*Taxus baccata*	Berries

* The plants asterisked are absent from the Berlin and Zürich lists (Tables 1 and 2). However, all the plants listed are discussed, or at least mentioned, in the main part of the book.

species (174 = 3%) are mentioned, i.e. plants that also figure prominently in the German and Swiss statistics. Ornamentals like *Philodendron* species (in first place with 645 cases = 11.3%), *Dieffenbachia* (257 = 4.5%), and *Solanum pseudocapsicum* (138 = 2.4%) are listed as in Europe. But others, like *Phytolacca* (402 = 7%) and *Colocasia* (116 = 2%), plants that do not occur naturally in Europe and are not well known as ornamentals, are rarely, if at all, found in the European reports indicated. On the other hand, the supposed or actual poisonous plants that top the European statistics – cotoneaster, rowan, cherry laurel, honeysuckle, as well as laburnum and mezereon – are less in evidence in the United States.

The experience of the United Kingdom National Poisons Information Service (N.P.I.S.), set up in 1963, is very much in line with that of the continental Toxicological Information Centres. The Service operates five centres – in London, Edinburgh, Cardiff, Belfast and Dublin† – and enquiries about 'poisonous plants', mostly concerning children, are currently running at about 2000 per year. Only two people are known to have died from plant poisoning in the last 15 years: one due to *Amanita phalloides* and the other to a *Laburnum* species [V11].

Plants which most frequently give cause for concern are either widely distributed or have a reputation for being poisonous. Table 3 lists the plants most commonly ingested in the United Kingdom, in alphabetical order. More than half of them are also in the Berlin and Zürich lists. Vale and Meredith [V11] note that several of these plants – cotoneaster, honeysuckle, firethorn, hawthorn, and berberis – are at most only slightly toxic and that with the amounts ingested by children, usually no treatment is necessary. As is evident from the monographs in the present book, the findings on the Continent are essentially the same.

'The fears of poisoning from plants and fungi in Britain are more imagined than real', and are often due to 'disproportionate and sensational reporting' – again, as on the Continent! Serious effects from poisonous plants are rare and, medically, it is nearly always considered sufficient to prescribe mild symptomatic and reassuring measures [V11].

To what extent are animals affected by poisoning?

Poisoning of farm animals can come about through eating plants growing in or near the grazing area. Often, cases of poisoning are a result of special weather conditions which change the food available: the usual forage plants are absent, so that the cattle feed on plants that they do not normally consider or that they instinctively avoid; or a few scattered poisonous plants have spread excessively and are then eaten. Particularly striking is the frequently observed difference in susceptibility of different animal species to plant poisons. Nevertheless, in many cases there are contradictory statements regarding this question in the literature.

With housed livestock, poisoning can take place through unnoticed contamination of the fodder with toxic plants or plant material. Press cake that is normally suitable as fodder may under certain circumstances contain poisonous constituents. Often in cases of fodder poisoning secondary changes in the plant materials are involved, which lead to the formation of poisonous substances, e.g. the presence of mycotoxins after fungal infection.

Finally, in the home, animals may suffer as a result of feeding on ornamental plants [B46; G19; J9; L21; P33; S91].

In the present book, poisoning in veterinary medicine has been included, as far as it concerns poisonous substances or plants of general interest or when epidemics of poisoning on an unusual scale have been observed. See also p.232. The following books and reviews deal in greater detail or exclusively with animal poisoning: Bentz [B23], Keeler, van Kampen, and James (eds.) [K17], Liebenow and Liebenow [L23], as well as Clarke, Harvey, and Humphreys [C34], Forsyth [F33], Humphreys [H63], Oehme [O7], and Smolenski [S66].

What possibilities are there of identifying poisonous plants and what information is available about their toxicity?

On the identification of poisonous plants. Plants that are poisonous have no special distinguishing features. Nature

---

† There are other centres in Birmingham, Leeds and Newcastle. In contrast to other countries, the Service handles enquiries only from medical doctors or their *bona fide* deputies.

has – certainly to the great regret of modern man – neglected to provide appropriate indications. Dangerously poisonous organs like the fruits of the deadly nightshade are attractive and taste sweet and so do not frighten off those who try them. There is no such thing as a universal test for recognising the poisonousness of a plant – that is true not only for mushrooms (silver spoon!).

In a case of ingestion, in order to identify a poisonous plant it is necessary first of all to have relevant knowledge of plants or the capability of establishing a plant's identity on the basis of a suitable identification key; see [C35; F34]. Photographs may be of help, but they are more useful to those who already have the requisite knowledge. For trees and shrubs it will be necessary to refer to special books for identification, such as: Bean [B60], Chittenden [C33], Everett [E17], Mitchell [M68], Krüssmann [K50], Fitschen [F11], or Eiselt and Schröder [E6].

In general, it can be said that the identification of a plant will be all the easier and quicker the more complete the material available for examination. Attempts to identify a plant by telephoning a Poison Information Centre or other source raise special difficulties. In such circumstances, use of a vernacular name (which may apply to more than one plant) and information obtained from the parents or other people concerned is often unclear and of little help in making an identification. Hence, in every enquiry by telephone pertinent questions that can be answered by the layman must be asked – in the case of having taken a 'berry' somewhat along the following lines:

- Kind of fruit? (berry, nut, etc.)
- Size, colour, nature of the fruit? (juicy, fleshy, firm, etc.)
- Number of stones or pips in it?
- Arrangement of the fruits on the plant? (singly, in pairs, many clustered together, stalked, unstalked)
- Were other parts of the plant also eaten? (leaves, roots, etc.)
- Appearance (habit) of the plant? (low herb, shrub, or tree)
- Where was the plant growing? (field, hedge, roadside, garden, park)
- Size, shape, and arrangement of the leaves (roundish, oval, pointed, prickly, stalked or not, with notches, run of the nerves)

How the problem of identification appears from the point of view of a Poison Control Centre is clearly explained by Lampe [L2]:

'One of the most perplexing problems facing those concerned with Poison Control Information Centers is the call from the panicky mother that her child has or may have swallowed a red berry growing on a bushy little plant with funny looking green leaves in the backyard. Equally frustrating is the parent who appears in the pediatrician's office with a wilted plant specimen announcing that this is growing all over the neighborhood, is it poisonous?'

It must be emphasised that an unequivocal statement that a plant or plant part is not toxic (or only very feebly so) is just as important as the identification of a questionably poisonous plant. For it is on that basis that therapeutic measures, which may well upset the patient

more than a possible mild intoxication, will be considered as necèssary or superfluous. Czech [C28] has discussed this problem in a general way, but his conclusion is particularly valid for cases in which 'poisonous plants' have been ingested:

Cases of poisoning are by no means as rare as is generally assumed. But even more frequent are situations in which it·is possible to clarify only on the basis of precise toxicological data relating to the substance that has been taken whether a case of poisoning is being dealt with or a harmless case of ingestion. Every time a substance is swallowed that does not belong to the recognised food intake – to call it a case of poisoning and to treat it by standard procedures such as gastric lavage and forced diuresis is the greatest mischief, which can only (if at all) be excused by the lack of knowledge of most doctors. Often, measures taken are determined not by clear clinical indications (feasibility + necessity) but rather by a kind of 'furor therapeuticus' intended to hide the doctor's own uncertainty.

Sources of information about the toxicity of plants. Just as the unequivocal botanical identification of a possibly poisonous plant is essential, so also is information about the supposed or real toxicity. Both are prerequisites for the medical decisions which have to be taken in the case at hand. If symptoms of poisoning have already occurred, it may be possible from their nature to obtain an additional indication as to the type of poisoning. In most cases, however, the symptoms will be relatively non-specific (vomiting, gastro-intestinal troubles), so that one has to be highly sceptical towards tables based on symptoms for the identification of poisonous plants [N 11].

There is an abundant but very heterogeneous literature dealing with poisonous plants, including books on medicinal plants.* We cite here a few lines from an introductory chapter in the book *Toxic Plants* [K 26; K 28]. They are by Kingsbury, whose book on the poisonous plants of North America [K 29] continues tò be a standard work, and they apply equally well to the European literature:

'The major human problems associated with poisonous plants derive from the basic problem of a confused, seriously inadequate, and often misunderstood body of literature on the subject . . . A significant amount of information in contemporary compendia is derived innocently from ancient sources or observations.'

---

* There is no fundamental difference between medicinal plants and poisonous plants. As pharmaceutical biologists – pharmacognosists – we are familiar with the old saying of Paracelsus 'Dosis sola facit venenum' and the double meaning of the Greek word φάρμᾰκον: medicine, poison.

A particularly critical point in many, especially older, works is the identification of the plants concerned. When critically evaluating the cases, again and again it turns out that an unequivocal identification has not been made, or it is unclear how much plant material has been ingested and whether in fact it really is responsible for the observed symptoms.

At the end of this chapter we have collected together a list of books in German and English. Besides a few with detailed accounts of the whole field of poisonous plants, there are a number of smaller, more popular, books. The subjects of poisonous plants is usually also dealt with in general works on poisoning and its treatment. Finally, mention may be made here of a few papers on poisonous plants which discuss in general terms the problems of plant poisoning or are extensive reports of the authors' own experience.

Poisonous plants are a popular subject in the daily press, where, usually at the beginning of the autumn, more or less (mostly less) authoritative articles appear and warn against 'poisonous berries' or 'deadly fruits'. In various parts of the book we have pointed out the problems connected with such publications.

What help does this book offer in identifying poisonous plants and in supplying information about them?

When some years ago we began to be closely involved with poisonous plants we soon found that, besides some reliable knowledge, there was much unclear and contradictory information. In enquiries dealing with acute cases the means of identifying poisonous plants then available were of little help, since the descriptions and – the often rather second-rate – photographs taken in their natural surroundings were inadequate.

We have therefore provided colour illustrations of the chosen selection of plants known to be or suspected to be poisonous (and a few others that have berries and frequently occur and are therefore of interest in connection with a differential diagnosis). These illustrations, together with a short description, will allow or, at least, suggest a probable identification of the plant concerned. Hence, conspicuous fruits, their arrangement on the twig (infructescence), number of seeds, and other features, together with the leaves and in some cases the flowers, are all illustrated; they are reproduced natural size, in order to facilitate a direct comparison. It must be remembered that, as is usual in living organisms, a certain variation in shape, colour, and size may occur. We have deviated from this scheme only in regard to house plants (and a few others) where we have shown the habit.

Apart from the macroscopically recognisable features, we have illustrated – and this is something new for a book on poisonous plants – microscopical characters, in particular those of the epidermis of the pericarp. The reason for this has been our experience in forensic investigations, which has repeatedly confirmed our view that microscopically recognisable structures can offer valuable pointers to the identification of a plant or plant part.

Owing to the resistance of plant wall structures, such features are usually still recognisable even after a long period in the gastro-intestinal tract. The structures shown here – partly as microphotographs and partly as drawings – can also be of use in the identification of plant materials in vomit or stomach contents.

Microscopy. We have attempted especially for the 'berries' of poisonous, as well as harmless, plants to show microscopical features. Naturally, the descriptions do not represent a detailed account of the anatomy of these fruits; moreover, an unequivocal identification solely on the basis of a few microscopical characters is usually not possible. Nevertheless, this type of feature can give important indications as to the plant species or genus that may be involved or else provide further evidence regarding the identity of an already suspected plant. Since it is not to be expected that the staff who deal with toxicological examinations necessarily have a broad experience of plant anatomy and daily use of the microscope, we have deliberately chosen a simple preparation that requires a minimum of technical equipment and chemical reagents and that will show such features as are easily observed by relatively inexperienced microscopists. The scale (|———|) drawn in on the illustrations, unless otherwise indicated, represents 50 μm.

Preparation. With the aid of a razor blade, a *ca* 5–10 mm^2 square piece is cut out of the fruit, laid with the outer surface down on a coverslip, and the pulp is separated from the exocarp by scraping with bent forceps or a micro-spatula. As a rule, the epidermis of the pericarp is tough enough to withstand such treatment and, at the same time, under the slight pressure it adheres to the coverslip. Finally, after adding a drop or two of water to the piece of plant material the coverslip is inverted and placed on a microscope slide. A drop or two of water is likewise added to the scraped-off pulp before it too is examined microscopically.

Further aids to identification are a key to the fruits and a compilation of macroscopically visible leaf characters (in black-and-white photographs), which can also help in recognition or, conversely, can confirm an identification already established on other grounds. Leaves also offer microscopical features (leaf structure, surface structures) that are suitable for characterisation. Haller and Bruder [H7] have demonstrated this very effectively in criminal investigations, making use of the scanning electron microscope.

In our statements about the supposed or actual toxicity of the plants discussed, we have attempted to evaluate the literature critically and in particular to consider newer publications dealing with case histories and experimental investigations. Much dead wood has thus been cut out; in some cases our own work has clarified the situation, while others have remained unexplained and require further study. It is noteworthy that in the recent German literature reports on cases of poisoning with plants are scarce. On the other hand, in conversation we have frequently been told about cases of poisoning that for the most varied reasons have never been published. A voluminous bibliography enables further information to be gathered about certain plants or problems.

It seemed to us that a short section on those constituents of plants that are of toxicological interest would be of use; it offers the interested user of this book a rapid orientation and shows what types of chemical substances are to be found in poisonous plants.

What is not included in this book? Although fungi not infrequently give rise to serious cases of poisoning, they are not included, since this special field has an extensive and adequate literature of its own, not only as regards the identification of fungi but also as regards the treatment of poisoning (Cetto, 1979; Dähncke and Dähncke, 1980; Flammer, 1980; Michael, Hennig, and Kreisel, 1978; Moser, 1978. See also: North, 1967; Forsyth, 1968; Vale and Meredith, 1981).

In order to keep the size of the book within limits, we have also omitted poisoning by bacteria, algae, mosses, and lichens, even though these groups of organisms can also form highly active compounds.

The toxic constitutents of timbers, with which people who are involved in the processing of this greatly versatile material come in contact, is a special field. Again, we have excluded this interesting aspect, since only a fairly restricted group of people is exposed to such dangers. Moreover, a book which deals with this subject has been written by Hausen: *Woods Injurious to Human Health*, 1981.

The discussion of those plants which cause injury to or illness involving the skin or mucous membranes is not complete. We have only dealt with a few known groups of substances which lead to contact dermatitis, e.g. sesquiterpene lactones, furanocoumarins, and have discussed the most important relevant plants. Further information can be obtained from several recent reviews (included in the list at the end of this chapter) and also in the comprehensive book by Mitchell and Rook: *Botanical Dermatitis*, 1979. It is clear that there is hardly a plant family without representatives having skin-irritant activity.

The problem of contamination of plants with pesticides or exhaust fumes is not covered. Undoubtedly, plants can become toxic through residues of such injurious substances, so that in enquiries dealing with poisonous plants the question of where the plant concerned is found acquires an added significance.

In regard to treatment, we have given general indications as far as possible, but we must refer the reader to the books on poisoning already mentioned, where further information can be found. In any case, frequently only symptomatic measures will be carried out as the doctor in charge judges to be appropriate.

What steps should be taken when plant material has been ingested?

It is relatively rare that soon after the plant material has been ingested clear symptoms of poisoning become evident, thus necessitating rapid hospitalisation (*Cicuta, Atropa, Aconitum, . . .*). Usually, the parents or other person(s) in charge* ascertain that children have eaten plant material without symptoms of poisoning being observable at that stage. Or it is discovered through interrogation, as a result of a conspicuous alteration in behaviour (headache, feeling of being unwell, exhaustion, 'bellyache', perhaps vomiting), that plant material has been eaten. And while in such cases it is advisable to consult a doctor, a paediatrics department, or a Toxicological Information and Control Centre, there should be no panicking. Instead, the following questions and considerations should be dealt with:

■ What plant has the child been eating? Can it be established (if necessary by getting hold of knowledgeable people, e.g. pharmacist, gardener, biology teacher) what the plant is?
■ Which parts of the plant have been eaten and how much?
■ How much time has elapsed since the ingestion?
■ Has vomiting already taken place?
■ When telephoning, information about the age of the child is important!

■ When going to a doctor or hospital, at the same time take along material of the plant in question – if possible, a complete twig with leaves, fruits, and, when present, flowers (see p.17). Keep any vomit, as this could help in identifying the species and determining the amount of plant material ingested.
■ Other possibilities of poisoning should be borne in mind: food poisoning? pesticides?
■ If a doctor cannot be reached, the first step to be considered should be to bring about vomiting – in children lukewarm water and tickling the throat; in adults ½ litre (somewhat less than 1 pint) of warm salt water. If appropriate, a slurry of activated charcoal can also be administered. It is inadvisable to get the person to drink milk (an old household remedy) as this can promote the absorption of lipophilic substances.

Ipecacuanha in the form of a syrup is a widely used emetic and is effective in children. In the United Kingdom the preparation can be obtained only from pharmacies, while in the United States it is freely available. Incidents may arise with its use partly through confusion of the syrup with the fluid extract which has a higher alkaloid content [S65; S68]. A daily intake of 90–120 ml ipecacuanha syrup (in order to lose weight!) over a period of 3 months led to the death of a 26-year old woman [A2]. Toxicological problems concerning the use of ipecacuanha preparations have been discussed in detail in recent reviews [F10; K24; M15].

Formula for the preparation of Paediatric Ipecacuanha Emetic Mixture B.P.:

Ipecacuanha Fluid Extract	70.0 ml
Hydrochloric acid	2.5 ml*
Glycerol	100.0 ml
Syrup	to 1000.0 ml

Should poisonous plants be rooted out?

Nobody would seriously consider attacking deadly nightshade, mezereon, or foxglove in their natural habitats just 'because they are dangerous poisonous plants'. On the other hand, the alpine farmer will take trouble to prevent the spread of false hellebore or senecio (*Senecio alpinus*) in his pastures since these plants can be a danger to his

---

* For the occasional cases of poisoning in adults what follows is valid *mutatis mutandis*.

* This component is omitted in the formula for Ipecac Syrup U.S.P.

cattle. At one time, the eradication of poisonous plants, e.g. cowbane, was officially regulated.

The eradication of plants in places where they are a danger to man and beast can thus be an essential precaution. This is also true for the frequently mentioned 'neighbourhood of kindergartens and playgrounds'. Undoubtedly, laburnum and mezereon should not be planted in such places or they should be positioned so that children cannot reach them. There are a few other plants with highly active constituents that should not be where there are infants. This requirement is equally true – which is often forgotten – in the home, where children readily have access to decorative plants and can stick bits of them in their mouth.

Those who know the serious consequences of ingesting dieffenbachia leaves or stems – fortunately, the burning in the mouth which soon intervenes stops most children from trying the plant and the poisoning does not become serious – will understand the demand put forward professionally for ending the sale of this plant (Farnsworth, cited from [O 17]). The same applies to *Primula obconica* [M 42] because it often causes serious dermatitis.

Nevertheless, voices which urge the general 'eradication of all poisonous plants', often raised by lay people or in the daily press, are highly questionable. Such demands always become louder when yet again there is a report about 'the deadly threat from poisonous berries and ornamental shrubs'* – beautiful but dangerous! – on the basis of incidents which, when looked at more closely, often turn out to be cases of ingestion with mild symptoms. See the report on 'cherry-laurel poisoning' on p. 194. This attitude obviously reflects an entirely incorrect appreciation of 'poisonous plants and berries', arising from the earlier literature and still being disseminated in popular articles.

Objections must be raised in the clearest terms possible to this mischievous general demand for the eradication of plants thought to be poisonous, especially as the concept 'poisonous plant' is usually taken in a very broad sense.

Instead of eradication, we should demand a better knowledge of the plants. And this knowledge should, together with the appropriate precautions, be passed on to children at an early age; for, nowadays children hardly know any poisonous plants at all.** Fundamentally, the precept formulated by Kingsbury [K 28] should be followed: 'Don't eat anything not commonly recognised as wholesome', and those who eat wild plants without taking the trouble to learn about them must accept the consequences: 'Society at large should not be penalised for the stupidity of a very few' [K 28].

Summarising, the better we know 'poisonous plants' and are able to assess their dangerousness, the sooner we shall be able to live with them and enjoy their beauty.

---

* 'My child is surrounded by poisonous shrubs; I'm worried about it' [S 11].

** In answer to a question no one in a class of 11–12–year old school children in Kiel was able to name a poisonous plant – except 'poisonous mushrooms': 'Are they plants, too?'

General literature on poisonous plants and poisoning

Books

ALTMANN, H.: Giftpflanzen – Gifttiere. Die wichtigsten Arten – Erkennen, Giftwirkung, Therapie, BLV, München, Bern, Wien, 144 pp., 1979.

BENTZ, H.: Nutztiervergiftungen. Erkennung und Verhütung, G. Fischer, Jena, 361 pp., 1969.

BRAUN, H.: Heilpflanzenlexikon für Ärzte und Apotheker. Anwendung, Wirkung, Toxikologie, 4th ed., G. Fischer, Stuttgart, New York, 302 pp., 1981.

BRAUN, W. and A. DÖNHARDT: Vergiftungsregister; Haushalts- und Laborchemikalien, Arzneimittel – Symptomatologie und Therapie, 2nd ed., G. Thieme, Stuttgart, 1975.

BRUGSCH, H. and O. R. KLIMMER: Vergiftungen im Kindesalter, 2nd ed., F. Enke, Stuttgart, 438 pp., 1966.

BUFF, W. and K. VON DER DUNK: Giftpflanzen in Natur und Garten, Augsburger Bücher, Augsburg, 352 pp., 1980.

CETTO, B.: Der Grosse Pilzführer, BLV, München, vols. 1–3, 1976–1979.

CLARKE, M. L., D. G. HARVEY, and D. J. HUMPHREYS: Veterinary toxicology, 2nd ed., Baillière Tindall, London, 328 pp., 1981.

CONNOR, H. E.: The poisonous plants in New Zealand, 2nd ed., Government Printer, Wellington, 247 pp., 1977.

DÄHNCKE, R. M. and S. M. DÄHNCKE: 700 Pilze in Farbfotos, AT Verlag, Aarau, Stuttgart, 686 pp., 1980.

DÄHNCKE, R. M. and S. DÄHNCKE: Beerenkompass, Gräfe & Unzer, München, 79 pp., 1977.

EVERIST, S. L.: Poisonous plants of Australia, 2nd ed., Angus & Robertson, Sydney, 966 pp., 1981.

FLAMMER, R.: Differentialdiagnose der Pilzvergiftungen, G. Fischer, Stuttgart, New York, 92 pp., 1980.

FORSYTH, A. A.: British poisonous plants, 2nd ed., Reference Book 161, Ministry of Agriculture, Fisheries and Food, Her Majesty's Stationery Office, London, 131 pp., 1968.

GESSNER, O.: Gift- und Arzneipflanzen von Mitteleuropa, 3rd ed. revised by G. Orzechowsky, C. Winter, Heidelberg, 582 pp., 1974.

HARDIN, J. W. and J. M. ARENA: Human poisoning from native and cultivated plants, Duke University Press, Durham, North Carolina, 194 pp., 1974.

HAUSEN, B. M.: Woods injurious to human health, W. de Gruyter, Berlin, New York, 189 pp., 1981.

JULLER, E. and R. KÖHLER-WIEDER: Tabellen zur Bestimmung der wichtigeren mitteleuropäischen Giftpflanzen im blütenlosen Zustand, G. Fischer, Jena, 105 pp., 1938.

KEELER, R. F., K. R. VAN KAMPEN, and L. F. JAMES (eds.): Effects of poisonous plants on livestock, Academic Press, New York, San Francisco, London, 600 pp., 1978.

KINGHORN, A. D.: Toxic plants, Columbia University Press, New York, 195 pp., 1979.

KINGSBURY, J. M.: Poisonous plants of the United States and Canada, Prentice-Hall, Englewood Cliffs, New Jersey, 626 pp., 1964.

KRIENKE, E. G. and K. E. VON MÜHLENDAHL: Vergiftungen im Kindesalter, F. Enke, Stuttgart, 273 pp., 1980.

LEWIN, L.: Die Gifte in der Weltgeschichte, J. Springer, Berlin, 536 pp., 1920.

LEWIN, L.: Gifte und Vergiftungen (= 4th ed. of Lehrbuch der Toxikologie), Berlin, 1929.

LEWIS, W. H. and M. P. F. ELVIN-LEWIS: Medical botany – Plants affecting man's health, John Wiley, New York, London, Sydney, Toronto, 515 pp., 1977.

LIEBENOW, H. and K. LIEBENOW: Giftpflanzen. Ein 'Vademekum für Tierärzte, Humanmediziner, Biologen und Landwirte', 2nd ed., F. Enke, Stuttgart, 248 pp., 1981.

LIENER, I. E. (ed.): Toxic constituents of foodstuffs, 2nd ed., Academic Press, New York, London, Toronto, Sydney, San Francisco, 502 pp., 1980.

LINDNER, E.: Toxikologie der Nahrungsmittel, 2nd ed., G. Thieme, Stuttgart, 200 pp., 1979.

LUDEWIG, R. and K. H. LOHS: Akute Vergiftungen, Ratgeber für toxikologische Notfälle, 5th ed., G. Fischer, Jena, 633 pp., 1975.

MICHAEL, E., B. HENNIG, and H. KREISEL: Handbuch für Pilzfreunde, G. Fischer, Stuttgart, New York, 1978.

MITCHELL, J. and A. ROOK: Botanical dermatology. Plants and plant products injurious to the skin, Greengrass, Vancouver, 787 pp., 1979.

MOESCHLIN, S.: Klinik und Therapie der Vergiftungen, 6th ed., G. Thieme, Stuttgart, New York, 640 pp., 1980.

MORTON, J. F.: Plants poisonous to people in Florida and other warm areas, 2nd ed., Fairchild Tropical Garden, Miami, 116 pp., 1977.

MOSER, M.: Die Röhrlinge und Blätterpilze, G. Fischer, Stuttgart, New York, 532 pp., 1978.

NIELSEN, M.: Giftpflanzen. 148 europäische Arten. Bestimmung – Wirkung – Geschichte, Kosmos Franckh, Stuttgart, 141 pp., 1979.

NORTH, P. M.: Poisonous plants and fungi in colour, Blandford Press, London, 161 pp., 1967.

OKONEK, S., G. FÜLGRAFF, and R. FREY: Humantoxikologie. Akute Vergiftungen – Giftinformation, G. Fischer, Stuttgart, New York, 202 pp., 1979.

PAHLOW, M.: Giftpflanzenkompass, Gräfe & Unzer, München, 79 pp., 1980.

ROTH, L. and M. DAUNDERER: Giftliste: IV. Giftpflanzen, 3rd ed., Ecomed, Landsberg/Lech, 1979.

SCHÖNFELDER, P. and I. SCHÖNFELDER: Der Kosmos-Heilpflanzenführer. Europäische Heil- und Giftpflanzen, Franckh, Stuttgart, 277 pp., 1980.

SPÄTH, G.: Vergiftungen und akute Arzneimitel-Überdosierungen, G. Witzstrock, Baden-Baden, Köln, New York, 584 pp., 1978.

TAMPION, J.: Dangerous plants, David & Charles, Newton Abbot, London, Vancouver, 176 pp., 1977.

TREASE, G. E. and W. C. EVANS: Pharmacognosy, 12th ed., Baillière Tindall, London, 812 pp., 1983.

TYLER, V. E., L. R. BRADY, and J. E. ROBBERS: Pharmacognosy, 8th ed., Lea & Febiger, Philadelphia, 520 pp., 1981.

WAGNER, H.: Rauschgift-Drogen, Springer, Berlin, Heidelberg, New York, 142 pp., 1969.

WATT, J. M. and M. G. BREYER-BRANDWIJK: The medicinal and poisonous plants of southern and eastern Africa, 2nd ed., E. & S. Livingstone, Edinburgh, London, 1457 pp., 1962.

WIRTH, W. and C. GLOXHUBER: Toxikologie – für Ärzte, Naturwissenschaftler und Apotheker, 3rd ed., G. Thieme, Stuttgart, New York, 414 pp., 1981.

Reviews

BARTELS, O.: Spezielle Probleme bei Vergiftungen mit Pflanzen. Intensivbehandlung **2**, 66–71 (1977).

COOPER, L., G. GRUNENFELDER, and J. BLACKMON: Poisoning associated with herbal teas – Arizona, Washington. Morbid. Mort. Weekly Rept **26**, 257–259 (1977).

EVANS, F. J. and R. J. SCHMIDT: Plants and plant products that induce contact dermatitis. Planta Med. **38**, 289–316 (1980).

FAWCETT, N. P.: Pediatric facets of poisonous plants. J. Fla Med. Ass. **65**, 199–204 (1978).

FISHER, A. A.: Contact photodermatitis. In: Contact dermatitis, 2nd ed., Lea & Febiger, Philadelphia (1978).

HAMMERSEN, G.: Vergiftungen im Kindesalter. Med. Monatschr. Pharm. **3**, 161–167 (1980).

HOWARD, R. A., G. P. DE WOLF Jr., and G. H. PRIDE: Living with poisonous plants. Arnoldia **34** (2), 41–96 (1974).

HUMPHREYS, D. J.: A review of recent trends in animal poisoning. Br. Vet. J. **134**, 128–145 (1978).

HUXTABLE, R. J.: Herbal teas and toxins: novel aspects of pyrrolizidine poisoning in the United States. Perspect. Biol. Med. **24**, 1–14 (1980).

JASPERSEN-SCHIB, R.: Pflanzenvergiftungen während 10 Jahren. Schweiz. Apoth. Ztg **114**, 265–267 (1976).

JASPERSEN-SCHIB, R.: Unsere toxischen Garten- und Zimmerpflanzen. Schweiz. Apoth. Ztg **117**, 398–416 (1979).

KINGSBURY, J. M.: Phytotoxicology. In: Casarett, L. and J. Doull (eds.), Toxicology. The basic science of poisons, MacMillan, New York, pp. 591–603 (1975).

KORNINGER, H. C. and K. LENZ: Vergiftungen im Kindesalter. Wien. Klin. Wochenschr. **20**, 1–7 (1978).

KRIENKE, E. G. and A. ZAMINER: Pflanzenvergiftungen auf Kinderspielplätzen. Öffentl. Gesundheitsw. **35**, 458–474 (1973).

KRIENKE, E. G.: Akzidentelle Vergiftungen durch Pflanzen aus der Sicht einer Giftinformationszentrale. Internist **17**, 399–410 (1976).

KRIENKE, E. G. and K. E. VON MÜHLENDAHL: Akzidentelle Vergiftungen durch Pflanzen. Notfallmedizin **4**, 486–495, 552–559, 619–627 (1978).

LAMPE, K. F.: Systemic plant poisoning in children. Pediatrics **54**, 347–351 (1974).

DER MARDEROSIAN, A., F. B. GILLER, and F. C. TOJA Jr.: Phytochemical and toxicological screening of household ornamental plants potentially toxic to humans. J. Toxicol. Environ. Health **1**, 939–953 (1976).

MOFFAT, A. C.: Forensic pharmacognosy – poisoning with plants. J. Forens. Sci. Soc. **20**, 103–109 (1980).

MÖSLEIN, P.: Pflanzen als Kontakt-Allergene. Berufsdermatosen **11**, 24–32 (1963).

OEHME, F. W.: Veterinary toxicology. In: Casarett, L. and J. Doull (eds.), Toxicology. The basic science of poisons, MacMillan, New York, pp. 701–727 (1975).

OEHME, F. W.: Veterinary toxicology: the epidemiology of poisonings in domestic animals. Clin. Toxicol. **10**, 1–21 (1977).

OPP, M.: Beautiful but dangerous. Med. World News **18** (10), 38–43 (1977).

ROOK, A., D. S. WILKINSON, and F. J. G. EBLING (eds.): Plant dermatitis. In: Textbook of dermatology, 3rd ed., Blackwell Scientific, Oxford, London, Edinburgh, Melbourne (1979).

SIEGEL, R. K.: Herbal intoxication – psychoactive effects from herbal cigarettes, teas and capsules. J. Am. Med. Ass. **236**, 473–476 (1976).

SIEGERS, C. P.: I. Vergiftungen durch Pflanzen. Z. Allg. Med. **54**, 1151–1158 (1978). II. Vergiftungen durch Pilze. Z. Allg. Med. **54**, 1190–1195 (1978).

VALE, J. A. and T. J. MEREDITH: Poisonous plants and fungi. In: Vale, J. A. and T. J. Meredith (eds.), Poisoning. Diagnosis and treatment, Update Books, London, Dordrecht, Boston, pp. 193–201 (1981).

2. Toxicologically significant plant constituents

The substances responsible for the toxic effects of plants arise through very different biogenetic pathways and are mostly so-called secondary metabolites, whose formation and accumulation so clearly distinguish plant metabolism from that of the animal organism. Many plant poisons are highly active substances, and since ancient times they have served the purposes of murder and suicide [L14; M51], but in suitable doses they are also of importance as medicines. The occurrence of other, pharmacologically less active, substances makes a plant a poisonous plant because they are present in high concentration or because they accumulate after chronic use.

The following sections provide a brief general account of the most important plant substances that function as poisons. Additional information on individual substances or groups of substances will be found under the discussions of the family characteristics or under the plants themselves. In a certain number of toxic plants, there are compounds present that are peculiar to those plants (or occur only rarely elsewhere) and are responsible for the toxic properties. A few of these substances are mentioned, but others do not come within the scope of the book. Finally, it must be pointed out that often the nature of the poisonous principle(s) in a plant is still unclear, even though a name may have been given to it and is still being used, e.g. such names as ligustrin, viburnin, or aroin.

Essential oils. Essential oils are mixtures usually of numerous steam-volatile, chiefly lipophilic, metabolites that in the plant are stored in special organs and are perceived by man through stimulation of the sense of smell. Essential oils often find use as scents and as constituents of spices and medicinal herbs. On the skin they have an irritant action and stimulate the flow of blood, e.g. pine oil. But essential oils may also act as contact allergens and an example of this is the laurel oil that at one time was used to impregnate hat bands [B6; S92].

Because of their lipophilic nature, they are well taken up by the skin and mucous membranes and after being absorbed they act as general cell poisons. Taken by mouth in large doses, they are not without harm in man, as is made clear in recent reports on cases of poisoning with eucalyptus oil [P11] and pine oil [K61], for example.

A few terpene and phenylpropane derivatives – both groups of substances are present in varying amounts and comprise the majority of constituents identified in essential oils – are marked by especially high toxicity, so that the essential oils in which they occur may give rise to serious poisoning. A few representatives may be mentioned by way of example:

Of the monoterpenes* (C_{10} aliphatic or cyclic compounds), thujone, which is present in oil of wormwood and other plants (see also Cupressaceae), comes to mind [V12]. Pulegone, from pennyroyal, *Mentha pulegium,* can give rise to serious, even fatal, cases of poisoning when the essential oil of the plant is misused as an abortifacient [G28; S96; V1]. Numerous cases of poisoning due to camphor, derived from the essential oil of the camphor tree, *Cinnamomum camphora,* have arisen either through taking camphor-containing liniments or through percutaneous absorption after external application [A17; P14; R13; T18].

Apiol, safrole, and myristicin are phenylpropane compounds known for their toxic effects: apiol is a constituent of parsley oil, from *Peterselinum crispum,* which, like parsley decoctions [G13], has been used to procure abortion. Safrole is a constituent of sassafras oil, from *Sassafras albidum* (Lauraceae), and is hepatotoxic and carcinogenic [S42]. Myristicin is the toxic principle [W12], and probably also one of the narcotic principles [W12; K67; S111], of nutmeg oil.

Alkaloids. Alkaloids are usually basic substances with nitrogen bound in a ring system. They mostly occur combined with plant acids and are widely distributed in the plant kingdom. Many, but by no means all, have

---
* For other toxic terpenes, see below under Terpenes.

marked physiological effects on the human and animal organism. The most important groups present as constituents of poisonous plants are:

■ **Quinolizidine alkaloids.** This group is derived from the nor-lupinan skeleton and is found scattered throughout the plant kingdom, e.g. in Lythraceae and Nymphaeaceae. Cytisine, sparteine, and similar alkaloids are toxicologically important and are present in the Fabaceae (see p.121), being responsible for the toxicity of laburnum, lupin (the 'sweet' mutants have little alkaloid present), and various kinds of broom.

■ **Indole alkaloids.** Powerfully acting compounds such as strychnine, etc., belong to this group. As constituents of European plants, however, their occurrence – and hence importance – is negligible.

■ **Isoquinoline alkaloids.** Benzyl-isoquinoline derivatives are toxic components of the Papaveraceae, e.g. chelerythrine, bulbocapnine, morphine, etc., and the alkaloids of ipecacuanha (ipecacuanha syrup), emetine and cephaeline, are also isoquinoline bases.

■ **Pyridine/Piperidine alkaloids.** These alkaloids, which often occur in the plant as *N*-oxides, are esters of amino-alcohols (substituted pyrrolizidines) with necic acids (mono- or di-carboxylic acids, some of which are branched-chain acids, e.g. tiglic acid and angelic acid). As constituents of the genera *Senecio* and *Crotalaria,* as well as of various Boraginaceae, e.g. *Heliotropium,* they have considerable toxicological importance because of their hepatotoxic and carcinogenic effects. Animal diseases and poisoning in man as a result of the chronic intake of preparations containing these plants are known; see Asteraceae (p.63).

■ **Steroidal alkaloids.** These comprise, on the one hand, the glyco-alkaloids of the genus *Solanum* and, on the other, the toxic constituents of *Veratrum, Zigadenus,* and *Schoenocaulon* (Liliaceae). It is particularly the esterified compounds of the protoveratrine type that are dangerous poisons; jervine derivatives are teratogenic [K16; K17].

■ **Terpenoid alkaloids.** The poly-esterified nor-diterpenes whose nitrogen is methylated or ethylated (alkamines) are highly toxic compounds and are found in monk's-hood and also in larkspur; see Ranunculaceae (p.172).

■ **Tropane alkaloids.** Esters of tropanol with various acids, including tropic acid, are constituents of the well-known poisonous (and narcotic) plants deadly nightshade, henbane, and thorn-apple. Hyoscyamine and atropine are parasympatholytics, at higher doses acting as central stimulants; the closely related scopolamine, however, has a mainly central-depressant action. See Solanaceae (p.201).

■ **Other alkaloids.** Colchicine and other structurally similar compounds are the dangerous poisonous substances (C-mitotic agents) of meadow saffron as well as the glory lily, *Gloriosa.* See Liliaceae (p.138). *Taxus baccata,* yew, contains labile and structurally complicated alkaloids called taxines. See Taxaceae (p.223).

Toxic amino acids. While the amino acids required for synthesising the body proteins are essential food constituents for the animal and human organism, among the more than 300 non-protein amino acids derived from plants there are some with toxic properties [U3]. As a rule, their toxicity is not great, so that it is only on chronic ingestion or in certain deficiency conditions that metabolic disturbances become apparent. Some of these amino acids are responsible for poisoning in grazing animals. Mimosine, which occurs in *Mimosa pudica* and *Leucaena leucocephala,* or indospicine, present in *Indigofera* species, are only of interest in tropical regions [H33]. Further details, also relating to those amino acids that can cause illness in man, e.g. lathyrism, are to be found under Fabaceae (p.121).

The hypoglycaemic amino acids hypoglycine A and B, from the tropical *Blighia sapida* (Sapindaceae), contain a cyclopropane ring in their molecules and quite often eating the fruits leads to symptoms of poisoning – akee poisoning or Jamaica vomiting disease [B29; S52].

Cyanogenic glycosides. The cyanogenic glycosides are cyanhydrins (α-hydroxynitriles) combined via a glyco-sidic linkage with one or two sugars. Their toxicity is due to the liberation of hydrogen cyanide (hydrocyanic acid). While HCN is undoubtedly one of the most toxic substances for man (the lethal dose is 1 mg/kg body weight), toxicologically the cyanogenic glycosides are usually overrated. They generally occur in plants in relatively small amounts; moreover, the liberation of HCN from them is a slow process that does not go to completion. Of the more than 2000 species from about 90 families in which the compounds have been found [S43; S44], some Rosaceae, especially their seeds, are of particular toxicological interest. See Rosaceae (p.186).

Many of the plant materials widely used in the tropics as foodstuffs contain cyanogenic glycosides, e.g. the manioc tubers from *Manihot esculenta,* and are not edible until they have been heat-treated, either by roasting or by prolonged boiling with water. As far as the pharmacist is concerned, the presence of cyanogenic glycosides in linseed should be noted; however, during the normal therapeutic use of the seeds as a laxative these substances do not constitute a danger [S16].

Cardioactive glycosides. These compounds, known as cardiotonic or cardiac glycosides because of their pharmacological effects, are steroidal glycosides with a characteristic lactone ring at C-17 of the cyclopentanoperhydrophenanthrene skeleton; cardenolides have a 5-membered lactone ring with one double bond and the bufa- or (scilla-)dienolides have a six-membered lactone ring with two double bonds.

The isolated pure substances are important medicinal agents which because of their low therapeutic index can lead to poisoning. Further, as constituents of plants, the cardiac glycosides also have toxicological importance. Thus, owing to their conspicuous fruits, lily-of-the-valley, *Convallaria majalis,* and spindle, *Euonymus europaeus,* figure prominently in advisory work on poisonous plants (see Tables 1 and 2). Another cardiac-glycoside plant that ought to be mentioned is the foxglove, *Digitalis* species. In contrast, yellow pheasant's-eye *(Adonis vernalis),* wallflower, *(Cheiranthus cheiri),* mustard species *(Erysimum* species), and crown vetch *(Coronilla varia)* rarely appear as poisonous plants. In the Mediterranean region, there are also the sea squill *(Urginea maritima)* and the very popular pot or tub plant oleander *(Nerium oleander).*

Despite the high toxicity and low therapeutic index of the constituents, the prognosis for those who have ingested material of plants containing cardiotonic glycosides is usually favourable, since (a) the very bitter taste normally prevents large amounts of plant material being taken, and (b) often spontaneous vomiting occurs. Moreover, since for a number of primary glycosides the proportion absorbed on oral administration is known to be low, unlike overdosing with medicinal preparations, glycoside concentrations that can bring about serious poisoning are not usually reached [M50]. Nevertheless, if poisoning as a result of ingesting material containing cardiac glycosides is suspected, medical help should certainly be sought. For further information, see Scrophulariaceae *(Digitalis)* and Apocynaceae *(Nerium).*

Furanocoumarins. Furanocoumarins are coumarin derivatives with a furan ring attached at the 6, 7- or 7, 8-position – psoralen type, linear compounds; angelicin type, angular compounds; see p.37. Furanocoumarins occur mainly in the Rutaceae* and Apiaceae (Umbelliferae) and are of toxicological importance because of their photosensitising properties. After percutaneous (also oral) absorption the effect of light is to bring about injury to the skin with erythema and blistering (meadow dermatitis).

The naphthodianthrone derivative hypericin is also a photosensitising agent and as a constituent of *Hypericum perforatum* can cause poisoning in animals [A14]. For photosensitising plant substances, see [T16].

Plant acids. While some of the acids accumulated by plants, especially in their fruits, are non-toxic and are therefore valued as flavour components (malic, tartaric, citric, and ascorbic acids), other plant acids may deploy very considerable toxic activity which is not due solely to their acidity. The most important of these compounds in European plants is **oxalic acid** and its soluble sodium, potassium, and ammonium salts. Through the formation of insoluble calcium salts they cause disturbances in the calcium economy of man and animals and more particularly in the mechanism of blood coagulation; for poisoning with pure oxalic acid and potassium hydrogen oxalate, see [F6; J11; M51; N8]. Along with the oxalis family (Oxalidaceae) may be mentioned sorrel and dock *(Rumex)* and rhubarb *(Rheum)* of the buckwheat family (Polygonaceae), which, together with much insoluble oxalate, accumulate soluble oxalic acid in high concentrations. However, the cases of poisoning as a result of eating rhubarb leaves described in the older literature were probably due to the presence of reduced anthracene glycosides [S93]. For animal poisoning by oxalate-containing plants, see [J3; J4] and by *Rumex venosus,* see [D7].

Oxalic acid is also the cause of poisoning by members of the goosefoot family (Chenopodiaceae [G2; H43]), grape family (Vitaceae) and begonia family (Begoniaceae), and it may likewise be involved in cases due to certain grasses (Poaceae (Graminae)) and members of the arum family (Araceae). Concerning the interaction of mechanical irritation of the mucous membranes and free oxalic acid as possible toxic principle, see p.51.

For sorbic and parasorbic acids, see *Sorbus aucuparia* (p.197).

Toxic amino acids: see Amino acids (above).

Fluorinated carboxylic acids (fluoracetic acid and related compounds) are very poisonous, but as constituents of European toxic plants are of no importance. They occur in South African Dichapetalaceae and also in non-European species of *Acacia, Gastrolobium,* and *Oxylobium* [E14].

---

* Recently it has been found that the furoquinoline alkaloids present in the family also have photosensitising properties [T17].

Poly-ynes (Poly-acetylene compounds). Accumulation of compounds with C≡C bonds in the molecule is found in the plant kingdom among the fungi (Basidiomycetes; here, some of the compounds have antibiotic activity) as well as higher plants. Apart from the ivy family (Araliaceae), it is particularly members of the carrot family (Apiaceae (Umbelliferae)) and composite family (Asteraceae (Compositae)) that are distinguished by the occurrence of these substances.

Recently, phototoxic effects caused by these compounds have been reported for the Asteraceae [T15], and as the highly toxic constituents of certain representatives of the Apiaceae they are of considerable toxicological interest (see p.37).

Proteins and peptides. Plant proteins, especially the reserve proteins of seeds, are an important food source. After enzymatic hydrolysis in the gastro-intestinal tract, the amino acids are absorbed and built up into the proteins of the body. Nevertheless, there are a number of proteins and peptides that are also of toxicological interest. They are not or only partially hydrolysed in the digestive tract and are evidently absorbed to a considerable extent so that they are also able to exert their specific action when taken by mouth. Among these toxic substances, formerly known as toxalbumins because of their solubility properties, are ricin and similar compounds from *Ricinus* seeds and other Euphorbiaceae (p.113), abrin, robin, and phasin from Fabaceae seeds (p.121), and modeccin from a member of the Passifloraceae. As regards their ability to agglutinate erythrocytes, these compounds exhibit some similarity to the lectins – phyto-haemagglutinins – which are widespread in the plant kingdom, more especially in the Fabaceae. However, as a rule, it is only on parenteral administration that they may be dangerous; and the same is true of the toxic proteins from mistletoe (viscotoxin, p.155).

It may be mentioned in passing that the dangerous poisons of the death cap, the amanitines, being cyclic peptides also belong to this group.

Saponins. Saponins are glycosides of terpenoid aglycones (steroid and triterpenoid) occurring widely in the plant kingdom and endowed with surfactant properties. On shaking, their aqueous solutions form a stable froth. Certain saponin drugs have long been known as fish poisons. The toxicologically interesting property of many saponins is their ability to bring about haemolysis, i.e. the release of haemoglobin from erythrocytes as a result of a change in membrane permeability. However, this only takes place on parenteral administration, since by mouth there is usually only limited absorption. Some saponins irritate the skin and mucous membranes and (perhaps as a result of damage to the mucosa?) are absorbed. Saponins are known to be the toxic constituents of several poisonous plants, including horse-chestnut, ivy, pokeweed, cyclamen (sowbread), and the corncockle *(Agrostemma githago;* now largely disappeared as a weed from cornfields).

Terpenes. Terpenes are substances biosynthesised by plants that in a formal sense contain the branched 5-carbon skeleton of isoprene. Depending on the number of isoprene units involved in the structure of the molecule, the terpenes are divided into several groups:

■ **Monoterpenes** (C_{10} compounds) have already been mentioned as components of essential oils. As a matter of interest, cantharidin may be singled out. It is an animal monoterpene from the blistering beetle or Spanish fly [S28] and, taken internally as a supposed aphrodisiac, it has often been the cause of serious poisoning [E16].

■ **Sesquiterpenes** (C_{15} compounds) can produce distinct pharmacological, including cytotoxic, effects [R14]. Picrotoxinin, from *Anamirta cocculus* (fish berries), and coriamyrtin, from *Coriaria myrtifolia,* are strong convulsant poisons. Anisatin, present in the poisonous shikimi fruits, gossypol, from the seeds of the cotton plant, and geigerin, found in *Geigeria* (Asteraceae) and responsible for the poisoning of sheep in Africa, are further examples of sesquiterpenes. As far as European plants are concerned, helenalin and its derivatives, which occur in the flowering heads of *Arnica* (p.63), and the numerous sesquiterpene lactones that can be the cause of contact allergies [M44] should be noted.

■ **Diterpenes** (C_{20} compounds). Andromedotoxin, present in Ericaceae (p.105), mezerein, isolated from mezereon (p.226), and phorbol esters, occurring in Euphorbiaceae (p.113), all have toxic properties. They are closely related structurally and, besides having a powerful irritant effect on the skin, some of them are co-carcinogenic. The alkaloids that are found in monk's-hood and larkspur (p.178) must also be regarded biogenetically as diterpene derivatives.

■ **Triterpenes** (C_{30} compounds). Included here are the cucurbitacins, the toxic bitter substances of the gourd family (p.92), and the constituents of lantana (p.230).

Also worth pointing out are the saponins with triterpenoid aglycones, the saponin-like steroidal alkaloids, and the compounds like those of the vincetoxin group.

3. The most important plants with alleged or actual toxic properties

AMARYLLIDACEAE

PLANTS of the **Amaryllis family** (Amaryllidaceae in the taxonomically narrow sense) are herbaceous perennials that produce bulbs. They are met with as wild or cultivated early-flowering plants (snowdrop, snowflake, daffodil) and as decorative house plants (kaffir lily, elephant's ear, amaryllis, narcissus, jacobean lily, etc.).

Many Amaryllidaceae are regarded as toxic, but reports of serious poisoning are rare and mostly rather old: the poisoning of five people after confusing daffodil bulbs with onions *(Allium cepa)* and taking *ca* 2.3 g of the boiled vegetable [J8]; fatal cases in cattle after being fed daffodil bulbs [cited from J8]. Essentially, recent statistics only show cases of ingestion with at most slight symptoms:

	According to [S38]	According to [K47]
Clivia miniata Kaffir lily	9	–
Galanthus nivalis Snowdrop	5	28
Narcissus pseudonarcissus Daffodil	33	16

(Cases of ingestion over a period of several years)

Toxic constituents. The so-called **Amaryllidaceae alkaloids,** which occur throughout the family and which so far have only been found in this family, are considered the toxic constituents; they are phenanthridine derivatives. The most frequently occurring of these alkaloids is lycorine; in small doses it causes salivation, vomiting, and diarrhoea, in larger amounts central paralysis and collapse. Galanthamine, likewise one of the more common alkaloids in the family, is a cholinesterase inhibitor. Nothing appears to be known about the effects of the other alkaloids, about 100 of which are known, apart from reported antiviral activity [I1; I2].

1 **Clivia miniata Regel**   **Kaffir Lily.**

The parts of the plants richest in alkaloids are the bulbs, especially the epidermis of the outer scale leaves. The mucilage-filled raphide cells (see **112a**) that occur in all parts of the plants also contain much alkaloid [C20]. Dermatitis is often observed as a result of contact with daffodil bulbs and is due to mechanical irritation by the oxalate needles [F9], which pos-

Galanthamine

sibly also brings about better absorption of the alkaloids.

A detailed discussion of toxic Amaryllidaceae has been published by Jaspersen–Schib [J8] and should be consulted for further information.

Lycorine

Symptoms of poisoning. On oral ingestion of small amounts (a few grams, especially of daffodil bulbs), after a short latent period severe vomiting and diarrhoea, coupled with outbreaks of sweating, may be expected.

Treatment. Direct removal of the poison; symptomatic measures.

Kaffir lily (*Clivia miniata*)
The kaffir lily comes from Natal and is a plant up to 50 cm in height produced from a corm. It flowers mostly between February and May and has ovoid red berries. Being a very popular house plant, it is often encountered. According to Amico *et al.* [A6], the kaffir lily contains 0.43% lycorine (calculated on a dry weight basis).

Daffodil (*Narcissus pseudonarcissus*)
The daffodil occurs wild in western Europe and the Iberian Peninsula as a 20–40 cm tall plant with ovoid bulbs *ca* 2–4 cm in diameter (see **111**). In western and central Europe it is an ever-popular early-flowering plant (March – April) and is found both cultivated and naturalised; it has been in cultivation since 1500. Cases of poisoning occur mainly as a result of eating the bulbs [J8; M50]. Jaspersen–Schib [J9] has reported on the poisoning of two children caused by daffodil leaves.

2 *Narcissus pseudonarcissus* L.
Wild Daffodil.

Rhus typhina L.   Stag's Horn Sumach

3 Stag's Horn Sumach

Shrub or tree up to 5 m in height with spreading branches and long creeping stolons; young twigs densely covered with soft hairs.

<u>Leaves</u> imparipinnate (11–13-membered), leaflets sharply toothed; autumn colouring (especially in dry years) scarlet.

<u>Flowers</u> in terminal panicles up to 20 cm long; male flowers yellow-green, female flowers reddish; VI–VII.

<u>Fruits</u> arranged in tomentose erect spikes comprising single small red drupes; VIII–X.

<u>Distribution:</u> Eastern North America; in Europe planted, rarely naturalised.

THE strange, usually picturesque, growth of the stag's horn sumach, its autumnal bright red-coloured foliage, as well as its great tolerance of habitat conditions, have led to the rapid spread of this impressive ornamental in Europe. Because of its close relationship with the highly poisonous *Toxicodendron* species (poison sumach) – they are sometimes included in the same genus, *Rhus* – it has repeatedly been confused with them in the sensational press and counted as one of the twelve poisonous plants most often encountered in playgrounds and public parks [R23]. But quite erroneously, since this sumach plant has not given rise to any ill-effects, and in its country of origin it is also called non-poisonous sumach [H9]. Its fruits are quite sour but are nevertheless used to prepare a refreshing drink. 'When the berries are placed in water for a short time, a pleasing and agreeable drink is formed, known to boys as "Indian lemonade" ' [M29].

Because of the high content of tannin and plant acids, ingestion of the raw fruits or leaves can lead to gastrointestinal upsets. However, compounds highly irritating to the skin, such as are present in poison sumach, are absent from the 'latex' of *Rhus typhina*. The only endemic member of the Anacardiaceae in Europe, Venetian sumach or smoke tree, *Cotinus coggygria*, is probably just as harmless.

On the other hand, some *Schinus* species (*S. molle, S. terebinthifolius*, etc.) can cause irritation of the mucous membranes. Especially in South America, the home of these plants, poisoning in man and animals has been observed [M67]; and in Germany there has been a warning against excessive consumption of their dry fruits [S104].

3-*n*-Pentadecylcatechol – a component of urushiol

Toxic sumach plants. Among the most toxic Anacardiaceae are *Toxicodendron diversilobium* (western poison oak), *T. quercifolium* (poison oak; formerly, *Rhus toxicodendron*), *T. radicans* (poison ivy), and *T. vernix* (poison sumach). Only the leaves of the last species (with up to 11 leaflets) have some morphological resemblance to those of the stag's horn sumach. The leaves of the others are reminiscent of ivy and are composed of three leaflets (see part 5: Compilation of leaf characters). In addition, the fruits of the poisonous *Toxicodendron* species are white and those of *Rhus typhina* are red.

With a few rare exceptions, in Europe these toxic sumach species will only be encountered in botanic gardens; and there they will be labelled as such and usually surrounded by a fence of some kind to prevent visitors coming into direct contact with them.

In North America, their homeland, they are a major problem. It is estimated that in the United States each year *ca* two million people suffer from Rhus dermatitis and that up to 70% of the population is sensitised to the skin-irritant constituents of *Toxicodendron* species. These highly allergenic substances, urushiols, are catechol derivatives with a 15–17(–19)-membered side-chain containing in some cases several double bonds. These compounds are constituents of the latex-like emulsion present in the schizogenous ducts and can therefore only reach the skin and make their unpleasant effects felt after the plant tissue has been damaged. Neither the pollen and flowers nor the smoke of burnt plant material gives rise, as is often alleged, to allergic reactions. After contact with the toxic excretion, immediate and thorough washing of the affected parts with soap will remove the poison from the skin and will occasionally prevent subsequent dermatitis.

Because these plants are of little importance in Europe, the numerous relevant investigations and case histories are not dealt with here, and the reader is referred to the literature [B2; D25; G8; G25; M42; R26].

APIACEAE (UMBELLIFERAE)

THE large **Carrot family** (Apiaceae, Umbelliferae) is divided into three subfamilies, but here only members of the Apioideae are of interest as poisonous plants. In western and central Europe, which has about 100 herbaceous species, the Umbelliferae are easily recognised as a group because of their typical habit, but not all of them can be distinguished individually without difficulty. The small, usually whitish, flowers occur in compound umbels; the alternate, as a rule pinnate or digitate, leaves have prominent sheaths and the cremocarps that split into two mericarps are also a characteristic feature.

Many representatives of the family have become important as vegetables and spices, and also as medicinal plants, because they accumulate essential oil (concerning apiol, see p.25) in vittae, i.e. schizogenous oleoresin canals. Apart from hemlock, which, because of its alkaloid content, was already known in antiquity as a poisonous plant (death of Socrates; cup of hemlock), the **toxicological significance** of the Apiaceae is due essentially to the occurrence of two types of compound – poly-ynes and furanocoumarins [F27].

Poly-ynes (Poly-acetylene compounds). These characteristic substances, already dealt with in the general introduction (p.28), are widely distributed in the family, but mostly in such low concentrations that poisoning does not take place. Thus, even the roots of *Daucus carota*, carrot, for example, contain a poly-yne, carotatoxin. However, some Umbelliferae accumulate poly-ynes in greater amounts and are therefore dangerously toxic plants. Among these are *Cicuta*

virosa, cowbane or water hemlock, as well as members of the genus *Oenanthe*, especially *O.crocata*, hemlock water-dropwort (dead men's fingers), and also the somewhat less dangerous *Aethusa cynapium*, fool's parsley, and *Chaerophyllum temulentum*, rough chervil.

While the poly-ynes of *Cicuta* and *Oenanthe (crocata)* are C_{17} compounds, those present in *Aethusa cynapium* are C_{13} compounds:

HOH₂C–(CH₂)₂–C≡C–C≡C | H₃C–(H₂C)₂–HOHC–(CH=CH)₂–CH=CH

Cicutoxin

H₃C–CH=CH–(C≡C)₂–(CH=CH)₂–CH₂–CH₃

Aethusin

Information on poly-ynes can be found in [H35] and in the more recent review by Bohlmann [B36].

Since all these substances are volatile and readily decomposed, danger from their toxic properties arises mainly through consumption of fresh plant material. Owing to the particular habitat of cowbane (water hemlock) and hemlock water-dropwort, cases of poisoning are fortunately rare but nevertheless have been described in recent years [A12; C7; C25; R12; W26]. Poisoning by poly-yne-containing plant material is characterised especially by persistent vomiting and the spontaneous occurrence of clonic-tonic convulsions, and it resembles picrotoxin poisoning. There is little certain knowledge regarding the point of attack of the poly-ynes in the animal or human body. Pharmacological and toxicological investigations are few

[G26; R4; S78]. Dubois and Schneider [D22] have recently been able to show that oenanthotoxin reversibly inhibits the sodium flux and action potentials in animal cell membranes. Cicutoxin is also an inhibitor of the electron transport that takes place during photosynthesis [R24].

Furanocoumarins. Coumarins with a condensed furan ring (see p.27) have phototoxic (photosensitising) and/or mutagenic and carcinogenic activity [F8; I7]. Under the influence of long-wavelength UV light, they form photo-adducts with DNA bases, especially thiamine. While linear compounds with two functional groups (double bonds in both the furan and pyrone rings) form bi-adducts and can therefore bring about cross-linking between two DNA strands, the angular compounds are only able to form mono-adducts. The bifunctional linear furanocoumarins are mutagenic and carcinogenic, and possible causes of phototoxicity are being sought in the formation of mono-adducts with DNA as well as interactions with proteins, enzymes, RNA, or ribosomes in epidermal cells [E12; S18; S19].

OCH₃

8-Methoxypsoralen (linear)

Angelicin (angular)

Furanocoumarins are present in all parts of the plants concerned, especially the rhizomes and/or fruits. They are localised in the oleoresin canals and the adjacent epithelial cells. The most important furanocoumarin-containing meadow plants belong to the genera *Heracleum* (hogweed), *Pastinaca* (wild parsnip), *Peucedanum* (hog's fennel), and *Angelica* (wild angelica). It is known that *Apium graveolens* (wild celery) after infection with *Sclerotinia sclerotiorum* can form furanocoumarins as lectins.

Photodermatitis resulting from contact between the leaves and the skin or through wetting with the juice of the plant, e.g. after cutting or breaking off the stems, and subsequent exposure to light causes serious damage to the skin which often goes hand in hand with increased pigmentation. It is because of this that plant extracts containing furanocoumarins have long been used in the treatment of pigmentation defects, e.g. vitiligo. More recently, the symptomatic treatment of psoriasis with the bifunctional 8-MOP (8-methoxypsoralen = xanthotoxin) and irradiation with long-wavelength UV light has met with considerable success [A 18; F 30; W 30].

Cicuta virosa L. Cowbane, Water Hemlock

4 Cowbane

1–1.5 m tall herb with hollow stems (and petioles) and tuberous, thickened, chambered rhizomes (5).
Water or marsh plant at the edges of ponds or river banks, usually in shallow water.
<u>Leaves</u> bi- to tri-pinnatisect; lower ones long-petiolate, upper ones short-petiolate or sessile; often doubly serrate; variable, depending on local habitat conditions, e.g. apex of leaf segments linear and sparsely toothed.
<u>Flowers</u> staminate or androgynous, white, with equal petals, in stalked umbels with 15–25 rays bearing many-flowered secondary umbels; bracts (usually) absent; VI–VIII.
<u>Fruits</u> ovoid and mericarps (carpels) usually not separating from each other.
<u>Distribution:</u> Northern and central Europe, in the south rarer to absent; in North America many other species, including *C.douglasii* and *C.maculata*, are likewise known as poisonous plants.

COWBANE or water hemlock is one of the most poisonous plants because of its poly-yne content and its extermination has been the subject of official regulations. All parts of the plant are highly toxic when fresh, particularly the underground organs (5) whose smell is reminiscent of parsnips or celery. On drying, the poly-ynes are largely destroyed (at least in the outer layers of tissue). In a case of suicide described by Berndt [B25], it was evidently chewing dried cowbane roots that led to death. Horses after being given 500 g of the dried herb have died within 15 hours [B23].

While in the older literature many cases of poisoning especially in children (with a mortality rate of over 30%) are to be found, there have been few reports from Europe in recent years [R18]. Not long ago, Bartel and Gerber [B15] described in detail the poisoning of two children through eating the tubers of cowbane:

An 8-year old boy who had eaten a tuber died from acute cardiac failure, in spite of being treated clinically for 12 hours.

The second patient, a 9½-year old boy who had only bitten off a piece of tuber and had spat it out because of the unpleasant taste, was saved after six

he was malingering and sent him out to do the work. About 15 minutes later his brother found him lying unconscious on the ground, frothing at the mouth, and with vomit close by. Violent convulsions then began and continued, along with vomiting, while the boy was being driven to hospital. It is believed that a new speed record for the journey (34 miles over gravel roads) was established. Administration of oxygen by mask with positive pressure and intravenous, later intramuscular, diazepam gradually brought the convulsions under control; four days later the boy was discharged, and six months after the incident there were no apparent ill-effects.'

Symptoms of poisoning. Even chewing small (thumb-size) pieces of rhizome or root soon (30–60 minutes) leads to burning pains in the mouth, severe and prolonged vomiting, and subsequent convulsions (see the above case history).

Treatment. Gastric lavage with activated charcoal. The most important therapeutic measure is the prevention of the convulsions; thiobarbiturates, e.g. thiopentone sodium (= Pentothal®) or diazepam, which according to [S78] is less active, have been indicated as antidotes. Thus, Starreveld and Hope [S78] in a case of serious poisoning in a 54-year old adult immediately after admission slowly injected a thiobarbiturate, 350 mg i.v., and followed this by infusing further thiobarbiturate over a period of eight hours, 2 mg/ml in isotonic saline, to give a total of 2.2 g.

5 **Cicuta virosa: (Left) Tuberous rhizome with root scars. (Right) Characteristic chambering and the golden-yellow juice on the cut surface.**

hours of treatment which included positive-pressure respiration and the administration of muscle-relaxants.

More recent reports of cowbane poisoning have come from North America, where, in addition to C.virosa, other Cicuta species, e.g. C.douglasii and C.maculata, occur and are likewise known as dangerously toxic plants [A12; C7; C25; W26]. In discussing a case of poisoning by C.douglasii, western water hemlock, which happened on 18.4.1974 in Vancouver, Mutter [M66] writes:

'While on a field trip with his class from school a 13-year old boy ate roots of a plant that some of the children identified as "wild carrot". When he arrived home about an hour later, he complained of abdominal pain and dizziness. But since he had been given garden chores to do his parents thought

Appendix. Of the other poly-yne-containing plants, the hemlock water-dropwort, *Oenanthe crocata,* merits special attention. It occurs in southern and parts of western Europe, including Great Britain where it is considered to be one of the most dangerous poisonous plants [M43; P30]. *O.crocata* – like *Cicuta virosa* or the Central European fine-leaved water-dropwort, *O.aquatica* – has a preference for wet and marshy localities. Although no cases of poisoning due to *O.aquatica* are known (it used to form the source of the now obsolete drug Fructus Phellandri; for the composition of the essential oil, see [V9; V10]), cases of serious poisoning with *O.crocata* are to be found both in the older and the more recent literature [A9; G26; M43]. Since the beginning of this century, at least 10 fatal cases have been published – the latest victim was a vegetarian hippie [A10].

It is true that the toxic poly-ynes in the juice (oenanthotoxin, etc.; for its fluorimetric assay, see [C30]) are rapidly decomposed in the air, but inside the fleshy roots they remain stable and hence active longer. The highest poly-yne content is in the roots in winter and the early part of spring [A9]. In the case described by Mitchell and Routledge [M43], an ecology student had been working on a farm during his holidays and had prepared a salad from the roots of some plants nearby, since a little piece of the raw root had a 'pleasant taste'. The serious poisoning that resulted was caused by the root of *Oenanthe crocata,* but fortunately was not fatal. However, the case does illustrate the point that without adequate knowledge the present-day fashionable endeavour to find an 'alternative' diet can have quite dangerous consequences (see also p.14).

Toxic concentrations of poly-ynes also occur in fool's parsley *(Aethusa*

6 Roots of Oenanthe crocata (Dead men's fingers).

cynapium) and in rough chervil *(Chaerophyllum temulentum;* **10)**. Both plants are also said to contain coniine-like volatile alkaloids [H35]. While *C.temulentum* is not involved in human poisoning, cases can arise with

---

Symptoms of poisoning and **treatment:** see *Cicuta virosa.*

---

rough chervil, a garden weed, through confusion with parsley, *Petroselinum crispum.* Since rough chervil does not produce crispate leaves, the form of parsley with crispate leaves is preferred for cultivation. Microscopically, parsley and rough chervil can be distinguished by the number of stomata on the under surface of their leaves **(7)**, rough chervil having about twice as many as parsley [M48].

In 1975 Swart [S 100] published an account of poisoning in goats by *Aethusa cynapium*.

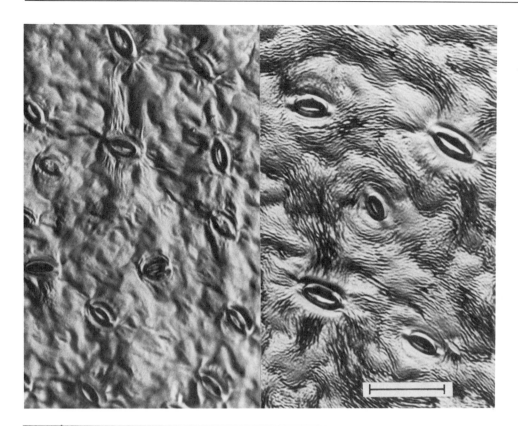

7 **Lower epidermis of the leaves of: (Left) Aethusa cynapium and (Right) Petroselinum crispum; gelatin impression. The scale marked corresponds to 50 μm.**

Conium maculatum L. Hemlock

8 Hemlock

1–2.5 m tall, annual or biennial plants with finely grooved, round, and, at ground level and higher up, spotted stem; distinctly smaller and with similarly spotted but dirty reddish stem: *Chaerophyllum temulentum* (see p.44). Growing along hedges, fences, roadsides, and on waste ground.
<u>Leaves</u> intense green, 2–4-pinnate, and glabrous.
<u>Flowers</u> whitish, umbels with bracts; VI–VIII.
<u>Fruits</u> ovoid with wavy ridges, glabrous (unlike aniseed).
<u>Distribution:</u> Throughout Europe, rarer in the north.

ALTHOUGH hemlock is one of the most widely known poisonous plants, the description has been kept brief and in what follows just a few points are mentioned. In poison control work only occasional enquiries are made regarding hemlock [K47]. The unpleasant odour of the plant – of mouse urine – is due to the free base coniine, and it becomes stronger after crushing the plant material and on making it alkaline. It effectively deters consumption of the plant. The presence of hemlock fruits in aniseed, which used to be mentioned often enough, rarely occurs nowadays. **9** shows some umbelliferous fruits, including the very similar ones belonging to hemlock and aniseed. Nevertheless, the report of a poisoning that took place in 1981, involving school children who had eaten *Conium* roots [D3], shows that this plant can still give rise to cases of poisoning.

Toxic constituents. The piperidine alkaloid coniine and related compounds are present in all parts of the plant and they accumulate in particularly high concentrations (up to 3.5%) in the fruit – mainly in the inner wall, the so-called coniine layer.

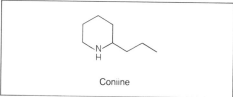

9 Fruits of several Apiaceae (Umbelliferae): (Left to right) Cicuta virosa, Aethusa cynapium, Conium maculatum, Pimpinella anisum, Heracleum sphondylium (showing the vittae).

Coniine

In addition to nicotinic activity, coniine also exhibits curare-like actions and it paralyses the striated musculature starting at the legs and rising until finally, while still fully conscious, death takes place as a result of respiratory paralysis. Plato's description of the death of Socrates gives rise to speculation even today. (Did Socrates die of hemlock poisoning? [O1]).

Treatment. Measures to prevent absorption of the poison (elicit vomiting, gastric lavage, activated charcoal), strychnine in small doses (2 mg/h), and in the case of respiratory arrest artificial respiration [M50].

10 Chaerophyllum temulentum L.   Rough Chervil.

Poisoning occasionally occurs in animals. Cases have been described [B23] in cattle with depraved appetite – an indication of a latent metabolic disorder. While animals such as goats and sheep are not very sensitive, pigs react to quite small doses with clear symptoms of poisoning. If pregnant sows survive ingestion of the plant, besides the acute symptoms limb deformations are observed in the piglets [D26; E4]. That coniine has such teratogenic effects has been demonstrated in cattle [K15].

Heracleum sphondylium L.   Hogweed, Common Cow Parsnip

11 Hogweed

0.5–1.5 m tall biennial or perennial herb with angular, grooved, mostly hispid stems and swollen leaf sheaths. On moist nutrient-rich soils, fertile meadows.
<u>Leaves</u> lobed or pinnatifid, also entire, on the whole very variable; lower leaves up to 60 cm long, petiolate; hispid, soft-haired, or even glabrous.
<u>Flowers</u> white, greenish, or reddish in large double umbels with rays unequal in length, bracteoles many; VI–IX.
<u>Fruits</u> flattened, usually elliptical with a broad marginal wing, 6–10 mm long (see 9).
<u>Distribution:</u> Throughout Europe; the plant varies greatly in many characters and it is divided into a series of subspecies and varieties.

THE hogweed is one of those plants which, as a result of the occurrence of 6,7-furanocoumarins (xanthotoxin = 8-methoxypsoralen, bergapten, imperatorin, etc.), display phototoxic properties and lead to the clinical picture of meadow dermatitis, characterised by reddening of the skin, swelling, formation of vesicles, lesions, and increased pigmentation [F8]. Strong illumination and high humidity intensify the reaction of the skin [F8]. Unless the case history is carefully recorded, it is easy to make an incorrect diagnosis. By way of example, the following report from the daily press [F21] may be cited:

Plant juice injured children! *It was not industrial acid but the caustic juice of the meadow plants cow parsnip and giant hogweed that some weeks ago in Hagen damaged the skin of eight children aged between 6 and 14. At first, it was believed that industrial effluents in a stream called the Volme in which the children had been paddling were responsible for the severe damage to the skin. . . . The error was rectified as a result of the definitive diagnosis established by the Dortmund and Düsseldorf Skin Clinic.*

According to the investigations of Weimarck and Nilsson [W 13], the leaves of five subspecies of hogweed (*transsilvanicum, pyrenaicum, montanum, orsinii,* and especially *alpinum)* were distinctly phototoxic in the Candida test; while the leaves of subsp. *sphondylium* and *sibiricum* yielded mostly negative, those of subsp. *granatense* and *ternatum* gave variable, results. The fruits of all the subspecies examined were phototoxic and so were the roots (except those of subsp. *alpinum).*

There are no specific **therapeutic** measures. Purely symptomatic treatment to reduce the swelling and inflammation can give relief. Once the blisters have become dry there are usually no complications, but full recovery of the skin requires a longer period.

Heracleum mantegazzianum. The giant hogweed, *Heracleum mantegazzianum,* is also distinguished by pronounced phototoxicity [M 42]. The plant often grows to a height of more than 3 m, and it has leaves with laminae as much as 1 m long and huge umbels. It comes from the Caucasus and was brought to Europe about 1890, where, because of its stately growth, it became popular as an ornamental in large gardens. The plant is frequently encountered wild and it spreads far and wide through the scattering of its fruits, so that in southern Bavaria, for example, investigations into its chemical control have already been undertaken [K 51]. In 1976 Camm *et al.* [C4] reported on photodermatoses caused by naturalised plants in America. With the giant hogweed they occur especially when the stems are being cut; again and again this leads to serious inflammation of the skin, as the juice runs out of the stem and drops on to the skin which is then exposed to the sun [F27]. **12** shows the course of an experimentally produced photodermatitis, brought about by placing a freshly cut piece of the stem on the skin of the forearm. Warnings of the dangers arising from too close an acquaintance with this plant have been repeatedly given: 'Keep away from that "tree", folks!' [G29]; see also [D 20; F 17; K 21; K 51].

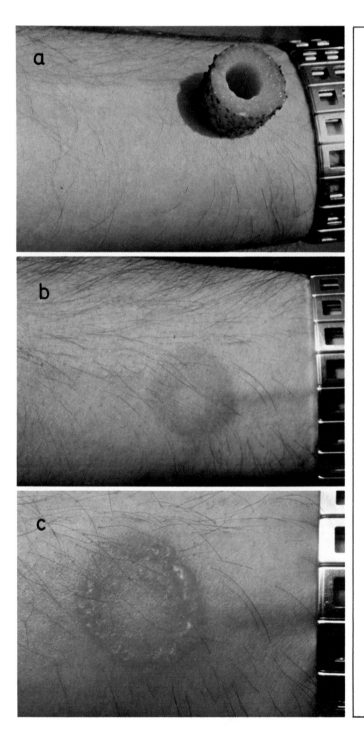

12   The phototoxic effects of Heracleum mantegazzianum:
(a) Contact between the skin and the freshly cut surface of the stem, followed by brief exposure to sunlight.
(b) Reddening of the place of contact on the forearm after 24 hours.
(c) Erythema with extensive blistering after three days.

APOCYNACEAE

Nerium oleander L.   Oleander

THE oleander, a member of the **Dogbane family,** comes from the Mediterranean region and is popular in western and central Europe as a pot and tub plant. Like the yellow oleander, *Thevetia peruviana*, it is widespread in tropical and subtropical regions as an ornamental. *Nerium* has long been known to be poisonous to animals and man and in antiquity was specially mentioned by Theophrastus, Pliny, and Galen. Cases of poisoning, including fatal ones, through drinking infusions of oleander as an abortifacient or for committing suicide have been described [B 40; S 69]. The oleander has been the subject of calls to Poison Control Centres [K 47], but after ingesting flowers or leaves evidently no serious symptoms have been observed. This finding from Central Europe agrees with the results of an Australian study. Shaw *et al.* [S 51] in a period of six years encountered only one serious case among children hospitalised after ingesting oleander *(Nerium + Thevetia),* and that was in a child who had a severe congenital heart defect.

The seeds of yellow oleander seem to be particularly dangerous and they are used in India to poison cattle and for murder. About the forensic detection of the constituents, see Tewari [T 7]. According to Kakrani *et al.* [K 62], 8–10 seeds are enough to kill an adult.

Toxic constituents. Both *Nerium* and *Thevetia* contain cardiac glycosides of the cardenolide type in all parts, but it is only from the seeds that a large number of such compounds has been isolated. Total extracts of the plants or pure glycosides, e.g. peruvoside from the yellow oleander, are used medicinally for cardiac insufficiency. What has been written further on (p.200) about other cardenolide-containing plants is just as true for the oleander: the bitter taste of the cardenolides is a deterrent to excessive consumption of the plant and the

vomiting which often occurs spontaneously prevents the absorption of
large amounts of poison. Hence,
although the plant is very dangerous,
serious poisonings are rare. Recently,
however, Ansford and Morris [A11]
have reported on the death of a 3-year
old child who had played near a yellow
oleander tree and was taken to hospital
for treatment showing the characteristic symptoms of cardiac-glycoside
poisoning. A concentration of
19 nmol/kg cardiac glycosides was
detected by radioimmunoassay in the
heart muscle of the child. The authors
concluded on the basis of this finding
that oleander poisoning had taken
place, although because of the persistent vomiting no remains of plant
material were found in the stomach.

> **Treatment.** See *Digitalis*, p.200.

Other Apocynaceae. The only genus
of the dogbane family indigenous in
Europe is *Vinca*, with *V.minor*, lesser
periwinkle, as the most widespread
species. It is often planted in gardens
and cemeteries. In recent years
Catharanthus roseus, a member of a
related tropical genus, has become a
common pot plant in nurseries and
flower shops. The two plants mentioned contain indole alkaloids with
pronounced pharmacological activity
(vincamine in *V.minor* and vinblastine
and vincristine in *C.roseus*), but so far
no cases of poisoning by these plants
have been reported.

Related to the Apocynaceae are the
Asclepiadaceae, the **Milkweed family,**
which has only one European representative, *Vincetoxicum hirundinaria*. It is rare to common, usually on
loose stony soil, throughout most of
Europe, but is absent from the British
Isles. Owing to its content of steroidal
glycosides with saponin-like properties
(vincetoxin), *Vincetoxicum* is considered as toxic, although, as far as is
known, no cases of poisoning have yet
been observed. Since the thin, whitish
roots look rather like those of the
primrose and are often found as an
adulterant in the drug, the 8th edition
of the German Pharmacopoeia includes an examination of Radix
Primulae for the presence of
Vincetoxicum roots.

AQUIFOLIACEAE

Ilex aquifolium L.   Holly

1–7 m tall evergreen shrub (rarely a tree). In woods in partly shaded humid spots, often associated with beech, on nutrient-poor, non-calcareous, acid soils.
Leaves evergreen, leathery; mostly ovate, but also elliptic, with glossy upper surface, margin more or less undulate, coarsely dentate with spine-tipped teeth; shape, colour, and dentation very variable, depending to some extent on locality and age of the plant; many cultivars with green, white, and yellow variegated leaves.
Flowers dioecious (in some cultivars also androgynous), small, in axillary cymes, creamy white; V–VII.
Fruits red, occasionally yellow, berry-like several-seeded drupes with an aromatic taste; IX–III.
Distribution: Western and central Europe, Balkans, Caucasus, northern Iran. Often planted as ornamental trees and hedges.

THE popularity of holly as a garden and Christmas decoration derives from the cheerful green of its glossy leaves and the bright red of its long-lasting fruits. So it is not surprising that children are quite often tempted to try these 'berries'. In 1977 alone, the Zürich Toxicological Information Centre logged 30 enquiries concerning *I.aquifolium,* and according to the records of other toxicological centres (Berlin, Freiburg, National Clearing-house U.S.A.) ingestion of the plant is not an unusual occurrence. Information about the possible toxic principles of holly, in particular of the fruits, is, however, limited. Leaves and twigs of many South American

Ilex species accumulate purine bases (especially caffeine; up to 1.8%) and have long been used for the preparation of stimulating drinks (maté tree, *I.paraguariensis*), but the leaves of the European holly apparently contain only traces of theobromine [B38]. Again in the leaves, Balansard and Flandrin [B3] found a saponin with distinct haemolytic activity. According to Ward [W9] extracts of the fruits and seeds have digitalis-like cardiotonic activity, and more recently other authors have isolated triterpene compounds [B52; T10] and a very small amount (30 mg from 20 kg fruits) of a bis-nor-monoterpene belonging to a new structural type [T9].

Symptoms of poisoning. The symptoms observed in poisoning by holly, occasionally after consuming more than two 'berries', are gastro-intestinal troubles such as abdominal pains, vomiting, and diarrhoea. Cases ending in death have been described exclusively in the older literature, and recent experience indicates that serious symptoms of poisoning are only likely to occur after consumption of a largish quantity of the fruit. Slight symptoms were noted in just nine out of 64 calls [K47].

Treatment. Symptomatic. When only a few berries have been eaten, as a rule it is not necessary to effect their removal by gastric lavage.

Microscopical characters of the fruit. The small-celled epidermis (**15a**) of *Ilex* fruits shows numerous stomata with 6–7 subsidiary cells (**15b**) and bulging guard cells. In the outermost layers of the pulp there are occasional thickened and pitted stone cells (**15c**). They are readily located in polarised light as bright spots shining through the epidermis. For additional features, see [G30].

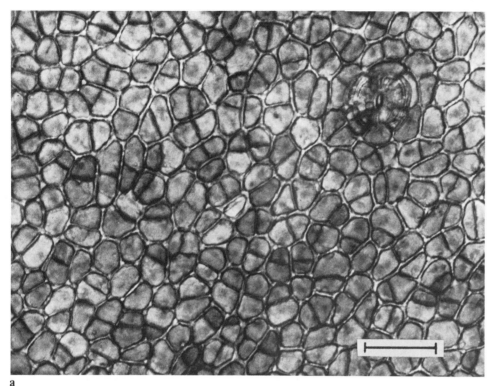

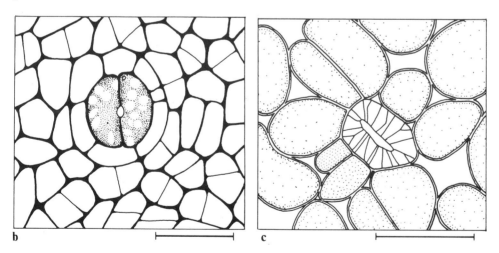

15 Ilex aquifolium. Pericarp: (a) Small-celled epidermis. (b) Stoma. (c) Stone cell in the mesocarp.

ARACEAE

THE large polymorphic **Arum family** has *ca* 1800 species, most of which are perennial herbaceous plants of tropical origin distinguished by striking morphological characters. The leaves often have reticulate venation and the inconspicuous flowers are united in a spadix that is more or less surrounded by a protecting spathe able to take on numerous other functions (a means of attracting pollinators [*Anthurium*], assimilative organ [*Acorus*], insect trap [*Arum*]).

The Araceae are grown for a variety of reasons in different parts of the world. In the tropics a number of genera are cultivated on a large scale – as green vegetables, starch-containing tubers, and pleasant-tasting fruits (*Colocasia* [taro, cocoyam, dasheen]; *Xanthosoma* [okumo, tannia]; *Amorphophallus* [elephant's foot, with tubers weighing up to 10 kg]; *Monstera* [ceriman]) [B 48]. In Europe, on the other hand, because of their attractive flowers or ornamental leaves, representatives of the family are popular as ornamentals and house plants *(Anthurium* [flamingo flower], *Aglaonema* [Chinese evergreens], *Caladium, Dieffenbachia* [dumb cane], *Epipremnum* [ivy arum], *Monstera* [ceriman, Swiss cheese plant], *Philodendron* [sweetheart vine], *Spathiphyllum* [white sails], *Syngonium* [goosefoot], *Zantedeschia* [calla]).

Araceae are generally warmth-loving plants and only a few of them are native to Europe, e.g. lords-and-ladies or cuckoo-pint *(Arum maculatum),* bog arum *(Calla palustris),* and sweet-flag *(Acorus calamus)* which was introduced from Asia in the 16th century and is now naturalised. In the Mediterranean region there are, among others, *Arisarum* and *Dracunculus* species.

A special **anatomical character** in the family is the presence of isolated oil cells, which sometimes occur in such profusion as to allow pharmaceutical use of their metabolic product, the essential oil, e.g. the rootstock of *Acorus calamus* (= Rhizoma Calami). In addition, all Araceae contain calcium oxalate, mostly in the form of raphides (exception: *Acorus*), but also as clusters, crystal sand, or larger single crystals.

Toxic constituents. The skin-irritant and toxic properties of the Araceae are, for want of more precise knowledge, ascribed to 'volatile acrid substances'. Over the years, greatly varying ideas as to the nature of these acrid substances have been put forward [B 10; C 11; F 13; L 1; M 3; O 3; O 19; W 5; W 6], but they have not always been confirmed upon subsequent investigation or they must be considered improbable because the supposed active constituent is present in too low concentration. Be that as it may, there is now little disagreement with the view that the numerous calcium oxalate crystals (raphides) present play a part in the strongly irritant action that most Araceae have on the skin and mucous membranes. These sharp raphides, which are grooved at both ends [B 45; W 8] (see **21**), are present throughout the plants in their millions, and are located in part in highly specialised ejector cells. Through mechanical irritation and perforation of the mucous membranes these raphides facilitate penetration of the acrid principles, as in an injection. In this connection it is worth mentioning that in addition to the crystalline (insoluble) calcium oxalate significant quantities of oxalic acid or its soluble salts are present (see *Dieffenbachia,* p.56).

Symptoms of poisoning. With the exception of *Acorus*, most Araceae have repeatedly given rise to symptoms of poisoning and in a surprisingly similar way. Frequently associated with a local action on the skin or after ingestion of fresh plant material, there is severe irritation of the skin and mucous membranes. Together with itching and burning, there is considerable swelling and inflammation which may give rise to blisters. Hoarseness, salivation, and vomiting are also often observed. The consumption of larger amounts (especially by grazing animals) can lead to severe gastro-enteritis with bleeding and cramps, ending in coma and death. Besides the skin-irritant properties, repeated contact with some species of Araceae, e.g. by florists and nurserymen, can cause genuine allergic reactions in the form of contact dermatitis (see *Philodendron*, p.60). Nothing is yet known about the nature of the allergenic substances.

Treatment. Initial removal of the poison by gastric lavage is only recommended after consumption of larger amounts. In general, medical care is limited to symptomatic treatment of the inflammation. In the case of allergic reactions, further contact with these plants should be avoided.

Appendix. A similar combination of mechanical irritation by raphides and plant toxic principles is also mooted in connection with several other plant families. Thus, in the bulb begonia *(Begonia tuberhybrida;* **Begoniaceae***),* in addition to oxalic acid, cucurbitacin B is present at least in the underground organs [D18]. In some ornamentals belonging to the **Bromeliaceae** (urn plant [*Aechmea fasciata*], green earth star [*Cryptanthus acaulis*], pink quill [*Tillandsia cyanea*], netted vriesea [*Vriesea fenestralis*], etc.), the skin-irritant action of the raphides is believed to be strengthened by proteolytic enzymes. It is suspected that the cause of the poisonings which used to be seen after eating large quantities of the fruit of the wild grape (*Parthenocissus quinquefolium;* **Vitaceae**) was the soluble form of oxalic acid (Warren, cited from [H35]). Although some non-European species of these families have been used in the preparation of arrow poisons, the representatives known in Europe as ornamentals are nowadays only occasionally encountered in toxicological practice.

Arum maculatum L.   Lords-and-Ladies, Cuckoo-pint

a

b

THE toxicity of lords-and-ladies has long been known. While the fresh tubers and other organs have a strong irritant action on mucous membranes, the plant material after boiling for a long time or drying becomes more or less innocuous. Supposedly, volatile acrid substances of unknown chemical structure are responsible for the toxic effect, and even in the more recent literature names such as aroin, aroidin, and aronin are mentioned and the substances sometimes characterised as a coniine-like alkaloid [L23; M50; N11], conicine-like glycoside [B50], or saponin. These can all be traced back

◁16 Lords-and-Ladies: (a) Infructescence. (b) Inflorescence, with the lower part cut open.

15–60 cm tall perennial herb with tubers brown outside and white inside.
In shady beech and mixed deciduous forests, hedges, and thickets, on moist nutrient- and usually humus-rich soil.
Leaves reticulately veined, long-petiolate, hastate, less often with red-brown spots (var. *maculatum*), mostly without spots (var. *immaculatum*).
Flowers unisexual; monoecious, united in a spadix; male flowers at the top, female ones at the bottom (lords-and-ladies!); upper part of spadix naked, clavate; violet-brown; inflorescence as far as the top of the spadix almost completely surrounded by a cone-shaped spathe (flowers forming a trap for insects, see 16b); IV–V.
Fruits few seeded, more or less round, red berries with a sweetish taste; VI–VII.
Distribution: Scattered throughout western, central, and southern Europe; in the Mediterranean region replaced by *Arum italicum*.

to investigations carried out in the middle (by Bird and Enz) or end (by Spica and Biscaro, Chauliaguet) of the 19th century [W10].

From 100 kg of fresh plant material Chauliaguet and co-workers were able to obtain by known methods 4–5 g of a dark-coloured base. Because of its volatility and smell resembling that of mouse urine, they assumed that it was coniine or a related alkaloid and that it was identical with the acrid principle [S73].

In 1965 Stahl and Kaltenbach [S73] repeated the investigation with the help of mild chromatographic micro-methods and obtained the following results:

(1) From 10 kg of fresh leaves of *Arum maculatum* they isolated 0.412 g of a crystalline product.
(2) The unpleasant-smelling volatile-alkaloid fraction consisted of a mixture of a little nicotine (0.7 mg/kg) and three primary amines (including *iso*butylamine; see also [S81]).
(3) Hemlock alkaloids and non-volatile alkaloids were definitely absent from the plant material examined.

It is therefore still an open question as to whether, in addition to the soluble and insoluble salts of oxalic acid, worthwhile amounts of other 'acrid substances' are present in the different organs of lords-and-ladies. From *Pinellia* tubers, which in East Asia are used medicinally for the same purpose as were the tubers of *Arum maculatum,* formerly an official drug (Tubera Ari) [W10], Suzuki [S99] obtained a glycoside of 3,4-dihydroxy-benzaldehyde (only 900 mg from 50 kg dry plant material). But, simply on the basis of the small amount present, it seems misleading to consider it to be the acrid substance responsible for the irritant action.

Fatal **cases of poisoning** by *Arum maculatum* occur mainly among grazing livestock [D1; M54]. When there is inadequate grazing in the spring and the animals are limited in their choice of forage, they are often no longer put off by the acrid taste of the juicy green leaves of the plant. The symptoms of poisoning observed in such cases (general weakness, motor disturbance, paralysis of intestinal peristalsis, convulsions, followed by collapse and death), as well as the pathological changes in certain organs (hyperaemia of the mucosa, haemorrhages, oedematous rumen walls, renal inflammation and swelling), are strikingly similar to those noted with pure oxalates [F6; N8] or other oxalic acid-containing plants (*Halogeton glomeratus* [U.S.A.], *Oxalis pes-caprae* [Australia]) [J4].

For human beings, especially children, the bright red berries of lords-and-ladies form a certain danger because of their sweet taste. In recent years only cases of slight poisoning (burning and prickling in the mouth, nausea) have been seen [K47], but the investigations carried out by Kann-giesser on himself [K6] show clearly that the toxicity of the berries varies considerably, depending on the degree of ripeness and the locality of the plants. This means that after consuming largish amounts more serious symptoms (gastro-intestinal pains, feeling of dizziness, cramps in the extremities) may be expected.

Treatment. See the introduction to the family, p.51.

Appendix. There are no new studies on the toxicity of the bog or water arum, *Calla palustris* (**17**). The rhizome of this plant, which is found on the banks of ponds and in peat bogs, has an acrid burning taste. This disappears after cutting into small pieces and thorough washing or after heating or drying, as is the case with all Araceae that are used as a source of food. Hence, it is not surprising that in Lappland the flour obtained from the rhizome has been used for making a tasty kind of bread known as 'misse-broed' [M29; P36]. Interestingly, pigs appear to be much less sensitive to the acrid substances of *Calla palustris*, which in certain parts of Germany is called 'Schweinekraut' (swine herb); the rhizome and the chopped leaves are said to provide good mast for them [H34; L11]. The red berries of *Calla palustris*, in contrast with those of *Arum maculatum*, have only a little calcium oxalate. No doubt because it is becoming rare in some of its localities, there have been just a few cases of otherwise symptomless ingestion in recent years [O10].

Microscopical characters of the fruits. The thin-walled finely pitted epidermal cells of *Arum* berries are characterised by the presence of carotenoids, localised in chromoplasts (recognisable as granular structure in the cell lumen; see **18**). In the epidermis there are anomocytic stomata, generally with 4–5 subsidiary cells. An important feature of the pulp is that, in addition to chromoplasts, there are numerous colourless round parenchyma cells, up to 300 µm in size and filled with vast numbers of calcium oxalate needles (*ca* 35 µm long).

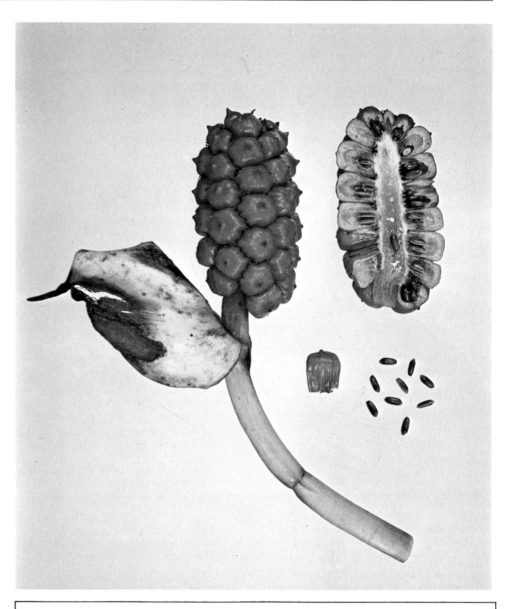

17 Calla palustris L.   Bog or Water Arum.

The epidermis of *Calla* fruits also consists of thin-walled, generally colourless cells which tend to be arranged in rows. In individual, sometimes paired, cells (see **19**) red colouring matter is present dissolved in the cell sap. Stomata are relatively rare, but are like those of *Arum*. The gelatinous pulp has occasional oval to saccate idioblasts containing a few raphides (up to 45 µm). In the outer layers there are cells with colouring matter like those occurring in the epidermis.

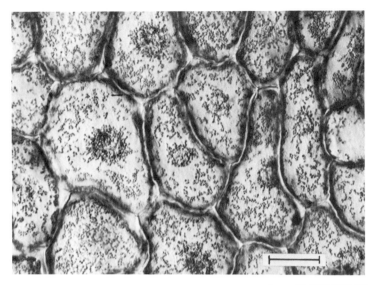

18 Arum maculatum: Epidermis of the pericarp.

19 Calla palustris: Epidermis of the pericarp.

Dieffenbachia Schott   Dumb Cane

THESE perennials come from Brazil and the West Indies and in their natural habitat can reach a height of 2 m. They have straight stems around which are clustered the thickly veined leaves on their sheath-like petioles. In many countries outside the tropics, species of this genus are kept as pot and house plants because of their conspicuously marked leaves and remarkable ability to adapt to the dry air of centrally heated rooms.

Their toxicity was already described at the end of the 17th century [W6]. When the juice of these plants comes into contact with mucous membranes or when the fresh plant material is chewed, the tongue and the mucous membranes of the mouth immediately swell up with reddening and stabbing burning pains. There is abundant salivation and difficulty in swallowing, and in serious cases loss of speech sometimes for several days. Because of these dramatic effects, in the West Indies during the slave era *Dieffenbachia* enjoyed a notorious reputation as a means of torture and it was sometimes used to silence temporarily unwelcome witnesses – hence the name 'dumb cane'. Even today, poisoning due to these plants is not unusual [B1; B45; F2]; over a period of 13 years, the Poison Information Centre at Utrecht alone dealt with 206 cases – 181 children, 11 adults, and 14 animals [E5; L26; R7; R17].

'A 13-year old Chinese schoolboy was plucking a plant when its sap squirted on to his left eye, causing immediate and intense pain. . . . On arrival at the General Hospital, he was unable to open his left eye-lids. . . .' [L26].

A patient came for treatment because the stem of a house plant that he wanted to remove had squirted juice into his left eye on being broken. Besides epiphora and blepharospasm, the conjunctivae of the eye showed the presence of much injected material; the surface of the cornea had a nodular appearance and in it could be recognised very fine needles [R17].

As a rule, these eye injuries heal spontaneously after 3–4 weeks without any permanent changes. Riede [R7] demonstrated in animal experiments that treatment with 1% ethylmorphine (improved permeability of the cornea) and 2% disodium edetate (dissolution of the calcium oxalate needles) as an eye ointment almost halves the period required for the injuries to heal.

Constituents and mechanism of action.
Although many investigations into the toxicity of *Dieffenbachia* species have been carried out [A24; B10; B11; C13; D19; F13; K52; K53; K63; L1; M4; M16; O3; W5; W6], views on the chemical nature of the active principle are widely divergent. As possible toxic constituents, saponins, glycosides, alkaloids, proteolytic enzymes, protein-like substances, and cyanogenic glycosides have all been mentioned. On the other hand, calcium oxalate needles (raphides) occur abundantly throughout these plants and their involvement is now hardly disputed.

The special shape (see **21** [W8]) and localisation of the raphides in explosive ejector cells (see **22** [B45; D15]), as well as the fact (ignored by many authors) that the plant tissues, besides containing insoluble calcium salts (in the form of clusters and raphides), also have free oxalic acid and its soluble salts in varying concentrations, provide grounds for believing that the *Dieffenbachia* syndrome may be the result of an ingenious combination of innumerable very fine mechanical injuries and subsequent oxalate poisoning. Slight pressure causes the caps of the ampoule-shaped raphide ejector cells to open and with a sudden swelling of the mucilaginous cell contents the raphides are instantly shot out of the cells. These fine needles, up to 250 μm long, are able to penetrate the mucosa of the mouth and throat very easily and by injuring the mast cells (where the local hormone histamine is stored) in the subcutaneous connective tissue can lead to a massive release of histamine. The grooved ends of the needles allow simultaneous injection of any adhering cell contents, as happens during an injection or bite by a venomous snake with grooved fangs. So far, nothing is known about the localisation of the free oxalic acid or the composition of the soluble content of the raphide

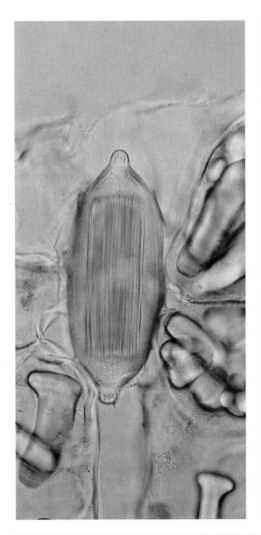

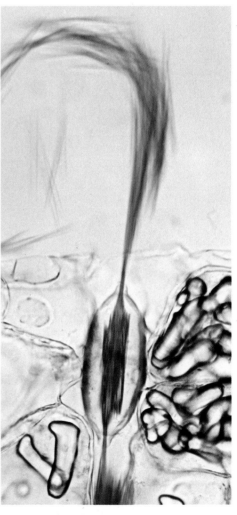

21 Calcium oxalate raphide with grooved ends from Dieffenbachia: (Left) In polarised light. (Right) Schematic drawing, according to [W8]: A, side view; B, cross-sections at various positions.

22 Dieffenbachia. Ampoule-shaped raphide ejector cell: (Left) before, and (Right) during the 'explosion'.

tissues (burning in the mouth, salivation, difficulty in swallowing, superficial inflammation, oedematous changes, swelling and proliferation of the endothelium, erosion and fissuring of the mucosal epithelium [A 20; F 6; H 51; J 3; N 8]) correspond largely with those observed in poisoning by pure oxalic acid.

The special toxicity of *Dieffenbachia* species and many other Araceae is thus not determined by the absolute amount of free oxalic acid present – many authors correctly point out that a whole series of non-poisonous foodstuffs (rhubarb, spinach, etc.) contain considerable amounts of oxalic acid – but probably through the special method by which this highly dissociated organic acid reaches the tissues. According to investigations carried

23 **Zantedeschia** Spreng.   **Arum Lily.**

Treatment. In most cases the poisoning takes a mild course, since the rapid local irritation in the mouth and throat prevents further consumption (cf. [B 45; D 19]). Greater danger will probably only arise when larger amounts of plant material are chewed and swallowed, as this may well result in massive injury to the gastric mucosa. As therapeutic measures, copious administration of fluid and, in more serious cases, gastric lavage as well as symptomatic treatment of the erosion and irritation with local anaesthetics and analgesics are recommended [D 19; K 47].

ejector cells. However, crystallographic examination of the calcium oxalate [F 22] suggests that a large part of the free acid is also to be found in the raphide ejector cells, since unlike the polyhydrate forms (clusters, prisms), the monohydrate (raphides) arises in a medium containing excess oxalic acid. This could therefore mean that with the help of the raphides a relatively concentrated solution of oxalic acid is transferred simultaneously. The symptoms of poisoning and the pathological changes in the

24 Anthurium Schott   Flamingo Flower.

out by us there is a clear parallel between the toxicity of certain *Dieffenbachia* organs (leaf < petiole < shoot axis) and their ratio of soluble to crystalline combined oxalic acid (0.03 < 0.12 < 0.29). If a fresh shoot is buried in the earth – a method for the detoxification of harvested taro tubers *(Colocasia esculenta)* practised by the people of the Fiji Islands [B48] – the ratio rapidly decreases from the initial 0.29 to 0.04 and lower, while the total oxalic acid content undergoes an insignificant increase.

As is clear from many publications, symptoms of poisoning similar to those encountered with *Dieffenbachia* have been observed after ingestion of fresh material of many other Araceae [B33; B48; E13; F19; H52; M42; O20; P36; S99; T20; W8; W10]. The morphological and anatomical peculiarities (raphide ejector cells, grooved needle ends, etc.) usually only show minor differences [S2; S3; S67; S98]. **23** and **24** illustrate two popular ornamentals belonging to this family; however, in contrast with *Dieffenbachia*, no cases of serious poisoning have been reported.

Philodendron Schott   Philodendron

IN tropical America there are 275 species of this genus; they comprise shrubby, tree-like, and occasionally climbing plants. Their leaves are often large and of very different shapes (entire, lobed, or pinnate). The spathe of the flower, typically araceous, is white, yellow, or red.

But, as a house plant, the philodendron rarely flowers and usually only offers the attraction of its leaves.

As regards it toxicity, basically the plants are no different from *Dieffenbachia* and other Araceae. Recent reports concern principally animal poisoning. Thus, Greer [G19] cites 72 cases involving cats, 37 of which ended in death. Pierce [P33] observed symptoms of poisoning in a 4-month old Siamese cat such as ready excitability, nervous spasms, convulsions occasionally accompanied by encephalitis, and he compared them with the symptoms due to cerebral meningitis. A piece of philodendron leaf ($6.5\,cm^2$) was found in the excrement. Sometimes, ingestion of philodendron leaves can give rise to renal failure [B46].

However, this genus deserves special mention, since it is also considered to be responsible for dermatological complaints:

'*In September 1940 a 23-year old woman developed an eruption on the eyelids. From then until January 1941 the dermatitis had periodic recurrences and exacerbations, with the latter appearing consistently in the early part of the week. The case history revealed that in her home the patient had eight philodendron (P. scandens) plants and that she washed and watered them every weekend. A patch test with a piece of the leaf of one of the plants was performed and after 48 hours the site of the test showed a definite erythematovesicular reaction.*' [H11]

As further reports have shown, people at risk are gardeners, florists, and housewives, through regular association with such plants [A21; D17; E7; M42].

In addition to *Philodendron* species, the devil's ivy (*Epipremnum aureum;* formerly, *Scindapsus aureus*) has been the cause of allergic reactions [M47]. Nothing is known yet about the chemical nature of the factors responsible.

ARALIACEAE

Hedera helix L.   Ivy

26 Ivy

A woody plant, up to 20 m in height, climbing by means of adhesive roots on trees and the walls of houses; also creeping along the ground.
<u>Leaves</u> evergreen, glabrous when old, very varied morphologically (heterophylly): lower ones lobed, nerves mostly white, upper ones of flowering shoots lanceolate and entire.
<u>Flowers</u> inconspicuous, greenish; in simple globose racemose panicles, with the terminal umbel the strongest; IX–XI.
<u>Fruit</u> globose berries with 3–5 seeds, ripening in spring and becoming black; III–IV.
<u>Distribution:</u> Throughout Europe, absent only in the far north; introduced into North America. Much cultivated as a shade plant.

LIKE many other Araliaceae, ivy contains triterpenoid saponins in all parts. Those compounds whose structures are known, e.g. hederasaponin C, have been isolated from the leaves. The leaf extracts used medicinally for whooping cough also contain saponin. As regards the berries, more especially the seeds, there are no recent investigations of the saponin content; nevertheless, it is probable that the saponins are responsible for their often reported toxicity, and certainly nothing is known about any other toxic constituents in the fruits. The fatal cases of poisoning in children recorded in the older literature must be regarded with scepticism; moreover, the berries when ripe are dry and taste bitter, and so are hardly likely to be consumed in large quantities. Kanngiesser [K5] described the following experiment on himself:

In May I ate a big greenish black ivy berry and, after chewing it thoroughly, swallowed it. I then drank some water. The taste was like grass but rather unpleasant. About 10 minutes later a slight burning sensation began in the throat and lasted for about ¼ hour. There were no other symptoms.

That touching ivy can also lead to contact dermatitis is known, but the

Treatment. Since consumption of largish quantities of berries is improbable, immediate removal of the poison is usually unnecessary; if need be, any gastro-intestinal troubles can be treated symptomatically.

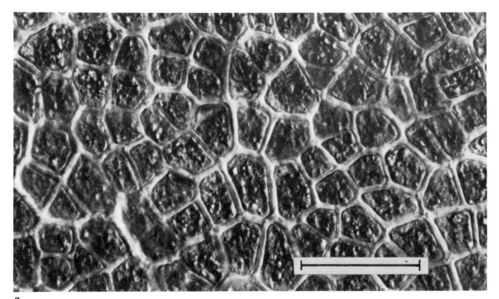

Hederasaponin C

reports concerned relate to leaves, stems, or roots, rather than fruits. Sensitisation to ivy is more frequent than generally recognised [G16; M45]. For further information, see Mitchell and Rook [M42].

Other Araliaceae. Stowe *et al.* [S91] reported the poisoning of a dog by *Schefflera actinophylla* leaves. The oxalate content was 0.9–1.5% (calculated on the fresh weight), and could have been the cause of the toxicity of this decorative ornamental.

Microscopical characters of the fruit. The deep violet colouring matter of *Hedera* fruits is to be found mainly in the thick-walled cells of the exocarp which exhibit a 'window-like' pattern

(27a).* Stomata are rare, although rather more frequent in the epidermis of the glandular disc. A diagnostic feature of the pericarp epidermis is the presence of occasional stellate trichomes **(27b).** They break off easily and, especially in older fruits, only the cells of the stalk, which are sometimes paired, can be seen. In the pulp there are large schizogenous oil glands and calcium oxalate in the form of clusters (*ca* 12 μm).

---

* This expression is used to describe groups of epidermal cells whose outside anticlinal walls appear to be slightly more prominent, giving the impression of panes of glass in a window frame. The microphotograph **146** shows most clearly what is meant by the term.

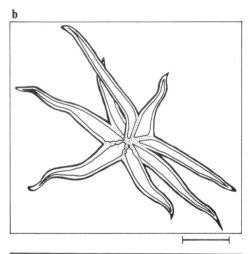

27 **Hedera helix. Pericarp:**
(a) **Epidermis.** (b) **Stellate trichome.**

ASTERACEAE (COMPOSITAE)

THE **Daisy family,** with about 15 000 species, is one of the largest plant families. It comprises annual or perennial herbs, less commonly shrubs or small trees, with a cosmopolitan distribution. Characteristic features include the arrangement of the small flowers (calyx absent or represented by a hair-like pappus) in anthodia which usually imitate large flowers (pseudanthia). The extraordinary polymorphism of the family is underlined by the presence of a wide range of chemical constituents [B37] which, on the one hand, are the reason why so many Compositae are medicinal and useful plants (e.g. chamomile, absinth, arnica, coltsfoot, milk-thistle, artichoke, sunflower, tarragon, pyrethrum) and, on the other, are responsible for the poisonous properties of many members. A detailed treatment of the biology and chemistry of this important family has been given by Heywood, Harborne, and Turner [H46].

Toxicologically important constituents.

Two groups of substances merit special attention: (1) terpenoid compounds, especially sesquiterpene lactones, and (2) pyrrolizidine alkaloids, especially of the genus *Senecio*. Other toxic compounds are of lesser importance or are only found in a few species.

Sesquiterpene lactones.

Although sesquiterpene lactones occur in other families, this class of substance, comprising *ca* 1000 compounds [B37], is a very prominent chemical feature of the Compositae. Here, it is not possible to deal in any detail with either the

structural diversity or the very varied biological activities of these substances; however, the following may be noted: the bitter taste; the antibiotic, anthelmintic, anti-inflammatory, and phytotoxic properties; and the cytotoxic activity, which has been extensively investigated in the last few years. Recent publications on the biological and toxicological actions of sesquiterpene lactones include those by Rodriguez *et al.* [R14], MacGregor [G20], Hall *et al.* [H6], and Kim [K22].

The great lettuce, *Lactuca virosa* (p.66), is an indigenous European plant whose toxicity is due to the presence of sesquiterpene lactones. Members of other genera are known to be the cause of poisoning in cattle. But, as they concern South Africa (*Geigeria* species) and North America (*Helenium* and *Hymenoxys* species), rather than Europe, it must suffice to give references to recent literature [H44; I5; I6; S79; W27; W28].

The allergenic properties of some sesquiterpene lactones are also of significance [H49; M44]. A well-known example is the hypersensitivity to chrysanthemums (*Chrysanthemum × hortorum* are hybrids of *C. indicum* and *C. morifolium;* newer hybrids also come from other parent species) that as an occupational dermatitis in gardeners and florists can lead to an allergic contact dermatitis in which the eyes and other parts of the face are affected (action of the released pollen) [B35; F9; H21]. Hausen and Schultz [H22; H25] were able to isolate a sesquiterpene lactone of the guaianolide type, arteglasin A, first found in *Artemisia douglasii,* as one of the active allergenic components of

the garden chrysanthemum. Arteglasin A is one of those sesquiterpene lactones that have an exocyclic α-methylene group attached to the γ-lactone ring (p.64).

A cross-link can result via this functional group and sulphhydryl groups of the body proteins, so that complete antigens are formed that stimulate the production of antibodies. It is these that after renewed contact between the organism and the allergen cause the allergic reactions.

Occasional allergic skin reactions have been described for several European Compositae, e.g. yarrow (*Achillea millefolium*) [G3; P29], wild chamomile (*Matricaria chamomilla*) and chamomile (*Chamaemelum nobile*) [B19; B22; C8], and also garden lettuce (*Lactuca sativa*) and endive (*Cichorium endivia*) [K49].

Appendix: *Arnica montana.* Although arnica is better known as a medicinal plant its toxic properties should be noted. In the first place, toxic-allergic skin reactions after applying tincture of arnica, often also an ingredient in cosmetics, hair shampoos, and bath preparations, are not uncommon [H19; H24]. Secondly, internal use of arnica preparations has been observed to bring about poisoning, with acceleration of the pulse, palpitation of the heart, and shortage of breath, and

Helenalin

Possible modes of cross-linking between helenalin and SH-groups of enzymes and proteins (accoding to [W21])

may even lead to death [W21].* Recent studies trace these effects to the helenalin ester characteristic of *Arnica montana* [H42] and also long known as the toxic principle of *Helenium autumnale*. As early as 1913 Lamson [L4] described helenalin as a substance with the following properties: it irritates the mucosa and in the gastro-intestinal tract causes vomiting, diarrhoea, and bleeding; it also gives rise to oedema and respiratory stimulation; and, after a brief positive inotropic action on the heart, it brings about paralysis of the cardiac muscle. Helenalin and other sesquiterpene lactones of similar structure (tenulin, parthenin) owe their special physio-

logical activity and greater degree of toxicity to the presence, in addition to the exocyclic α-methylene group on the γ-lactone ring, of a second group that can link with SH-functions (see reaction scheme).

This means not only particular allergenic but also high cytotoxic activity, explicable by addition to SH-functions (alkylation) in enzymes such as those taking part in cell division. From a review of arnica research published recently by Willuhn [W21] it is clear that the helenalin esters are the most important constituents giving rise to the anti-inflammatory, positive inotropic, and respiration-accelerating, as well as allergenic and general toxic, effects.

Pyrrolizidine alkaloids. This toxicologically important group of constituents is discussed further under the genus *Senecio*.

Other toxic compounds. Essential oils occur extensively in the Compositae and may contain pharmacologically highly active components. The monoterpene thujone, found in *Artemisia absinthium*, etc., is an example.

The toxic principle of *Atractylis gummifera*, a Mediterranean plant, is believed to be atractyligenin, a nor-diterpene with a phyllocladene skeleton that has structural similarities with the aconitine-delphinidine alkaloids; the same is also true of the diterpenes present in *Inula royleana*. Carboxyatractyloside is responsible for the toxic effects of the rough cocklebur *(Xanthium strumarium)*, according to Stuart *et al.* [S95].

In contrast with the poly-ynes of the Apiaceae (Umbelliferae), little is known about the pharmacological activity of those present in the Asteraceae (Compositae). Towers [T15] points out that S-containing poly-ynes (thiophene derivatives), which occur particularly in the tribes Helenieae, Heliantheae, and Tageteae, e.g. in *Tagetes* species (African marigold, etc.), can cause photodermatitis; see also [A16].

---

* Following the recommendation of arnica tea by Köhnlechner in a magazine, there has recently been the first warning in West Germany against the use of arnica [A19], after a case of poisoning had already occurred. Schoenemann [S29] reported poisoning after drinking arnica tea in 1938.

Senecio L.   Ragwort, Groundsel

THE genus comprises *ca* 1300 species with cosmopolitan distribution, but many species are confined to smaller regions. Only herbaceous representatives grow in Europe; many occur widely, sometimes very abundantly, as weeds, e.g. groundsel *(Senecio vulgaris)*. The so-called Senecio

alkaloids, characteristic of the genus, have so far been found in more than 100 species and in recent years have been attracting increasing toxicological interest [H66; R16; S62].

Pyrrolizidine alkaloids. Esters of necine bases with necic acids (see p.26) are

known to be constituents not only of many *Senecio* species but also of the other genera of the Senecioneae and Eupatorieae.* In the plant the pyrrolizidine bases frequently occur as *N*-oxides.

As early as 1920 it was suspected that constituents of *Senecio* bring about liver damage. Intensive research undertaken around 1950 confirmed this and led to definite statements about the toxicity of the pyrrolizidine alkaloids [M26]. They are hepatotoxic and carcinogenic, but certain structural conditions have to be met:

- A 1, 2-double bond must be present in the necine part.
- If possible, both hydroxyl groups of the pyrrolizidine moiety (amino-alcohol) must be esterified.

Retronecine

It is believed that the actual toxic agents are pyrrole derivatives with alkylating properties, formed after metabolism of the pyrrolizidine alkaloids by liver microsomes in mammals or man [H68; M26; N3].

Symptoms of poisoning. Clinical picture. Acute poisoning in man has never yet been observed. Symptoms usually first make their appearance after weeks or months and to begin with are non-specific: loss of appetite, exhaustion, and abdominal pains. Increased consumption leads to swelling of the abdomen (with veins appearing on the surface), the lower extremities may become oedematous, and lung damage is also possible. As the intoxication progresses, there are characteristic changes in the

liver: enlargement, hardening, and later cirrhosis. The condition described as hepatic veno-occlusive disease (V.O.D.) – comparable with the Budd-Chiari syndrome – can be brought about in man in two ways:

(1) By drinking teas prepared with the leaves of *Senecio* (and also *Crotalaria*) species. The use of such teas in folk medicine is known from South Africa, Jamaica, and also from some parts of North America (the bush teas of the poor) [C22; F16; G6; H67; S84]. The widely used name 'Gordolobo tea' relates to the leaves of *Senecio longilobus,* but other plants, such as *Gnaphalium* species, may be a component of the tea. In 1980 Huxtable [H66] published a detailed report in which he pointed out the problems – in America often not yet properly understood – of such herbal teas. In Germany an anti-diabetic tea was for long (still is?) commercially available under the name 'Kruziflora'. It consisted of the green parts of *Senecio nemorensis* subsp. *fuchsii;* for the carcinogenic and mutagenic action of the alkaloids of this plant, see the recent work of Habs [H70]. *Senecio* extracts are still being offered as a styptic in medicinal preparations available today. Attention should also be drawn to the fact that the hepatotoxic and carcinogenic pyrrolizidine alkaloid senkirkine may occur (at least in small concentrations) in colt's-foot leaves from certain sources [H48; L34].

(2) Contamination of grain with the seeds of plants containing pyrrolizidine alkaloids. In Afghanistan and India, seeds of, respectively, *Heliotropium* (p.73) and *Crotalaria* (p.123) species have been recognised as the cause of serious poisoning epidemics with a high mortality rate.

In South Africa the fruits of *Senecio* species are said to have led in the same way to cases of poisoning.

According to Huxtable [H66] the LD_{50} i.p. in rats is $85\,mg/kg$ for senecionine, $77\,mg/kg$ for seneciphylline, and $35\,mg/kg$ for retrorsine. Since it is evident that pyrrolizidine alkaloids are accumulated, with long-continued ingestion of preparations containing them such dosage levels will undoubtedly be reached.

Poisoning in animals. Generally, *Senecio* species are avoided by livestock. In the absence of other food, or if fed on hay or silage containing much *Senecio,* a group of diseases can occur which are known by the name pyrrolizidine-alkaloidosis (seneciosis). While cases of acute poisoning, with colic, cramps, and diarrhoea, have been described, usually in animals as well the disease takes a chronic course and in the late stage there are, along with other symptoms, the typical cirrhotic changes in the liver. Pohlenz *et al.* [P37] have quite recently reported on liver cirrhosis in cattle as a result of eating *Senecio alpinus* and Lüthy *et al.* [L35] have detected nine alkaloids, with seneciphylline as the main one, in the plant; see also [K31]. The total alkaloid content was 0.3–0.4% (calculated on the dry weight). See also p.232.

Treatment. There are no specific antidotes. Because of the long latent period, in animals once the symptoms have been recognised as due to poisoning by pyrrolizidine alkaloids treatment is hopeless. In the cases of human poisoning described so far, the mortality rate has been high; as regards treatment, the most appropriate measures are those recommended in liver cirrhosis.

---

* Pyrrolizidine alkaloids occur elsewhere, especially in the Boraginaceae (p.73) and in the Fabaceae (Leguminosae) (the genus *Crotalaria*) (p.121), both of which are of considerable toxicological importance. For the distribution of these alkaloids in the plant kingdom, see the recent review by Smith and Culvenor [S62].

Senecio jacobaea L.   Common Ragwort, Tansy Ragwort

28 Common Ragwort

30–90 cm tall biennial to perennial plant with erect angular grooved stems, branching above halfway with the branches pointing upwards. In sparse woods and at the edges of woods; in pastures, along waysides and on banks, mostly in the lowlands but also up to 1500 m.
<u>Leaves</u> light green, firm, basal ones lyrate-pinnatifid, usually dead before flowering; middle ones eared and like upper ones pinnatifid.
<u>Flowers</u> golden yellow, in large flat-topped compound corymbs; VII–IX.
<u>Fruits</u> indistinctly longitudinally grooved, pappus caducous.
<u>Distribution:</u> Throughout Europe; naturalised in North America, Australia, and elsewhere.

Senecionine

COMMON ragwort contains at least six pyrrolizidine bases with jacobine as the main one. Recent animal experiments on the toxicity of the plant have been carried out by Gopinath and Ford [G17] and Miranda *et al.* [M39; M40]. Honey derived from *S.jacobaea* may contain pyrrolizidine alkaloids [D6], as did the milk of cows in whose feed ragwort was present [D8].

Lactuca virosa L.   Great Lettuce

29 Great Lettuce

0.6–1.5 m tall annual or biennial plant
with terete erect stems branching in
upper part to form a panicle. On sunny
slopes (vineyards), waysides, railway
embankments, usually scattered.
<u>Leaves</u> glabrous, bluish green, toothed
with thorns and spinulose on lower
surface of midrib; entire, sinuate-lobate.
<u>Flowers</u> pale yellow, only ray florets,
these longer than the involucral bracts;
capitula in panicles.
<u>Fruits</u> blackish, ribbed, narrowly
winged.
<u>Distribution:</u> In western and central
Europe; formerly occasionally cultivated
for production of lactucarium and
therefore possibly sometimes run wild
from old plantations.

Lactucin

GREAT lettuce, belonging to the
subfamily Cichorioideae, contains in all parts a white latex that
turns brown in the air. The presence of
latex is a chemical characterstic of the
subfamily. When the plant is in flower
and its stem is cut, there is a copious
flow of sticky latex, which, after being
collected and dried, forms the drug
lactucarium – at one time used as a
sedative. The components responsible
for the sedative, as well as the toxic,
effects are the sesquiterpene lactone
bitter substance lactucin and its
p-hydroxyphenylacetic ester lactupicrin. Characteristic triterpene alco-

hols of the latex, such as lactucerol, have no toxicological significance. There is no recent confirmation of the presence of a hyoscyamine-like alkaloid, frequently mentioned in the older literature, which was supposed to explain the 'narcotic effects' of lactucarium.

Lactucin and lactupicrin are found in the latex of other Cichorioideae.

The dandelion, *Taraxacum officinale,* whose root is known in folk medicine as a cholagogue, is also sometimes called a poisonous plant. Hänsel *et al.* [H2] were able to isolate four new sesquiterpene lactones from the plant, but were unable to find any lactupicrin. A rare case of allergic contact dermatitis due to dandelion (with an already existing chrysanthemum allergy) is reported by Hausen and Schultz [H26].

Poisoning in man and animals is rare; the only **treatment** that can be suggested is direct removal of the toxic material and symptomatic measures.

BERBERIDACEAE

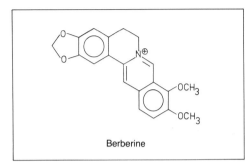

Berberine

MEMBERS of the **Barberry family** are indigenous to the extra-tropical regions of the northern hemisphere. There are many genera and species, particularly on both sides of the Pacific Ocean. Although in western and central Europe *Berberis vulgaris,* barberry, is the only native species, many *Berberis* and *Mahonia* species are used as ornamental shrubs. There are three groups of compounds in the family that are of toxicological interest:

(1) **Isoquinoline alkaloids,** with the characteristic alkaloid berberine. Their occurrence is limited to the Berberidoideae (including *Berberis, Mahonia*), but within the subfamily they are present in all genera. They accumulate preferentially in the root and stem bark, where, through deposition of berberine in lignified cell walls, they are sometimes recognisable macroscopically as an intense yellow coloration.

Berberine is readily absorbed orally. It stimulates smooth-muscled organs (increase in intestinal peristalsis). It also affects the respiratory centre, but only in high doses does it lead to primary respiratory arrest (LD 0.1 g/kg in rabbits); lethal doses produce haemorrhagic nephritis as well [H3].

(2) **Lupin alkaloids,** which belong to the quinolizidine group (see also p.26). Several species of the Berberidoideae contain, in addition to the above-mentioned isoquinoline bases, or in some cases exclusively, alkaloids of the cytisine or sparteine type [H35]. Thus, in *Caulophyllum thalictroides* (blue cohosh), for example, found in eastern North America, *N*-methyl-cytisine is present in the leaves and fruits. Children exhibit symptoms of poisoning after consuming the dark blue berry-like seeds [H9; L8; L20].

(3) **Lignan β-glycosides** of the podo-phyllotoxin group. In contrast with the Berberidoideae, alkaloids appear to be absent from the subfamily Podophylloideae. They are replaced especially in the subterranean parts of *Podophyllum peltatum* (may apple) and *P. emodi* by water-soluble lignan glycosides. In addition to podophyllo-toxin, a further 15 physiologically active compounds have been isolated from the crude resin of the plant extracts [R5]. Their strong laxative action has long been known, but nowadays they are used principally as cytostatics (antimitotics) in the treatment of tumours.

Understandably, poisoning after ingestion of plant material is only known from North America, the natural home of *P. peltatum.* Use of the young plants as kitchen herbs or after eating unripe fruits has some-times resulted in fatal cases of poison-ing [F31; H9; M17]. According to several authors the large plum-shaped berries can be eaten in small amounts when ripe (yellow-red).* But intraperitoneal administration of their extracts in rats leads to the same toxic reactions as do the unripe fruits [K26]. Moreover, topical use of podophyllin resin (treatment of papilloma with a 20% tincture) can give rise to toxic symptoms [S58].

---

* Medsger [M29] tells the story of what happened to him at the tender age of eight: '. . . it was the first time that I could eat all the May Apples that I wanted and not have someone around to say 'no'. Half an hour later I was rolling on the ground with the worst colic that one could imagine. I felt certain that I was going to die but hoped to put off the fatal moment until my parents returned. An hour or two later the discomfort left me without any ill effects; but I shall never forget the agonizing experience.'

Berberis L.   Barberry, Pipperidge

**30 (Left) Berberis vulgaris
(Right) B. x hybridogagnepainii**

1–3 m tall shrub, with usually 3-partite spines and much-branched twigs.
At the edges of woods and in thickets, on dry calcareous soils and loam.
<u>Leaves</u> deciduous, elliptic to obovate, upper surface dull dark green, lower surface lighter, with finely toothed margin; in clusters.
<u>Flowers</u> pendent many-flowered racemes, inner perianth segments yellow; V–VI.
<u>Fruits</u> oblong-cylindrical, orange-red, sour-tasting berries with 1–2 finely wrinkled red-brown seeds; IX–XII.
<u>Distribution:</u> Central Scandinavia to southern Europe; frequently planted in gardens and as hedges; many other species, some having fruits with a blue-black colour or a bluish bloom.

THANKS to the extensive investigations of Petcu [P14–20] there is much information available on the distribution of the isoquinoline alkaloids in *Berberis vulgaris* and some other *Berberis* species (see Table 4).

Leaving aside the seasonal variations (the alkaloid content reaches its maximum when the plants are dormant), it can be seen that the root bark is the plant part richest in alkaloids, followed by the stem bark. As a rule, the leaves and flowers are free of alkaloids. In the fruits (pulp + seeds), which are of particular interest in the present context, *B. vulgaris* is evidently in an isolated position: isoquinoline bases could not be detected in either the pulp or the seeds. On the other hand, the seeds at least of the other species examined by Petcu in some cases contain noteworthy amounts of alkaloids.

Table 4. Total alkaloid content (%) of the organs of various *Berberis* species.

		B. vulgaris	*B. dielsiana*	*B. guimpelii*	*B. hakodate*	*B. hauniensis*	*B. serrata*	*B. virescens*
Root	Bark	12.8	7.9	12.9	13.2	14.7	15.3	12.6
	Wood	–	1.1	3.6	2.0	1.1	0.2	1.6
Stem	Bark	5.5	5.3	5.8	9.9	6.9	5.8	7.4
	Wood	–	1.1	1.7	1.6	0.4	0.1	0
Leaves		+	0	–	0	0	–	0
Flowers		–	0	–	0	–	–	–
Fruit pulp		0	0	–	–	0	–	0
Seeds		0	1.4	3.8	4.3	2.7	1.8	2.5

+ = Alkaloids present; 0 = Alkaloids absent; – = No data.

31 **Berberis vulgaris: Epidermis of the pericarp.**

The red berries of barberry are thus harmless, and owing to their content of fruit acids and vitamin C they are also used to prepare jams and refreshing drinks.

Since in three cases slight symptoms of poisoning (fever, stomach-ache) have been observed after eating unknown amounts of barberry leaves [K46] and since in the fruit (seeds) of other *Berberis* species presumably alkaloids are normally present, the possibility must be borne in mind that after eating a large amount of such plant material symptoms may occur such as can arise after taking medicinal doses of berberine: confusion, nosebleeding, vomiting, diarrhoea, and renal irritation.

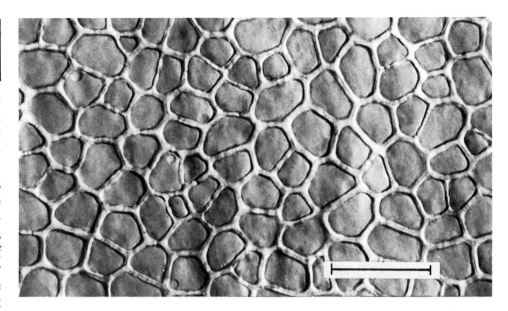

Treatment. Symptomatic. Because of the low toxicity of berberine and its accompanying alkaloids (a single therapeutic dose lies between 0.03 and 0.2 g), gastric lavage will only be required after the ingestion of a large amount of alkaloid-containing plant material.

Microscopical characters of the fruit. The epidermis is largely free of stomata (**31**) and numerous large (*ca* 20 μm) clusters of calcium oxalate occur in the pulp.

Mahonia aquifolium (Pursh) Nutt.   Oregon-grape, Trailing Mahonia

32 Oregon-grape

Up to 1 m tall, bushy erect shrub.
<u>Leaves</u> evergreen, imparipinnate,
(5–11) leaflets ovate and spinose dentate.
<u>Flowers</u> in dense erect racemes with
golden yellow, often reddish tinged,
perianth segments; IV–V.
<u>Fruits</u> globose, bluish pruinose, very
sour-tasting berries with dark red juice
and 2–5 shiny red-brown seeds;
VIII–XII.
<u>Distribution:</u> Western and Pacific North
America. Cultivated in Europe as an
ornamental shrub.

THE berries of the Oregon-grape are just as harmless as those of the barberry and are used in North America in the making of wine and spirits [H57]. Older data suggest that the fruits contain only 0.06% alkaloid [W11].

In the Berlin, Hamburg, and Zürich Toxicological Information Centres, in a total of 247 enquiries no toxic symptoms have been reported.

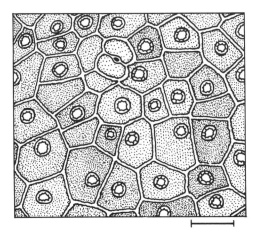

Microscopical characters of the fruit.
The epidermis has numerous stomata with 5–6 subsidiary cells and it also features thick-walled papillae. Small isolated calcium oxalate prisms (*ca* 5 μm) are present in the pulp.

33 Mahonia aquifolium: Epidermis of the pericarp.

BORAGINACEAE

THE **Borage family,** represented in the temperate zone only by herbaceous species, is of no importance in the statistics of the European Toxicological Centres. But, because potentially poisonous substances occur in the family it is mentioned here.

Toxic constituents. Pyrrolizidine alkaloids and their *N*-oxides have been detected in two subfamilies, Heliotropioideae and Boraginoideae, and owing to their hepatotoxic and carcinogenic effects attract considerable toxicological interest (see pp. 26 and 64). Fatal cases of poisoning in horses after eating *Echium lycopsis,* purple viper's-bugloss, have been described [S39], as well as the death of chickens, ducks, and pigs through the admixture of *Heliotropium* seeds in their feed [E15; P5; P6; J15]. Contamination of bread cereals with *Heliotropium* seeds was also the cause of a serious poisoning epidemic in Afghanistan resulting in many deaths [M52]. Following a dry period lasting two years, the widespread occurrence of *Heliotropium porovii* led to the contamination of the cereal with its seeds and, after two years during which the contaminated cereal formed the staple diet of the poor, to the outbreak of the illness.

Heliotropium arborescens

The ornamental sweet heliotrope comes from Peru and Ecuador, and because of its pleasant-smelling flowers, reminiscent of vanilla, used to be very popular; it is now experiencing a revival. Certainly, there is no fear of acute poisoning. Nevertheless, it contains – as does also the heliotrope, *H.europaeum,* which comes from the Mediterranean region – pyrrolizidine bases. Birecka *et al.* [B30] have reported on the alkaloid content of 24 species of *Heliotropium,* chiefly of Mexican origin.

Appendix. Extracts of common comfrey, *Symphytum officinale,* because of their allantoin content, are used externally in the healing of wounds. However, under the name 'comfrey', leaves, roots, or extracts from *S.peregrinum* or hybrids are being sold for internal use [S106]. As pyrrolizidine alkaloids are also present in *Symphytum* species, in recent years studies on the detection of these substances in drug preparations have appeared [S106; T13; W3]. Brauchli *et al.* [B42] investigated the percutaneous absorption of the alkaloids and found, in contrast with oral administration, that only very small amounts appeared in the urine of experimental animals.

34 Heliotropium arborescens L.   Sweet Heliotrope.

BUXACEAE

Buxus sempervirens L.   Box, Boxwood

35 Box

0.3–4 m tall, very bushy shrub to small tree with 4-angled shoots. In oak scrub on warm, base-rich, stony, loam.
<u>Leaves</u> **evergreen, leathery, opposite, upper surface glossy dark green, lower surface light yellow-green (garden forms also have white variegated leaves or yellow streaks along the margins), ovate to elliptic, slightly revolute margins.**
<u>Flowers</u> **in axillary clusters, unisexual, monoecious, yellow-white, inconspicuous; III–IV.**
<u>Fruits</u> **blue-green, glaucous, 3-horned capsules with six black glossy seeds; IX–X.**
<u>Distribution:</u> **Indigenous to southern Europe, North Africa, and Asia Minor; has been cultivated for many centuries and therefore occurs widely as hedges and in cemeteries.**

THE **Boxwood family** is a relatively small family of only six genera. In the species which have been examined so far, steroidal alkaloids of the pregnane group, such as cyclobuxine, have been found. These bases are responsible for the toxicity; and they are present in all parts of the plants, more especially in the leaves (1% of the dry weight) and in the bark. A system of secretory cells whose contents give precipitates with reagents for alkaloids and tannins penetrates the individual organs in the form of long, articulated cells [H35].

Cyclobuxine D

The leaves of the box have occasionally given rise to animal poisoning when freshly cut twigs have been used in the stall as straw [B23; L23]. A case involving the poisoning of pigs recently reported to us from the rural district of Steinburg [O4] shows that the animals are endangered particularly by cut plant material, while according to the owner of the animals box hedges usually remain untouched:

In the afternoon a neighbour of the pig breeder had pulled up 30–40 cm tall

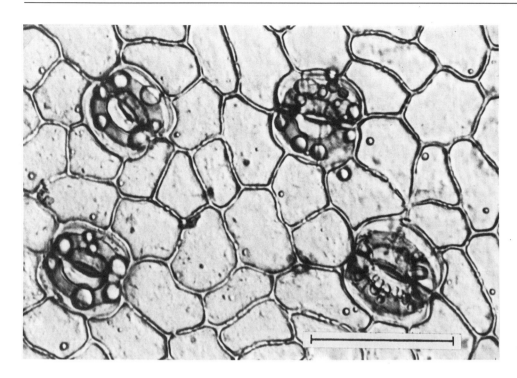

spurge, often planted as green manure, which has 12 mm long, ovoid, glassy white fruits, and *Sarcococca humilis*, sweet box, an occasionally cultivated 50 cm high shrub with 6 mm globose, blue-black (slightly horned) berries.

Treatment. Removal of the poison should as a rule be possible after dealing with the convulsions; for the rest, symptomatic measures.

plants from her box hedge and after work had thrown them over the hedge to where the pigs foraged. The next morning three were dead and then one after the other three seriously ill sows were discovered and had to be destroyed. The symptoms of poisoning were described by the owner as follows: The animals appeared to be healthy until shortly before they had to be slaughtered. Then quite suddenly they exhibited a nervous and awkward gait, difficulty in breathing, and, after falling over on their side, tonic-clonic convulsions; in addition, before collapsing some of the animals screamed loudly, showing clearly that they were in pain. All the pigs examined had box leaves in their stomach (in one case almost 500 g).

Hauschild indicates that 0.1 g buxine/kg is the lethal dose for a dog, while 750 g leaves are said to be sufficient to kill a horse [L23]. Up till now, no cases of poisoning in man appear to have been reported, even though box leaves can sometimes occur as an adulterant in Folia Uvae Ursi (*Arctostaphylos uva-ursi*, bearberry) [H3].

A warning note must be sounded about two other ornamentals, since they also have toxic alkaloids. They are *Pachysandra terminalis*, Japanese

Microscopical characters of the leaf. The leaves of *Buxus sempervirens* are dorsiventral with 3–4 palisade layers below the upper surface of the leaf. The numerous stomata (36) are present only on the lower surface (hypostomatal leaf). Their guard cells are distinguished by a ridge-like swelling along the outer margin. Unicellular thick-walled trichomes are rare. Calcium oxalate is present in the mesophyll in the form of clusters, along the nerves as individual prisms, or in cells as crystal sand (now and then the crystals appear to be corroded).

CAPRIFOLIACEAE

THE **Honeysuckle family** comprises 15 genera with about 400 species, most of which occur in the northern hemisphere. Besides the few indigenous species of *Lonicera* (honeysuckle), *Sambucus* (elder), and *Viburnum* (guelder-rose), many foreign species of these and other genera (*Symphoricarpos* [snowberry], *Kolkwitzia* [beauty bush], *Weigela)* are cultivated in Europe. In town parks, private gardens, cemeteries, or along streets, there is scarcely a corner without at least one representative of the family. With the exception of *Kolkwitzia* and *Weigela,* they bear conspicuous, fleshy and juicy fruits, usually in large numbers and during several months of the year. So it is not at all surprising that children are always trying the berries and as a result the Toxicological Information Centres receive many enquiries (see Table 5).

In striking contrast is the paucity of our knowledge about the chemical nature of the constituents and the possibly toxic principles in these plants. Many species have long been considered poisonous or at least suspected of being so. It is chiefly in the older literature that cases with serious symptoms of poisoning have been described. From the present-day experience of the Toxicological Centres it seems that little danger may be

Table 5. Number of enquiries about Caprifoliaceae.

	Berlin 1964–78	Zürich 1973–79
Lonicera species (*xylosteum, tatarica*, etc.)	244	205
Sambucus species (*ebulus, nigra, racemosa*)	59	67
Symphoricarpos albus (= *rivularis*)	141	57
Viburnum species (*opulus, lantana*)	49	50

expected from the fruit of Caprifoliaceae. Only in about 16% of the enquiries made have symptoms – and mild ones at that, such as feeling unwell and perhaps vomiting – actually been noted.

Chemical characters. An important chemical feature of the Caprifoliaceae is the accumulation of phenolic compounds in the form of glycosides (flavonoids, anthocyanins, etc.) [B56; C14; C15; G14; H35; P50]. In addition, cyanogenic glycosides [J12], alkaloids, and iridoids [B57; C10; S102] have been found, albeit in very small amounts. But it seems probable that the mild symptoms seen after the ingestion of plant material are due to **saponins,** which occur throughout the family [L12]. They are said to have relatively weak haemolytic activity, but so far neither the amounts present in the various plant parts nor the structures of their aglycones have been determined.

Treatment. When only a few berries have been swallowed, it is best to wait and see. With larger amounts, especially of the unripe fruits, symptomatic measures and, if necessary, emptying of the stomach are recommended [K47].

Lonicera xylosteum L.   Fly Honeysuckle

37 Fly Honeysuckle

1–2 m tall shrub with spreading, almost hollow, branches and grey-pubescent young twigs; very variable. In mixed deciduous forests, thickets, and hedges on nutrient-rich sandy soils and loam. <u>Leaves</u> deciduous, broadly elliptic, on short pubescent petioles; upper surface dark or greyish green, lower surface lighter, often with soft hairs, but also with both surfaces glabrous. <u>Flowers</u> in pairs, pedunculate, axillary, yellowish white, also tinged with red, two-lipped; bracteoles half as long as the ovary; V–VI. <u>Fruits</u> scarlet, juicy, many-seeded berries, in pairs on a single pedicel, rarely white or yellow; VIII–X. <u>Distribution:</u> Throughout Europe; in Asia as far as the Altai Mountains.

ABOUT 200 *Lonicera* species occur in the northern hemisphere. As already mentioned in the introduction to the family, in Europe besides the indigenous species many others and cultivars, some of which are highly variable morphologically, are grown as ornamentals. The fruit of the honeysuckles vary greatly in form and colour (white – yellow – red – blue – black). Depending on the arrangement and extent to which the flower parts have coalesced, the juicy berries may be grouped in infructescences, in pairs on a single common pedicel (more or less fused, sometimes enclosed by bracts), or united to form a double berry **(40)**. The plant may grow as an erect shrub, dwarf shrub, and climber. The various characters are set out in Table 6 for the more commonly occurring species. Accurate identification necessitates reference to more detailed accounts [B 60; C 33; E 6; E 17; F 11; K 50].

Toxicity. The berries of the fly honeysuckle **(37)** are generally considered in the literature to be toxic. However, reports of poisoning are rare and mostly old. Thus, Kroeber [K 48] recalls the mass poisoning in school children that took place in Münich in 1929 as a

38 Lonicera ledebourii Eschsch.   Ledebour's Honeysuckle.

bitter-tasting berries that symptoms such as abdominal pain and vomiting have been noted. Also the detailed investigations of Leveau *et al.* [L12] confirm the slight toxicity of the berries when taken orally. The most important findings of this work may be summarised as follows:

(1) The fruits of *L. alpigena, caerulea, henryi, maakii, nigra, periclymenum, pyrenaicum,* and *xylosteum* all contain traces of alkaloids, but for the symptoms observed it seems that saponins are responsible.

(2) The toxicity of fresh fruit of *L. xylosteum* on being taken by mouth is relatively slight. Rabbits given a dose of 25 g (dry weight)/kg body weight showed within 24 hours diarrhoea and some lack of movement as the only symptoms of poisoning.

(3) On intraperitoneal administration in mice of alcoholic fruit extracts clearer symptoms of poisoning were observed. After a brief excitation phase there was a lengthy period of drowsiness, abdominal spasms, disturbances of equilibrium and respiration, sometimes followed by death within 10 minutes to several hours. In this study, the amounts injected were very high, 20–40 g (dry weight)/kg mouse. In addition, a connection between the saponin content (foam index) and the toxicity was established.

The berries of some other *Lonicera* species, in contrast, are recorded as non-toxic or even edible [H3; H9]:

'*Twinberry or Honeysuckle, Lonicera involucrata, has dark purple berries that are eaten by the Indians and considered good by hunters and miners'.* [M29]

result of eating the ripe fruit of cultivated honeysuckle plants. The most recent case of poisoning by berries of this genus in which serious symptoms were seen is due to Schurno [S37]. Nevertheless, even in this report the causal connection between ingestion and observed symptoms is not free of uncertainty:

One day before admission, in the course of the morning the child is supposed to have eaten berries from the shrub growing in the local park identified as Lonicera tatarica. The amount of fruit taken is not known. The clinical picture resembled that of atropine poisoning.

On the other hand, there is the wide experience of the Toxicological Centres in Berlin and Zürich which shows that it is only after consumption of a largish number (*ca* 30) of the

Constituents. The frequently mentioned bitter substance xylostein, found by Hübschmann in 1845, has not been further characterised. More recently, Chaudhuri and Sticher [C10] have isolated xylostosidine, a monoterpenoid glyco-alkaloid, from *L. xylosteum;* unfortunately, however, data on the content and the pharmacological activity are lacking.

Microscopical characters of the fruits. The bright colour of honeysuckle fruits is due to anthocyanins. These pigments occur in varying concentrations in both the epidermis and the underlying cells of the pulp. The radial walls of the epidermal cells are usually relatively thin and distinctly pitted (**42c**). In some species, e.g. *L. caerulea* and *L. henryi,* there are granular deposits of wax (**41d**) on top of these cell walls. The epidermis of the pericarp in many *Lonicera* species, e.g. *L. caprifolium, L. caerulea,* and *L. nitida,* has anomocytic stomata usually with 5–6 subsidiary cells. Where stomata are absent, as in *L. xylosteum,* their function is taken over by large lenticels (**41a**).

Another conspicuous character is the occurrence of two forms of trichomes: multicellular glandular scales or relatively thick-walled unicellular hairs (**41b**). They are quite common particularly on the berries of *L. xylosteum* and *L. tatarica.* The pulp of honeysuckle fruits usually has numerous sharply pointed calcium oxalate clusters of varying sizes (5–35 μm).

Table 6. Fruit morphology and colour, as well as habit, of frequently occurring *Lonicera* species.

Lonicera species	Fruit	Fruit colour	Habit
alpigena	Double berry	Red	Erect
caerulea	Double berry	Dark blue	Erect
caprifolium	Up to several on a leaf pair	Reddish orange	Twining
etrusca	Infructescence	Red	Twining
henryi	Mostly paired	Black	Twining
ledebourii (**38**)	Paired, surrounded by red bracts	Purplish black	Erect
maakii	Paired	Red	Erect
nigra	Paired	Blue-black	Erect
nitida	Fused	Purple	Trailing
orientalis (**40**)	Double berry	Black	Erect
periclymenum (**39**)	Infructescence	Red	Twining
tatarica	Paired	Red	Erect
xylosteum (**37**)	Paired	Red	Erect

39 Lonicera periclymenum L.   Honeysuckle.

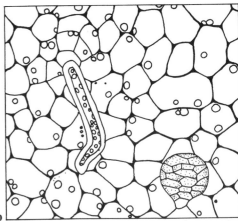

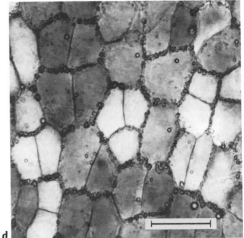

40 Lonicera orientalis L.   Eastern Honeysuckle.

**41 Epidermis of the pericarp of various Lonicera fruits: (a) and (b) L. xylosteum.
(c) L. periclymenum. (d) L. caerulea.**

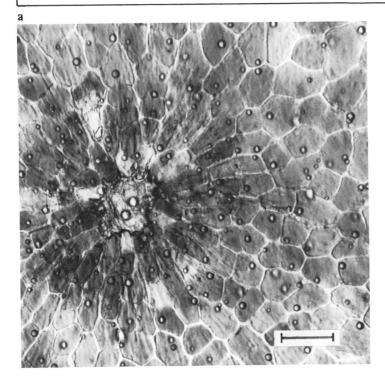

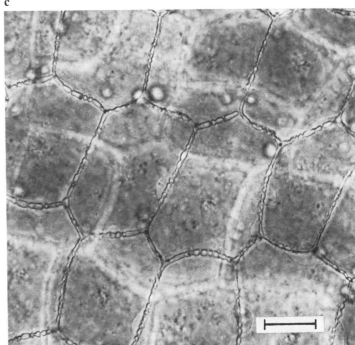

Sambucus ebulus L. Dwarf Elder, Danewort

42 Dwarf Elder

0.5–1.5 m tall perennial herb with creeping rhizome and mostly unbranched grooved stems; plant with foetid smell. In moist forest glades and meadows, in ravines and waste places; prefers fresh nutrient-rich loam.
<u>Leaves</u> imparipinnate (5–9-membered), leaflets acutely serrate and with asymmetric base.
<u>Flowers</u> in terminal corymbose inflorescences, with reddish white petals and purple anthers; smelling of bitter almonds; VI–VIII.
<u>Fruits</u> ellipsoid, shiny black, usually 3-seeded drupe, less often greenish or white; VIII–IX.
<u>Distribution:</u> From southern Sweden to North Africa, in Iran and western Asia; formerly cultivated as a medicinal plant and naturalised.

ALL parts of the plant, but especially the roots and fruits (Radix, Fructus Ebuli), were used in folk medicine as a diuretic and diaphoretic. Cases of poisoning occurred and sometimes the roots were adulterated with, or replaced by, those of belladonna [J13; U2]. It is known also that drinking large amounts of dwarf-elder tea leads to violent vomiting and diarrhoea [B24]. Nowadays, the plant is little used as a medicament and its fruits find scant use in dyeing textiles and making wine.

Many *Sambucus* species – the red berried elder *(S. racemosa* **(43)**) and elder or bourtree *(S. nigra),* as well as the Canadian elder *(S. canadensis),* are repeatedly mentioned along with the dwarf elder *(S. ebulus* **(42)**) – appear to contain **substances which cause vomiting and purging.** According to Scheerer [S12], the consumption of **raw** elder berries should be avoided because of the frequent ill-effects. In some children even a few fruits may bring about serious vomiting [K47]. The resinous substances responsible

for the effects are present mainly in the seeds; there is less in the oil of the pulp. Heating destroys the toxic activity [S12].

Pharmacological investigations enabled Petkov *et al.* [P21] to confirm the diuretic activity of aqueous preparations of *S. ebulus.* The extracts also showed an inhibiting effect on the motor activity of the experimental animals and, depending on the amount injected, also caused a distinct reduction in the arterial blood pressure.

Microscopical characters of the fruits.
A feature that the drupes of *Sambucus*
species have in common is the almost
parallel cuticular striations on the
epidermis of the pericarp (**44a;** see
also [P22]). The radial walls of the
prismatic epidermal cells also have
numerous pits and in the case of
S. nigra the cells are partly thickened
and beaded (**44b**). Anomocytic stomata
with 6–7 subsidiary cells are usual in
S. racemosa, but otherwise occur only
sporadically. Unlike the anthocyanin-
containing blue-black fruits of *S. nigra*
and *S. ebulus,* the pulp of the drupes
of the red-berried elder, *S. racemosa,*
contains an oil which is intensely
yellow-coloured owing to the presence
of carotenoids. The detailed anatomy
of the pyrenes (stones) is set out in
[M48].

43 Sambucus racemosa L.   Red-berried Elder.

44 Epidermis of the pericarp of
Sambucus species: (a) S. ebulus.
(b) S. nigra.

a

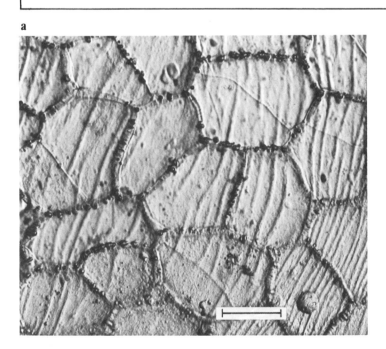

b

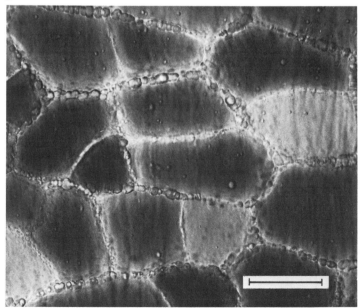

Symphoricarpos albus (L.) S.F. Blake   Snowberry

45 Snowberry

1–2.5 m tall shrub with slender stems.
<u>Leaves</u> opposite, elliptic to more or less
round, entire, on sucker shoots lobed.
<u>Flowers</u> campanulate, single or in
terminal spike-like racemes; reddish
white; VI–VIII.
<u>Fruits</u> white berries with small black
calyx remains and large-celled juicy
pulp; VIII–XI.
<u>Distribution:</u> Indigenous to western
North America, long cultivated in
Europe as an ornamental and widely
distributed.

THE conspicuous white berries of this shrub are very popular with children as missiles, since on reaching their target they burst with a satisfying little pop. Opinions as to their toxicity differ widely:

The berries are poisonous. In children . . . after eating them, irritation of the gastro-intestinal tract has been observed [H3].

There is saponin in the white berries and a highly irritating active principle which has not yet been studied [A5].

'They are edible but relatively tasteless and rarely used' [P30].

Occasionally, in serious cases confusion and deep unconsciousness are mentioned as symptoms of poisoning. This appears to be based on the brief, rather dramatic report by Amyot [A7], dating from 1885:

'Some time ago I was called to attend four children of one family, who were all suffering from vomiting, purging, and delirium, after which they became semi-comatose. They all recovered, but one of them had a narrow escape from death. I was anything but easy about the other three. Their vomit left no doubt of their having eaten largely of snowberries.'

Szaufer *et al.* [S102] indicate that in Poland children have been poisoned by eating the berries. These workers isolated a little chelidonine (see p.161) from the leaves and roots, but it cannot be held responsible for any toxic properties the plant may exhibit.

However, from the experience of the Berlin and Zürich Toxicological Centres it is clear that 3–4 berries generally do not cause any symptoms. Larger amounts may perhaps give rise to abdominal pains and vomiting. From America, Lewis [L17] has reported similar observations.

Chavant *et al.* [C12] came to the following conclusion as a result of their phytochemical and toxicological work on the fruits: 'These preliminary tests seem to show the fruit to be non-toxic.' On oral administration of an aqueous extract of the fresh fruit to young mice they found LD_{50} 435 g (!)/kg. With amounts of up to 2 g/kg body weight of the marc left after pressing the fruit the mice ex-

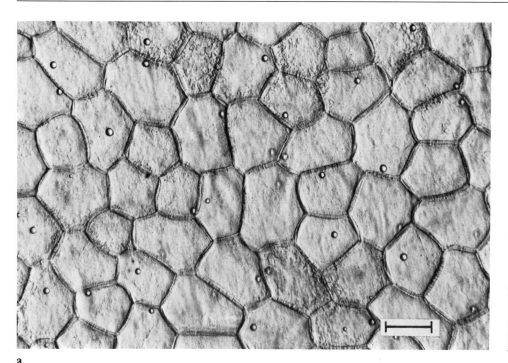

a

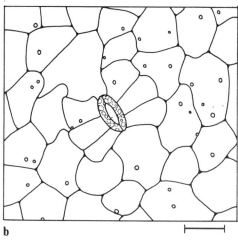

b

46 Symphoricarpos albus: (a) Epidermis of the pericarp. (b) Epidermis of the pericarp with stoma.

hibited no symptoms at all [N 10]. The lipophilic constituents of the berries have just as little toxicity, for Merfort [M 32] determined LD$_{50}$ 1266 g/kg (calculated on the fresh weight).

Besides the snowberry, in Europe a few other *Symphoricarpos* species are planted as ornamentals, in particular *S. orbiculatus,* coral berry or Indian currant, which also comes from North America. Its purplish red fruits are no doubt to be considered just as harmless as those of the snowberry. At any rate, there is no information about any cases of poisoning.

Microscopical characters of the fruits. The pericarp epidermis of the snowberry consists of colourless, polygonal, relatively thin-walled cells with fine pitting **(46a).** Stomata are rare, but have a conspicuous arrangement of the subsidiary cells **(46b).** Large (*ca* 100 μm) thin-walled parenchyma cells, which, through dissolution of the middle lamella during ripening, are very loosely bound to each other, make up the soft mealy pulp. They contain many calcium oxalate clusters (*ca* 15 μm); for an account of the anatomy of the seeds, see [G 30].

The pericarp of the red-spotted *S. orbiculatus* has distinctly smaller, but otherwise similar, colourless epidermal cells and a few short (*ca* 65 μm), thick-walled bristly hairs. The colouring matter is limited to a few regions in the hypodermal cell layers. The berries of both *Symphoricarpos* species have fine granular waxy deposits, chiefly on top of the anticlinal (radial) walls of the epidermal cells.

Viburnum opulus L.   Guelder-rose, High-bush Cranberry

47 Guelder-rose

1–3 m tall shrub or small tree with glabrous twigs. In wet thickets, deciduous and lowland forest on nutrient-rich mostly loam and clay soils.
<u>Leaves</u> opposite, maple-leaf shaped, with irregularly dentate lobes; upper surface glabrous, lower surface pubescent.
<u>Flowers</u> in terminal much-branched cymose corymbs; marginal flowers sterile and much larger than the inner ones, white; V–VIII.
<u>Fruits</u> scarlet, globose drupes with a flat red pyrene; VIII–XI.
<u>Distribution:</u> In Europe, western and northern Asia; several varieties are in cultivation in gardens.

AS with other Caprifoliaceae, the red berries of *Viburnum opulus* and the shiny black (when ripe) drupes of *V. lantana*, wayfaring-tree or mealy guelder-rose (see **48**), are generally suspected of being poisonous. Old reports suggest that they cause inflammation of the digestive tract and that they may even have caused death. However, there are no reports from this century of serious poisonings due to *Viburnum* fruits, although children quite often try them (see Table 5). In contrast, there are several indications in the literature that ripe fruits of various kinds of guelder-rose *(V. alnifolium, cassinoides, lentago, opulus, prunifolium)* are not only made into jellies and jams but also eaten raw [M29; S12]. About the berries of the Canadian guelder-rose *(V. prunifolium)*, whose bark was included in many pharmacopoeias and used on the uterus because of its spasmolytic action, Medsger [M29] has written: 'I do not recall any other wild fruit that I enjoy more.'

There is no doubt that the bark and leaves of some *Viburnum* species contain pharmacologically active compounds (coumarins, diterpenes) [H50; K13; V4]. The fruits, however, appear to do no more than bring about a mild upset (vomiting, diarrhoea) when they are eaten unripe or in largish amounts.

Microscopical characters of the fruits. The pericarp epidermis of the guelder-rose *(V. opulus)* is distinguished by relatively thick, mostly straight, cell walls in which the middle lamella is clearly seen. The extra thickening at the corners of the cells gives the epidermis an almost collenchymatous appearance **(49a)**. Stomata are relatively few; they have 6–8 subsidiary cells and are surrounded by a ring of very much smaller epidermal cells.

The berries of *V. lantana* and *V. rhytidophyllum* are anatomically very similar, but differ from that just described in a number of features. The epidermal cells are more beaded **(49b)** and the pericarp, which is largely free of stomata, bears large multicellular stellate trichomes **(49c)**. The pulp has many calcium oxalate clusters, larger (*ca* 65 μm) than those of *V. opulus* (*ca* 25 μm), and occasional calcium oxalate prisms (*ca* 25 μm). Characteristic of all three species are the hypodermal cells, which are very much larger than those of the epidermis and which in surface view usually shine through **(49b)**.

48 Viburnum lantana L.   Wayfaring-tree, Mealy Guelder-rose.

49. V. opulus: (a) Epidermis of the pericarp. V. lantana: (b) Epidermis of the pericarp; (c) Stellate trichome.

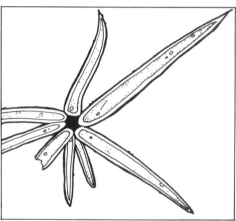

a

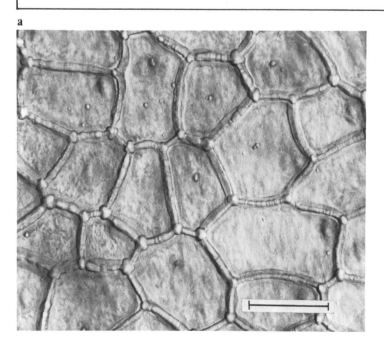

b

c

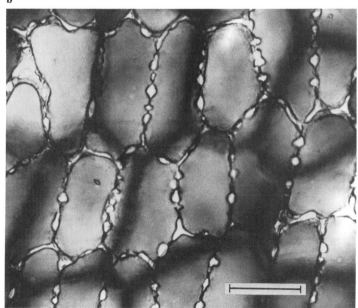

CELASTRACEAE

Euonymus europaeus L.   Spindle

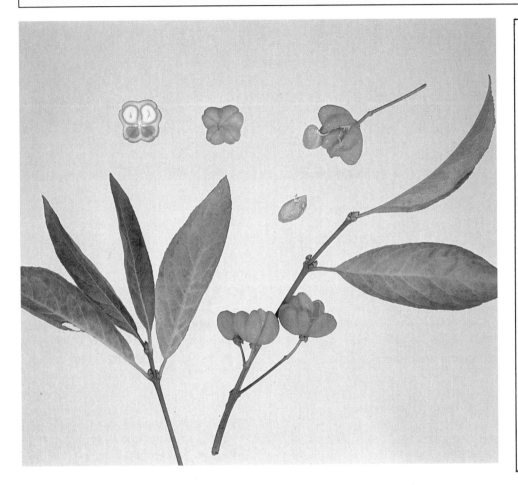

50 Spindle

3–6 m tall shrub with rounded 4-angled twigs, sometimes with cork ridges. In woods, thickets, and hedges on humic, moist to dry soil.
Leaves deciduous, ovate-elliptic to oblong, up to 8 cm in length, with jagged serrate margin, upper surface deep green, lower surface lighter; with yellow or red autumn colouring.
Flowers yellowish green, small and inconspicuous, in axillary cymes; V–VI.
Fruits 4-merous, pink to reddish capsules, 4(–5)-locular each with 1(–2) seed(s), whose whitish epidermis is enclosed by a bright orange-red aril; capsules dehisce in August and allow the conspicuously coloured seeds which are attached by a filament to be exposed; VIII–X.
Distribution: Throughout most of Europe as far as western Asia; many garden forms have been cultivated since olden times.

THE fruits of spindle with their arillate seeds are conspicuous structures and entice children in particular to eat them, so that cases of ingestion are regularly noted by the Toxicological Centres; see Tables 1 and 2. In contrast with the descriptions of serious poisonings found in the older literature [H41; U4], in recent times only cases with mild symptoms have been observed.

Constituents. Cardiotonic glycosides and alkaloids are present in the seeds and to both these, possibly together with as yet unknown substances, is ascribed the toxic action. The **cardiac glycosides** present are (a) evonoside, (b) evobioside, and (c) evomonoside; the aglycone is digitoxigenin, while the sugars are, respectively, (a) rhamnose + 2 glucose, (b) rhamnose + 1 glucose, and (c) rhamnose [H35].

The **alkaloids,** occurring to the extent of *ca* 0.1% in the seeds, are described as poly-esters of a C_{15} poly-alcohol, yielding on hydrolysis acetic acid and evonic acid – 3-[α-(β-carboxypyridyl)]-2-methylbutanoic acid. Besides evonine, quantitatively the major base, 6-*O*-deacetylevonine (= neo-evonine) and 4-deoxyevonine [B51] have been identified. As far as is known, the toxicity of these com-

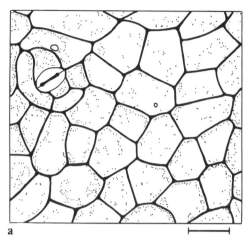

51 Euonymus europaeus: (a) Epidermis of the pericarp. (b) Aril in surface view.

a

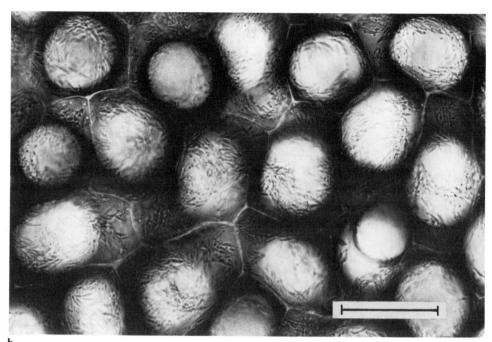

b

pounds has not been studied. Structurally similar alkaloids, isolated from the roots of another member of the Celastraceae *(Tripterygium wilfordii),* have insecticidal properties. This activity could explain the former common use of powdered *Euonymus* seeds against itch mites (in scabies) and lice and, at the same time, may be an indication of the pharmacological activity displayed by evonine and related compounds. Whether the seed oil is toxic on its own or because of the admixture of alkaloids is not clear; and it is not known whether the fruit pericarp has toxic substances in it.

Leaves and bark of spindle are also regarded as being poisonous, and they contain cardiac glycosides. In the leaves, stems, and roots there are also very low concentrations of alkaloids [B61] which, however, probably contribute little or nothing to the effect.

Symptoms of poisoning according to the older literature [H41; U4] are: colic, severe diarrhoea, fever, disturbances of the circulation, and symptoms of collapse; they may not appear until after a longish latent period (8–15 hours).

Treatment. When a large number of seeds have been eaten, gastric lavage may be carried out, with activated charcoal if thought appropriate; otherwise, symptomatic measures are sufficient.

Several other *Euonymus* species are planted as ornamentals. As far as is known, the range of constituents in their seeds is much the same as in spindle.

Another member of the Celastraceae, *Catha edulis,* 'khat', is worth a mention. Its leaves are chewed as a psycho-analeptic – a brief review has recently been published by Mebs [M28]. The toxicity of *Catha* extracts in animals has been investigated by Maitai [M8].

Microscopical characters of the fruit. The epidermis of the pericarp is made up of polygonal cells differing greatly in size. It has stomata (**51a**) whose relatively small guard cells lie distinctly below the level of the epidermis. Large calcium oxalate clusters (*ca* 25 μm) occur in the mesocarp. The thin-walled cells of the aril are distinguished particularly by their large transparent vacuoles and numerous spindle-shaped, intensely yellow-orange coloured chromoplasts (**51b**); a detailed account of the various parts of the fruit has been given by Guse [G30].

CORNACEAE

Cornus sanguinea L.   Dogwood, Dogberry

52 Dogwood

1–5 m tall perennial shrub with branches reaching upwards and bending over; 1-year old twigs blood red in autumn and winter. In thickets, hedges, and mixed deciduous forests, on dry to moist soils, calcicole.
<u>**Leaves**</u> **ovate to elliptic, acuminate; upper surface pale green, lower surface bluish green; in autumn changing to dark red.**
<u>**Flowers**</u> **in dense, flat, pubescent terminal corymbs; white, fragrant; V–VI (sometimes flowering a second time in autumn).**
<u>**Fruits**</u> **violet-black drupes, marked with white dots (trichomes) and tasting bitter; IX.**
<u>**Distribution:**</u> **In Europe and Asia Minor; because of its far-reaching root system, often planted in order to consolidate steep slopes.**

THE black berries of this shrub are believed in some parts of Germany to be poisonous [H34], perhaps because with insufficient botanical knowledge they can be confused with those of the elder buckthorn or black dogwood. They are unpalatable when raw, but not toxic. Because of its vitamin C content, the pulp, like that of the cornelian cherry, *Cornus mas* (53), is sometimes used in fruit juices and for making jam. There are no reports of poisoning by the fruits of *Cornus* species, Nestler [N5] points out that after contact with the leaves of these plants sensitive skins may show signs of irritation (reddening, continuous itching). He ascribes this effect solely to the trichomes, which are extensively encrusted with calcium carbonate.

Verbenalin

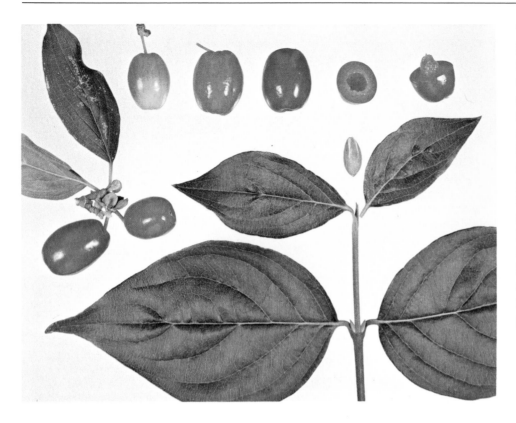

The symptoms only occur when the leaves are moved over the surface of the skin in the direction of the parallel warty T-shaped trichomes. Such trichomes are also found on the skin of the fruit **(54b)**. Highly active constituents are not known to be present in the family, and the iridoid cornin (= verbenalin), which is located especially in the leaves, has little toxicity. Children sometimes exhibit slight symptoms (fever, vomiting) after taking a few berries of *Aucuba japonica* (also Cornaceae), which is cultivated in France and the Mediterranean region, but these are ascribed to the triterpenoid saponins of the β-amyrin group that it contains [L 13].

53 Cornus mas L.   Cornelian Cherry.

a

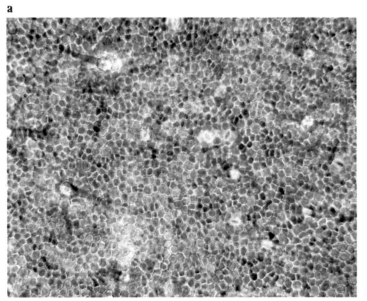

b

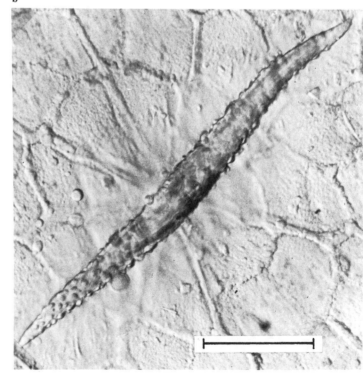

54 (a) Cornus sanguinea: Epidermis of the pericarp (photographed in polarised light). (b) C. sericea: Trichome.

Microscopical characters of the fruits.
The most prominent feature of *Cornus* fruits is the pubescence of their epidermis, which, in the case of the dark coloured berries of *C. sanguinea,* can be seen with a hand lens as white spots on the surface. In **54a** this dense pubescence is revealed by the blue colour that the individual trichomes exhibit under polarised light. These structures are unicellular, T-shaped, warty trichomes, and they are pointed at each end (**54b**) and encrusted with calcium carbonate. The fruits of different *Cornus* species are distinguished not only by their pigmentation but also by the denseness of the pubescence *(C. sanguinea > C. sericea > C. mas);* moreover, the trichomes of the cornelian cherry often appear to be longer and to have arms of unequal length.

55 Cornus sericea L.   Red Osier.

CUCURBITACEAE

TO the **Gourd family** belongs a whole group of species with considerable importance as sources of food (cucumbers, melons, water melons, pumpkins, etc.). Even though these plants have long been in cultivation, occasionally (as a result of mutation) toxic constituents are formed in their fruits such as are found in the organs of the wild plants (p.14). Thus, in South Africa cases of poisoning by gourds and other cultivated species keep on cropping up [S83]. Wild plants of these species are also known to be the cause of poisoning in cattle.

The toxicological problems were the motive for detailed investigations of the bitter and toxic constituents, the **cucurbitacins,** which are tetracyclic triterpenes [L7]. The most important biological problems have been summarised by Rehm [R3].

The cucurbitacins are apparently formed *in situ* and are not transported within the plant. While the embryos of the ripe seeds, as far as they have been studied, are entirely free of bitter substances, as soon as germination starts often the formation of large amounts of cucurbitacins is initiated. Their distribution in the various parts of the plants depends very much on the species and variety and at the same time to a great extent on the stage of development of the plant – in ripe fruits the total content is higher than in unripe ones. In the plant tissues they are often present in glycosidic form and are usually accompanied by a very active enzyme, elaterase (a β-glucosidase).

David and Vallance [D4] have reported the results of preliminary studies on the toxicity of pure cucurbitacins. For example, LD i.v. in the cat is 1 mg/kg and in the rabbit 6 mg/kg, and LD_{50} i.p. in the mouse is *ca* 1 mg/kg. After giving a lethal dose, the animals suffered from dyspnoea and lung oedema. All the compounds with a double bond in the side-chain are

Cucurbitacin J

said to be strongly cytotoxic and in animal experiments to suppress the growth of certain tumours [L7; T5]. Toxicological investigation of oral doses of the bitter substances would be especially interesting, as in this respect the older literature indicates wide differences in the toxic activity of the same plant in different animals [R3].

In folk medicine parts of the fruit of gourd species are occasionally used as a vermifuge. While shelled pumpkin seeds (*Cucurbita pepo,* Semen Cucurbitae Decorticatum) are not known to have any side-effects [B44], Lewis and Elvin-Lewis [L20] mention fatal cases in children who had been given the pulp of *C. lagenaria,* the bottle gourd. The seeds of this plant are also supposed to be highly toxic.

From the seeds of the bitter gourd, *Momordica charantia,* a fruit popular in the East as a food and stimulant, Lin *et al.* [L27] have isolated toxic lectins, which, like abrin and ricin (see p.121), act through the inhibition of protein synthesis. In contrast with them, however, momordin carries the various active groups on a single polypeptide chain.

Bryonia cretica L.   Red Bryony

56 Red Bryony

2–3 m tall perennial herbaceous plant, climbing by means of simple tendrils, and thick (up to 2.5 kg) napiform, foul-smelling roots (those of *B. alba* white). Along roadsides and hedges, in scrub, on fresh nutrient-rich loam.
<u>Leaves</u> cordate, 5-lobed, toothed, minutely hirsute, opposite each leaf a tendril.
<u>Flowers</u> dioecious; those of the male plant in long pedunculate racemes, those of the female plant in short pedunculate clusters, greenish white; corolla twice as long as calyx, stigma pubescent; VI–VII.
<u>Fruits</u> 1–2-seeded, thin-skinned, globose berries; when ripe those of *B. alba* black and those of *B. cretica* scarlet; VIII–X.
<u>Distribution:</u> Throughout southern, central, and eastern Europe; formerly cultivated as a medicinal plant and often naturalised further to the north and west.

THE drastic purgative action of bryony was already known to the doctors of antiquity. On the skin, the juice from the fresh roots first causes reddening, then painful inflammation with the formation of blisters. It is the cucurbitacins, nine of which have so far been isolated from *Bryonia* root [L7; P4; P38; R8], that are responsible for these irritant effects. However, the active principles are evidently not very stable, since on drying the tubers the activity decreases very considerably.

The acrid-tasting, shiny berries of *Bryonia* species are likewise toxic, but there are no data available about their cucurbitacins content. According to the older literature 40 berries are lethal to adults and 15 to children. And according to the experience of the Toxicological Information Centres these fruits are to be grouped with those which give rise to serious symptoms after a largish number have been eaten. Krienke and von Mühlendahl [K46] saw mild symptoms of poisoning (repeated vomiting) in three out of six cases after ingestion of only 6–8 berries. Other reported **symptoms** of *Bryonia* poisoning are abdominal pains, bloody diarrhoea, dizziness, renal inflammation, and in serious cases respiratory paralysis.

Treatment. Immediate gastric lavage with much activated charcoal. If there is vomiting and severe diarrhoea, the gastric lavage should be omitted and only the activated charcoal given. For the rest, symptomatic treatment (if necessary, fluids should be supplied and respiration assisted) [M50].

Microscopical characters of the fruits.
The epidermis of the pericarp of red bryony *(B. cretica)* fruit comprises polygonal cells with straight, thickened walls **(58a).** It has stomata whose guard cells are surrounded by several small epidermal cells arranged in the form of a rosette. In the mucilaginous pulp, as well as in the epidermis, carotenoid pigments are present.

On the other hand, the epidermis of the black berries of *B. alba* is colourless; however, it has similar stomata **(58b)** with guard cells which clearly protrude above the level of the epidermis. The fruit pulp is marked by an abundance of chloroplasts in the outer layers and starch grains ($<12 \mu$m) in the inner layers.

57 Bryonia alba L.   White Bryony.

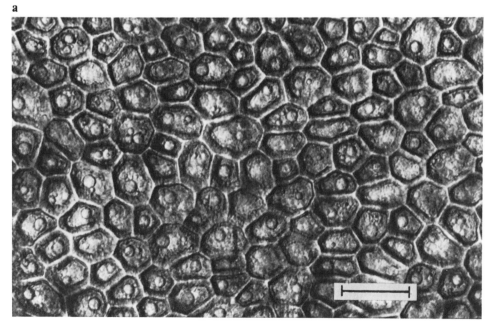

a

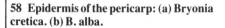

58 Epidermis of the pericarp: (a) Bryonia cretica. (b) B. alba.

b

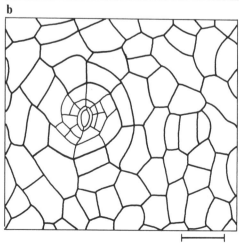

CUPRESSACEAE

EXCEPT for the yew (Taxaceae) with its conspicuous arillate seeds, conifers, to which the Cupressaceae belong, hardly figure in the statistics of the Toxicological Information Centres. This does not mean, however, that conifers have no highly active compounds. Their needle-shaped leaves and woody cones are no inducement to consumption, so that accidental poisonings are a rare occurrence. Only the (former, certainly more frequent) misuse of extracts or infusions of certain conifers as aborti-facients can lead to serious or, under certain circumstances, fatal poisoning.

Three Cupressaceae are illustrated and discussed below, in order to draw attention to the potential danger of some conifers.

Juniper (*Juniperus communis*)
The juniper is indigenous to Europe and usually grows as an erect shrub or small tree on heaths and in open conifer forests; it is also often planted. The globose, berry-like cones ripen on the female tree in the course of three growth periods, so that there are un-ripe (green) and ripe (brown-black, bluish glaucous) juniper berries on the tree at the same time. Fructus Juniperi contain a terpene-rich essential oil, with, among other things, the irritant α-pinene and the diuretic terpinenol. They are a usable diuretic drug, but in excess can bring about renal in-flammation and damage. Eating just a few juniper berries is in most cases probably harmless.

Savin (*Juniperus sabina*)
The savin occurs naturally in the mountains of southern and central Europe, but since it was formerly cultivated for pharmaceutical purposes here and there it may be encountered as an escape. It is a prostrate, un-pleasant smelling shrub or small tree initially with acicular and later with scale-like leaves.

In contrast with the essential oil of the juniper, that of the savin is a dangerous poison with a violent irritant action on the gastro-intestinal tract and on the renal epithelium. Poisoning with savin extracts or decoctions – formerly used to procure abortion – leads to the occurrence of convulsions and finally to central paralysis. In contact with the skin, savin oil causes blisters and deep-seated necrosis and, like the powdered branch tops (Summitates Sabinae), was used against warts and condyloma acuminatum. As regards the drug, it may be that podophyllotoxins, which have been detected in the scale-like leaves, are also involved in the activity. The major

59 Juniperus communis L.   Juniper.

60 Juniperus sabina L.   Savin.

61 Thuja occidentalis L.   White Cedar.

constituents of the essential oil are the terpene derivatives sabinene and sabinyl acetate.

White Cedar *(Thuja occidentalis)*
This 20 m tall evergreen, from eastern North America, is much planted in Europe, partly as a low hedge shrub ('thuja hedges'). In its scale-like leaves there is an essential oil which has a strong local irritant action. Taken by mouth, it leads to very serious poisoning with long-lasting clonic-tonic convulsions and de-generative changes in the liver, renal damage, and bleeding from the mucosa of the stomach. The toxic action is due mainly to the monoter-pene thujone, whose dangerous prop-erties have been known from the properties exhibited by the essential oil of absinth [V 12].

Treatment. In the case of poisoning by savin or white cedar: firstly, removal of the poison by gastric lavage with activated charcoal; symptomatic measures against convulsions and, if necessary, artificial respiration.

Other toxicologically interesting constituents of the Gymnosperms worth mentioning are the skin-irritant substances of the fleshy seed coat (sarcotesta) of *Ginkgo biloba* [B 18] – substances which resemble the urushiols of the Anacardiaceae [A 22] – and the carcinogenic pseudo-cyano-genic compounds of the Cycadaceae, e.g. macrozamin or cycasin.

DIOSCOREACEAE

Tamus communis L.   Black Bryony

62 Black Bryony

0.5–3 m tall perennial herb with twining stem and tuberous sometimes branched rootstock. At the edges of woods and hedgerows, in thickets, on rich mostly calcareous soils.
<u>Leaves</u> alternate, long-petiolate, undivided, cordate-ovate to hastate, acuminate, reticulate venation, glossy.
<u>Flowers</u> dioecious, greenish, as loose axillary racemes; male perianth campanulate, female perianth divided almost to the base; V–VI.
<u>Fruits</u> scarlet, trilocular, few-(3–5)-seeded berries; VIII–X.
<u>Distribution:</u> Southern and western Europe, Balkans, Near East, North Africa, Canary Islands; in England and Wales, probably introduced in Ireland.

LESS reputable companies sometimes market the dried rhizome of *Tamus communis* and praise it as an anodyne and panacea ('unexcelled for head-, tooth-, or ear-ache, which disappears in 2–3 minutes') [S21]. Even today, the freshly dug up rootstock is used by Hungarian country people for rheumatic conditions [B7]. If the freshly cut sticky and shiny surface is rubbed on the skin, it stimulates the circulation and, depending on how heavily it is used, causes severe burning with general reddening, formation of painful swellings, and sometimes allergic reactions.

Toxic constituents. The irritant action on the skin is said to be due to a histamine-like constituent [H54]. An essential role is undoubtedly played by the calcium oxalate needles [C24], which, by damaging the skin, facilitate penetration of the irritant substance (see also Araceae, p.51). There are, in addition, in the leaves and tubers of the plant traces of alkaloids, saponins (20 mg diosgenin/kg tuber) [H35], and also photosensitive phenanthrene derivatives [L9; S103], that in view of the small amounts present can have little influence on the toxic action of the plant material. Young shoots do not contain any idioblasts with needles of calcium oxalate [H35] and are evidently not toxic; in Dalmatia they are eaten as a vegetable.

The fruits of black bryony are red, owing to the presence of carotenoids,

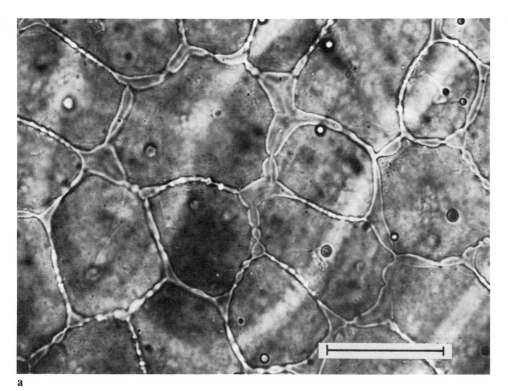

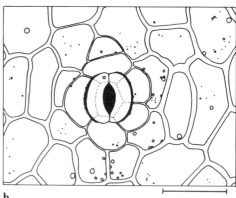

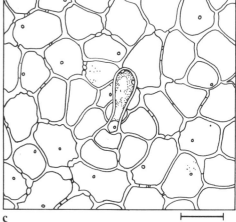

63 Tamus communis: (a) Epidermis of the pericarp, with (b) an anomocytic stoma and (c) a single glandular trichome.

and because of their attractive appearance are the part most likely to be eaten by children. Because of the considerable calcium oxalate (raphides) content, the symptoms produced are like those caused by the fruit of lords-and-ladies (severe irritation of the mucosa, nausea, diarrhoea).

Treatment. Symptomatic; see also p.51.

Microscopical characters of the fruit. As is evident from the name black bryony for *Tamus communis,* the macroscopic appearance of the plant (habit, leaf shape) and its fruits (size, colour) closely resembles that of *Bryonia* species (bryony, see p.93). Microscopically, at least, the red fruits of the black bryony are readily distinguished by a number of features.

The epidermis of *Tamus* fruits is distinctly collenchymatous **(63a)** and has anomocytic stomata **(63b);** there are also very occasional unicellular glandular trichomes **(63c).** The pulp has numerous mucilage-containing idioblasts with large (*ca* 230 μm) raphides.

ELAEAGNACEAE

THE small **Oleaster family** is distinguished by the occurrence of conspicuous, mostly red to orange-yellow berry-like fruits. These are drupe-like – the dry fruit being surrounded by a fleshy hypanthium. They are **not toxic** – on the contrary, most of them can be eaten raw or cooked and some actually have a pleasant taste. Two representatives of the family are illustrated here as an aid to identification, so that these harmless, but not uncommon, fruits can be the more readily differentiated from potentially or genuinely toxic 'berries'. As shown in **66,** the peltate, scale-like trichomes of the Elaeagnaceae are a very good diagnostic feature.

64 Hippophae rhamnoides L.   Sea-buckthorn.

65 Elaeagnus umbellata Thunb.

Sea-buckthorn *(Hippophae rhamnoides)*

This shrub or small tree is widespread throughout Europe on sandy coasts, but also in the Alps along river banks; moreover, it is often planted. The ovoid fruits, which are orange-red from August onwards, contain much ascorbic acid, carotenoid pigments, and fixed oil, not only in the seeds but also in the 'pulp' [A1; H3]. In times of emergency, they have been collected for the purpose of producing vitamin C, and nowadays they are used in making ascorbic acid-rich preparations (sea-buckthorn juice).

Oleaster *(Elaeagnus)*

The genus *Elaeagnus* is found mainly in eastern Asia and is represented in the Mediterranean region only by *E. angustifolia*. This and some other species are quite often planted in Europe and attract attention because

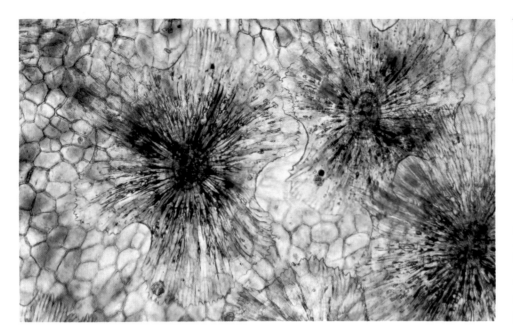

66   **Elaeagnus umbellata: Epidermis of the pericarp with characteristic peltate trichomes (photographed in polarised light).**

of their dense covering (at least on the young organs) of silvery trichomes. The *E. umbellata* illustrated here (**66**) also has fruits with a scurfy surface owing to their covering of characteristic peltate scale-like trichomes.

EMPETRACEAE

Empetrum nigrum L.   Crowberry

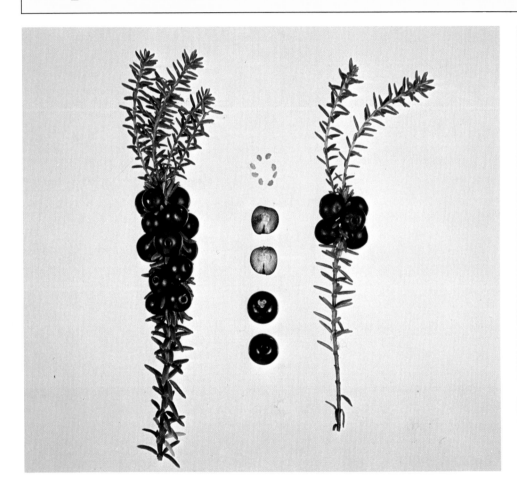

67 Crowberry

Profusely branched, up to 25 cm high, dwarf shrub; with procumbent grey-green branches and a heath-like appearance, forming a carpet of vegetation. In sparse coniferous forests and moors, but also on sandy heath soils and dune sand.
<u>Leaves</u> often verticillate to opposite, shortly petiolate and needle-shaped, with strongly revolute margins; evergreen, glossy.
<u>Flowers</u> mostly dioecious; inconspicuous, in short lateral racemes; corolla pink to dark purple; V–VI.
<u>Fruits</u> glossy black drupes with 6–9 1-seeded pyrenes (stones); VII–IX.
<u>Distribution:</u> Throughout the northern hemisphere.

THIS plant, which resembles members of the heath family, has so far been little investigated. The unsupported suggestion by Gessner [G11] that it contains the toxic andromedotoxin (= acetylandromedol) is contradicted by other authors [H34; H35], according to whom neither alkaloid nor andromedotoxin nor arbutin is present. More recently, however, traces of alkaloid have been detected in the leaves [S94]. That the highly pigmented (anthocyanins) berries are

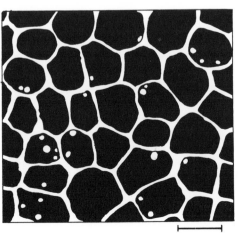

harmless is also evident from the fact that in many countries they are considered to be edible whether raw or made into a jelly [H9]. Thus, Hegi [H34], for example, writes:

They are one of the few berries indigenous to northern Scandinavia

68 Empetrum nigrum: Epidermis of the pericarp.

and northern Russia that are enjoyed in considerable quantities both fresh and prepared. The frozen berries are especially pleasant-tasting . . . according to Rink more than 139 000 litres of them being collected annually.

Microscopical characters of the fruit. The epidermis of the pericarp of the crowberry has no stomata **(68)** and is coloured dark reddish violet (anthocyanins). Its mostly thick cell walls are sometimes beaded. In the outer layers of the pulp there are also pigments, but in the anthocyanin-free deeper layers of thin-walled parenchyma chloroplasts and roundish starch grains (up to $10\,\mu$m in size) may be present.

Equisetum palustre L.   Marsh Horsetail

69 Marsh Horsetail

0.2–0.6 m tall perennial herb with simple branched and grooved stems (4–8 grooves). Fertile (sporangia-bearing) and sterile stems similar and appearing simultaneously; narrow central hollow (70). Sheaths loose, with white-edged lanceolate teeth (up to 10). Lowest branch joint always distinctly shorter than the sheath. Spores ripen V–IX. <u>Distribution:</u> In Europe, temperate Asia, North America; on nutrient-rich, damp meadows and marshes.

THE marsh horsetail is generally looked upon as being poisonous because of its alkaloid content. Since the pharmacopoeial drug Herba Equiseti, from *E. arvense,* often enters commerce admixed with other *Equisetum* species [L5; S15], the 8th edition of the German Pharmacopoeia specifically requires examination for adulterants, in particular *E. palustre.* So far, however, cases of poisoning are only known from veterinary practice. They represent a local, but for the agricultural concerns in question very serious, problem [B23; H64; N9; see also F33].

Constituents. The principal alkaloid, palustrine, was first isolated in a pure state by Karrer and Eugster [K7] and its chemical structure was elucidated by Mayer *et al.* [M27]. In extensive investigations Holz and Richter [H53] showed that the alkaloid content of *E. palustre* can undergo very rapid and extreme fluctuations (96–302 mg/100 g dry weight), which have no demonstrable connection with either locality or weather. Nevertheless, once the frost starts, the content decreases to such an extent that the horsetail is then almost alkaloid-free. On the other hand, the alkaloid content of air-dried plant material can remain unchanged for years [W29].

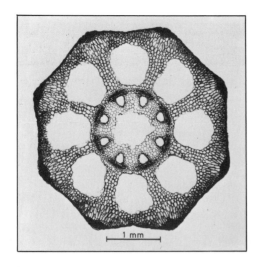

70 Equisetum palustre: Transverse section through the stem.

71 Epidermal protuberances in: (a) Equisetum palustre. (b) E. arvense. See Table 7.

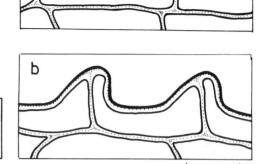

In the great horsetail *(E. telmateia)* and wood horsetail *(E. sylvaticum)*, which are also considered to be toxic, apart from traces of nicotine no other alkaloids have been found [P31].

A further toxic principle occurring in horsetails is believed to be the vitamin B_1-degrading enzyme thiaminase [H40; L20; L23]. Horses in particular are susceptible to a lack of vitamin B_1, for, unlike ruminants, it is an essential factor for them. The folk wisdom regarding the suitability of horsetail enshrined in the German proverb 'Der Pferde Brot – der Kühe Tod' (bread for the horse – death for the cow) does not appear to be confirmed by these investigations.

Cases of poisoning. The symptoms of poisoning seen in horses comprise excitability, twitching of facial muscles, reeling gait, falling over, until finally the animal dies of exhaustion. This condition is traced to the decomposition of the vitamin B_1. In cows the more prominent symptoms include a decrease in the yield of milk, loss of weight, diarrhoea, and in acute cases symptoms of paralysis. Fatal cases have also been observed. The symptoms are ascribed to the alkaloids of *Equisetum*, since ruminants are able to synthesise vitamin B_1 for themselves.

Palustrine

Treatment. When the illness is correctly diagnosed, recovery can be ensured within a few days by changing the diet. For horses, giving 100–150 g baker's yeast in addition is recommended [B23; L23].

Macroscopical and microscopical characters of the marsh horsetail. To distinguish the marsh horsetail with certainty from other *Equisetum* species, especially the very similar field horsetail, *E. arvense*, both morphological and microscopical features can be a great help; see **70** and **71** and Table 7.

Appendix. The Lycopodiaceae, **Club Moss family,** which is near the Equisetaceae, is also noted for the presence of toxic alkaloids. Bergemann [personal communication] has come across the substitution of Herba Nasturtii (water cress) by Herba Lycopodii (club moss), and this shows the necessity of a careful check when dealing with drugs for therapeutic use.

Table 7. Differentiating characters of *Equisetum palustre* and *E. arvense*.

	E. palustre	*E. arvense*
Teeth of sheath	Broad, white-edged	Narrow, white-edged
Branch sheaths	Black	Light to dark brown
Lowest joint	Shorter than	Longer than
	stem sheaths	
Central hollow	Smaller than	Larger than
	lateral hollows	
Epidermal protuberances	1-Celled	2-Celled

ERICACEAE

THE **Heath family** has considerable importance as a source of ornamentals (azalea, mountain laurel, wild rosemary, rhododendron, checkerberry or wintergreen), while others are medicinal (bearberry leaves in the 8th edition of the German Pharmacopoeia; whortleberry in the German Pharmaceutical Codex and German Homoeopathic Pharmacopoeia) or yield wild fruit (bilberries, cowberries). Many members of the family are nevertheless markedly toxic to both man and animals. The genera which are of especial importance in this respect belong to the subfamilies Arbutoideae (*Andromeda, Gaultheria, Pernettya, Pieris*) and Rhododendroideae (*Kalmia, Ledum, Rhododendron*).

Like the rose family (p.186), the Ericaceae are typical polyphenol-containing plants. They accumulate high concentrations of tannins (of different biogenetic origins), flavonoids, or phenolic glycosides (arbutin, pyroside, rhododendrin, etc.) [T8] in all parts. Except for the occasional gastro-intestinal troubles caused by eating unripe fruits with a high tannin content, these **phenolic constituents** are rarely (see *Gaultheria*) the cause of toxic symptoms. Rather, it is the **toxic diterpenes** of the acetylandromedol type that since antiquity (large-scale poisoning by Pontic honey) have been responsible time and time again for poisonings. These compounds are

Acetylandromedol
(= Grayanotoxin I)

C_{20} poly-ols, some of which are acetylated, that show a degree of resemblance to other, likewise toxic, compounds present in the spurge family (see p.113) and the mezereum family (see p.226). It was not until 1955 that the group of toxic principles which in the course of time had been isolated from various Ericaceae was recognised as having the same type of structure. Thus, the names andromedotoxin, asebotoxin, grayanotoxin I, and rhodotoxin all represent the same substance, viz acetylandromedol [S20]. Since then, the structures of further derivatives of this parent compound have been elucidated [Z2].

The toxic actions of acetylandromedol are many-sided and in several respects resemble those of aconitine [P48; Z3]. In addition, the substance has a positive inotropic effect [R25; T14] and, in low doses, a long-lasting hypotensive effect that can be used in therapeutics [T19]. After administering a lethal dose, paralysis starts at the extremities and progresses until finally it reaches the respiratory centre when death occurs. Trunzler [T19] determined LD_{50} p.o. in rats as 2–5 mg/kg. In working with concentrated solutions of the compound almost always hypersensitivity develops, in the form of severe irritation of the skin and mucosa [S20].

Many Ericaceae are characterised anatomically by the occurrence of glandular trichomes which in some cases produce considerable amounts of **essential oil.** Bearing in mind the general toxic action on cells and the narcotic action of this group of substances, plant extracts containing them, e.g. of *Ledum,* particularly when misused as an abortifacient used to give rise to symptoms of poisoning.

Gaultheria procumbens L.   Checkerberry, Creeping Wintergreen

72 Checkerberry

Creeping dwarf shrub, up to 15 cm in height, with some branches bearing glandular trichomes, spreading underground and in time forming a dense ground cover. In woods and glades, on sandy sterile soils.

<u>Leaves</u> alternate, evergreen, with a short petiole, elliptic, clustered on the branches; upper surface glossy dark green, lower surface lighter; turning reddish in autumn.

<u>Flowers</u> single, axillary, nodding; corolla white to light pink, conical to urceolate; VI–VIII.

<u>Fruits</u> globose, red, 5-locular capsules enclosed in a fleshy calyx and resembling a berry; with an aromatic fragrance, mealy; IX–IV.

<u>Distribution:</u> Eastern North America; much planted in parts of western Europe; important ground cover, for planting round graves, in heath and rock gardens.

DURING the American War of Independence the evergreen leaves of the checkerberry were used to prepare a tea, known by the names 'salvador' or 'mountain' tea. Pouring boiling water over the fresh or dried leaves is supposed to yield a pleasant-tasting and refreshing tea. The berries, which remain on the plant until well into the spring, are sold at local markets and are used in fruit tarts and cakes [M29].

At the turn of the century, gaultheria or **wintergreen oil** was steam-distilled from fresh plant material on a large scale (annual production 10000 kg). Depending on the time of year the yield varies be-tween 0.55 and 0.8%, and the main constituent of the oil is methyl salicyl-ate (96–99%). This substance does not occur as such in the plant but is liberated by hydrolysis from the glyco-side monotropitoside (= gaultherin). The very penetrating characteristic odour and taste of the oil is due to the presence of various esters and alcohols.

Monotropitoside

Nowadays, the oil is still used in America to flavour confectionery, chewing gum, toothpaste, and certain drinks, e.g. root beer [G12]. Its thera-peutic application as an antirheumatic has decreased in importance, since methyl salicylate is now made more cheaply by synthesis.

Poisoning has only occurred after the pure oil has been taken internally or through percutaneous absorption. Because of the toxicity of methyl salicylate, cases have quite often been fatal. Between 1940 and 1949 16 chil-dren died, mostly as a result of licking from containers which had gaultheria oil in them.

In view of the wide distribution of this plant as an ornamental and as the berries, which are indeed harmless, because of their strong taste and odour are often suspected by the layman of being poisonous, it is worthwhile indicating the microscopical characters of the fruit as a help in identification.

Microscopical characters of the fruit. The red-coloured epidermis of the fruit (fleshy calyx) bears only a few stomata; some groups of cells show a 'window-like' pattern* and have a clearly striated cuticle with granular wax deposits (73). In the pulp (mesophyll) there are occasional calcium oxalate clusters ($<25\,\mu$m). The outer layer of the seed coat (testa) consists of wavy- and thick-walled extensively pitted cells.

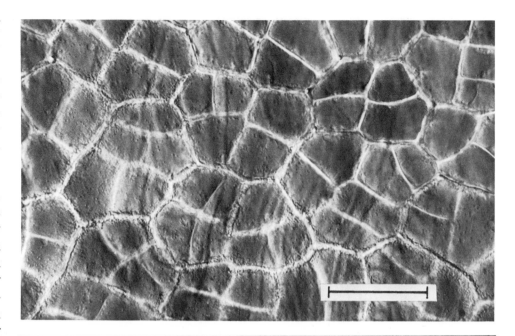

73 Gaultheria procumbens: Epidermis of the pericarp.

*See footnote on p.62.

Ledum palustre L. Wild Rosemary

74 Wild Rosemary

0.5–1.5 m tall shrub with erect spreading juvenile branches; rusty-tomentose.
In birch and coniferous forests and on moors, mostly on wet, non-calcareous, poor peat soils or cliffs.
__Leaves__ evergreen, entire, linear; upper surface glabrous, glossy, lower surface densely rusty-tomentose; margin revolute.
__Flowers__ in terminal umbel-like racemes; white, fragrant; V–VI.
__Fruits__ inconspicuous capsules, opening from below, pendent.
__Distribution:__ Northern and central Europe, Asia; rare in western Europe.

THIS shrub with its evergreen lanceolate leaves, which are rusty-tomentose beneath, resembles the true rosemary. Since it mostly grows on peat soils, its rare localities in central Europe are threatened by the draining of many moors.

Owing to their penetrating camphor-like odour, the dried branches used to be used against moths and (bed) bugs. The Vikings employed the leaves and shoots to give taste and, at the same time, strength to their beer. It is the intoxicating effect of this beverage that is supposed to have been the basis of the often-mentioned frenzy of the berserkers [S 10].

In contrast with older data, wild rosemary appears not to contain arbutin [K 41] or toxic diterpenes (acetyl-andromedol) [H 35]. The intoxicating and narcotic action of the plant is attributed solely to the essential oil, whose chief components are two sesquiterpene alcohols, ledol and palustrol [S 10; T 3]. Ledol first brings about central stimulation (psycho-motor excitation, and sometimes convulsions) with subsequent paralysis [H 3]. Using the oil, MacDonald *et al.* [D 14] were able to demonstrate a dose-dependent reduction in motor activity and ability to maintain balance, as well as an increase in the sleeping time after giving barbiturate or alcohol.

Nowadays, because of its remote habitat, this plant no longer has any special toxicological interest.

Rhododendron L.   Rhododendron, Azalea

75 (Left) Rhododendron   76 (Right) Azalea

Trees or (in Europe exclusively) shrubs with laurel-like evergreen or deciduous leaves and mostly handsome, splendidly coloured flowers.

<u>Leaves</u> alternate, entire, undivided.

<u>Flowers</u> mostly in terminal racemes, less often axillary, sometimes single; corolla usually campanulate, rotate, disc-shaped, or funnel-shaped, generally 5-merous.

<u>Fruits</u> woody septicidal capsule with numerous very small seeds.

<u>Distribution:</u> Mainly East Asia, temperate North America; only about four species in the mountains of Europe.

OPINIONS as to the number of *Rhododendron* species vary enormously. It is estimated that there are 500–1000 natural species and several thousand hybrids and cultivars, many of which are grown in temperate regions as ornamentals and pot plants (azaleas). Many of these species contain in their flowers (including the nectar), fruits, leaves, and shoots the poisonous diterpene acetylandromedol. However, it is difficult to say anything about the toxicity of any particular rhododendron in the absence of exact investigations. This is clear from the example of a hybrid derived from four different parent species, which, in contrast with three of the parents, does not produce toxic nectar [C6]. On the other hand, a table of the *Rhododendron* species examined so far will be of limited value to most readers of this book since only a few specialists are in a position to identify these plants with certainty; those interested are referred to the review by Hegnauer [H35].

Poisoning due to rhododendron is seen mainly in ruminants (sheep, goats, cattle) [B23]. Bolton [B39] points out that every year many cases of poisoning occur in the winter months when the animals are limited by frost and snow in their choice of forage. Plants containing acetylandromedol also cause special problems in zoos, where visitors frequently offer the caged animals bits of leaf from ornamentals growing near at hand [S63]. Finally, people, more especially small children, who are fond of trying conspicuously coloured plant parts are endangered by the poisonous nectar. Hardin and Arena [H9], for example, report that children who sucked the flowers or made a tea from the leaves exhibited symptoms of poisoning.

The effects of toxic Ericaceae honey have been described by many writers, from ancient times (Xenophon, Pliny, Strabo) right up to the present day [C6]. It seems that the unpleasant bitter taste of the product, which comes principally from Asia Minor and Japan, is not enough to prevent some people from consuming toxic amounts of it. Of interest biologically is the fact that the bees producing this honey are themselves not insensitive to the acetylandromedol [C6] and also that, in addition to toxic diterpenes [W14], phenolic constituents (arbutin or its derivatives) can get into the honey via the nectar [D23].

Besides rhododendrons, among the ornamental Ericaceae lambkill or dwarf laurel *(Kalmia angustifolia)*, mountain laurel *(K. latifolia), Pernettya mucronata*, and *Pieris japonica* contain acetylandromedol and have occasionally given rise to cases of poisoning [H9; L20; M13; S63; S64; S105]. Surprisingly, in contrast to the often repeated old assertion, toxic diterpenes have **not** been detected in bogrosemary *(Andromeda polifolia)* [C17; P1]. Also of interest is the indication by Schindler [S20] that *Kalmia latifolia* leaves, at least those of central European origin, i.e. from cultivated plants, contain at most only traces of or even no acetylandromedol at all. Such a change in metabolism is not known to take place with *Rhododendron* species.

Symptoms of poisoning. According to Trunzler [T19], among the symptoms encountered in the course of poisoning with acetylandromedol-containing plant materials or products are: copious salivation, nausea, vomiting, diarrhoea, pain and cramp in the intestines, dizziness and excitation, as well as burning and itching of the skin and mucous membranes. Smith [S63] has shown in feeding experiments that as little as 1 g fresh leaf material of *Pieris* per kg body weight leads to serious poisoning in goats. The symptoms may take 4–6 hours to develop and, depending on the circumstances, may last for several days. It seems, however, that in animals the grayanotoxins tend not to accumulate, since Hikino *et al.* [H47] observed after feeding sub-lethal amounts ($\frac{1}{5}$th of the LD_{50} p.o.) only very slight toxicity (loss of weight, increase in serum aspartate aminotransferase (AST) and alanine aminotransferase (ALT)). Recent investigations into the structure-activity relationships of various substituted grayanotoxins have been carried out by Mager *et al.* [M5].

Treatment. A specific antidote for acetylandromedol and related compounds is not known, but in certain cases gastric lavage using activated charcoal and symptomatic measures can be recommended. Smith [S63] suggests in the case of animal poisoning the application of purgatives, calcium injections, and antibiotics for dealing with the pneumonia that often ensues.

For the **detection** of acetylandromedol and related compounds a saturated solution of antimony trichloride in chloroform can be used. This reagent enables as little as 2 μg to be satisfactorily detected on thin-layer chromatograms through the intense red fluorescence produced under UV light [S20].

Vaccinium uliginosum L.   Bog Bilberry

77 Bog Bilberry

0.5–1 m tall dwarf shrub with terete, glabrous, erect branches and creeping rhizomes. In peat forests, moors, and alpine heaths; requires acid nutrient-poor peat and virgin humus soils.
<u>Leaves</u> deciduous, short-petiolate, obovate to elliptic, glabrous, margin often slightly revolute, lower surface especially bluish green.
<u>Flowers</u> in few-(1–4)-flowered terminal racemes on short lateral branches; pink to white corolla; V–VI.
<u>Fruits</u> bluish glaucous many-seeded berries with colourless juice having a sourish taste; VIII–IX.
<u>Distribution:</u> Europe, North America, northern Africa.

IN many parts of the world, the berries of several *Vaccinium* species (*V. corymbosum, V. macrocarpon, V. myrtillus, V. oxycoccos, V. vitis-idaea*) are among the most popular wild fruits. Owing to their content of plants acids, sugars, and vitamins, they are used to prepare refreshing drinks, pleasant-tasting stewed or preserved fruits, and jams, and they are also eaten raw. The only one suspected of being toxic is the bog bilberry, *V. uliginosum*. Undoubtedly, after eating these berries (the identity of the plants is certain) symptoms of poisoning have occasionally been observed: psychomotor excitation, vomiting, pupillary dilatation, feeling of dizziness [Z1]. On the other hand, two authors, experimenting on themselves, have come to entirely opposite findings. While Kreuder after taking *ca* 300 g of *V. uliginosum* berries noted 'dizziness, feeling hot in the head, lassitude, visual disturbances, inability to swallow, etc.', Moeschlin [M50] reported: 'We have enjoyed large quantities of the berries in Sweden and Switzerland without detecting any side-effects at all'. And in spite of intensive examination, neither toxic diterpenes [P1] nor other constituents that might be responsible for the symptoms have been found in the fruits of *V. uliginosum*. Zipf [Z1] therefore wonders whether a fungus *(Sclerotinia megalospora)* which sometimes parasitises the berries might perhaps be responsible for the toxic symptoms.

Thus, in general, the fruits appear to be harmless, and it is only in rare cases that on eating large amounts symptoms are likely to develop.

For the macroscopic **identification, 78,** in which the berries and leaves of several *Vaccinium* species are compared, will be of help. The very similar berries of *V. myrtillus* and *V. uliginosum* are clearly distinguished through the juice – that of *V. myrtillus* is dark blue-violet and that of *V. uliginosum* is colourless.

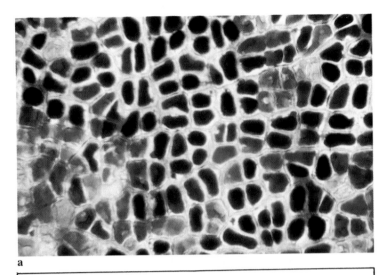

78 **Leaves and fruits of various Vaccinium species:**
(From left to right) V. myrtillus, V. oxycoccos,
V. uliginosum, and V. vitis-idaea.

79 **Epidermis of the pericarp of various Vaccinium species:**
(a) V. uliginosum. (b) V. myrtillus. (c) V. vitis-idaea.
(d) V. oxycoccos.

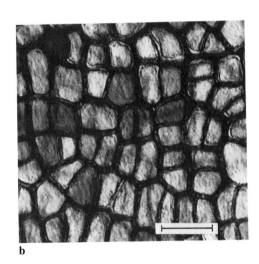

b

c

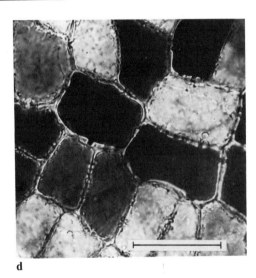

d

Microscopical characters of some Vaccinium fruits. A feature common to the illustrated *Vaccinium* berries is the more or less distinct 'window-like' pattern (see footnote on p.62) exhibited by the pericarp epidermis (**79a, b**), below which is a hypodermis consisting of large thin-walled parenchyma cells.

The externally very similar fruits of *V. uliginosum* and *V. myrtillus* are distinguished not only in the distribution of the pigment but also in the appearance of the endocarp (inner fruit wall). In both fruits part of it consists of sclerenchymatous cells, and those present in *V. myrtillus* are distinctly smaller and thicker-walled (up to $45\,\mu$m wide and $140\,\mu$m in length). Such cells also occur regularly in the central part of the pulp, as do also calcium oxalate clusters ($<18\,\mu$m); both these features are absent from the mesocarp of *V. uliginosum*.

The small-celled epidermis of the cowberry (**79c**) is largely colourless (pigments are concentrated chiefly in the hypodermis) and there are only a few stomata, with bulging guard cells and 5–6 subsidiary cells. The pulp is characterised by the occurrence of numerous calcium oxalate clusters (up to $25\,\mu$m). With the mostly spotted fruits of the cranberry *(V. oxycoccos)*, pigmented cells are present both in the epidermis, whose walls exhibit distinct pitting (**79d**), and in the deeper layers. The pulp does not contain either sclereids or calcium oxalate.

Detailed accounts of the anatomy of the fruits have been published by several authors [C27; G5; G24; K3; M48].

EUPHORBIACEAE

OWING to their content of rubber (Hevea), fixed oil (Ricinus, Aleurites), or carbohydrate (Manihot), several genera of the **Spurge family** are of great economic importance. In addition to its morphological heterogeneity, this family is notable for its wide range of chemical constituents. Thus, alkaloids originating via the most diverse biosynthetic pathways, cyanogenic glycosides, and polyphenols occur widely. Other species accumulate volatile oils, saponins, or mustard-oil glycosides (glucosinolates) [S27]. Apart from the cyanogenic glycoside linamarin, which can be present in bitter cassava (starchy tuberous roots of Manihot esculenta) in amounts of up to 0.4% [F19; H69; Y1] and therefore does not allow the tubers to be eaten raw [S45], the substances mentioned above are of little importance toxicologically. The main compounds responsible for the toxic properties are lectins and esters of certain diterpene alcohols.

Toxic lectins (Toxalbumins). Lectins are proteins which bind specifically to carbohydrates. Some of them are highly toxic to man and animals, as a result of the inhibition of ribosomal protein synthesis. As far as the Euphorbiaceae are concerned, toxalbumins have been found in, e.g. the seeds of Jatropha curcas (curcin), Hura crepitans (hurin), Croton tiglium (crotin), and Ricinus communis (ricin). This last one, ricin, closely resembles abrin from jequirity (Abrus precatorius; p.126), so that it is not necessary to discuss the mechanism of action here. Their remarkable stability towards proteolytic enzymes is of importance in connection with their toxic action after being taken by mouth. Detailed accounts of the occurrence, isolation, action, and physiological significance of plant lectins have been published by Liener [L24], Kauss [K11], and Schneider [S26].

Irritant diterpene esters. The seed oil of Croton tiglium has long been known as a drastic purgative, but because of its great toxicity (20 drops are lethal) is no longer used medicinally. As active principle, altogether 14 different fatty-acid esters of the tetracyclic diterpene alcohol phorbol have been isolated from the oil [H30]. Similar substances occur in the latices and seed oils of other Euphorbiaceae, especially in species of genera belonging to the subfamilies Crotonoideae and Eu-

Ingenane

Daphnane

Phorbol
(Tigliane skeleton)

phorbioideae [K27]. Here, in addition to phorbol (Croton, Euphorbia, Aleurites) derivatives, esters of two other structurally related diterpenes, daphnane (Euphorbia, Hura; see also p.117) and ingenane (Euphorbia), are found [E11].

These toxic diterpene esters cause inflammation of the skin, with reddening and the formation of oedematous swellings and vesicles. If these poisonous latices get into the eyes they can cause inflammation of the cornea and conjunctiva, sometimes leading to blindness. When taken internally, poisoning with severe gastro-enteritis, vomiting, and colicky diarrhoea has occasionally been observed.

From the News Reports of the *Pharmazeutische Zeitung* [A25] the following case may be cited:

Injury to health by tung oil. A Hamburg druggist picked up a barrel of oil at an auction of stranded goods. Without assuring himself of the nature of the oil it contained, he sold it to a Hamburg baker for less than the going price of rape oil for use in food. The baker made pancakes with the oil and thereby ensured diarrhoea and vomiting in 190 of his customers.

Tung or wood oil is obtained by warm expression from the seeds of various Aleurites species and is used in making water-resistant boat varnishes and waterproof fabrics and paper [F19]. The toxic principles of tung seeds are esters of 16-hydroxyphorbol [O11].

In recent years, this group of substances has become of considerable interest as a result of their co-carcinogenic properties [E11; H30; K27].

Ricinus communis L. Castor Oil Plant

80 Castor Oil Plant

1–4 m tall annual bushy shrub, with erect glabrous stems and a much-branched root system (in the tropics up to 13 m in height, perennial arborescent).
Leaves verticillate, long-petiolate (excentrically peltate) with palmately divided laminae.
Flowers in terminal panicles usually overtopped by lateral shoots; male flowers clustered at the bottom, female flowers above, with inconspicuous caducous perianth.
Fruits globose, trilocular, soft-spiny or smooth capsules, with 3 almost oval seeds surrounded by a hard brownish red mottled testa bearing a caruncle, and, depending on the variety, varying between 0.8 and 2.2 cm in size; VIII–X.
Distribution: Believed to have originated in tropical Africa; nowadays worldwide, cultivated in the tropics and subtropics and in temperate regions often kept as an ornamental in gardens.

THE seeds of this very ancient oil plant have been found in Egyptian graves dating from around 4000 BC [H34]. Nowadays, *Ricinus communis* is cultivated all over the globe for the production of castor oil (about 800000 tonnes per year [F19]), which is used mainly for technical purposes but also in medicine as a purgative. In addition to 45–55% fixed oil, the seeds contain up to 25% protein, so that the press cake, some of it after further extraction of the residual oil and detoxification by heat treatment, is often used as feed and fertiliser. Among the proteins of the seeds there is the highly toxic lectin ricin; and low-molecular weight glycoproteins with allergenic activity are also supposed to be present [H35]. Both components have repeatedly given rise to serious cases of poisoning.

In 1955 there were 120 cases of poisoning with the seeds of Ricinus communis. *Of these . . . 113 were admitted to hospital. The treatment lasted 4–7 days, but for many as much as 29 days' treatment was required. Pathological-histological changes in the gastro-intestinal tract could be demonstrated in a deceased patient* [K14].

On 31.5.1958 10 children from a school in Debrecen suffering from Ricinus-seed poisoning were sent to our clinic. From the case histories it emerged that the Ricinus seeds . . . had been brought to school by a pupil . . . as 'foreign nuts'. The number of seeds eaten varied between ¹/₂ and 6. In general, the severity of the poisoning was related to the number of seeds taken . . . [K10].

A three-year old child ate 5–6 Ricinus seeds from a packet of the seeds and had to be taken to the University Clinic Homburg/Saar suffering from severe symptoms of poisoning [S75].

In September 1974 four patients who had eaten 2–10 seeds were admitted to the Policlinico Umberto I in Rome. 13 days of intensive treatment enabled the lives of all four to be saved. '. . . even a single seed can cause a lethal intoxication, as happened to a child recently in Italy' [M11].

There are three principal factors which make *Ricinus* seeds so dangerous:

(1) Their attractive appearance and alleged hazelnut-like taste [B50; M21] tempt even adults to try them.

(2) The high content, relative to its toxicity, of ricin. 1 mg of pure toxin can be isolated from 1 g of seed [O16]. This means that in a single seed, weighing *ca* 0.25 g, the lethal dose for an adult is already present.

(3) The great stability of ricin towards the proteolytic enzymes of the gastro-intestinal tract, so that when taken by mouth a relatively large amount of toxin can be absorbed and take effect. Understandably, the data in the literature regarding the lethal dose differ considerably, because often the genuine toxin is contaminated with less active protein fractions, e.g. *Ricinus* agglutinin mol. wt. 120000. For highly purified ricin on parenteral administration Olsnes and Pihl [O16] determined a lethal dose of 1 μg toxin/kg body weight in the mouse, rat, and dog; rabbits were 10 times more sensitive. That the toxicity is of the same order of magnitude in man is evident from the recent sensational murder of the 49-year old Bulgarian exile and journalist Georgi Markov [K34]:

'According to Mrs Markov while her husband was waiting for a bus he had felt a jab in the back of his right thigh and looking round had seen a man drop an umbrella. After apologising, the man immediately made off in a taxi. Within a few hours he became very sick, with a high fever. On the third day
after the "injury" had been inflicted, Georgi Markov died in St James's Hospital. During the necropsy, a metallic sphere about the size of the head of a pin was found below the wound. It was composed of a platinum/iridium alloy and was 1.52 mm in diameter, with two minute holes bored right through it, so that the volume available for the retention of the toxin was ca 0.28 mm³. This means that it would contain at most ca 250 μg of poison. Such a small amount can, of course, no longer be detected in the body, but consideration of all the circumstances (course and symptoms of the poisoning, subsequent animal experiments, high toxicity) led the experts to the view that ricin was the only poison likely.'

On oral ingestion of the seeds, the toxicity doubtless depends on how well the kernels are chewed. It is understandable, therefore, that adults as well as children have survived doses of several times the lethal amount, especially when it has been possible to start clinical treatment in time – even before the occurrence of the first symptoms.

However, it is not only the consumption of a single seed that can be dangerous, but also the wearing or playing with exotic necklaces [J10; S75]. Often, decorative but toxic seeds and fruits from exotic plants, including *Ricinus communis,* are strung together on these necklaces [K23]. Since for this purpose a hole has to be bored through the generally hard seed coat, toxic substances from the inside can reach the skin directly and be absorbed via insignificant injuries, e.g. little scratches, or the mucosa of the mouth. Lockey and Dunkelberger observed a
severe anaphylactic reaction in a 21-year old female student caused by wearing a Mexican necklace put together from seeds of *Ricinus communis* and those of the harmless ornamental *Canna indica*:

'The patient had marked periorbital edema with complete closure of the left eye and partial closure of the right eye. The rest of the face was also swollen with marked erythema and numerous urticarial wheals' [L31].

Contact with the dry, mealy press cake of *Ricinus* seeds or simply handling jute bags in which it has previously been transported has in many cases led to allergic reactions [B49].

Treatment. According to Malizia *et al.* [M11] the symptomatic treatment should concentrate on the following three aspects: (1) Removal of the toxin from the gastro-intestinal tract by gastric lavage, purgatives such as sodium sulphate, adsorption on mucilage-containing suspensions of activated charcoal. (2) Maintenance of the circulation; transfusion of blood or plasma expanders. An adequate supply of fluids prevents dehydration and promotes renal excretion of the poison. If there is decreased urinary output, mannitol diuresis may be useful. To prevent haemoglobin precipitation in the renal tubules, it is important to make the urine alkaline by administering sodium bicarbonate. Maintenance of the electrolyte balance. (3) If necessary, treatment of the haemolytic anaemia and erythrocyte agglutination.

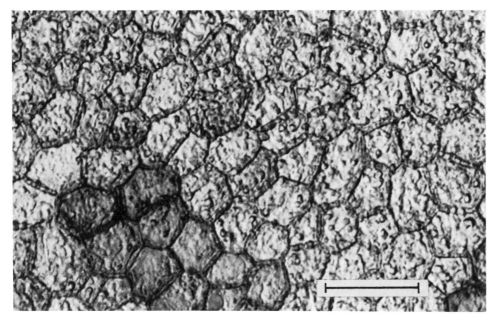

81 Ricinus communis: Epidermis of the testa.

and alanine aminotransferases (AST, ALT) and lactate dehydrogenase (LDH) in the extracellular volume are found, as well as raised total bilirubin and lowered blood sugar values [L3]. The pathological changes seen in fatal cases are characterised by severe gastro-enteritis with erosion, necrosis of the liver, kidneys, spleen, and lymphatic tissue [M11].

Microscopical characters of the testa. There are detailed accounts of the anatomy of the testa and endosperm by Moeller and Griebel [M48], Gassner [G5], and Hummel [H62], so that here only a description of the epidermis need be given. It comprises polygonal cells whose external periclinal walls are irregularly thickened, so that in surface view (81) the partly colourless, partly brown coloured, cells appear minutely papillose.

In acute cases the symptoms take some time to appear. As a rule, this latent period is 2–24 hours, rarely less, but under certain circumstances as much as three days. It is determined by the size of the dose [W4] and the mechanism of action of ricin itself. The inhibition of protein synthesis does not take place until the enzymes essential for life present in the cells have been used up [S26]. The symptoms listed are nausea, vomiting, abdominal pains, bloody diarrhoea, tenesmus, drowsiness, cyanosis, convulsions, circulatory collapse, and death, possibly with anuria, due to nephro-toxicity. As regards the enzyme picture, clearly increasing values for serum aspartate

Euphorbia L.   Spurge

*E*UPHORBIA is one of the largest genera in the family and has about 680 species throughout the world. Generally, they are annual to perennial herbs, bushes, or shrubs with copious latex; the habit is sometimes cactus-like.

The **leaves** are mostly alternate, less often verticillate or opposite. The **flowers** are much reduced and united to form cyathia (pseudanthia). The cyathia resembling a single flower consist of numerous male flowers (reduced to a single stamen) and a likewise perianth-less female apical flower. From the superior trilocular ovary a 3-valved **capsule** develops. The great majority of these species prefer dry localities, and in western Europe wild spurges are among the weeds encountered in field and waste-ground vegetation.

The best known representatives of the genus include the cypress spurge (*E. cyparissias*, see **82**), petty spurge (*E. peplus*), sun spurge (*E. helioscopia*, see **83**), and caper spurge (*E. lathyrus*).

Usually, these plants are avoided by grazing animals; nevertheless, feeding with hay containing much spurge can lead to poisoning, especially as the toxic substances present in the latex and seeds do not lose their activity on drying and storage [B 23].

For man it is particularly the whitish, fresh latex of many *Euphorbia* species that is potentially dangerous to children who play with the plants (*E. helioscopia* [M 42], *E. myrsinites* [S 70]), to adults who come into contact with them while gardening (*E. lathyrus* [G 7], *E. peplus* [C 3]), or because the latex is used according to old, handed-down recipes as a depilatory or for the removal of warts and freckles. If the abundant latex comes into contact with the skin or mucosa, whether on purpose or not, inflammation to a greater or lesser extent may well follow.

The substances responsible are irritant and co-carcinogenic diterpene esters, which in *Euphorbia* species are mainly ingenol derivatives [E 11]. Kinghorn and Evans [K 25] have investigated 60 species of the genus and only a few had no irritant activity towards the skin. Table 8 summarises information on some of those which are either indigenous to or are grown as ornamentals in western Europe.

82 **Euphorbia cyparissias L.**   **Cypress Spurge.**

Table 8. Toxic diterpenes in *Euphorbia* species (according to [E 11]).

Species	Toxic diterpenes
E. cyparissias	Unknown ingenanes
E. erythraea	Ingenol derivatives
E. esula	Ingenol derivatives
E. helioscopia	12-Deoxyphorbol
E. lathyrus	Ingenol derivatives
E. milii var. *milii*	Ingenol derivatives
E. myrsinites	Ingenol, 5-Deoxyingenol
E. peplus	Ingenol, 5-Deoxyingenol
E. pulcherrima	None
E. stricta	Ingenol, 5-Deoxyingenol
E. tirucalli	4-Deoxyphorbol

There is still some uncertainty about the intensity of action. In 1926 Nestler carried out numerous experiments on himself and found that there were seasonal variations in the effects. While the latex of *E. cyparissias* was irritant to the skin in August and September, it was inactive in April and May. Two-year old specimens of *E. lathyrus* afforded latex extracts which were five times as active as those from first-year vegetation [K 25]. What must also be borne in mind in evaluating the results of animal experiments are the differences in sensitivity of the various kinds of animal.

83 **Euphorbia helioscopia L.** **Sun Spurge.**

Geidel [G7] established that the latex of *E. lathyrus,* while without effect on the eyes of rabbits and dogs, in guinea pigs and also man leads to serious inflammation in the form of swelling of the eyelids, conjunctivitis, and damage to the corneal surface.

But development of the individual symptoms certainly depends on the amount of latex and the duration of contact with the skin. The initial symptoms, reddening and swelling of the affected parts, usually occur after 2–8 hours and increase in intensity in the following 12 hours (formation of blisters and pustules). Within 3–4 days these inflammatory reactions fade and healing generally ensues without the formation of permanent scars. Taken internally it results in painful inflammation of the mucosa of the mouth and throat, severe gastro-enteritis, vomiting, and diarrhoea. As consequences of the absorption, dilatation of the pupils, giddiness, and delirium may be observed, in certain cases accompanied by convulsions and systemic collapse [M50]. However, because of the unpleasant burning taste, it is rare that large amounts of latex or plant material are taken.

Microscopical characters of the latex. All *Euphorbia* species have a whitish latex, characterised especially by the occurrence of peculiarly (rod-, spindle-, or bone-)shaped starch grains (see **84**).

Treatment. Essentially symptomatic. (1) If the affected parts of the skin are cleansed thoroughly and in time, no symptoms are likely. (2) If the latex gets into the eyes, after washing them out immediately with water it is essential to seek medical help. The prognosis in such cases is favourable, and even severe conjunctivitis and choroiditis [G7; H16] heal after several weeks' medical attention without after-effects. (3) If large amounts have been taken internally, direct removal of the poison by gastric lavage, activated charcoal, and laxatives may be considered.

Other European Euphorbiaceae of interest are annual mercury and dog's mercury (*Mercurialis annua* and *M. perennis*). They do not contain a white latex, but are nevertheless considered to be poisonous [G11; L23; N11].

A recent case involving *M.perennis* [R29] is instructive. Owing to the use of an inadequate means of identification, this typically woodland plant was gathered in mistake for the widely occurring and edible brooklime, *Veronica beccabunga* L., usually found in streams and ponds and other wet places. As a result, two people

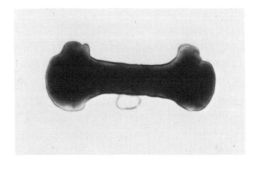

84 **Bone-shaped starch grain (stained with iodine).**

who ate a large quantity of the boiled herb became ill with nausea, vomiting, and bilateral colicky pains; malar erythema was also a noticeable feature, and in one patient there were traces of haemolysed blood in the urine.

This case shows once again how essential it is for untrained people to use a reliable and unequivocal means of identification, especially when looking for unusual plants as an addition to the diet.

Both *Mercurialis* species have even been thought to be responsible for deaths in grazing cattle [B 32]. The toxic action is said to result in severe diarrhoea, blue coloration of the milk, and bloody urine. Jaretzky and Risse [J 7], however, showed that, as compared with the usual purgative drugs, fresh plant material harvested before the flowering stage has a fairly gentle laxative action. The dried herb or material collected later is almost inactive. The red staining of the urine is not in any way due to blood but rather to the presence of a colouring matter from the plant.

Euphorbiaceae as house plants. Many Euphorbias and representatives of other genera are widespread as indoor ornamentals (succulent habit or conspicuously coloured leaves and inflorescences) and are often the subject of calls for toxicological advice. Undoubtedly, as a general recommendation care should be exercised in dealing with these plants and they should be kept out of reach of small children. However, some of the species through being cultivated appear to have become less dangerous than might be expected.

Poinsettia (*Euphorbia pulcherrima;* see **85**), met with in many households during the (pre-)Christmas period, is a good example. Most of the data in the literature on the toxicity of this plant are based on a case of hearsay: In 1919

85 Euphorbia pulcherrima Willd.   Poinsettia.

the 2-year old son of an army officer at Fort Shafter, Hawaii, died after eating a few leaves [W 22]. Moreover, there are only two reports of poisoning that include details of actual investigations.

Case 1. 'In 1973 a 66-year old man sought medical advice because of large, inflamed areas on the arms and chest. The case history brought to light the fact that 10 days previously, because of the high temperature, he had been working stripped to the waist in a greenhouse cutting and bundling large poinsettias (white and red forms). Taking into consideration the well documented course of this dermatitis, the doctor was of the opinion that it was a case of allergic hypersensitivity' [A 15].

Case 2. From the Swiss Toxicological Information Centre: After eating a few poinsettia leaves, a dachshund which had been left at home on its own developed severe gastro-enteritis with progressive apathy, high fever, and after 10–12 hours, in spite of infusions and circulatory stimulants, it died. The post-mortem on the poisoned animal revealed extensive acute pulmonary oedema and congestion, acute stomach oedema, and congestion of the internal organs; death followed circulatory failure [J 9].

In contrast, there are detailed investigations by several different groups [D 13; K 25; M 19; P 40; R 28; S 88; W 22] which can be summarised as follows:

The experience of the Toxicological Centres tends to support the inoffensive nature of this plant. In 1973 the National Clearinghouse for Poison Control Centers, Bethesda, registered a total of 228 cases of poinsettia ingestion. Only 14 of them exhibited symptoms: among the 'most severe' were a feeling of being unwell and vomiting. Krienke and von Mühlendahl [K 47] in discussing 62 cases, seven of which had slight symptoms, express the view that 'the "acrid principle" appears to have decreased through cultivation, so that in general the occurrence of serious symptoms is unlikely.'

Another widespread ornamental is the so-called 'croton', *Codiaeum variegatum,* which should not be confused with the quite different *Croton tiglium*! In 1976 in Germany alone more than 300 000 'croton' plants were sold [H23]. Its colourless latex has in several cases, especially gardeners having frequent contact with such plants, given rise to contact eczema [H23; K20; S24; T1]. According to the preliminary investigations of Hausen and Schulz [H23] compounds similar to phorbol esters are present in *Codiaeum* extracts. Morton [M59] states that the chewed bark and roots cause burning, also seen in three children who had chewed the flowers, together with slight irritation in the mouth.

The chenille plant or redhot catstail, *Acalypha hispida,* is a handsome tub plant originating from Australia and New Guinea. The whitish latex of this and other *Acalypha* species is also said to cause skin and gastro-intestinal inflammation [M42].

86 Codiaeum variegatum Muell.-Arg. 'Croton'.

(1) No toxic diterpenes or other compounds which could exert a strong toxic action were detected in the plant.
(2) On feeding fresh or dried plant material (flowers, leaves, latex, stem) to rats and mice there were no symptoms of any kind or changes in the behaviour or weight, even at maximum doses of 25 g fresh plant material per kg body weight.

(3) On repeated treatment with aqueous suspensions of the plant, albino rabbits showed slight irritation of the skin, but shaved guinea pigs, in contrast, only after subsequent UV irradiation (photosensitivity).
(4) The eyes of rabbits were not anaesthetised or damaged in any way on instilling latex into them.

FABACEAE (PAPILIONACEAE)

THE **Bean family** is a large family of cosmopolitan distribution which is represented in western Europe by many, chiefly herbaceous, species. Numerous cultivated ornamentals and garden plants, including trees and shrubs, also belong to the family.

In addition to the typical dorsiventral flower, the usually alternate, mostly compound, leaves and the fruit derived from a single carpel in the form of a pod are characteristic features of the family. Their economic importance is considerable: besides important food and fodder plants (peanuts, soya beans, lentils, peas, beans, lupins, clover, etc.), there are commercial timbers from the tropics, plants yielding colouring matters and tannin, as well as plants that are sources of pharmaceutical drugs (tragacanth, balsam of peru, liquorice).

Toxicological significance. A not inconsiderable number of Fabaceae can bring about poisoning in man and animals. The toxicity is due to highly active constituents of greatly differing structures and effects. Attention will be focused on two particular groups of substances: toxic proteins (and amino acids) and alkaloids, especially quinolizidine derivatives.

Toxic proteins. Lectins (for their general properties, see p.28) are present in the seeds and other organs of the Fabaceae. They agglutinate – to some extent depending on the blood-group – erythrocytes, but are only active on parenteral administration. On the other hand, there are a number of dangerously toxic proteins that, in addition to attaching themselves to animal membranes, exert toxic actions in the cells themselves and when taken by mouth are scarcely or not at all attacked by the enzymes of the digestive tract. Among them are **abrin** [P27] from the seeds of *Abrus precatorius,* **phasin** from *Phaseolus vulgaris* (common bean), **robin** from *Robinia pseudacacia,* and (less active) some of the lectins mentioned in Table 9.

Abrin, like the equally active ricin from *Ricinus communis* (cf. Euphorbiaceae, p.113) and modeccin from *Adenia digitata* (Passifloraceae [G41]), comprises two peptide chains linked by a disulphide bridge:

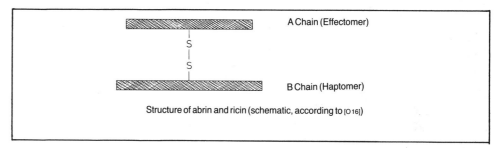

Structure of abrin and ricin (schematic, according to [O16])

While the B chain, the haptomer, is responsible for the attachment of the toxin to the surface of the cell, the A chain is the toxic agent, the effectomer. It attacks the 60S subunit of the ribosomes and by cutting out the elongation factor EF2 brings protein synthesis to a standstill [O16].

Opinions differ about which organs abrin attacks preferentially. Niyogi [N14] has determined changes in serum enzymes (aspartate and alanine aminotransferases, isocitrate dehydrogenase) values in various experimental animals, and he concludes that liver necrosis plays an important part in abrin poisoning. On the other hand, Barbieri *et al.* [B8] have shown by light-and electron-microscopical studies the occurrence in rats of serious necrotic lesions in the pancreas after the injection of abrin, but they did not observe any damage to the cells of the liver or spleen (as is the case with ricin).

Symptoms of poisoning usually appear only 2–3 hours after the ingestion: severe vomiting and serious, often haemorrhagic, enteropathy ('small intestine shock') with heavy loss of fluids and symptoms of shock. As regards **treatment,** no specific antidotes are known (an abrin antiserum, which used to be available commercially as jequiritol serum, is no longer in use). The emphasis of the symptomatic measures is on the treatment for shock with the corresponding administration of fluids and electrolytes, and, if required, support for the circulation.

Toxic amino acids. Of the non-protein amino acids mentioned on p.26, many are present in the seeds, as well as other parts, of Fabaceae. Particularly important toxicologically are the lathyrogenic amino acids L-α, γ-diaminobutyric acid in the seeds of *Lathyrus silvestris* and *L. latifolius* and α-amino-β- (or α-) -oxalylaminopropionic acid in *L.sativus,* which, when large amounts of Indian pea or chick-

Table 9. Fabaceae as the cause of animal poisoning.

Plants	Constituents	Symptoms of poisoning	References (in addition to [K17] and [S66])
Crotalaria species	Pyrrolizidine bases	Pneumonia, renal and liver damage	[H55]
Lupinus species	Quinolizidine bases	Dyspnoea, ataxia, cramps	[D24]
Astragalus species on Se-containing soils (North America)	Toxic, e.g. Se-containing, amino acids	Alopecia, leucopenia, infertility	[H10; H33]
North American *Astragalus* species; in European species the compounds indicated occur only sporadically	Aliphatic nitro compounds, e.g. 3-nitro-propionic acid and -propanol (as the glycoside miserotoxin)	Anorexia, emaciation, diarrhoea, salivation, inco-ordination of the hind legs	[J5; S82; W15-18]
Canavalia ensiformis Glycine max, Arachis hypogaea, Phaseolus lunatus	Lectins (in addition to those already mentioned), e.g. concanavalin A	Haemorrhagic enteropathy	[D24]
Glycine max	Protease inhibitors	Hypertrophy of pancreas	[L25]
Medicago sativa (alfalfa), *Glycine max*	Saponins	Growth retardation, bloat, respiratory depression	[B31]
Psoralea species	Photosensitising furanocoumarins	Photodermatitis	[T21]
Medicago sativa, Trifolium species	Isoflavones (genistein, formononetin) and benzo-furanocoumarins (coum-oestrol) and phyto-oestrogens	Infertility, growth disorders	[B27; K18; S54]
Lotus corniculatus, Phaseolus lunatus, Trifolium repens	Cyanogenic glycosides	Dyspnoea, coughing, giddiness, convulsions	[K29]
Astragalus species, *Oxytropis* species (locoweeds), *Swainsona* species	Unknown	Neurological disorders	[D16; H15; H56; S97]

ling vetch are consumed, as in the Indian subcontinent, leads to the nerve disease known as neurolathyrism [L28; N7]. On the other hand, β-*N*-(γ-L-glutamyl)-aminopropionitrile in the seeds of *Lathyrus odoratus*, sweet pea, in experimental animals causes a condition of the joints known as osteolathyrism. Such lathyrogens are also present in the seeds of some *Vicia* species.

Alkaloids. As already mentioned, the alkaloids of the family do not all belong to one particular structural group. The following may be briefly discussed: Physostigmine, the alkaloid of the (tropical) calabar bean, is a cholinesterase inhibitor and is known as an antidote in atropine poisoning, but also as a drug used in ophthalmology (indirect parasympathomimetic).
Pyrrolizidine alkaloids (pp. 26 and 64) of the genus *Crotalaria* have hepatotoxic and carcinogenic activity. In 1975 admixture of *Crotalaria* seeds in food cereals led to a serious poisoning epidemic in the Sarguja District of Madhya Pradesh, Central India [T2]. Of 67 patients ill with the typical symptoms of pyrrolizidine-alkaloid poisoning (liver necrosis), 28 died – a mortality rate of 42%.
Isoquinoline alkaloids in *Erythrina* species. *Erythrina crista-galli,* coral tree, occasionally found as an ornamental in sheltered spots, is supposed to be toxic.

The toxicologically significant compounds in western European poisonous plants belong to the group of **Quinolizidine alkaloids,** with the two most important substances being **Cytisine,** present especially in

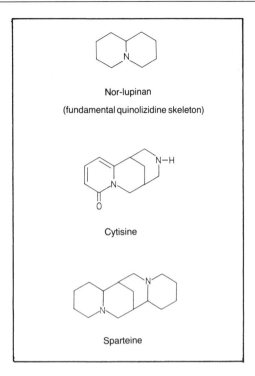

Nor-lupinan
(fundamental quinolizidine skeleton)

Cytisine

Sparteine

Laburnum anagyroides (laburnum), and
Sparteine, occurring in *Cytisus* (broom) and *Lupinus* (lupin) species, etc. Further, minor, alkaloids derived from the nor-lupinan skeleton are in the plants mentioned as well as in several other Fabaceae.

While sparteine exhibits quinidine-like effects and is therefore applied medicinally in the treatment of cardiac arrhythmias, cytisine has principally nicotine-like actions in which the ganglion-stimulating activity is more marked than the ganglion-blocking activity.

Symptoms of poisoning, particularly in the case of cytisine, are abdominal pains, circulatory disorders, and convulsions; higher doses result in death through central respiratory paralysis. Vomiting usually sets in early and as a

rule prevents the absorption of large amounts of poison, so that the number of serious cases is small. The **treatment** comprises symptomatic measures and, if convulsions are occurring, the administration of anticonvulsants.

Many Fabaceae are forage plants poisonous to cattle when eaten in large amounts. See the extensive work of Smolenski *et al.* [S66] and the book by Keeler *et al.* [K17]. Here a tabular summary must suffice.

As already indicated in Table 9, a number of the saponin-bearing plants belonging to the family may be responsible for poisoning in animals. The saponin-containing extracts of the roots and rhizomes of *Glycyrrhiza glabra,* liquorice, are used medicinally. The triterpenoid saponin glycyrrhizin and its aglycone glycyrrhetinic acid have a certain structural similarity to the corticosteroids. Taking a gross overdose of stick liquorice as in self-medication for stomach ulcers, for example, can give rise to oedema as a

Glycyrrhetinic acid

result of strong water retention, to dangerously high blood pressure, and to congestive heart failure [C9; K40]. The chemistry and therapeutic use, as well as side-effects, of liquorice have recently been reviewed by Lutomski [L36].

Laburnum anagyroides Medic.   Laburnum, Golden Chain

87a Laburnum

Up to 7(–10) m tall shrub or small tree with light green branches and mostly wide-spreading pendent twigs.
Leaves alternate, grouped on short shoots; long-petiolate, trifoliate, leaflets elliptic, lower surface light grey (pubescence).
Flowers yellow, 10–20 in curved pendulous racemes; IV–VI.
Fruits silky-haired pods with flat dark brown seeds; VII; remaining long on the plant and then becoming brown.
Distribution: Northern Mediterranean species; in western Europe an often planted ornamental (mostly as the hybrid L. × watereri) and partly naturalised; similarly, L. alpinum, Scotch laburnum.

THE laburnum is a very popular winter-hard ornamental requiring little in the way of soil conditions and therefore often seen in gardens and parks. It is, on the other hand, known as a dangerous poisonous plant, and time and time again warnings are issued especially against planting it near children's playgrounds [B 53; K 44; P 35].

Poisonous constituents. The toxicity of laburnum is due chiefly to cytisine, which occurs throughout the plant. Besides N-methylcytisine, another quinolizidine derivative, there are small amounts of the pyrrolizidine bases laburnine and laburnamine [J 16]. N-methylcytisine, which is much less toxic than cytisine, is found preferentially in meristematically active tissues and may be the main alkaloid in, for example, young shoots. In dormant seeds, however, the cytisine: N-methylcytisine ratio is 150:1 and is thus shifted almost entirely in favour of the cytisine [J 16].

It is particularly children who are endangered, when they play with the fruits and especially the pea-like seeds and chew and swallow them. But even sucking the conspicuous flowers has its dangers. As Tables 1–3 show, the laburnum is high on the list of enquiries made to Toxicological Information Centres. However, the number of serious poisonings is relatively small. Recent publications give a similar picture [B 58; C 16; F 14; M 46; M 55]. Mořkovský and Kučera [M 56] reported the poisoning of 13 children in a kindergarten in 1980. In addition to vomiting and diarrhoea, three children suffered from colicky pains. Six children sent to hospital were discharged after one day.

While in the older literature fatal cases of poisoning were quite often mentioned, there is only one such case

87b Flowers of Laburnum.

from recent times [R6]. From the stomach of the dead person (a 50-year old) 23 laburnum pods were recovered and a cytisine content of 3 mg was determined; in the blood 0.68%, corresponding to about 35 mg cytisine in the body, was found.

Normally, the rapid onset of vomiting after the plant material has been ingested prevents the absorption of large amounts of cytisine. This also explains why in most cases where a call is made to a Toxicological Information Centre only slight symptoms of poisoning are noted. In the above-mentioned fatal case it is possible that previous treatment with a massive dose of the central depressant chlorpromazine (Largactil®) may have inhibited this protective measure of the body itself.

Symptoms of poisoning. The symptoms are like those seen in nicotine poisoning: ½–1 hour after ingestion salivation, outbreaks of sweating, burning in the mouth and throat; centrally-stimulated vomiting, which may persist for 1 or 2 days. In serious cases of poisoning, the central-stimulating effects of the cytisine cause delirium, excitation, and clonic-tonic convulsions, and death through respiratory paralysis.

Quite recently, Leyland [L21] has reported on the poisoning of two dogs by laburnum.

Treatment. Direct removal of the poison; gastric lavage with activated charcoal, if vomiting has not already started. Short-acting barbiturates, chlorpromazine, or diazepam against the convulsions. If respiratory paralysis threatens, prethcamide (Micoren®) or (better) artificial respiration.

Abrus precatorius L.

Jequirity, Crab's Eyes,
Indian Liquorice,
Rosary Pea, Prayer Bean

Reports from Florida [D 5; F 5; H 13; K 23] concern cases of serious poisoning in adults who had eaten ½–2 seeds and the deaths of children after chewing 1–2 seeds. Apart from sensational accounts in the daily press [B 28], there are no reported cases of poisoning from western Europe.

Symptoms of poisoning. After a variable latent period – 3 hours to two days – severe gastro-enteritis develops, with vomiting, diarrhoea, and cramps. Bleeding from the retina and serous membranes is a characteristic feature.

Treatment. Immediate removal of the poison by bringing about vomiting or by gastric lavage; because of the necrotic action of abrin, care is essential in applying these measures. Further, symptomatic treatment under hospital supervision, as is recommended in ricin poisoning, p. 115.

JEQUIRITY is a pantropical plant that climbs by means of tendrils. Its seeds (Semen Jequiriti) were at one time used in medicine to bring about inflammation of mucosa, particularly in ophthalmology. Because of their decorative appearance, prayer beans have long been used in the tropics for making ornaments or as playthings. While rosaries from the seeds are only of historical interest and account for the various names with a religious connotation, the seeds, as well as those of *Ricinus communis,* have in recent years reached Europe as a component of exotic decorative necklaces, thereby acquiring added toxicological significance. It is true that their inclusion in such necklaces is only sporadic [J 10; S 74], but owing to their abrin content they represent a considerable danger. This is all the more true because in order to string them they have to be pierced, so that on chewing or sucking them constituents from the inside of the seeds can be extracted. On the other hand, intact seeds, because of their hard testa, when swallowed whole are harmless.

Appendix: Other, similar looking Fabaceae seeds are used in the same way as jequirity for the purpose of adornment [J 10; L 29]. The seeds of various *Erythrina* species are somewhat larger and contain alkaloids with a curare-like action. There are also the seeds of *Ormosia dasycarpa,* which have lupinine-type alkaloids; according to comparative investigations, by Genest *et al.* [G 9], the toxicity of *Ormosia* seeds in various animals is much less than that of *Abrus* seeds. *Rhynchosia phaseoloides* has seeds which look like those of *Abrus precatorius* but are rather smaller – they contain as yet uncharacterised alkaloids; no data on their toxicity appear to be available. For the microscopy of the testa, see von Lingelsheim [L 29].

Phaseolus vulgaris L.   Common Bean

89 Common Bean

Annual plants, either with twining stems and 3–4 m in height (var. *vulgaris*, French climbing bean) or shrubby and only *ca* ½ m tall (var. *nanus*, French dwarf bean); cultivated plant.
Leaves **long-petiolate, with three usually ovate, more or less acuminate leaflets; shortly pubescent and therefore somewhat rough.**
Flowers **fairly long pedicellate, usually 2–6 pairs in erect inflorescences; corolla, whitish, less often pink or violet; VI–VIII.**
Fruits **pendent; several-seeded mostly green somewhat curved pods. Seeds highly variable in shape and colour, usually white to yellowish.**
Distribution: **Originally from South America; in Europe since the 16th century, but now worldwide in a multitude of cultivated forms.**

THE common bean is cultivated chiefly for its protein-rich seeds. In the temperate regions of Europe the green unripe pods remain tender and edible longer, and they form an important foodstuff. In folk medicine the dried pods without the beans (Fructus Phaseoli sine Semine) are considered to be diuretic.

In the seed, as well as the pericarp, of the common and many other kinds of bean there are lectins, the agglutinating properties and molecular structure of which have been the subjects of a series of studies [K 11]. No thorough investigation of the toxic effects after oral administration has yet been carried out. At the moment, it can only be surmised that the proteins comprised under the old collective name phasin act as inhibitors of protein synthesis in the same way as ricin and abrin. The clinical picture of phasin poisoning certainly resembles that of ricin or abrin poisoning, but altogether phasin seems to be rather less dangerous.

Phasin, being a protein, is denatured and thus rendered inactive by heating. Although it is generally known that beans should only be eaten after cooking, cases of poisoning by raw beans are not uncommon (cf. Table 1). It is particularly children who are involved, as they eat the uncooked beans through ignorance [H14], but serious cases have also been met with among adult vegetarians who live on a diet of raw food [R1]. Severe haemorrhagic gastro-enteropathy occurs after eating a few of the seeds or green pods.

Symptoms of poisoning. 2–3 Hours after ingestion nausea and vomiting commence, followed later by colicky stomach pains, diarrhoea, and circulatory collapse.

Treatment. Symptomatic, with emphasis on combating the shock by administration of fluids and electrolytes. The prognosis is favourable.

Of other *Phaseolus* species, the (scarlet) runner bean, *P. coccineus,* may be mentioned. It has larger pods and reddish, black-speckled seeds, which, like those of *P. vulgaris,* can lead to poisoning [H4]. In Europe, species such as the lima bean, *P. lunatus,* whose seeds also contain cyanogenic glycosides, have only a very limited importance as a source of food.

Robinia pseudacacia L.   (False) Acacia, Black Locust

90 (False) Acacia

Tree up to 20 m in height with glabrous spreading branches and twigs; trunk often branching early.
<u>Leaves</u> up to 30 cm long, imparipinnate with ovate-elliptic leaflets. Stipules in lower part of crown spinose.
<u>Flowers</u> white, up to 15–25 in pedunculate, initially erect, later pendent, inflorescences; V–VI.
<u>Fruits</u> parchment-like to leathery flat pods, brown to purple, with 4–10 olive-green to brown seeds (ripe from X); not dehiscing until winter.
<u>Distribution:</u> Originating in North America and now naturalised throughout Europe; often planted.

IN the bark, especially, and in the seeds *Robinia pseudacacia* contains a lectin (mixture?) named robin. Like ricin and abrin, it is built up from two peptide chains; these are not, however, cross-linked via disulphide bridges [P25; P26; P28]. Robin has haem-agglutinating and mitogenic proper-ties, and its toxicity on oral administration appears to be very much less than that of ricin, abrin, and phasin.

In addition to the Fabaceae discussed so far, there are further representatives of the family which are often mentioned as poisonous plants or which at least are suspected of being poisonous. No serious poisonings by these plants have been recorded in the more recent literature. The section below summarises what reliable information there is available about them. Several illustrations are included, to aid possible identification should advice be sought. This appears to be necessary, since they grow or are grown in western and central Europe and occasionally (in some cases oftener) give rise to enquiries.

Herbs and shrubs

Crown Vetch (*Coronilla varia*)
The crown vetch is a shrub with long, mostly procumbent, stems and imparipinnate leaves; it occurs in central and southern Europe and it has now become naturalised in western and northern Europe, including parts of Great Britain, and in North America.

Two groups of constituents may be responsible for its toxicity: cardiac glycosides and aglycones, whose presence in the plant has long been known, or nitropropionic acid derivatives [G31; M10]. The latter are mentioned as the cause of animal poisonings in North America [S66]; ruminants appear to be less endangered, since they are able to detoxify these compounds [G32; G33]. Hyrcanoside and similar cardiac glycosides have cytotoxic activity [H39].

Lupin (*Lupinus*)
Lupins are usually stately herbs much planted as green manure (nitrogen fixation) and fodder crops and as

91   Coronilla varia L.   Crown Vetch.

garden ornamentals. Besides the sweet lupin, *L. luteus,* and the annual lupin, *L. angustifolius,* the large-leaved lupin, *L. polyphyllus,* from North America may be mentioned.

Cases of poisoning in man are relatively rare and usually involve children who have eaten seeds or fruits. The toxic principles are sparteine and similar quinolizidine alkaloids; in the so-called 'sweet' varieties, the content of lupin bases is drastically reduced. When more than two pods have been eaten and spontaneous vomiting has not already occurred, removal of the poison should be ensured first of all.

Animal poisonings after eating lupins have long been known under the name 'lupinosis'. While it may be assumed that the lupin alkaloids are responsible for acute cases of poisoning accompanied by restlessness, convulsions, and icterus, in cases of chronic illness it is suspected that the condition is due to fungal toxins (crushed lupin rapidly becomes mouldy).

Vetch, Tare (*Vicia*)
The genus *Vicia* comprises about 150 species which grow chiefly in the northern temperate zone. A number of them are important as fodder and food plants, e.g. *V. faba,* broad bean, or as garden ornamentals. *V. faba* causes favism, a disease which mani-

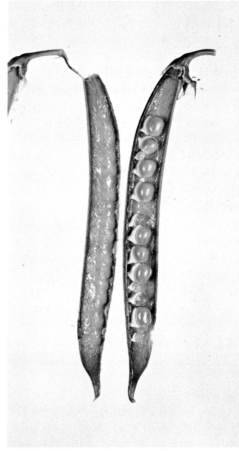

92a Lathyrus odoratus L.   Sweet Pea.

92b Sweet Pea: Unripe fruit.

fests itself as acute haemolytic anaemia. It occurs more frequently in southern Europe, where a deficiency of glucose-6-phosphate dehydrogenase in the erythrocytes is a common hereditary condition among the population [G1]. Under certain circumstances the disease can be fatal; the biochemical mechanism that gives rise to it has been extensively investigated and further details can be found in [L28].

Sweet Pea *(Lathyrus odoratus)*
The sweet pea, often planted along garden fences, arbors, or on balconies, is quite frequently the subject of toxicological enquiries [K47]. The seeds contain – as do those of the Indian pea or chickling vetch, *L. sativus,* a plant of some importance as a source of food – β-N-(γ-L-glutamyl)-aminopropionitrile, continuing ingestion of which can lead to lathyrism (cf. pp. 26 and 123). However, there need be no fear that eating a few seeds will give rise to any serious poisoning. According to Krienke and von Mühlendahl [K47] there were 137 calls for advice in which no symptoms were reported as against only 13 in which slight symptoms were indicated.

Shrubs

Broom *(Cytisus scoparius)*

Broom can grow to a height of 2 m and is widespread, locally abundant, on silicate soils throughout western and central Europe (but absent from the Alps). The virgate twigs are bright green, angular, with small pubescent trifoliate leaves; these are mostly caducous, but some continue to grow after the flowering period and assimilate until the winter. The yellow flowers (V–VI) give way to compressed and densely pubescent pods.

As Herba Spartii, the plant has a modest role in medicine. The most important constituent is sparteine, which is accompanied by other quinolizidine alkaloids. Sparteine, as already pointed out, acts like quinidine, i.e. it delays the formation and conduction of the cardiac impulse; peripherally, its effects are similar to those of nicotine and, like coniine, gradually lead to paralysis. Poisoning (including fatal cases, e.g. in an infant [S23]) by sparteine-containing drugs occurs, but hardly as a result of ingesting plant material. The case of broom poisoning in man described in the literature is not very convincing. After reporting the death of a 45-year old farmer, the account goes on [M62]:

A long time after the death (!) I was informed that the patient, whose farm lay on a road along which a lot of broom was growing, had gathered some fresh shoots of it. From the partly dried twigs he had prepared what he considered to be a strong infusion and had drunk several cups of it every day. He had begun this cure about 6 days before the start of the ileus and severe peripheral circulatory insufficiency. There is no doubt that the serious condition which ended in death was poisoning with the infusion of broom.

93 Cytisus scoparius (L.) Link   Broom.

94 Colutea arborescens L.   Bladder-senna.

95 Caragana arborescens Lam.   Pea Tree.

Quinolizidine alkaloids, including sparteine or cytisine, are also to be found in various kinds of whin or greenweed and gorse *(Genista* and *Ulex)*.

Pea Tree *(Caragana arborescens)*
The pea tree, which grows to a height of 5 m, comes from Siberia, and is not infrequently planted in gardens and parks. Its pods, unlike those of *Laburnum*, are acute and mucronate; they are many-seeded and when ripe spring open on touching. The plant is said to be poisonous, but precise information is apparently lacking. The occurrence of cytisine in the seeds is doubtful. 'The fat-containing seeds are a good poultry-food and have also been recommended as an emergency food for human beings' [H34].

Bladder-senna *(Colutea arborescens)*
Bladder-senna is a shrub often planted in western and central Europe, and it has become naturalised in Great Britain. It grows to a height of 2–3 m and is noteworthy for its pods with parchment-like pericarp which swell when ripe. The small black seeds contain canavanine (p.26). Here again, reports of the presence of cytisine must be treated as doubtful.

Wisteria or Chinese Kidney Bean *(Wisteria sinensis)*
The wisteria is a woody liane that can reach a height of 20 m. Its pendent racemes with their many light blue-violet scented flowers make a striking picture. Wisteria flowers from April to June, and often again in the late summer, but north of the Alps it very rarely sets fruit.

A poisonous glycoside wistarin, according to [T22] a 'sapotoxin', is indicated to be a constituent of the bark and roots. In all parts of the plant (and in other species such as *W. floribunda)* there are lectins, whose structure and haem-agglutinating or mitogenic effects have recently been studied [K1; K57; U1]. Attention has repeatedly been drawn to the toxicity of the seeds [L18; L20]. Just two of them are said to cause serious poisoning in children, with vomiting and gastro-enteritis. No information has been found concerning the constituents responsible.

GROSSULARIACEAE

THE **Gooseberry family** comprises only one genus, *Ribes,* with *ca* 150 species distributed chiefly in the northern temperate zone. Among the species are various fruit-producing bushes, such as the gooseberry and currant, which were taken into cultivation early on. But there are also many ornamentals that, because of their unexacting requirements regarding soil and position as individual or hedge plants, are often grown along roads and in gardens and parks. They are low to moderately tall bushes, never trees, which form mostly racemose inflorescences on short shoots, while the partly thorny long shoots carry out the vegetative function. Juicy berries develop from the inferior ovary, differently coloured according to the species. Only a few of them are pleasant tasting; most of them are hardly edible, **but are in no way poisonous.**

Commonly planted species. The following list shows some of the species that have become wild or are planted in built-up areas, together with the colour of their fruits:

Mountain currant (*Ribes alpinum*)	Dark red (bland, mucilaginous)
Golden currant (*Ribes aureum*)	Purplish brown to black
Black currant (*Ribes nigrum*)	Black
White currant (*Ribes niveum*)	Blue-black
Red currant (*Ribes rubrum*)	Translucent red
Flowering currant (*Ribes sanguineum*)	Black with blue-white bloom
Gooseberry (*Ribes uva-crispa* var. *sativa*)	Yellow-green or reddish

A conspicuous feature of most of these berries is that the bottom end of the fruit bears the persistent dried remains of the calyx.

Constituents. In addition to polyphenolic substances (tannins and pigments), *Ribes* species are characterised by a high plant acid (malic and citric acids, etc.) and vitamin C content. Further, there are traces of cyanogenic compounds and essential oil. The latter is responsible for the sometimes harsh fragrance of the leaves and fruits, e.g. the bedbug smell of black currants. Possibly because of this, but certainly also because of the wide distribution

96 Ribes sanguineum Pursh   Flowering Currant.

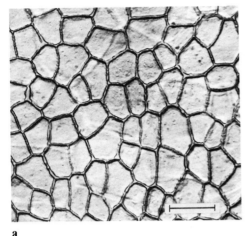

a

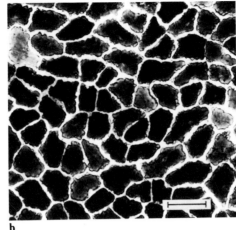

b

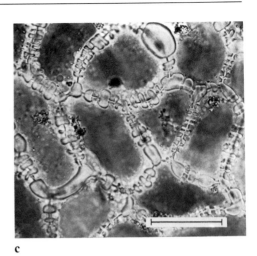

c

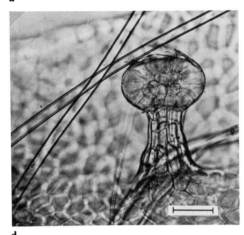

d

97 Epidermis of the pericarp of various Ribes species: (a) R. rubrum, (b) R. nigrum, (c) R. alpinum, and (d) different types of trichome on that of R. sanguineum.

of these bushes and the conspicuous colouring of their fruit, they give rise to frequent calls to the Toxicological Information Centres. It is on these grounds that the otherwise essentially harmless fruits of the Grossulariaceae are included here, together with illustrations of some of the microscopical characters. If the fruits are eaten when unripe or to excess, sensitive people may develop gastro-intestinal troubles, but these hardly require treatment.

Microscopical characters of the fruits. Typical of the berries of some *Ribes* species *(R. uva-crispa, R. nigrum, R. sanguineum)* is a polymorphic pubescence, which includes capitate or blunt protuberances, long thin-walled, curved trichomes, as well as

disc- or mushroom-shaped glandular trichomes **(97d)**. The pulp usually contains numerous calcium oxalate clusters *(ca 20 μm)* and occasionally small prisms in the hypodermal layers *(R. nigrum)*.

Detailed descriptions of the anatomy of edible *Ribes* berries are to be found in [C27; G5; M48], so that it suffices here to deal with the variation in the epidermis of the pericarp. That in *R. rubrum* **(97a)** and *R. aureum* comprises relatively thin-walled polygonal cells, below which is visible the large-celled hypodermis. The walls of the epidermal cells in *R. nigrum* **(97b**; very similar in *R. niveum)* are beaded – a feature that is most clearly seen in the walls of the epidermal cells of *R. alpinum* **(97c)**.

Toxic Crassulaceae. The **Stonecrop family** is closely related to the gooseberry family, and both of them belong to the order Saxifragales. Several genera of the Crassulaceae (*Cotyledon, Kalanchoe = Bryophyllum*) are known to have been the cause of an epidemic among grazing animals – krimpsiekte – in South Africa. The responsibility lies not so much with the small amounts of piperidine alkaloids present, but more probably with isoprene derivatives of still unknown structure [F23]. Quite a few *Kalanchoe* species that are kept as (indoor) ornamentals have the toxic principle in their roots, but they are of as little importance in toxicological practice as our own *Sedum* and *Sempervivum* species, which belong to the same family.

HIPPOCASTANACEAE

Aesculus hippocastanum L.   Horse-chestnut

98 Horse-chestnut

Tree up to 30 m in height with dense crown and on the outside ultimately pendent twigs; large conical and sticky buds remaining conspicuous until the start of the vegetation period. Frequent along streets, in parks, less often found along the edges of woods (wild).
<u>Leaves</u> large, 5–7-partite, on grooved petioles up to 20 cm long; leaflets up to 20 cm long, obovate.
<u>Flowers</u> whitish, stamens longer than petals; in many-flowered, terminal erect panicles; V.
<u>Fruits</u> softly spinose, spherical capsules; flattened globose seeds with a hard testa; VIII–X.
<u>Distribution:</u> Planted throughout almost the whole of Europe and locally naturalised; in northern Greece and Bulgaria also occurring naturally.

IN contrast with the seeds of the real chestnut, *Castanea sativa*, those of the horse-chestnut are inedible and are considered to be poisonous. The bitter taste undoubtedly prevents the consumption of large amounts; at any rate, no serious cases of poisoning have been reported in recent years.

Toxic constituents. Horse-chestnut seeds contain, in addition to much starch, 3–5% of a mixture of saponins – aescin – which consist of short-chain fatty-acid esters of various triterpenoid aglycones, including protoaescigenin. Aescin and horse-

Protoaescigenin

chestnut extracts are used in medicine for their anti-oedema and capillary-sealing actions. Incidents of anaphylactic shock after i.v. injections of horse-chestnut extracts are known [W1]. However, taken by mouth, and provided that the mucous membrane of the gastro-intestinal tract is whole, the toxicity is slight because the saponins are poorly absorbed. An irritant effect on the mucous membrane, possibly leading to gastro-intestinal upsets, is all that is likely.

> **Treatment.** If action is really necessary, purely symptomatic measures.

Appendix. Some points about the toxicology of the nuts from two of the most widespread forest trees – oak and beech – may be discussed here. The two genera, *Quercus* and *Fagus,* belong to the **Beech family** (Fagaceae).

Acorns. Especially the unripe fruits and young leaves of oak can lead to the poisoning of grazing cattle; and all the more so when other forage is insufficient or when there has been an overabundant crop of acorns [D12; D27; P3; S8; S87]. The acorn and oak-leaf poisoning described in the veterinary literature is marked by lack of appetite, diarrhoea, colic, and renal damage. It is generally agreed that the toxic principles are tannins and their degradation products (or precursors?) such as gallic acid or pyrogallol.

Poisoning in children from chewing a few acorns need cause little worry [S72]; before the introduction of the potato, acorns were a (starch-containing) food in times of emergency.

Beechnuts. The seeds of the beech when taken in large amounts are considered to be toxic. But it is still not clear what the responsible constituents are: along with saponins, the relatively high content of oxalic acid (0.54% soluble and 2.41% insoluble [K42]) has been mentioned. A now somewhat dated summary of the problem has been published by Hotovy [H59]; there appear to be no recent toxicological studies.

IRIDACEAE

THE **Iris family,** related to the Liliaceae and Amaryllidaceae, is represented in Europe by just a few perennial species that form rhizomes, corms, or bulbs. Nothing is known about poisoning with the spring-flowering *Crocus* species. On the other hand, the true saffron crocus, *Crocus sativus,* that flowers in the autumn and is found only in cultivation or as an escape, requires mention because the expensive spice and colouring agent saffron derived from it has toxicological importance. A plant that occasionally gives rise to poisoning in animals is *Iris pseudacorus.*

Saffron – the dried, dark orange-red, aromatic and spicy, bitter-tasting stigmas of *Crocus sativus* when used in small amounts as a spice or a colouring matter are harmless. But ingestion of only a few (5–10) grams is sufficient to bring about symptoms of serious poisoning and can lead to death. An amount of this order is supposed to be an 'effective' dose in the misuse of saffron as an abortifacient. Frank [F18] has reported on a case of abortion after taking 5 g saffron powder in which there was extensive bleeding from the skin and severe collapse with nephro-toxicity.

Safranal, a dehydro-β-cyclocitral, or other monoterpenoid components of the essential oil that arise, together

99 **Crocus L.** (Early spring flowering garden variety).

Safranal

with constituents responsible for the colour, taste, and aroma, from the common tetraterpene glycoside precursor protocrocin, are most probably responsible for the toxic effects.

The **yellow iris,** *Iris pseudacorus,* commonly occurs along ditches and river banks, on rich muddy soils. In its stems and ensiform leaves it contains acrid poisonous principles whose activity remains even after drying the plant material. There does not appear

to be any new information on the nature of these substances – a glycoside iridin is mentioned in the older literature. After feeding on the plant, animals suffer from severe, bloody diarrhoea; according to the older literature, serious gastro-intestinal troubles are also caused in man. No new relevant observations have been reported. Other, rarer, *Iris* species should probably be regarded toxicologically in a similar light.

LILIACEAE

THE **Lily family** is large and comprises plants of greatly differing habit. Most of the more than 3500 species grow in warm climates, but many species that survive the winter by means of tubers, bulbs, or rhizomes are to be found in the European flora. Some are important as food plants, e.g. asparagus, onion, chive, garlic, and leek; others serve as ornamentals, e.g. tulip, hyacinth, and martagon lily; and still others are used as medicinal plants, e.g. *Convallaria, Urginea,* and (as extra-European genus) *Aloe.*

A number of Liliaceae are of **toxicological interest,** because of very different types of constituents:

Saponins. Steroidal saponins occur widely in the family. Although saponins taken orally are as a rule poorly absorbed, it is nevertheless assumed that the toxicity of several Liliaceae is due to their presence. This is particularly the case for herb-Paris, *Paris quadrifolia,* with its blue-black fruits, and also for Solomon's-seal, *Polygonatum* species, the fruit of asparagus, *Asparagus,* etc. In the case of bog asphodel, *Narthecium ossifragum,* a saponin has been recognised as a liver poison, which secondarily leads to photosensitisation and is the cause of the disease in sheep known in Norway as 'alvelden' [H35].

Alkaloids. The steroidal alkaloids present in false hellebore, *Veratrum,* but also detected in fritillary, *Fritillaria,* are highly dangerous poisonous substances that in addition have teratogenic activity [K16; K17]. The same can be said of colchicine, a very toxic compound present in meadow saffron, *Colchicum autumnale.*

Cardiotoxic substances. While in lily-of-the-valley, *Convallaria majalis,* besides saponins there are cardenolides present which are the source of the toxic properties, the sea onion, *Urginea maritima,* and several *Scilla* species contain bufa- (or scilla-)dienolides; these latter compounds are also found in the well-known South African poisonous plant *Bowiea volubilis.*

Other poisonous constituents. The methylenebutyrolactones (tulipalins) found in the tulip and other Liliaceae are contact allergens and can cause skin troubles; see also p.149. Cases of contact dermatitis are known to have occurred with garlic, *Allium sativum* [B34]. Of the sulphur-containing constituents in the oils formed by *Allium* species, *n*-propyl disulphide has haemolytic activity [P32]. The occurrence of haemolytic anaemia (connected with the formation of Heinz bodies in the erythrocytes) in horses, cows, and sheep has been seen after feeding on *Allium* species, both wild (*A. canadense, A validum* [North America]) and cultivated (e.g. *A. cepa,* the ordinary onion) [H65; P32; T23]. Recently, Stallbaumer [S77] has reported on a similar disease in a dog that liked to eat raw onions.

Asparagus officinalis L. Wild Asparagus

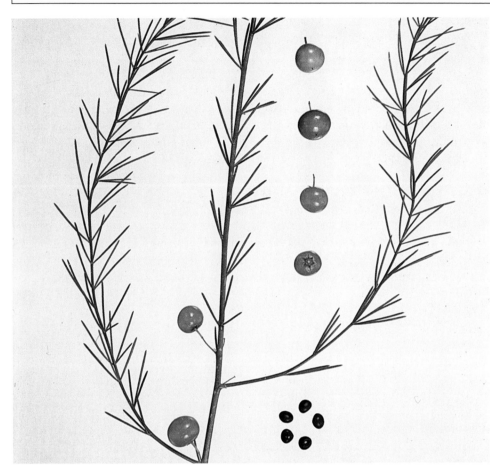

100 Wild Asparagus

0.3–1.5 m tall perennial plant with woody rhizomes and erect, later often pendulous, pedicels; cultivated and naturalised, occurring preferentially in dry places.
Leaves brownish, scale-like, from whose axils lateral branches grow, which after further branching form short needle-shaped green branchlets (clusters of phylloclades).
Flowers mostly dioecious, with funnel-shaped perianth, whitish to greenish; perianth of the female flowers smaller; IV–V.
Fruits brick-red berries, usually with 6 black, rugose, striated seeds; VI–VII.
Distribution: Central and southern Europe, originating in the Near East; in cultivation since antiquity.

WHILE the widely appreciated vegetable asparagus tips is said occasionally to give rise to allergic skin reactions, the red fruit of asparagus is regarded as poisonous. No reliable information about the toxic constituents is available. If anything, (steroidal) saponins are most likely to be involved, but the toxicity of these substances is reckoned to be slight.

Along with sitosterol and stigmasterol and their glucosides, Sharma *et al.* [S47] have isolated from the fruits of *A. racemosus* sarsasapogenin and four (steroidal) saponins in which it is the aglycone.

According to older data [G5; M48], in regions where asparagus was cultivated the roasted fruits were often used as a coffee substitute.

Eating the red berries will give rise to at most a slight indisposition, probably requiring only symptomatic **treatment**. This is also the case with asparagus dermatitis, which only occurs after contact with young asparagus shoots [M42].

The rhizomes and roots of asparagus (Radix Asparagi), employed as a diuretic, contain asparagine.

Sarsasapogenin

Microscopical characters of the fruit.
The hard-skinned epidermis of the
pericarp is free of stomata and is
unmistakably characterised by the
swollen thickening of the cell walls
(101). Numerous raphides ($<70\,\mu$m)
of calcium oxalate are present in the
spongy parenchyma of the pulp.

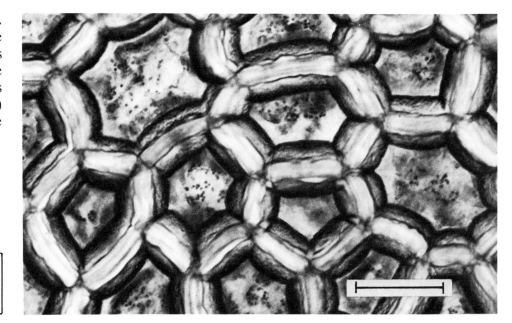

**101 Asparagus officinale: Epidermis of
the pericarp.**

Colchicum autumnale L. Meadow Saffron

102 Meadow Saffron

8–25 cm tall perennial herb with basal leaves and flowers and large corms with brown outer scales. In fertile meadows and at the edges of woods, sometimes abundant.
Leaves oblong-lanceolate, appearing in spring, up to 40 cm in length.
Flowers usually in autumn, pale pink (rarely white), perianth lobes fused at the bottom to form a long tube; until the flowering period, ovary deep underground; stamens 6 (cf. crocus, 3); VIII–XI, occasionally also in the spring.
Fruits together with leaves first appearing above ground when ripening in early summer; oblong-ovoid capsule with numerous small black-brown seeds, these with an initially sticky appendage; when ripe, capsule swollen; V–VI.
Distribution: Western, central, and southern Europe, in the north rare to absent.

THE meadow saffron is a poisonous plant dangerous not only to livestock at pasture but also to man, since in early summer children like to play with the capsule, in which, when ripe, the seeds rattle.

Constituents. The highly active 'alkaloid'* colchicine and other structurally related compounds are present in all parts of the plant; the greatest concentration is in the seeds, especially the testa.

Colchicine

Effects of colchicine. The effects of colchicine are many. It is a capillary poison, causing dilatation and ultimately serious damage to the blood vessels. Its excitant, and subsequent depressant, action extends to medullary centres, smooth and striated musculature, and sensory nerve end-ings (which is the reason for resemblances with the symptoms observed in poisoning by aconitine and the *Veratrum* alkaloids). Finally, colchicine is a mitotic inhibitor; the high toxicity (LD p.o. for adults is *ca* 20 mg) and the low therapeutic index have prevented its introduction as a cytostatic.

Symptoms of poisoning. When taken by mouth the first symptoms appear after a relatively long latent period (2–6 hours), which is due to conversion in the body of warm-blooded animals and man to the actual toxic agent. In many respects, colchicine poisoning is like arsenic poisoning ('vegetable

---

* The nitrogen is present in the form of an acetylated primary amino group and is thus not heterocyclic; being an acid amide, the compound is not basic.

103 Meadow Saffron, showing the parts of the flower.

on people who have died from drugs, the presence of colchicine has frequently been detected, having been used to 'cut' the hard drugs. Pharmacies in Germany have therefore been warned against handing over colchicine supposedly 'for purposes of experiment' [A 26].

A thin-layer chromatographic method for estimating colchicine in the rumen contents of ruminants has been developed by Kasim and Lange [K 9].

Treatment. Because of the relatively long latent period, measures taken to ensure removal of the poison as soon as the first symptoms appear are usually too late. Hence, when there are good reasons for thinking that *Colchicum* may have been ingested, such measures should be instituted immediately and the patient subsequently transferred to hospital for further treatment. The therapeutic measures are, for the rest, symptomatic: replacement of fluids and electrolytes, and circulatory support; atropine or papaverine against intestinal cramps and diarrhoea; if necessary, artificial respiration. The prognosis is serious.

arsenic'). There is a feeling of burning and tingling in the mouth, along with difficulty in swallowing. Besides nausea and vomiting, the occurrence of acute gastro-enteritis with slimy-watery, partly bloody, diarrhoea is characteristic; the body temperature and blood pressure are lowered, convulsions and paralysis appear, and finally death takes place through respiratory paralysis. These are further stages in serious colchicine poisoning, but fortunately they rarely occur after ingestion of plant material. The lethal dose is put at *ca* 5 g for adults and *ca* 1–1.5 g for children.

The therapeutic use of pure colchicine, e.g. in the treatment of gout,

can lead to accidental poisoning through overdosage. In the period 1947-1979 16 fatal cases of colchicine poisoning were described in the literature (for a review, see [S 76]). The lethal dose varied from 7 to 200 mg, but lay mostly between 30 and 80 mg, and death took place 36 to 72 hours after ingestion. In the case reported by Caplan *et al.* [C 5], that of a (successful) suicide attempt, 30–35 tablets each containing 0.6 mg colchicine were taken and death occurred 40 hours later. *Colchicum* seeds have also been used to commit murder [M 33].

More recently, another source of colchicine poisoning has become known: in post-mortem examinations

Appendix. Colchicine and similar compounds are also present in the tubers of the glory lily, *Gloriosa superba*. The plant grows in tropical Africa and Asia, and in Europe and elsewhere may be encountered as an ornamental. Nagaratnam *et al.* [N 1] have reported on six cases of poisoning resulting from eating *Gloriosa superba* tubers, all of which ended in death. The symptoms corresponded with those due to colchicine poisoning.

Convallaria majalis L.   Lily-of-the-Valley

104 Lily-of-the-Valley

10–20 cm tall perennial with far-reaching creeping rhizome, scape leafless with several flowers in one-sided raceme at the top. On sandy loam, widespread in mixed deciduous woods.
<u>Leaves</u> long-petiolate, sheath-like, elliptic to lanceolate and acuminate.
<u>Flowers</u> nodding, with fused perianth lobes, campanulate, white, pleasantly fragrant; V–VI.
<u>Fruits</u> globose red berries, trilocular, with 2–6 seeds; VII–VIII.
<u>Distribution:</u> Throughout almost the whole of Europe; also planted as an ornamental in gardens.

LILY-of-the-Valley is an old medicinal plant which has held its own right up to the present day. It contains cardioactive glycosides of the cardenolide type (p.27) in all its parts, as well as steroidal saponins. The cardenolide content in the flowers is relatively high – up to 0.4% (calculated on the dry weight), which is 2–3 times greater than the amount in the leaves. While the pulp of the fruit has only traces of cardenolides, the seeds contain *ca* 0.45% of readily water-soluble glycosides with convalloside as the main component [S25]. The cardenolides of *C. majalis* are present chiefly in the cell vacuoles [L32].

Cardenolides of lily-of-the-valley. The composition of the cardenolide mixture present in *Convallaria majalis* varies according to its geographical source. Convallatoxin is the main

R = Rhamnosyl	Convallatoxin
R = Glucorhamnosyl	Convalloside

glycoside in herb of western and north-western European origin; on the other hand, in central European plants there is a considerable amount of lokundjoside; and in herb from eastern Europe there is much convalloside.

Effects. The glycosides in lily-of-the-valley are very strongly cardioactive, but are poorly (up to 10%) absorbed orally. Serious cases of poisoning are therefore hardly likely to occur after ingesting the fruit, or indeed other parts of the plant, and have not been described in recent years, even though *C. majalis* looms large in the statistics

105 Convallaria majalis: Epidermis of the pericarp.

of the Toxicological Information Centres. Both Krienke [K45; K46] and Jaspersen-Schib [J9] indicate that lily-of-the-valley (and the data relate almost exclusively to the fruit) belongs to the group of plants about which enquiries are most often made. Furthermore, it is repeatedly asserted that water in which lily-of-the-valley has stood for some time is poisonous; but animal experiments have yielded no evidence to confirm this [W23]. Nor can the case reported in 1954, which evidently relied on information in the older literature, be seen as proof of the assertion:

Case of poisoning. In Osterburken, in the district of Burken, a 3-year old girl died in tragic circumstances. The child had eaten withered gooseberries and then drunk some water from a glass in which lily-of-the-valley had been standing. All attempts to save the child's life were in vain.

The questions raised by the uncritical reporting of such 'cases of poisoning' are discussed elsewhere (p.18).

The *Convallaria* saponins are described as having local irritant effects. Dried and powdered lily-of-the-valley flowers were a sternutatory component of the formerly very popular German Schneeberg (Snow-mountain) snuff. The pulp and seeds of the fruit are free of saponins, but according to Roberg [R10] the 'skin of the berries', i.e. the epidermis, contains haemolysing substances, so that after ingesting the fruits a certain degree of saponin activity should perhaps be borne in mind.

Treatment. If it does not occur naturally: elicit vomiting; administer demulcent preparations against gastro-intestinal irritation. Only after consuming larger amounts of plant material is it necessary to take therapeutic measures, such as are described under *Digitalis* (p.200).

Symptoms of poisoning. These include gastro-intestinal irritation, nausea, and vomiting. Cardiotoxic effects (see *Digitalis*, p.200) are unlikely.

Appendix. According to old statements *Maianthemum bifolium*, May lily, has no cardenolides. The effects of the fruits, as in the case of other Liliaceae fruits, are most probably due to saponins.

Microscopical characters of the fruit. The pericarp of *Convallaria* fruit has stomata with 4–5 subsidiary cells. The beaded radial walls of the epidermal cells have a thick waxy deposit on top **(105)**. Roundish-oval to tubular idioblasts with raphides (25–45 μm) occur in groups only in the inner layers of the pulp. All parts of the pericarp are extremely rich in carotenoid pigments.

Paris quadrifolia L. Herb-Paris

106 Herb-Paris

10–40 cm tall perennial with subterranean creeping rhizome; flowers terminal, pedicels with two-part cataphylls, leaves (mostly) 4 in a whorl. Frequent in somewhat damp woods and thickets.

<u>Leaves</u> elliptic-lanceolate, subsessile, glabrous, venation reticulate.

<u>Flowers</u> usually 4-merous, with narrow inconspicuous greenish petals; V.

<u>Fruits</u> 4-locular, several-seeded blue-black berries; seeds brown with rugose epidermis; VI–VIII.

<u>Distribution:</u> Throughout almost the whole of Europe; rare in the Mediterranean region.

THE blue-black berries, and indeed the whole plant, are considered to be poisonous on the basis of their saponin content. The (steroidal) saponins (old names: paristyphnin, paridin) are supposed to have local irritant properties and to be toxic after oral ingestion as well, since they are to some extent absorbed.

Symptoms of poisoning. According to old information, the symptoms of poisoning by herb-Paris fruits are nausea, vomiting, diarrhoea, and miosis. Occasionally, *P. quadrifolia* turns up in the statistics of the Toxicological Information Centres, but no serious cases have been encountered. There appear to be no recent investigations on the toxicity of the plant.

Treatment. If need be, when a largish amount has been ingested direct removal of the poison should be considered; otherwise, symptomatic treatment should be undertaken.

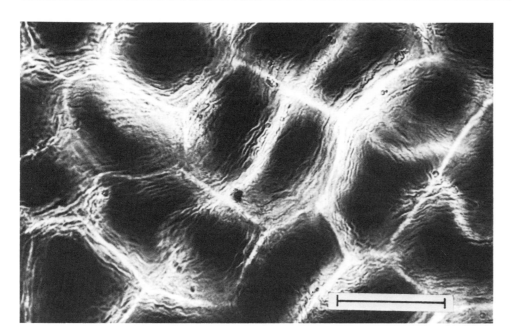

Microscopical characters of the fruit. The epidermal cells of the pericarp of *Paris* fruits are filled with dark red sap; they have thin but distinctly pitted walls. A notable feature is the highly striated cuticle (**107**). The pulp contains numerous raphides (up to *ca* 80 μm).

107 Paris quadrifolia: Epidermis of the pericarp.

Polygonatum multiflorum (L.) All.   Solomon's-seal

108 Solomon's-seal

30–60 cm tall perennial with terete (cf. *P. odoratum*) stems and whitish rhizomes; not infrequent in shady woods.
Leaves **ovate to elliptic, upper surface dark green, lower surface grey-green.**
Flowers **with tubular perianth, whitish green, in pendent several-flowered racemes; unscented; V–VI.**
Fruits **blue-black berries with globose brown seeds; unpleasant sweetish taste; VII–X.**
Distribution: **Throughout most of Europe.**

THE fruits, like those of herb-Paris, are considered to be poisonous, but rather less so. In contrast with earlier reports, according to Horák and Horáková [H58] cardioactive glycosides do not occur in the genus *Polygonatum*. It seems that it is only the saponin content, said to be very high in the seeds [H35], that can be implicated in possible cases of poisoning. As far as is known, there is no recent work on the toxic constituents of the fruits. The structures of the sugar chains present in two saponins from the roots of *P. multiflorum* have been elucidated by Janeczko [J6]; the aglycone is diosgenin.

Treatment. If at all necessary, purely symptomatic.

The fruits of angular Solomon's-seal, *P. odoratum,* which as a rule are somewhat larger, must be treated as toxicologically equivalent to those of Solomon's-seal. The plant differs in having pleasant-smelling flowers usually in 1–2-flowered inflorescences, angular stems, and thicker erect leaves.

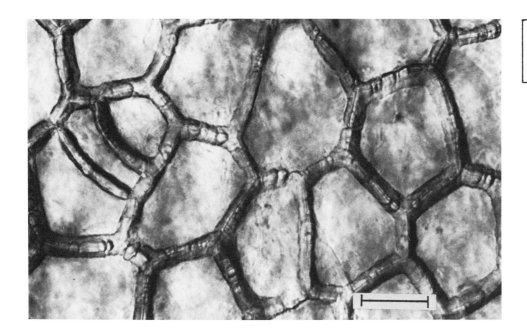

109 Polygonatum multiflorum: Epidermis of the pericarp.

Microscopical characters of the fruit. The fruits of *Polygonatum* species are characterised by a particularly thick-walled, colourless, and strongly pitted epidermis **(109)**. They have only a few stomata, mostly with four subsidiary cells and an unusually small pair of guard cells. The hypodermal cells are somewhat smaller than those of the epidermis and shine through in surface view; they contain many chloroplasts. In addition, the pulp has many large raphides (*ca* 85 μm).

Tulipa L.   Tulip

THE genus *Tulipa* comprises more than 50 species, but only one, *T. sylvestris*, occurs wild in the western part of Europe. Garden tulips, which are offered in many forms and hybrids (cultivars) and whose cultivation can be traced back to medieval times, are usually gathered together under the collective name *T. gesneriana*. They are presumed to derive from species that were distributed from Asia Minor to Iran (Persia), but that for centuries were cultivated in gardens in the Near East and about 1550 were brought from Turkey to Central Europe.

Tulips are perennial bulbous plants; their leafy stem usually only has one large terminal flower. The leaves are broadly linear to lanceolate. The bulbs, which are the toxicologically important organ, are made up of closely imbricate fleshy scales.

Tulip finger. Tulip bulbs – as well as other parts of the plant, especially the flowers [S60] – contain substances that can bring about severe dermatitis. People affected by the condition are, e.g. those in nurseries who have to handle tulip bulbs a great deal [B20]. The dermatitis (tulip finger, tulip nails) is characterised by eczematous changes in the skin of the contact surfaces of the hand, especially the finger tips, and by damage to the nails, e.g. increased brittleness [F9]. Other parts of the skin may be affected. On the reddened, swollen, and itching or burning skin, fissures may develop and in places scaling. These symptoms, the clinical picture of an allergic eczema, only occur after prolonged contact with tulip bulbs or their juice [K30].

Tuliposides. The causative agents of the condition are substances localised mainly in the outer layers of the bulbs and known as tuliposides. In the plant they act as protective antibiotics. Chemically, they are esters of glucose with α-methylene-γ-hydroxybutyric acid (tuliposide A) or α-methylene-β-hydroxybutyric acid (tuliposide B) [S59; V3], and after hydrolysis the acid components lactonise spontaneously.

Of the two lactones, it is tulipalin A that is primarily responsible for the effects on the skin and tulipalin B is only weakly active. Among the

Tulipalin A

Tuliposide A

111 (Left to right) Bulbs of the daffodil, onion, hyacinth, and tulip.

112 Occurrence of calcium oxalate in the scales of different bulbs: Raphides arranged in rows in (a) Narcissus and (c) Hyacinthus. Prisms in (b) Allium. The absence of oxalate in (d) Tulipa.

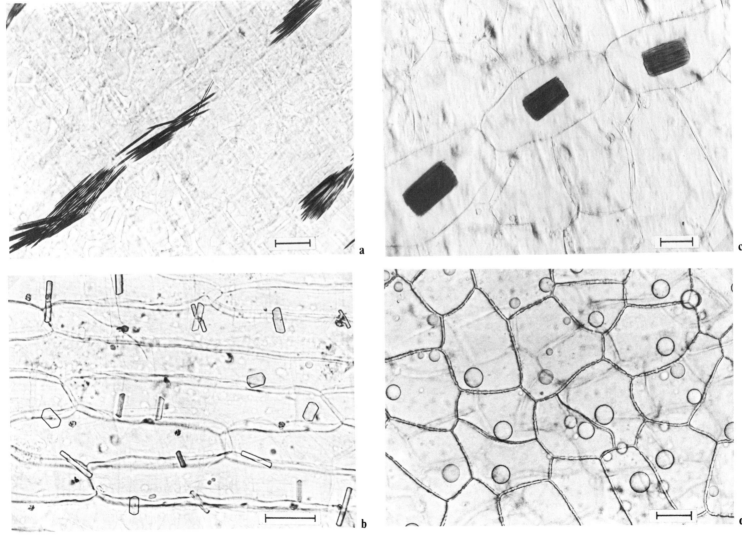

numerous cultivated forms, the cultivar 'Rose Copeland' appears to be particularly active in causing tulip finger [R21]. Other cultivars, e.g. 'Madame Lefeber', also known as 'Red Emperor', a hybrid of *T. fosteriana*, owing to a smaller tulipalin A content are less active in causing allergy. Slob and Varekamp [S60] give a detailed review of the tuliposide content of many *Tulipa* species and cultivars.

In contrast with the dermatitis due to hyacinth or daffodil bulbs, there is no mechanical component in the irritation since raphides (cf. **112**) are absent. According to Slob *et al.* [S59], tulipalin A also occurs in dog-

tooth violet, *Erythronium* species, and star-of-Bethlehem, *Gagea (Ornithogalum)* species, in high concentrations (>0.1%), as well as in Peruvian lily, *Alstroemeria* species (Amaryllidaceae or Alstroemeriaceae).

Irritation of the skin by active principles similar to the tuliposides, i.e. lactones of short-chain hydroxy-acids, occurring in the plant chiefly as glycosides, is also known to be brought about by a few Ranunculaceae (p.172).

Poisoning by eating tulip bulbs is rare; up to 5 bulbs a day are said to give rise to only slight gastro-intestinal symptoms [M20]. Maretić *et al.* described a case in which a goulash was prepared with tulip bulbs instead of

onions, but whether the toxic symptoms were due to the tuliposides or other substances could not be established.

Treatment. After contact with the tulips has ended, the skin lesions heal in the course of a few days with or without the use of an ointment. Renewed contact can bring about a relapse within a few hours. Protective ointments are generally of little help. Wearing gloves is the best preventive measure, but is often felt to be a hindrance in working.

Veratrum album L.   White Hellebore

113 White Hellebore

(Photograph: M. Wichtl)
0.5–1.5 m tall herb with stout erect stem, pubescent in the upper part, and spirally arranged leaves. Occurring in the montane and alpine regions of mountain ranges, in damp meadows, especially subalpine pastures and hay meadows between 700 and 2000 m. Characteristic plant of lower alpine damp grassland.
<u>Leaves</u> large, longitudinally plicate, lower ones broadly elliptic, upper ones lanceolate, lower surface pubescent, upper surface glabrous.
<u>Flowers</u> pedicellate, white or yellowish green, in a terminal 30–60 cm long much-branched panicle, lower ones bisexual, upper ones chiefly male; VI–VIII.
<u>Fruits</u> sparsely pubescent, many-seeded capsules with curved apices.
<u>Distribution:</u> Alps; in the mountains of central and southern Europe.

THE white hellebore is known as a poisonous invasive weed of alpine hay meadows, and farmers eradicate it as far as possible from their pastures. Cattle usually leave it alone; calves, sheep, and goats are particularly susceptible to its poison.

As far as man is concerned, its toxicological significance lies in the fact that in the vegetative stage white hellebore bears a certain resemblance to the great yellow gentian, *Gentiana lutea*, except that its leaves are opposite rather than spirally arranged. Because the distribution of the two plants overlaps and because the great yellow gentian, although a protected plant, is subject to regulations so that its roots can be collected and used in making enzian, mistakes have often been made by non-experts. The case described by Jaspersen-Schib [J9] illustrates the dangers of such a mistake:

On an alp, three recruits dug up 'gentian roots' and chewed them to relieve their thirst. One of the recruits was admitted to hospital four hours later in a coma, with strong convulsions and moderate salivation. The other two recruits, who had evidently only chewed a little of the root, remained free of symptoms. After telephoning the botanical expert (of the Swiss Toxico-

logical Information Centre), it became clear that the plant that had been consumed was Veratrum album. *Since* Veratrum *alkaloids are re-absorbed from the kidney, in spite of the relatively long period that had elapsed since the plant had been taken, repeated gastric lavage was carried out on the recommendation of the Toxicological Centre. The patient was further treated with valium and atropine. Recovery was slow.*

Mistaking the thin roots of *V. album* for the relatively thick brown ones of gentian is only possible when experience is lacking, but the cases described in the literature involving confusion with valerian roots are more understandable **(114)**. It was because of this, according to Seeliger [S41], that a tea made from 'valerian roots' resulted in a serious case of poisoning. As appeared subsequently, the drug in question had been borrowed from a neighbour and it turned out to be roots of white hellebore. In the case reported by Haas and Poethke [H1] a tincture of valerian contained *Veratrum* alkaloids. It had evidently been prepared entirely or in part from Radix Veratri – at one time also an official drug.

Veratrum constituents. The toxic substances in white hellebore are alkaloids with a C_{27} steroidal skeleton. Besides the oxygen-rich compounds of the protoverine type, which can be esterified to a greater or lesser extent (protoveratrines A and B are tetraesters), alkaloids of the less oxygenrich jerveratrum group, having a characteristic furano-piperidine structure in rings E/F, e.g. jervine, are also present.

Pharmacological effects. The ester alkaloids of *Veratrum* are highly toxic substances (the lethal dose in man is *ca* 20 mg, corresponding to 1–2 g dried root), probably because of their ability to increase the permeability of cell membranes to sodium ions. As a reflex effect, through depression of the impulses from the sympathetic centres, the heart rate and blood pressure are reduced. Because of this property, an attempt was made to introduce the drug into medicine, but it was given up again because its therapeutic index was too low. As it first stimulates, then paralyses, the sensory nerve endings, it leads to pains, hyperaemia, and

Protoverine

Jervine

114 Dried roots of: (Left) White Hellebore (Radix Veratri). (Right) Valerian (Radix Valerianae).

subsequent anaesthesia of the mucous membranes and extremities.

The alkaloids of the jerveratrum group, which occur partly as glycosides, are much less toxic, but more recently have attracted attention in North America owing to their teratogenic effects. Growth abnormalities in the heads of new-born lambs were traced to the eating of *Veratrum viride* by the pregnant ewes. Jervine and 11-deoxyjervine (= cyclopamine) were shown to be particularly active teratogenically [K 16; K 17].

Symptoms of poisoning. A few minutes after taking a toxic dose by mouth, burning and tingling sensations are already felt in the mouth and throat (and, through irritation of the mucous membrane, sneezing: Radix Veratri = 'Nieswurz' = sneeze herb), followed by a feeling of numbness and roughness and dryness in the mouth. The paraesthesia includes the extremities and gradually extends over the whole body; for the similarity with the symptoms of aconitine poisoning, see p.179. It is followed by vomiting and violent diarrhoea and, as a result of a drop in body temperature, there is a feeling of cold. In serious cases of poisoning, respiratory difficulties, arrhythmia, lowered blood pressure, and collapse, while remaining fully conscious, precede death, which may occur after a period of only 3 hours. The prognosis is poor; nevertheless, if the acute poisoning is successfully overcome, there is no permanent damage.

According to a report by Hruby *et al.* [H72] *V. album* is one of the few poisonous plants in Austria that in recent years has caused serious poisoning. The authors document seven cases that occurred in a 5-year period. The patients exhibited severe emesis, muscular twitching and cramp, CNS (hallucinations) and especially cardiac (e.g. sinus bradycardia, intermittent atrio-ventricular arrhythmia) symptoms. Besides the mistaken consumption of a leaf, several times pieces of root, as well as supposed enzian which had been made from *Veratrum* root, were taken.

Veratrum nigrum, black hellebore*, is similar; it is a representative of the southern European-Pontic flora and is very rare north of the Alps. In America there is *V. viride,* green hellebore†, which is common in certain regions. Both have a range of constituents like that in *V. album.*

Structurally related alkaloids are present in the genus *Zigadenus* (death camas). Cases of poisoning after eating its tubers have been reported by Spoerke and Spoerke [S71].

Treatment. Elimination of the poison by gastric lavage; since no specific antidotes are known, only symptomatic therapeutic measures are possible: peripheral circulatory agents, atropine for bradycardia; against convulsions, if present, short-acting barbiturates, warmth; against threatened respiratory paralysis, artificial respiration.

---

* In the British Isles this name is applied to *Helleborus niger*, better known as the 'Christmas rose'. Cf. p.176.

---

† This, and the name 'white hellebore', are two of the many that are given to the plant in America, but in the British Isles 'green hellebore' is the recommended name for *Helleborus viridis*. Cf. pp.176–177.

LORANTHACEAE

Viscum album L.   Mistletoe

115 Mistletoe

Evergreen partial parasite, up to 1 m in diameter, branching dichotomously and growing on the branches of woody plants. A number of forms are distinguished as a result of adaptation to certain host plants: deciduous (subsp. *album*), fir (subsp. *abietis*), and pine/larch (subsp. *austriacum*) mistletoe.
<u>Leaves</u> opposite, sessile, leathery, obovate-oblong, yellowish-green.
<u>Flowers</u> inconspicuous, unisexual, dioecious, up to 3–5 in sessile cymes; III–V.
<u>Fruits</u> white, berry-like (formed from the floral axis), with viscid, slimy pulp; in subsp. *austriacum* often yellow; XI–XII.
<u>Distribution:</u> Throughout Europe, in North Africa, and in Asia as far as Japan.

MISTLETOE plays a large part in ancient and Germanic mythology. As told by Julius Caesar and Pliny, it was used by the Druids – Gallic and Celtic priests – as a medicament and in religious and cult ceremonies. The reported cancerostatic effect of mistletoe extracts has given rise to extensive animal, clinical, and biochemical investigations. Moreover, mistletoe preparations find by no means uncontroversial therapeutic application in hypertony and arteriosclerosis.

Toxic constituents. Semi-parasites (Australian Loranthaceae) as a rule are able to accumulate pharmacologically active constituents (alkaloids, cardenolides) from their host plants *(Duboisia, Nerium)* [H35]. But the toxicity of mistletoe is due, among other things, to a mixture of toxic proteins – viscotoxins [K36; S4; S5; S85; W33]; nevertheless, here also it has been observed that the activity depends on the nature of the host plant [P41]. These toxic proteins are found especially in the leaves and stems.

Toxic effects from mistletoe extracts only appear on parenteral administration (possibly with participation of the lectins which are also present [F32]). Only after taking large quantities orally is there likely to be a local irritant and necrotising effect. The potential hazard of (self-)medication with mistletoe preparations because of their content of toxic components – alkaloids, viscotoxins, and lectins – has been pointed out [A23].

However, the viscotoxins appear to be completely absent from the berries

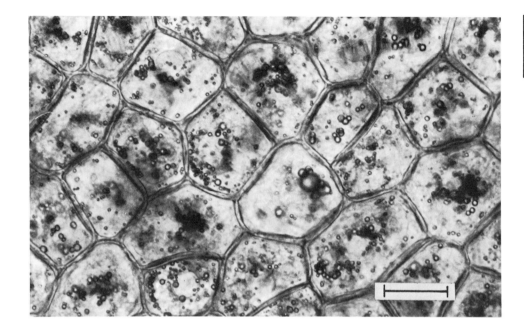

116 Viscum album: Epidermis of the berry.

[K47], and this presumably explains why in many cases where berries have been ingested the Poison Information Centres have not noted any symptoms and why they consider their toxicity to be very slight.

Microscopical characters of mistletoe berries. The pericarp of *Viscum* berries consists of colourless polygonal cells **(116)** with relatively large nuclei (*ca* 18 μm). In this layer there are more or less large intercellular gaps where the walls of the surrounding cells have become considerably thickened (cf. also **118a** and **146c**). As these epidermal gaps become larger, the underlying parenchyma cells may invade the resulting spaces. The stringy fruit pulp contains calcium oxalate clusters (*ca* 30 μm), while in the greenish seeds there are chloroplasts and starch grains (<25 μm).

OLEACEAE

Ligustrum vulgare L.   Wild Privet

117 Wild Privet

Up to 4 m tall, dense, erect shrub. In light woods, copses, and thickets, mostly on dry, calcareous, warm soils.
<u>Leaves</u> opposite, entire, highly variable in shape – obovate, elliptic, and lanceolate; upper surface deep green, lower surface lighter, glabrous; mostly deciduous, in protected places evergreen.
<u>Flowers</u> in up to 8 cm long panicles; corolla lobes flattened, white, greenish at the tips; strongly fragrant; VI–VII.
<u>Fruits</u> in dense erect panicles, glossy black berries with two violet seeds; often remaining on the shrub throughout the winter; garden form 'xanthocarpum' has yellow fruits; IX–X.
<u>Distribution:</u> Europe, North Africa, western Asia; in parks and gardens as hedges and undershrubs; other species, e.g. *L. ovalifolium* and *L. obtusifolium*, used similarly.

ALTHOUGH most privet hedges when regularly trimmed do not set fruit, children still find the opportunity in disused allotments and neglected parks to experience the unpleasant consequences of eating the berries of this shrub. The Toxicological Centres in Berlin and Zürich average 6–7 calls for advice each year.

Up until now, no information about the chemical constituents of privet fruits has become available. However, investigation of related species and genera [H35; I3] suggests that lignan glycosides, saponins, and seco-iridoid bitter substances are likely to be present.

In the literature, the berries of privet are often indicated to be highly toxic and, among other things, mention is made of '. . . the several fatal cases of poisoning by the black berries observed in children . . .' [B50; D2; G11]. Critical examination brings to light the fact that these statements refer to fatalities which occurred 100 or more years ago. Of the fatal cases supposedly caused by privet berries which have taken place during the present century [F12; G10; R23; S101], in spite of an intensive search only one case history has been found which goes beyond a simple factual report. Moreover, it allows room for doubt as to whether the death of the child really was caused by eating plant material [G10]:

According to a report which reached me by the general practitioner Dr M. the 5-year old child of the worker J. was suddenly taken ill with convulsive abdominal pains, and severe vomiting and watery yellowish diarrhoea. The

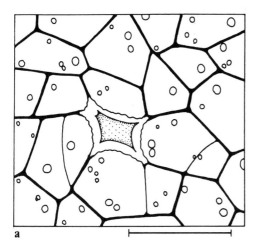

a

118 Ligustrum vulgare: (a) Epidermis of the pericarp. (b) Epidermis of the testa in surface view. (c) Epidermis of the testa in transverse section.

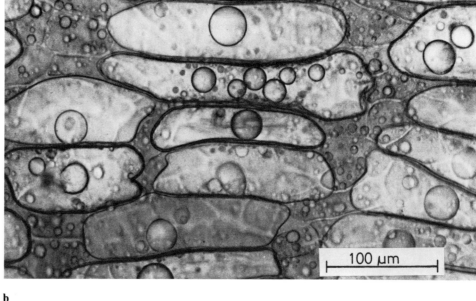

b

c

100 μm

pulse was rapid and there was no fever. The pressing recommendation by the doctor that the child should be admitted to hospital was refused by the parents. During the afternoon of the same day, the doctor was again called urgently but found the child already dead. The possibility of poisoning was first raised when, after the death of the child, the parents stated that the child had . . . eaten berries from ornamental shrubs. As appeared from the details of a request to me by an insurance company for an expert opinion, initially the fruits of a medlar tree were thought of. But since the fruits of the rose family do not contain any poisonous substances in the pulp . . ., this assumption became even less likely when the father asserted that the child had eaten the berries . . . of cultivated privet bushes. However, what is particularly suggestive of

poisoning by privet berries is the circumstance that the observed symptoms of poisoning . . . corresponded with the symptoms of privet-berry poisoning.

The supposition that eating privet berries caused the death of the child is thus based essentially on a quite unspecific array of symptoms and on the questionable statement of a father, who, on the one hand, refused hospital treatment for his child and, on the other, apparently put in a claim to an insurance company.

An entirely different impression of the toxicity of privet fruits is evident from the recent experience of the Toxicological Information Centres [K 46]:

In 55 cases, some with a known number – 12 – of berries and some with unknown numbers of berries, no symptoms occurred. On one occasion, a 2-year old, after eating two berries, had vomiting and diarrhoea. In nine other cases, the symptoms were similar (some vomited twice) after consuming an unknown number of berries.

Treatment. If necessary, administration of activated charcoal – otherwise, symptomatic. If, when a large quantity of the berries has been taken, vomiting has not taken place spontaneously, direct elimination of the poison should be considered.

Microscopical characters of the fruit. The pericarp of privet berries has distinct cuticular striations; as a result of secondary division, the epidermal cells are in part arranged in two or more groups and exhibit considerable thickening at the epidermal gaps **(118a)**. Stomata are very rare, while trichomes are completely absent. Highly characteristic is the surface view of the testa **(118b)**. Large light-coloured cells with lipid content are arranged in rows interrupted by small pigmented cells. In transverse section, depending on the direction of the cut surface of the section, they occur either singly **(118c)** or as a chain of large cells in the epidermis of the testa. Additional features are described by Guse [G 30].

PAPAVERACEAE

THE **Poppy family** comprises mainly herbaceous annuals or perennials, whose occurrence is restricted essentially to the temperate zone of the northern hemisphere. In addition to the species of *Chelidonium, Corydalis, Fumaria, Glaucium,* and *Papaver* indigenous to Europe, the Californian poppy, *Eschscholzia californica,* and bleeding heart or Dutchman's breeches, *Dicentra spectabilis,* are very frequently encountered in gardens as ornamentals. All the genera are characterised by having articulated laticifers (Papaveroideae) or alkaloid idioblasts (Fumarioideae). Their particular chemical characteristic is the abundance and diversity of their alkaloids.

Pharmacologically interesting constituents

(1) The **alkaloids** of the Papaveraceae are benzyl-tetrahydroisoquinolines or biogenetically derived variants. They can be divided into at least 10 different groups; of these, the protopine group can be looked upon as the characteristic alkaloid type of the family. The favoured site of accumulation in the plant tissues is the laticifers [F1; J17] or the vacuoles of special idioblasts in which they often occur combined with fumaric, chelidonic, or meconic acid.

Since 1806 when Sertürner isolated a pure alkaloid for the first time – morphine, from opium, the dried latex of the opium poppy, *P. somniferum* – and thus became the founder of alkaloid chemistry [M60], phytochemists have continued to investigate the alkaloids of the Papaveraceae. In this connection, the summary of Papaveraceae phytochemistry by Hegnauer [H35] should be consulted. Since the cases of poisoning with plant material relevant in the present context are determined by the interplay of all the components of what is usually a very complex mixture of alkaloids, there is little point in enumerating the pharmacological effects of the individual, therapeutically much used, pure alkaloids – morphine, codeine, papaverine, etc.

(2) Of the non-alkaloidal constituents of the poppy family, possibly the **triterpenoid saponins** are responsible for so far unexplained pharmacological effects [K60]. But from a toxicological point of view, because of their weak haemolytic activity, they are likely to be without significance.

Microscopical detection. Traces of the alkaloids combined with chelidonic and meconic acid can be detected by means of an interesting micro-reaction [G22; K58; K59]. If a pinhead-size amount of the substance to be examined – powdered drug, dried latex, opium, etc. – is placed on a microscope slide and to it a few drops of 5% tannic acid solution are added and then a cover slip immediately placed on top, the formation and slight 'ballooning' of fine 'strands' can be observed, from whose initially open ends there streams a very fine granular precipitate **(119)**. Neither the pure acids or alkaloids nor the alkaloid salts of inorganic acids give this reaction.

Protopine

HOOC — O — COOH

R = H   Chelidonic acid
R = OH   Meconic acid

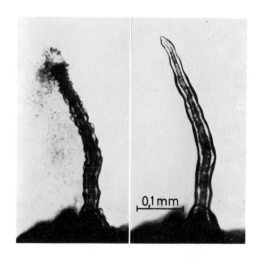

0,1 mm

119 Micro-reaction. Strand-like structure: (Left) During its formation. (Right) After the reaction has finished.

Chelidonium majus L.   Greater Celandine

120 Greater Celandine

30–60 cm tall perennial herb with erect, branched, sparsely pubescent, hollow stems and orange-yellow latex.
In waste ground and as a weed on rich loam.
<u>Leaves</u> alternate, pinnately cut (upper) to lobed (lower); tip roundish, crenate or serrate; upper surface dark green, lower surface blue-green; sparsely pubescent.
<u>Flowers</u> radiate, in few-(2–6)-flowered loose umbels, yellow; V–IX.
<u>Fruits</u> pod-like capsule, without septum, dehiscing from the bottom by two valves; numerous ovoid, black seeds; VI–X.
<u>Distribution:</u> Europe, Mediterranean region, Asia; naturalised in Atlantic North America. Widely distributed weed, growing in undergrowth, waste ground, and on walls.

BECAUSE of its conspicuously coloured latex, the greater celandine has attracted man's attention and has lent wings to his fantasy. The alchemists called this plant a gift from heaven *(coeli donum)*, since they imagined all four elements, and the philosophers' stone, the art of making gold, to be in the yellow juice, while at the same time the genus name is of Greek origin (χελῑδών = swallow) and is associated with great healing power in the plant. Thus, Pliny tells that young, blind swallows were healed by the ancients with the yellow juice of the greater celandine [H34] and in folk medicine the fresh latex is considered a remedy against cancerous swellings and warts [H3]. This may perhaps explain why old information on the effects and toxicity of the plant has been more or less uncritically taken over into the more recent literature:

Allowed to act externally on the skin, blisters and subsequently abscesses form. [A5; H3]

As (already) mentioned, the latex is highly caustic. . . . [N11]

(It) has an effect similar to that of ricin. . . . [M50]

The fresh, very bitter, orange-yellow latex is burning and acrid. . . . [B50]

'Chelidonium majus has extremely acrid orange-yellow juice. . . .' [L20]

However, in 1940 Schmaltz *et al.* [S22] already showed by extensive ex-periments on animals and on themselves that neither the fresh latex nor extracts or tinctures made from the fresh plant give rise to irritation of the skin. We also have been unable to bring about any irritant effects after repeated external application of the latex. Critical consideration of the often cited fatal case of poisoning in a 4-year old boy, observed in 1936, suggests that it is by no means certain that it should be ascribed to the effects of greater celandine [K37].

The boy was admitted to hospital with the diagnosis 'suspected greater-celandine poisoning' and in spite of medical treatment died the next morn-ing. Although the post-mortem ex-

amination, as well as the chemical and botanical investigation of the specimens removed for analysis, did not allow any conclusion as to the cause of death, except that there was severe inflammation of the large intestine, in essence, on the basis of a yellow fluorescence exhibited by the contents of the small intestine, the report comes to the conclusion that . . . 'in the present case poisoning due to the greater celandine with fatal outcome (may) definitely be accepted'.

Constituents. Up until now, 21 alkaloids have been isolated from the plant. Most of them are benzophenanthridine and protoberberine bases, in part combined with chelidonic acid, and their content in the different parts of the plant (herb 0.3–1.0%, root up to 2%, fruits *ca* 0.15%) is subject to considerable seasonal variation. The main alkaloid in all parts is chelidonine, and it is accompanied principally by sanguinarine, chelerythrine, and berberine. The seeds are an exception, as the reports on their alkaloid composition are quite contradictory [B47; H3].

121 Ramstad reaction.

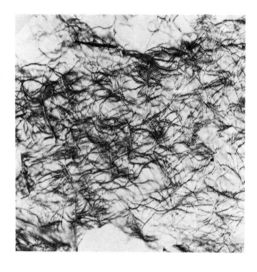

Chelerythrine

Pharmacological effects. As a result of the very different activities of the individual alkaloids, the pharmacodynamics of the fresh plant are very complex. Following oral administration in mice and rabbits of extracts or tinctures of fresh plant material, several authors have observed a weak sedative action (inhibition of motor activity), a lasting decrease in blood pressure, as well as a spasmolytic effect on the stomach and intestines [K43; M6; S22]. This spasmolytic effect on smooth-muscled organs provides a possible explanation for the use of the drug against inflammation of the bile duct. Nevertheless, on drying the plant much of the activity is lost. Chelerythrine is usually considered to be responsible for the toxicological phenomena, although used as a pure substance it acts as a sternutatory and causes vomiting in cats without being particularly toxic [K43]. However, because of the small amount of the alkaloid present in the aerial parts of the plant [S30], the afore-mentioned view is unlikely to be correct.

Symptoms of poisoning. In view of what has been said above, external application can hardly be expected to lead to toxic symptoms. Although Schmaltz *et al.* [S22] also report that there are no pathological effects on the sensitive mucous membrane of the rabbit's eye, contact of the fresh latex with the human eye should be avoided, since there is the possibility, as in the case of *Euphorbia* latex, of a difference in the sensitivity of the two organs (p.117). One of the pure alkaloids, sanguinarine, is used to produce ex- perimental glaucoma; furthermore, there is a report in the older literature (1916) of inflammation of the iris resulting from the action of *Chelidonium* latex (cited from [M42]).

Ingestion of plant material is stated to give rise to 'severe irritation of the entire digestive tract (burning, blistering in the mouth and throat, nausea, severe bloody diarrhoea accompanied by colic)' [H3]. In animal experiments, however, no such symptoms and no pathological changes in the digestive organs have been seen [K43; M6; S22].

In practice, poisoning with *Chelidonium* is rare, which is no doubt also because of the unpleasant smell and taste of the crushed plant material. More than 500 g of greater celandine is said to be required to cause toxic effects in horses and cattle [B23].

Treatment. After taking small amounts of the aerial plant parts, treatment is not likely to be necessary. With larger amounts, after direct removal of the poison (gastric lavage, activated charcoal), only symptomatic treatment need be recommended.

Detection of the constituents. Several alkaloids present in the latex, e.g. chelidonine and berberine, are yellow and/or on irradiation with long-wavelength UV light develop a strong yellow fluorescence [S30]. On the skin the latex produces yellow spots that even after several days and frequent washing still fluoresce yellow in UV light [K37]. Microchemical detection of alkaloid chelidonates with tannic acid solution has already been suggested in the review of the family (above). In addition, there are several possible ways of identifying free chelidonic acid, one of which, the reaction due to Ramstad [R2], is a simple microscopical means of detection with high specificity. Dry plant materials containing chelidonic acid with 20% aqueous potassium hydroxide solution give first of all a yellow solution from which yellow branched and bent crystal threads of potassium xanthochelidonate are immediately deposited. Of course, it must not be forgotten that chelidonic acid occurs widely in the plant kingdom.

Corydalis cava (L.) Schweigg. et Körte   Bulbous Corydalis

122 Bulbous Corydalis

10–35 cm tall perennial with erect stems; tubers usually globose, soon becoming hollow; latex absent.
In mixed deciduous forest and beech woods on wet loam and nutrient-rich soils; mostly gregarious in light undergrowth, under hedges, in orchards and nurseries.
<u>Leaves</u> glabrous, blue-green, 2-ternate, leaflets cuneate at the base, obovate.
<u>Flowers</u> in many-flowered erect racemes; spurred, dull red or yellowish white (rarely lilac or blue); III–V.
<u>Fruits</u> small, pale green, many-seeded capsules; seeds up to 3 mm broad, globose, black, with an aril.
<u>Distribution:</u> In Europe except the north and mouth of the Mediterranean, western Russia.

THE Central European species of *Corydalis** flower in the spring and have a subterranean tuberous storage organ. In addition to *C. cava*, whose tubers become hollow as parts of them die off **(122)**, and *C. solida (bulbosa)*, *C. lutea* (yellow corydalis or fumitory) and *C. ochrolutea* (pale yellow corydalis or fumitory) of southern Europe are popular ornamentals. The tubers of *C. cava* (Tubera Aristolochiae Cavae) used to be an official drug and were used as a vermifuge and in gynaecological practice.

Alkaloids. The alkaloid-richest organ is the tuber (up to 6% calculated on the dry weight). Along with the principal alkaloid bulbocapnine, there are more than 20 others. In animals and man pure bulbocapnine has an unusual action on the central nervous system in that it brings about a catatonic state ranging from reduced motor activity to suppression of all voluntary and reflex movements. In this state the musculature is quite flaccid and, rather like a piece of lead piping, the limbs can be moved and bent into bizarre postures [H17]. Extracts of the drug have spasmolytic activity and can be used in dealing with hyperkinetic states [O5].

Poisoning. Cases of poisoning by *Corydalis* plant material have not so far been reported and are unlikely; the tubers do not invite consumption and, in any case, they lie deep in the ground. Neither has the frequently cultivated ornamental *Dicentra spectabilis,** bleeding heart or Dutchman's breeches, been the source of any poisoning reports. Here, the alkaloid content is much smaller – root 0.76%, herb 0.17% [H35].

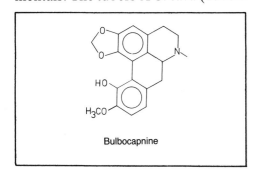

Bulbocapnine

---

* The genera *Corydalis* and *Dicentra* belong to the same subfamily Fumarioideae, characterised *inter alia* by the absence of latex, which is often treated as a separate but related family, Fumariaceae.

Papaver somniferum L.   Opium Poppy

123 Opium Poppy

0.3–1.5 m tall herbaceous annual with a single erect, usually glabrous, blue-green glaucous stem.
Leaves oblong, more or less amplexicaul, irregularly toothed, lower ones undulate, upper ones entire.
Flowers single, pedicel long and usually with spreading hairs; petals white or violet; numerous stamens, broadening towards the top; VI–VIII.
Fruits large globose capsules, opening just under the stigma disc by the bending back of many small flaps to form pores; numerous reniform seeds with reticulately wrinkled surface and white, grey, yellow, or black in colour; VII–IX.
Distribution: Probably originating in the Near East or Mediterranean region; nowadays only known in cultivation or as an escape.

THE opium poppy has been known as a medicinal plant for more than 2000 years. Today, it is cultivated in almost all parts of the globe for the production of opium, alkaloids, seeds, or oil. Many forms and races are distinguished, depending on the shape of the capsule, the colour of the seeds, the mechanism by which the capsule opens, and the amount of alkaloid present in the latex. Of the more than 100 species and subspecies belonging to the genus *Papaver*, in Europe the common poppy, *P. rhoeas,* long-headed poppy, *P. dubium,* and oriental poppy, *P. orientale,* are widely distributed as wild or cultivated plants.

Alkaloid composition. Chemically, the genus is characterised by the general occurrence of rhoeadine-type alkaloids. Also belonging here are the papa-verrubines (*N*-demethylrhoeadines), which on heating with mineral acids are converted into intense red-coloured bases. So far, over 100 alkaloids derived from benzyl-isoquinoline have been isolated from more than 30 species; quite often, morphologically related species produce a similar range of alkaloids (see reviews by [H35; H57; K55; P23; S110]. For example, the medicinally very valuable alkaloids morphine, codeine, and noscapine are present only in the species *P. somniferum* (including its var. *setigerum* – by some considered as a separate species). On the other hand, thebaine and papaverine, which are also used therapeutically, also occur in wild poppies [P23]. The proportions of these five principal bases in the latex of the opium poppy depend on the form, but can also vary within limits according to the soil conditions and climatic factors. On average, in the dried latex (opium) there are 15% morphine, 5% narcotine, 1% codeine, 1% papaverine, and 0.5% thebaine. The oil-rich poppy seed (Semen Papaveris), the one plant part without latex, contain not more than traces of alkaloid – 0.005% [P43]. As a rule, the amount of alkaloid present in the latex of other poppy species is small.

Poisoning. Acute cases usually arise as a result of faulty medical treatment or

Morphine

Papaverine

of attempted suicide with the pure alkaloids or opium. Neither these cases nor the innumerable cases of chronic morphine poisoning (morphinism) are discussed here, but rather cases due to carelessness or ignorance of the poisonous properties of the plant material. Thus, poisoning often used to be reported after administering 'calming tea' to infants, e.g. [E1]:

On 19.2.1952, at the age of six weeks, because the infant was in a generally restless state it was given 100 g 'calming tea' at 7 o'clock in the morning. The child then fell asleep and did not waken again until the late afternoon.

These teas usually contained pericarp material derived from unripe or ripe poppy capsules, whose morphine content was considered not to be dangerous. Investigation in the above case showed that the infant had nevertheless received six times the maximum dose for a 1-year old child. Thanks to medical care the infant's life could be saved. In another case, that of a 3-year old boy who had eaten freshly broken poppy capsules while they were being harvested, help came too late [K39]. Children and infants are not more sensitive to morphine than adults, as is often stated, it is simply that in the newborn the newly functioning respiratory centre is particularly reactive to this alkaloid [H17].

Not long ago, the death of a 20-year old man was occasion for the West German Ministry of Health to draw attention to the toxic effects of poppy capsules [A27]:

Death through 'O tea'. A young man had taken poppy capsules, used in making flower arrangements, and had boiled them up with water in order to make what is known in the drug scene

as 'O tea'. He died after drinking a large amount of the tea.

There are no recent reports of poisoning with fresh plant material derived from other *Papaver* species, and confusion of the poppy seed used in the bakery trade with tobacco or henbane seed [G23] no longer plays any significant part in present-day toxicological work.

Symptoms of poisoning. Acute poisoning is characterised essentially by the toxic effects of morphine on the central nervous system, in particular the respiratory centre. Typical symptoms are a narcotic state with muscular relaxation, extremely slow respiration (2–4 breaths per minute; sometimes, Cheyne-Stokes respiration), and pinpoint pupils. Because of the inadequate oxygen supply, those tissues still being supplied become cyanotic. Death normally follows from respiratory failure. For adults the acute lethal dose of morphine may be as little as 0.2 g, although with proper medical treatment people have survived considerably larger amounts.

Treatment. Gastric lavage is only of use shortly after (1–2 hours) the poison has been taken. Particularly important are artificial respiration continued over many hours, measures to support the circulation, and emptying the bladder (catheterisation) [H17]. As specific antidote levallorphan (Lorfan®) may be recommended: 0.5–2 mg per dose, administered slowly i.v. For further measures, see the specialist literature [M50].

PHYTOLACCACEAE

Phytolacca americana L.   Pokeweed, Pokeberry

124 Pokeweed

Up to 2 m tall perennial herb with erect
stem and napiform thickened root with
several crowns. Naturalised in vineyards
and waste places.
<u>Leaves</u> ovate-elliptic and entire,
glabrous, short-petiolate.
<u>Flowers</u> greenish white, in
dense racemes; terminal on a
sympodially branched stalk and
therefore apparently opposite the leaves;
VII–VIII.
<u>Fruits</u> dark red to black berry-like
syncarp, flattened globose; from VIII.
<u>Distribution</u>: Originally from North
America. In Europe planted and also as
an escape; in the south partly
naturalised.

POKEWEED used to be cultivated in Europe, as extracts of the fruits were used for colouring wine and sweets. Nowadays, it is no longer employed as a colouring matter. All parts of the plant are considered to be poisonous, especially the roots. Since these are used in North America in folk medicine as an antirheumatic, cases of poisoning through drinking poke root tea have often occurred. But there are also recent accounts of poisoning with the leaves [C2; J18; L19; S80].

'In New Jersey, after eating a salad prepared with pokeweed leaves 52 people became ill, 21 of them with symptoms such as nausea, headache,

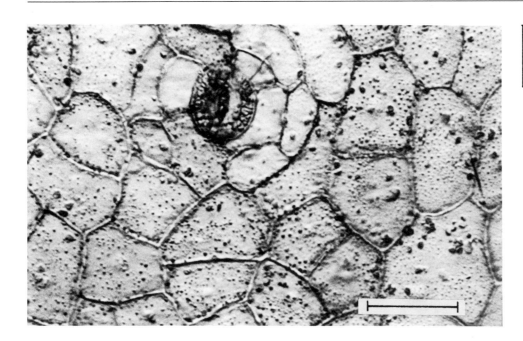

125 **Phytolacca americana: Epidermis of the pericarp.**

vomiting, and stomach cramps. Owing to protracted vomiting and dehydration, four people had to be hospitalised for 24–48 hours' [C2].

A few (up to 10) raw pokeweed berries can be looked upon as harmless for adults and older children, but may lead to serious poisoning in infants, manifested as severe gastrointestinal troubles, vomiting, diarrhoea, and cramps. While cases of poisoning are evidently not infrequent in North America [L8], pokeweed berries do not figure in the statistics of the European Toxicological Centres.

Toxic constituents. Triterpenoid saponins are found in all parts of the plant, especially in the roots and seeds, and are believed to be responsible for the toxic properties [L18; L20]. Besides phytolaccatoxin (aglycone: phytolaccagenin [S89]; cf. structure), whose

Phytolaccagenin

structure was elucidated in 1964, further triterpenoid saponins, among them those from the berries [K4], have been isolated. The nitrogen-containing colouring matter in the berries, a betacyan similar to the colouring matter of red beet, has no toxicological significance. In recent years the so-called pokeweed mitogens, i.e. lectins with mitogenic (lymphocyte-growth stimulating) activity, have been much in-

vestigated [P25; P26]. If there are skin injuries, these substances can get into the bloodstream percutaneously and cause plasmacytosis and other haematological abnormalities [B9; L18].

Treatment. Only if large amounts of the berries or in the case of infants if just a few have been taken, is direct removal of the poison required. Otherwise, symptomatic measures are sufficient.

Microscopical characters of the fruit. The thin-walled epidermal cells of the berry are covered with a finely granular layer of wax. Stomata with relatively large guard cells occur sporadically (**125**). In the pulp, chloroplasts and large numbers of calcium oxalate needles (*ca* 30 μm) are present.

POLYPODIACEAE

Dryopteris filix-mas (L.) Schott   Male-fern

126 Male-fern

0.3–1.4 m tall perennial fern with rhizomes having one to few crowns.
In deciduous and coniferous forests, on fresh to moist nutrient-rich soils.
<u>Leaves</u> summer-green, elliptic-oblong fronds; pinnae alternating, upper surface dark green, lower surface lighter and with reniform sori; spores ripe VI–IX.
<u>Distribution:</u> Almost cosmopolitan; this polymorphic forest plant appears to be absent from the Arctic zone, Africa, and Australia.

AS one of the most active remedies against tapeworms, the male-fern, *D. filix-mas,* was already known to the doctors of antiquity. Nowadays, owing to the low therapeutic index, the drug Rhizoma Filicis and its extracts have been largely replaced by synthetic products; for not infrequently fatal cases of poisoning occurred, sometimes because of overdosage and sometimes because of the hypersensitivity of the patient [G21; H45]. Only in veterinary medicine do reports still occasionally appear of accidental poisonings after feeding *Dryopteris* species [E2; M2].

Toxic constituents. The anthelmintic and toxic principle of almost all male-ferns is crude filicin – a mixture of dimeric, trimeric, and tetrameric butanone phloroglucides, which are more or less unstable compounds of butyric or isobutyric acid with phloroglucinol or its homologues. The mixture is localised in the hair-like excretory cells (scales) of the rhizomes and frond bases [M30]; it occurs very rarely outside the genus *Dryopteris* [H35].

Among the many symptoms of male-fern poisoning, in addition to the local irritant action on the gastrointestinal tract, there are, particularly in serious cases, cramps and disturbances of vision which may end in blindness. In view of the negligible occurrence nowadays of such poisonings, the reader is referred elsewhere for more detailed accounts of the symptoms [H3] and treatment [M50].

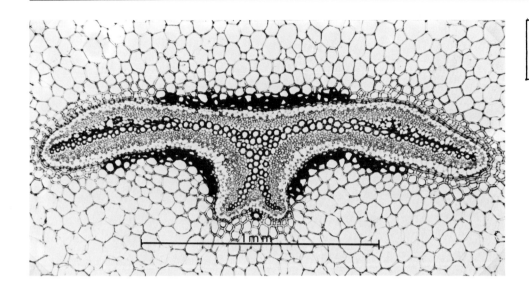

127 Asplenium nidus: Typical fern vascular bundle with internal xylem.

Microscopical characters. An important microscopical character of all ferns is the arrangement of the conducting tissue in amphicribral bundles (see **127**). Braun [B 43] has dealt at length with the macroscopical and microscopical characters of pharmaceutically important Polypodiaceae, in the form of both illustrations and a key.

Albaspidin

Other toxic Polypodiaceae. Since 1952 many ferns, including the widely distributed bracken, *Pteridium aquilinum,* have attracted toxicological interest because of the presence of carcinogenic constituents. Cf. also p.232. Owing to the lack of other plant materials yielding starch, 'fern roots' are used as a source of food and fodder in very different parts of the world [C 1; M 63], and this gives rise to the danger of chronic poisoning in both man and animals [P 44; Y 2]. The water-soluble carcinogenic substances (sesquiterpenes?) can be absorbed not only by eating the fern as a tasty wild vegetable (as in Japan) but also indirectly through the milk of grazing cows [E 9]. If the proportion of fern in the animals' forage is very high it can bring about acute poisoning which may end in death [E 10; K 64]. As the cause, both the carcinogens and an enzyme which destroys vitamin B_1, thiaminase, have been implicated [E 8; K 19].

Ferns as house plants. Because of their great morphological diversity, ferns are becoming ever more popular and this means that they are within 'grabbing' range of the fingers of infants bent on investigating their surroundings. Among the genera most often found in living rooms and offices are the maidenhair fern *(Adiantum),* spleenwort *(Asplenium),* sword fern *(Nephrolepis),* stag's-horn fern *(Platycerium),* and brake *(Pteris).* Apart from an occasional case of ingestion, no reports of poisoning due to these ferns have been encountered.

PRIMULACEAE

THE **Primrose family** comprises mostly herbaceous plants that overwinter by means of rhizomes or tubers and that are marked by the abundant occurrence of triterpenoid saponins. Two representatives of the family frequently encountered as house plants are poisonous, viz a primrose from China and cyclamen or sowbread.

Primula obconica

This plant comes from China and has been in Europe as a house plant for about a century. In its glandular trichomes, found especially on the calyx and flower stalks, there is a skin-irritant benzoquinone derivative, primin.

Primin

The compound, 2-methoxy-6-*n*-pentyl-*p*-benzoquinone, is a contact allergen that after sensitisation causes severe dermatitis (primula dermatitis) in the people concerned. Simply touching the plant, e.g. in removing dead leaves or flowers, may lead to contact between the skin and the resinous secretion which is then carried by the fingers to other parts of the skin. There is an extensive literature on primula dermatitis, summarised in [M42]. Rook and Wilson [R22] have carried out a detailed study, while Hausen [H18] has investigated the distribution of primin and other quinonoid compounds in the family.

128 Primula obconica Hance

Treatment. Avoidance of further contact with *Primula obconica*. Symptomatic measures, using, for example, anti-inflammatory and anti-histamine drugs.

129 Cyclamen purpurascens Mill.   Cyclamen, Sowbread.

Cyclamen

In the round tuberous rhizomes of the cyclamen there are triterpenoid saponins, including cyclamin, which have a local irritant action and (as a result?) are absorbed from the gastro-intestinal tract. Poisoning, which, besides causing gastro-intestinal troubles, may lead to convulsions and paralysis, can occur after ingesting only a small piece of the tuber. But in recent years such cases have been very rare (formerly, Rhizoma Cyclaminis was employed as a drastic purgative).

Cyclamin

RANUNCULACEAE

THE **Buttercup family** consists mostly of annual or perennial herbs, rarely undershrubs or shrubs, distributed largely outside the tropics in the northern hemisphere. It includes many ornamentals (e.g. columbine, anemone, hellebore, monk's-hood, and delphinium) and also a number of medicinal plants that are still in use (e.g. *Adonis, Aconitum, Cimicifuga, Helleborus*) and a 'horde of poisonous plants' (Hegnauer [H35]), a considerable number of which grow in western and central Europe.

Toxic constituents. The spectrum of poisonous substances in the Ranunculaceae ranges from alkaloids to cardiotoxic compounds to skin-irritant lactones of short-chain acids; and some of them are characteristic of certain parts of the family. Cyanogenic glycosides and saponins, which are not unusual in the family, on the other hand, are of very minor toxicological interest.

Alkaloids. Different types of isoquinoline alkaloids are widespread in many Ranunculaceae. Many of these alkaloids are pharmacologically interesting compounds, e.g. the alkaloids of meadow-rue, *Thalictrum,* have hypotensive or anti-cancer activity and have been much investigated [H3]. But from a toxicological point of view this group has little importance; see the discussion on berberine (p.69), which has also often been detected in Ranunculaceae. On the other hand, the diterpene alkaloids of the aconitine type, which occur only in the genera *Aconitum* and *Delphinium* (including *Consolida*), are highly poisonous [P13].

Cardiotoxic substances. Cardioactive glycosides of the cardenolide type have been found in numerous *Adonis* species, but the rarer bufadienolide type occurs in the genus *Helleborus.*

Skin-irritant substances. It is particularly in the genus *Ranunculus,* but also in *Anemone, Pulsatilla, Clematis,* and *Helleborus,* that skin-irritant acrid substances of the protoanemonin type are to be found and they determine the toxicity of many representatives of these genera. Interestingly, the accumulation of such compounds and the occurrence of isoquinoline alkaloids appear to be mutually exclusive.

Protoanemonin

Protoanemonin, the lactone of a γ-hydroxyvinylacrylic acid, is formed from glycosidic precursors (ranunculin?) and is converted fairly readily into the inactive dimer anemonin. Studies by Burbach [B45] show that protoanemonin has a marked ability to combine with SH groups. Its toxic effects as a sub-epidermal vesicant depend perhaps on inactivation of enzymes containing SH groups, e.g. those involved in glycolysis.

Ranunculus acris L.   Meadow Buttercup

130 Meadow Buttercup

30–80 cm tall perennial herb with erect sparsely branched stem. From low up to alpine altitudes, in meadows, along roadsides, and in undergrowth, often abundant.

<u>Leaves</u> lower ones palmate, 5–7-partite, initially pubescent; upper ones simpler and short-petiolate or sessile.

<u>Flowers</u> golden yellow, conspicuous, on terete pedicels; V–X.

<u>Fruits</u> numerous, small, on glabrous receptacle.

<u>Distribution:</u> Throughout Europe.

THE genus *Ranunculus* comprises *ca* 300 species of annual or perennial herbs found mainly in the temperate zone of the northern hemisphere. A few species are aquatic (partly submerged) or grow in wet, muddy localities, while the others are in part widespread representatives of the European-Asiatic forest flora or characteristic weeds of meadows and pastures. All *Ranunculus* species contain the acrid, skin-irritant constituent protoanemonin or its glycosidic precursors. The work of Burbach [B54] on the blistering action of the buttercup has already been mentioned. The plants are considered to be more or less toxic, depending on the proto-anemonin content. From a toxicological point of view, *R. sceleratus,* celery-leaved buttercup, and (the rare) *R. thora,* crowfoot, are important; in addition, *R. acris,* meadow buttercup, and *R. flammula,* lesser spearwort, and *R. bulbosus,* bulbous buttercup, should be mentioned.

Poisoning is rare and is limited essentially to animals when the proportion of toxic *Ranunculus* material in their food intake is large. With hay there is no problem, since, as already pointed out, the protoanemonin on drying is converted into the inactive dimer anemonin.

Symptoms of poisoning. Gastro-intestinal irritation with colic and diarrhoea occur; and nephritis and central stimulation or else symptoms of paralysis are also possible. In man, irritation of the skin as a result of percutaneous absorption must also be borne in mind.

Treatment. If necessary, symptomatic; demulcents against the irritation of the mucous membranes; also, if required, activated charcoal and purgatives.

Ranunculus sceleratus L. Celery-leaved Buttercup

131 Celery-leaved Buttercup

Annual or biennial, 20–50 cm tall plant with erect hollow stems and, depending on the locality, varying habit; on dry soil dwarf forms, in marshy and muddy places luxuriant growth, in inundated localities forms with floating leaves.
Leaves petiolate, somewhat fleshy; lower ones 3–5-partite, upper ones simpler and smaller; with crenate margin.
Flowers yellowish, relatively small and inconspicuous; peduncle with numerous flowers; VI–IX.
Fruits small, numerous, on ovoid receptacle.
Distribution: Throughout the whole of the northern hemisphere; scattered.

MISRA and Dixit [M41] have investigated the fungitoxic principle of *R. sceleratus*. They isolated protoanemonin and anemonin from the leaves and were able to show that their inhibitory activity towards different test fungi varied considerably. Anemonin only effected complete inhibition of growth down to a dilution of 1:100, while protoanemonin was still fully active at a concentration of 1:10000.

Clematis vitalba L.   Traveller's-joy, Old Man's Beard

132 Traveller's-joy

Perennial climber with stems up to 5 m long, becoming woody. Frequent in damp woods, undergrowth, meadows; climbing on a great variety of trees and shrubs.
<u>Leaves</u> with long winding petioles, imparipinnate, with 3–5 stalked leaflets.
<u>Flowers</u> long-pedicellate, with whitish downy perianth segments and long stiff spreading stamens; in many-flowered panicles; VI–IX.
<u>Fruits</u> oblong, red-brown, with a 2–3 cm long silky-haired beak (old man's beard); IX–X.
<u>Distribution:</u> West, central, and southern Europe; also frequently planted.

TRAVELLER'S-joy is one of the few European lianes. It holds on to trees and shrubs and climbs up them with the help of the petioles of its leaves. *Clematis vitalba* is often planted as a climbing ornamental because of its conspicuous fruits. The plant is one of the Ranunculaceae that accumulates protoanemonin and at the same time has a low saponin content; nevertheless, cases of poisoning are only mentioned in the older literature. More recently, Moore [M53] has described a case of animal poisoning due probably to *C. vitalba*. Less common European species of *Clematis* are *C. recta* (non-climbing) and *C. alpina*, and like the many popular large-flowered garden hybrids, they contain protoanemonin. As already indicated, protoanemonin is of general occurrence in the tribe Anemoneae. Other plants belonging to this tribe include *Anemone nemorosa*, wood anemone, and *A. ranunculoides*, yellow anemone; *Hepatica nobilis*; and *Pulsatilla pratensis*, small pasqueflower, and *P. vulgaris*, pasqueflower.

Symptoms and **treatment:** see *Ranunculus*.

Although protoanemonin is present in all these species – but often only in small amounts – their toxicity is to be considered relatively slight. Regarding possible symptoms of poisoning and the treatment to be applied, see the indications given under the genus *Ranunculus*.

Caltha palustris, marsh-marigold or kingcup, which is often mentioned in the literature as containing protoanemonin, according to Hegnauer [H35] does not have any. Possible cases of poisoning would best be explained by the occurrence of alkaloids and saponins.

Helleborus niger L.   Christmas Rose, Black Hellebore

133 Christmas Rose

Perennial 15–30 cm tall plant with a stout rhizome bearing one or more stems. On stony slopes; on calcareous soils.
<u>Leaves</u> basal, long-petiolate, leathery; remaining throughout the winter; pedate, with 7–9 segments.
<u>Flowers</u> white or reddish, terminal on thick erect pedicels with 1–3 green scale-like bracts; (XII–) II–IV.
<u>Fruits</u> many-seeded follicles, *ca* 7 on short stalks.
<u>Distribution:</u> Southern and eastern calcareous alps; often encountered in gardens and occasionally found as an escape.

THE Christmas rose is an old medicinal and poisonous plant. It is reported to have been used in ancient times, *ca.* 600 BC, as a 'chemical weapon':

'. . . *Solon invented another trick to outwit the Cirrhaeans. The water of the river Pleistus ran along a channel to the city, and Solon diverted it in another direction. When the Cirrhaeans still held out against the besiegers drinking well-water and rain-water, Solon threw into the Pleistus roots of hellebore,* and when he perceived that the water held enough of the drug he diverted it back again into its channel. The Cirrhaeans drank without stint of the water, and those on the wall, seized with obstinate diarrhoea, deserted their posts, and the Amphictyons captured the city.'* [P51]

Toxic constituents. Cardiotoxic bufadienolides (p.27), as well as saponins and protoanemonin, occur in the genus *Helleborus*. At the present time, the following picture of the Christmas rose can be built up from the numerous old and new, partly contradictory, data:
(a) Hellebrin and other bufadienolides are **not** present in the underground organs [W25]; aerial parts have not been examined for these compounds.

(b) The saponin mixture described in the older literature – helleborin – consists chiefly of steroidal saponins. For the identification of individual components, see the work of Kating and Wissner [K12].
(c) Aerial parts (leaves, stems, flowers) contain ranunculin or protoanemonin [M22].

The partly contradictory findings may be explained by the use of the commercial drug as starting material for the chemical investigations: Rhizoma (Radix) Hellebori may be derived from either *H. niger* or *H. viridis;* a clear-cut pharmacognostical identification, which also excludes other *Helleborus* species, is, however, not possible. It is for this reason that

---

* It should be noted that the account by Pausanias in the classical literature only speaks of ἐλλέβοροσ, so that other species could also have been intended.

Wissner and Kating carried out their extensive investigations, which were published in several papers [K12; W24; W25] in 1971–1974, exclusively on unequivocally identified material that they had collected or cultivated themselves.

Thus, only the combination saponins/protoanemonin remains as an explanation for the symptoms of poisoning described in the literature.

Symptoms of poisoning. These include tingling in the mouth and throat, increased salivation, gastro-intestinal troubles with vomiting, colic, and diarrhoea, and dilatation of the pupils. The cardiac symptoms that are said to occur in poisoning by Christmas rose must be considered doubtful (see above), but are indeed conceivable with other species. Be that as it may, cases of *Helleborus* poisoning are rare.

Johnson [J14] has reported on animal poisoning by *H. viridis*.

Treatment. Direct removal of the poison; activated charcoal, purgatives. Symptomatic measures.

Aconitum napellus L. Monk's-hood

134 Monk's-hood

0.5–1.5 m tall perennial herb with tuberous fleshy roots and erect stout stems. Frequent in wet places, on well-manured soil, along waysides and the banks of streams in montane to alpine regions. Highly polymorphic species.
<u>Leaves</u> 5–7 segments, deeply divided, dark green; towards the top becoming smaller.
<u>Flowers</u> in dense racemes; violet-blue; with helmet-shaped hood; VI–VIII.
<u>Fruits</u> follicles with shiny black triangular seeds, winged at the angles; VIII–IX.
<u>Distribution:</u> In the Alps and other mountainous regions of Europe; in the west as far as south-west England and Portugal; frequently planted in gardens.

MONK'S-hood is often called 'the most poisonous plant in Europe', and within the genus its toxicity is supposedly only exceeded by the Indian *A. ferox,* an extract of which has been in use as an arrow poison. The poisonous properties of monk's-hood were already known in antiquity, and extracts of the plant have often been employed to commit murder [L14]. The daughter tubers of *A. napellus,* Tubera Aconiti, have been prescribed as a drug since the 18th century, but their use is now obsolete.

Toxic constituents. In the genus *Aconitum* there are diterpene (C_{20}) and nor-diterpene (C_{19}) alkaloids, whose nitrogen is usually ethylated or methylated (alkamines). While the C_{20} compounds are not very toxic, the esterified nor-diterpene bases are distinguished by a high toxicity. Hydrolysis of the ester functions leads to a reduction in the activity, so that the unesterified C_{19} alkamines can be grouped toxicologically with ordinary diterpenes. Differences in alkaloid composition and transformations that occur during drying and storage determine the variability in toxicity of individual species and of the drug formerly used. Aconitine is present in

[D21] – rarely occurs nowadays, since the alkaloid is no longer part of the drug armamentarium. Fiddes [F29] reported aconitine poisoning in two students who, when clearing out a collection of medicines, tried one or two of the bottles (fortunately, only small quantities), in the course of which they tested some aconitine on the tongue. A fatal case due to the confusion of horse-radish root with aconite root has been documented by Kalbfleisch [K2]. This disastrous error occurred in the month of December, a point worth remembering as the aconitine content of the roots attains it highest value in winter. In recent times as well, there have been a number of fatal cases resulting from the use of aconite root in order to get 'high' [M25].

Symptoms of poisoning. On taking a toxic dose by mouth the effects appear rapidly (sometimes within 10–20 minutes) and first manifest themselves by burning and tingling in the mouth and also in the fingers and toes. Accompanied by bouts of sweating and feeling chilly, the paraesthesia extends over the whole body and gradually alters to a feeling of roughness and dryness in the mouth, numbness, and being icy cold (anaesthesia dolorosa). This is followed by agonising vomiting, colicky diarrhoea, paralysis of the skeletal musculature, and evidently intense pain. A case of a fatal overdose (100 times!) of aconitine was described [D21] thus:

A few minutes after taking the powder, the patient became ill; agonising vomiting was soon followed by diarrhoea . . . 10 minutes after taking the dose the patient complained of severe pains in the head, neck, and back, and especially that 'his heart was painful', and also that his eyesight had gone. The pains were so severe that the patient's cries could be heard through the whole house. When the woman was tele-

135 Aconitum vulparia Reichb. ex Spreng.   Wolfsbane.

fresh material of monk's-hood, e.g. 0.3–2% in the tubers and 0.2–1.2% in the leaves [B23], and the plant is indeed very poisonous. The lethal dose of aconitine for an adult is 3–6 mg, so that only a few grams of plant material may already be dangerous.

Cases of poisoning. Medicinal poisoning through overdosage with aconitine – impressively described by Druckrey

R_1 = Benzoyl

R_2 = Acetyl

R_3 = Ethyl

Aconitine

136 Delphinium elatum L. Larkspur.

Treatment. Immediate removal of the poison by eliciting vomiting; gastric lavage, activated charcoal; no specific antidote is known. In hospital, intensive care with emphasis on measures in support of the cardiac and respiratory functions; if necessary, Mg/Ca infusion against cardiac disturbances. Prognosis poor.

Nor-diterpene alkaloids, including lycaconitine, are present in wolfsbane, *A. vulparia* **(135),** whose extract was formerly employed as a poison for wolves. The plant is to be considered toxicologically on the same level as *A. napellus,* even though there are no reported cases of poisoning due to it.

Diterpene and nor-diterpene alkaloids are found elsewhere in the Ranunculaceae, in the larkspur. Three of the species occurring throughout a large part of Europe and (in the British Isles mainly) as garden ornamentals are:

Consolida regalis, forking larkspur, calcicole weed in fields;

Delphinium elatum (0.6–1.5 m high; **136**); and

Consolida ambigua (ajacis), larkspur (0.3–1 m high).

Although aconitine-like alkaloids are present in all three species listed, the toxicity appears to be less. However, concrete data on poisoning are absent from the central European region. On the other hand, larkspur poisoning is a serious veterinary toxicological problem in the western mountainous region of North America. The losses of grazing animals through larkspur toxicosis may amount to as much as 12% [O15]. The poisonous herbs concerned are especially *Delphinium barbeyi* (a tall larkspur) and *D. andersonii* (a low larkspur). For some reviews on larkspur poisoning, see [C26; O13; O14].

phoning the doctor, the latter heard the screaming through the telephone even although it was situated on another floor. . . . Two hours after taking the powder, the patient died in hospital.

As the body temperature sinks, death takes place through respiratory paralysis or heart failure, consciousness being maintained to the end. Aconitine is also well absorbed percutaneously through mucous membranes and the undamaged skin, so that children may be endangered when, for example, they play with the flowers.

Actaea spicata L.   Baneberry, Herb Christopher

137 Baneberry

40–70 cm tall perennial herb with tubercular rhizomes and erect more or less branched stems. In shady damp deciduous forests, especially associated with beech; widespread, but usually occurring singly.
Leaves long-petiolate, (bi)ternate with more or less dentate margin.
Flowers whitish, with numerous stamens longer than the sepals; usually in many-flowered racemes; V–VII.
Fruits ovoid shiny black berries; brown seeds in two rows, flattened; VII–IX.
Distribution: Throughout most of Europe; widespread in mountain forest. Occasionally, forms with red (A. erythro-carpa) or white (A. alba) fruits are found as ornamentals in gardens and parks.

BANEBERRY has long been known as a poisonous plant. However, protoanemonin, often stated to be the toxic principle, does not occur in the plant [H35], nor do other highly active constituents, so that poisoning after eating the fruits is unlikely. Nikonov and Syrkina-Krugljak [N12] found the cancer-inhibiting substance *trans*-aconitic acid to be present.

Microscopical characters of the fruit. The thin-walled epidermal cells of *Actaea* berries, like parts of the spongy parenchyma of the pulp, contain a dark red pigment in varying concentrations. In the intact cytoplasm, the brightly translucent nucleus in the lumen of these cells is a prominent feature (**138**). In addition, the epidermis has stomata with large guard cells usually surrounded by eight subsidiary cells. Calcium oxalate is not present in the fruit.

138 Actaea spicata: Epidermis of the pericarp.

Adonis vernalis L.   Yellow Pheasant's-eye

139 Yellow Pheasant's-eye

10–30 cm high perennial herb with dark stout rhizomes and erect stems with scales at the base; on dry grassland, calcareous and sandy soils.
Leaves 2–4-pinnate, feathery with narrow linear lobes.
Flowers yellow, single, terminal, and erect; IV–V.
Fruits small, almost globose, wrinkled, with a hook-like beak.
Distribution: Central and south-eastern Europe; rare in parts of western Europe.

SPECIES of the genus *Adonis* have cardiotonic glycosides of the cardenolide type (p.27) which are poorly absorbed and show little tendency to accumulate. In *A. vernalis* adonitoxin is the principal component of a mixture containing about 20 glycosides; it is isomeric with convallatoxin and its aglycone is isomeric with k-strophanthidin. The total content when harvested is about 0.25%.

Poisoning is hardly likely and is not mentioned in the literature; see further under *Convallaria. A. vernalis,* a plant with constituents that are potentially cardiotoxic, is only included here for the sake of completeness (and also because it is the source of Adonis Herb, an official drug in the 8th edition of the German Pharmacopoeia).

Other *Adonis* species, like *A. aestivalis,* red-flowering summer pheasant's-eye, *A. autumnalis,* autumn pheasant's-eye, *A. flammea,* large pheasant's-eye, also contain cardiac glycosides, but in smaller amounts than *A. vernalis,* so that poisoning is even less likely.

RHAMNACEAE

Rhamnus frangula L.   Alder Buckthorn

140 Alder Buckthorn

Up to 4 m tall shrub or small tree, with smooth thornless branches and twigs; bark with long horizontal lenticels. Mostly on more or less damp nutrient-poor soils, on heaths and in undergrowth and forest communities.
Leaves broad-elliptic, cuspidate; predominantly entire, with 6(–11) prominent lateral veins.
Flowers greenish white, in several-flowered axillary cymes, not conspicuous; V–VI.
Fruits globose drupes, on ripening becoming first yellow-red and then black; usually fruits at different stages of maturity occurring together; VIII–IX.
Distribution: Throughout most of Europe except the extreme north and much of the Mediterranean; naturalised in North America.

ALDER buckthorn, like the closely related buckthorn, *Rhamnus catharticus* **(141),** and other *Rhamnus* species, contains strongly purgative anthracene glycosides that act on the large intestine. While the bark of the alder buckthorn is an important drug, and is included in the pharmacopoeias along with the American cascara bark from *R. purshiana,* it is more often the fruits of buckthorn (Fructus Rhamni Cathartici) that are used as a purgative. But the fruits of the alder buckthorn, especially the seeds, also have anthracene glycosides, including glucofrangulin, and these can bring about drastic purging – in animal experiments in some cases with fatal results [H3].

Gluc.~O   O   OH

Rham.~O   O

Glucofrangulin

buckthorn berries. On the other hand, in the statistics of the Toxicological Centres over a long period no serious cases of poisoning have been noted, but only cases of ingestion (possibly with slight symptoms) [K47]. With children who take only a few berries, parents certainly need not fear any threat to life; but the patient must nevertheless be kept under observation.

> **Treatment.** Emptying the stomach, administering activated charcoal; symptomatic measures, replacement of fluids and electrolytes.

In addition to anthracene glycosides, cyclopeptide alkaloids have also often been found in the Rhamnaceae [H35]. So far, however, little seems to be known about the toxicity of these substances. From the fruits of *Karwinskia humboldtiana*, which in America are known to be poisonous [H9], Arai *et al.* [A13] have isolated neurotoxic C_{15} polyphenols.

Microscopical characters of the fruits. The drupes of *Rhamnus* species have several characteristic features. Below the colourless epidermis with its shallow and radially thin-walled cells **(142a),** there is a hypodermis comprising several layers of distinctly larger cells which are coloured and almost collenchymatous **(142b).** Clusters of calcium oxalate occur in the chlorophyll-containing parenchyma of the pulp and in addition there are solitary crystals in the outer layer of the endocarp. Details of the transverse section of these fruits have been given by Esdorn (cited from [B24]).

141 Rhamnus catharticus L.   Buckthorn.

The fresh bark of buckthorn is known to be a particularly strong laxative, which can cause nausea and lead to intestinal colic. The explanation put forward is the predominance of reduced anthrone/anthranol derivatives, in part also dianthrones, which have a strong irritant action on the skin and mucous membranes. Although the fruits have not been examined, it may be assumed that the situation will be much the same. The fruits of alder buckthorn, buckthorn, and other *Rhamnus* species thus cannot be considered as harmless. This is confirmed by the report of Banach [B5] concerning the deaths of two children (aged 20 months and 3 years) after eating

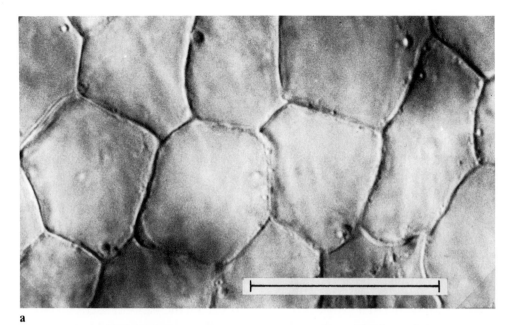

a

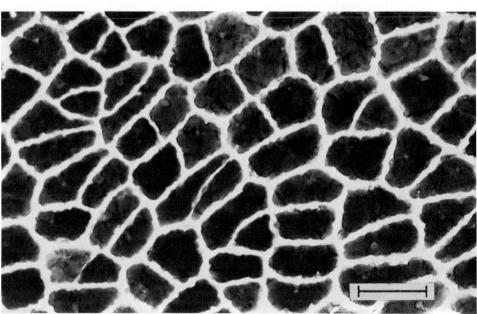

b

142 Pericarp of Rhamnus fruits: (a) Epidermis of R. frangula. (b) Hypodermis of
R. catharticus.

ROSACEAE

THE **Rose family** occurs worldwide, especially in the northern temperate zone, and comprises more than 3000 species of herbs, shrubs, and trees. Among them are more than 100 species in western and central parts of Europe. Owing to their conspicuous flowers and great variety of fruits with edible pulp, many Rosaceae are ornamental and useful (fruit) plants, while others because of their accumulation of tannin (a characteristic of the family) are sources of useful drugs.

The **toxicological significance** lies particularly in the wide occurrence of **cyanogenic glycosides** (p.26 and [M37]), which appear to be absent only in the subfamily Rosoideae. **Prunasin** [D-(–)-mandelonitrile β-D-glucoside; racemate: prulaurasin] dominates in the vegetative organs and **amygdalin** [D-(–)-mandelonitrile β-D-gentiobioside] is found exclusively in the seeds.

The reactions which lead to the liberation of hydrocyanic acid are: (a) glycosidic hydrolysis, and (b) decomposition of the α-hydroxynitriles (cyanhydrins) formed to give a carbonyl compound and free hydrocyanic acid.

These reactions take place under suitable conditions of pH with or without participation of enzymes (β-glucosidases, lyases) already present in the plant material and that after disruption of the tissue structure come into contact with their substrate.

However, cyanogenic glycosides when taken orally are not as a rule under optimal conditions for the liberation of HCN – neither in the stomach (too acid) nor in the small intestine (too alkaline). Moreover, the body's own detoxification mechanisms are able to convert *ca* 30–60 mg CN^-/hour into the much less toxic thiocyanate. Hence, concentrations of hydrocyanic acid that are dangerous to the human organism can only be reached after massive ingestion of those plant parts which have a high content of cyanogenic compounds. According to [C21] the lethal dose after oral administration lies between 0.5 and 3.5 mg HCN/kg body weight.

This, it is true, can be attained with the vegetative organs of a number of Rosaceae, e.g. leaves of the cherry laurel (p.193), but these are hardly attractive to eat. Thus, potentially poisonous plants are those representatives which contain high concentrations of cyanogenic glycosides in their seeds. In this connection, a group of *Prunus* species merits particular mention (p.195), and also some genera of the subfamily Maloideae (p.190) even though the amygdalin content of the seeds is lower. Such compounds are entirely absent from the seeds of the Spiroideae.

It has long been known in the case of bitter almonds that the strong bitter taste of the cyanogenic glycosides is an effective protection against taking potentially dangerous amounts of seeds – at any rate, as long as there is no genetically caused defect in the ability to taste bitterness. Hence, in the more recent literature there are only occasional reports of dangerous poisonings with bitter almonds, apricot stones, and apple pips, or the seeds of the choke cherry, *Prunus virginiana;* nevertheless, among them there are some fatal cases. Mostly, the ingestion of cyanogenic fruits or seeds gives rise to only slight gastro-intestinal symptoms; dramatic pictures of poisoning with pure hydrocyanic acid as described in many popular-scientific books, e.g. in connection with *Cotoneaster* fruits [N11], are entirely out of place.

While on the subject, a dangerous source of HCN poisoning may be pointed out here: the much praised (but also much disputed) preparation for cancer therapy 'laetrile' [F25; G15], made from apricot or peach kernels, contains a high concentration of amygdalin* and in America has already led to a number of serious cases of poisoning. Moreover, the innocent-sounding name 'vitamin B_{17}' for amygdalin, which has been used in connection with certain preparations, is quite misleading. In one case [H61] where the father of an 11-month old girl, believing his 'vitamin' tablets to be harmless, simply kept them in a vial together with a collection of other vitamin tablets, this had tragic consequences and the child died after accidentally ingesting some of them.

Liberation of HCN by glycosidic hydrolysis

---

* According to the investigations of Nahrstedt [N4], the indication that it contains mandelonitrile β-glucuronidate is incorrect.

When using linseed in the ordinary way as a laxative and for 'looking after the bowels', the cyanogenic glycoside content – *ca* 0.3%, linamarin and lotaustralin – is no cause for worry; see the data of Schilcher [S16] relating to the liberation of HCN and detoxification by the body. From a veterinary point of view, however, there are reservations as regards the feeding of large quantities of linseed press cake.

Symptoms of sub-lethal HCN poisoning. Headaches and a feeling of dizziness, local irritation of the mucous membranes, salivation, also nausea and vomiting (the vomit smelling of bitter almonds), pink skin colour, dyspnoea, and unconsciousness are among the symptoms; cf. [V6].

Although as already mentioned the dangers of HCN poisoning on ingestion of plant materials rich in cyanogenic glycosides are slight, a few pointers regarding the treatment are given in the following paragraphs. Basically, it is true to say that the earlier the antidote is given, the better the prognosis [F25]. CN⁻ ions block cellular respiration by attaching themselves to cyto-

---

Treatment. Direct removal of the poison by bringing about vomiting or by gastric lavage (if necessary, with potassium permanganate); administration of activated charcoal. As first aid in mild cases, inhaling amyl nitrite (ampoules); according to [A28], in serious cases Kelocyanor®, 1–2 ampoules i.v., is the remedy of choice. Further, 4-dimethylaminophenol (4-DMAP) and sodium thiosulphate.

---

chrome oxidase. Hence, substances are in use as antidotes which effectively bind the CN⁻ ions by complex formation or which speed up the body's own detoxification mechanisms (conversion of CN⁻ to thiocyanate).

The most important antidote of the complex-forming type is cobalt EDTA (ethylenediamine-tetraacetic acid) = Kelocyanor®. Since methaemoglobin binds CN⁻ ions more strongly than does cytochrome oxidase, compounds which form methaemoglobin are also used as antidotes, but

cannot be applied repeatedly (excessive methaemoglobin formation). Besides amyl nitrite, of this group 4-DMAP may be mentioned; according to [S36] it is to be preferred to complexing agents because it has less side-effects on the circulation and its action begins more rapidly.

The body's own system of detoxification is accelerated by S-donors; and sodium thiosulphate (6–10 ampoules i.v.) is used as an antidote.

Frankenberg [F20] has recently published the results of animal experiments on the injection of rhodanase (a thiosulphate : cyanide sulphur transferase) in order to augment the effect of S-donors as antidotes.

As indicated at the beginning, **tannins** of different kinds are widespread in the Rosaceae. Fruits, especially when unripe, may have an astringent action and because of this may occasionally be the cause of – mostly harmless – gastro-intestinal symptoms. In the stomach contents of a child that had eaten 'unknown berries' and had been taken to hospital we were only able to detect (mainly unripe) brambles.

Cotoneaster horizontalis Decne. Wall Cotoneaster

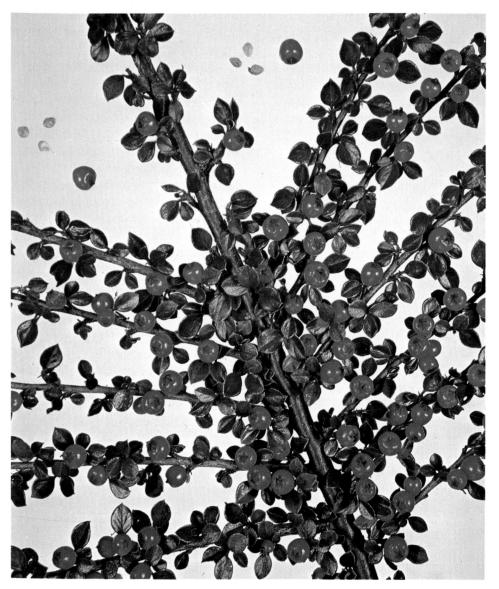

THE genus *Cotoneaster* has numerous species, the majority of which come from the Himalayas and the rest from other mountain ranges in Asia, Europe, and North Africa. They are almost all **shrubs** (rarely small trees) with extensively ramified, non-thorny, erect or prostrate branches.

The **leaves** are deciduous (rarely lasting), undivided and entire, with narrow-lanceolate stipules, often arranged distichously.

The rather small **flowers** are either solitary or in many-flowered racemes (also panicles) and are usually terminal on short lateral shoots; the petals are white to pink.

The **fruits** are small fleshy pomes with 2–5 (rarely one) stones (pyrenes) surrounded by a mealy flesh and they have a red or sometimes blackish skin.

Many species and cultivated forms of cotoneaster are popular ornamentals, partly as ground cover, in parks and gardens.

The interest in the genus in the present context is because all its species are cyanogenic. Investigations reported so far show that the cyanogenic glycoside prunasin occurs in the bark, leaves, and flowers, while prunasin and also amygdalin have been detected in the fruits [N2]. It appears that the cyanogenic glycosides – unlike those in *Prunus* species – are localised chiefly in the fleshy part rather than the stones; but it has to be remembered that the type of fruit in the two genera is not the same.

On the whole, the glycoside content in the vegetative organs is greater than in the fruit, but, as far as toxicological information work is concerned, only the conspicuous red fruits* are involved since they often remain on the plant far into the winter and so it is not only birds that they attract.

There are only two recent studies on the cyanogenic glycoside content of *Cotoneaster* fruits [N2; T12] and, as Tables 10 and 11 show, there are considerable differences between one species and another.

If it is accepted that more than 20 mg HCN/100 g (= 200 ppm = 0.02%) fresh material is potentially dangerous [K29; S43; S44], then most of the values determined lie well below that figure.

---

* *Cotoneaster* species with dark-coloured fruits;
  C. acutifolius: fruit ellipsoid, black with 2 stones;
  C. lucidus: fruit purple-black, with 3 stones;
  C. niger: fruit ovoid-oblong, black-red, glaucous, with 3 stones;
  C. nitens: fruit after a long time red, later purple-black, mostly with 2 stones;
  C. insignis: fruit black, with a bluish bloom, almost globose, with 1–2 stones.

Nahrstedt [N2] likewise found greatly differing HCN values in six species, which also depended on the degree of ripeness of the fruits (Table 10).

In order to determine the toxicity of *C. divaricatus,* Tidwell *et al.* [T12] also carried out animal experiments. Neither 6 g dried fruit material/kg body weight in the cat nor 10 g fresh material/kg in the dog caused toxic symptoms. 0.5 g/kg in the rat proved to be non-toxic; the ED_{50} was about 3 g/kg body weight.

Extrapolating from the non-toxic dose, for a child weighing 15 kg about 80 fruits can still be considered as a non-poisonous dose.

The results are thus largely in agreement with the data furnished by the various Toxicological Information Centres, according to which *Cotoneaster* fruits are often the subject of enquiries but are very rarely the origin of serious poisoning [K47; S38]. Nevertheless, along with Hegnauer [H35], it must be said that the findings regarding the extent of cyanogenesis obtained with fruits from only a few species of *Cotoneaster* cannot be considered as being valid for the genus as a whole.

144 **Cotoneaster insignis Pojark.**

Table 10. Cyanide content of *Cotoneaster* fruits (from [N2]).

Species	Harvested	Ppm Dry Weight
C. hybridus	July	185
C. integerrimus	July	15
C. congestus	July	1350
C. praecox	July	1772
C. bullatus	September	18
C. dielsianus	September	15

The **symptoms** of hydrocyanic-acid poisoning (p.187), even after eating large amounts of *Cotoneaster* fruits, are certainly only to be expected in a mild form; special **treatment,** as discussed for HCN poisoning on p.187, is probably superfluous.

145 Amelanchier lamarckii Schroeder.   Juneberry.

Appendix: In the Maloideae, to which *Cotoneaster* and *Pyracantha* both belong, cyanogenesis is not observed throughout the subfamily. Hegnauer [H35] sketches the following picture:

Crataegus, Hawthorn
Mespilus, Medlar
Pyrus, Pear

↓

No cyanogenic glycosides

Amelanchier, Juneberry
Chaenomeles, Ornamental Quince
Cydonia, Quince
Sorbus, Whitebeam, Rowan,
    Service-tree

↓

Cyanogenic glycosides in leaves and seeds, in some cases only small amounts

Malus, Apple

↓

Amygdalin in the seeds

That apple pips can be a 'deadly poison' is proved by the following often cited case [L20]:

'*A man who enjoyed apple seeds saved a cupful of them, which he proceeded to eat all at once; he died of cyanide poisoning. Therefore, do not eat large quantities of apple seeds, but enjoy the rest of the apple!*'

Table 11. HCN content of fruits of *Cotoneaster* species (from [T21]).

Species	Ppm	
	Fresh Weight	Dry Weight
C. adpressus	5.3	14.0
C. apiculatus	8.8	15.9
C. divaricatus	10.0	18.0
C. horizontalis	12.0	24.0
C.lucidus	1.6	6.2
C. racemiflorus	10.0	26.0
C. zabelii	15.0	60.0
C. roseus	2.3	4.8

Microscopical characters of the fruits. The fruits of the numerous *Cotoneaster* species are understandably very similar to each other in their anatomical structure, and they are even difficult to distinguish from those of closely related genera such as *Pyracantha* and *Crataegus* on the basis of their microscopical characters. As with many Rosaceae fruits, their more or less thin-walled epidermal cells exhibit a 'window-like' pattern (see footnote on p.62) **(146a)** and only in the regularly occurring epidermal idioblasts **(146c)** is there typical thickening. Stomata are more frequent on the upper part of the fruit near the remains of the sepals; the guard cells in *Cotoneaster* **(146b)** and *Crataegus* are more oblong than those present in *Pyracantha*. Although the fruits of *Cotoneaster* and *Pyracantha* vary considerably in the density of their pubescence, in both genera it comprises unicellular trichomes with the same 'crook' shape **(146d)**. In the pulp there are calcium oxalate clusters and prismatic crystals of similar size (*ca* 25μm) and, especially in *Crataegus*, stone cells arranged singly or in groups.

a

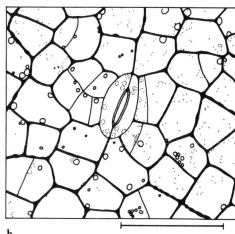

b

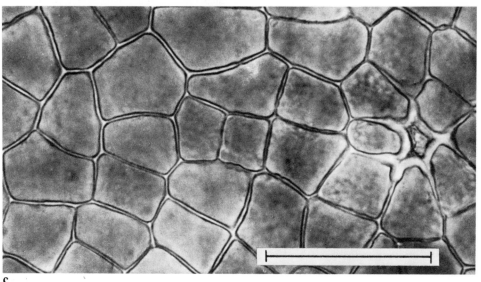

c

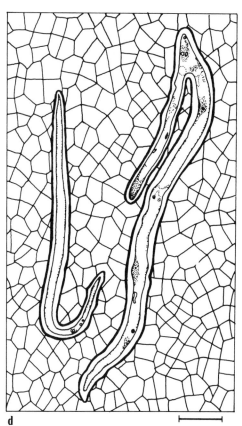

d

146 Epidermis of the pericarp in: (a) Cotoneaster bullatus. (b) C. dammeri. (c) Pyracantha coccinea. (d) C. congestus, with characteristic crook-shaped trichomes.

Pyracantha coccinea M.J. Roemer   Firethorn

147   Firethorn

Up to 3 m tall shrub with spreading, closely set branches and short shoots with thorns.
<u>Leaves</u> evergreen, elliptic to lanceolate, finely toothed, with a dark green glossy upper surface and lighter lower surface; some pubescence, but only when young.
<u>Flowers</u> white, in dense, up to 4 cm broad, compound corymbs; V–VI.
<u>Fruits</u> small bright red (occasionally also yellowish) pomes with 5 stones (pyrenes) and adhering calyx; remaining long on the shrub; VIII–XII or longer.
<u>Distribution:</u> Originally in Italy to western Asia. Popular ornamental in western and central Europe; available in many forms and planted either singly or as a light hedge; sometimes an escape.

THE characters of the firethorn are intermediate between those of *Cotoneaster* and *Crataegus* and the plant has in the past been referred to both these genera (as *Cotoneaster pyracantha* or *Crataegus pyracantha*). Phytochemically, it is distinguished from *Cotoneaster* by the presence of non-cyanogenic vegetative organs (leaves, twigs) and from *Crataegus* by the presence of cyanogenic seeds [H35]. However, the content of cyanogenic glycosides appears to be low [P22]. It is hoped later to be able to furnish more accurate data on this point.

The indications regarding the **symptoms** and **treatment** of poisoning with cyanogenic plant materials (p.187) are probably not important as far as firethorn fruits are concerned.

Enquiries about firethorn loom large in the statistics of the Toxicological Information Centres [K47; S38]. Up until now, however, only mild gastro-intestinal symptoms have been observed, and never more serious consequences.

Microscopical characters of the fruit. The microscopical characters of the firethorn fruit correspond in essential details with those of *Cotoneaster*.

Prunus laurocerasus L.   Cherry Laurel

148 Cherry Laurel

2–4(–8) m tall shrub, in warmer climates a small tree, erect or growing laterally. <u>Leaves</u> evergreen, thick and leathery, glabrous and glossy, upper surface dark green, lower surface pale green, with slightly revolute margin, entire or slightly toothed, very variable in length, width, and shape; glands usually present on the lower surface near the petiole. <u>Flowers</u> white, *ca* 8 mm broad, in dense erect many-flowered racemes; V, often flowering again in autumn. <u>Fruits</u> first red, then black, ovoid, slightly narrower towards the top; seeds with smooth surface, swollen longitudinally and tapering towards the top; VIII–X. <u>Distribution:</u> Indigenous in south-eastern Europe and Asia Minor to the Caucasus. As a cultivated shrub brought via northern Italy and Switzerland to central (and western) Europe, where it is planted as a popular, but not always winter-hard, ornamental; in gardens, parks, and cemeteries; many cultivated forms, sometimes an escape.

THE cherry laurel contains in both the vegetative organs, especially the leaves, and the seeds a considerable amount of cyanogenic glycosides. Fresh leaves have *ca* 1–1.5% prunasin.* Their toxicity has long been recognised, and cases of poisoning were first described in 1728 [H34]. Since the thick leathery leaves are no incitement to consumption (except perhaps to crush them and enjoy the bitter-almond smell), they are not the subject of toxicological enquires. The position is quite different with regard to the fruits,

which, because of their appearance and unobjectionable taste, are often tried. Contradictory statements relating to the toxicity of the cherry laurel are encountered, but these can probably be explained as follows: The content of cyanogenic glycosides in the fruit pulp is very low (our experiments do not agree with other reports of their complete absence). In the seeds, on the other hand, there is a considerable quantity of amygdalin, which can be detected, after crushing, by the strong bitter-almond smell and also microchemically. Nothing can be said about the amount present, since there are no quantitative data in the literature. As long as the seeds are spat out or swallowed whole, there is,

as a rule, little fear of serious poisoning as a result of eating the fruits. This is confirmed by the experience of the various Toxicological Information Centres, so that the sensational reports emerging from time to time in the press about cherry-laurel poisoning are completely without foundation.*

---

* According to the Swiss Pharmacopoeia, which has the fresh leaves as starting material for the preparation of *Aqua Laurocerasi*, cherry-laurel water, the minimum HCN content should be 0.15%.

---

* For example, in the *Bildzeitung* dated 31.8.76: Children poisoned nibbling at the 'cherries' on a shrub!. . . Eleven children hovered between life and death: they had been nibbling the highly poisonous berries of the oriental 'cherry laurel' . . . by evening 11 children lay in hospital. They all had their stomach pumped out and all were saved. A doctor said: 'Only two hours later and some of the children would have been dead!'. . .

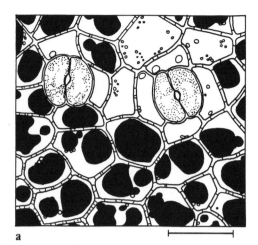

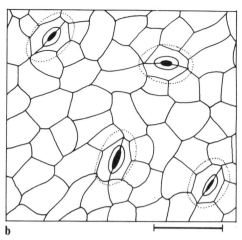

149 Epidermis of the pericarp of:
(a) Prunus laurocerasus, and
(b) P. virginiana.

Serious **symptoms** (p.187) are thus only to be expected after ingesting chewed seeds; in appropriate cases, the **treatment** indicated on p.187 should be applied.

Microscopical characters of the fruits.
The drupes of the cherry laurel, as well as the distinctly smaller ones of other kinds of cherry tree which have them in racemes *(P. padus, P. serotina, P. virginiana)*, have similar microscopical features. The epidermis has numerous stomata **(149b)** whose guard cells are in part at or below the level of the epidermis. The epidermal cells are usually thin-walled, less often beaded *(P. serotina)*, and they show little of the 'window-like' pattern (see the footnote on p.62) usual with other Rosaceae that arises through secondary division. The anthocyanin pigments are confined almost entirely to the epidermis **(149a)** and peripheral layers of the pulp. Calcium oxalate occurs as clusters and prisms *(ca* 25 μm), but in *P. laurocerasus* they are rather larger (35–60 μm) and are present in cells which are noticeably smaller than the surrounding parenchyma.

150 Prunus serotina Ehrh.   Wild Black Cherry.

Other Prunus species. Almost all representatives of the genus contain cyanogenic glycosides. However, the way in which and the extent to which the glycosides are accumulated varies considerably. Of the numerous species, only those in which large amounts of amygdalin are stored in the seeds are of toxicological interest, especially [H3]:

Prunus armeniaca, apricot: up to 8% amygdalin (seeds);
Prunus domestica, plum, damson: up to 2.5% amygdalin (seeds);
Prunus dulcis var. *amara,* bitter almond: up to 5% amygdalin (seeds);
Prunus persica, peach: up to 6% amygdalin (seeds).

Prunus armeniaca: Sayre and Kaymakgalan [S9] have reported on poisoning by apricot stones in children. Their analyses of wild and cultivated apricots showed high CN⁻ values (>200 mg HCN/100 g fresh seeds) only for the seeds of the wild forms; the amygdalin content of the seeds from cultivated forms, which in any case do not taste bitter, was low. Stoewsand *et al.* [S86] obtained similar results: cultivars with sweet seeds had only 11.7 mg CN⁻/100 g, while those with bitter-tasting seeds had values in the range 130–180 mg CN⁻/100 g.

A case of serious poisoning by hydrocyanic acid after eating 20–40 apricot stones has been published by Rubino and Davidoff [R27]. In the blood of the woman, admitted to the casualty department of the hospital and only saved through intensive care, a cyanide value of 3.2 mg/l was determined (values above 1 mg/l are considered to be highly toxic).

151 *Prunus dulcis:* Barrel-shaped cells from the epidermis of the seed testa (<200 μm).

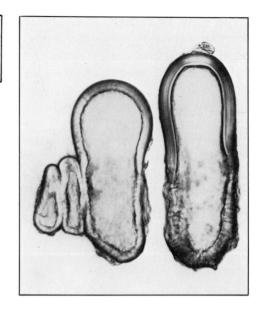

About the 'cancer drug' laetrile, prepared from apricot or peach stones, see p.186.

Prunus dulcis var. *amara:* The poisonousness of bitter almonds does not appear to be generally known. According to Klöver and Wenderoth [K33], it was familiar to only 16 out of 100 housewives; however, as already mentioned, the bitter taste as a rule prevents the consumption of large amounts (but cf. [K33]).

For children about 10, and for adults about 60, bitter almonds are considered to be the lethal dose, provided they are taken quickly in one go and conditions for the liberation of HCN in the gastro-intestinal tract are optimal. That such a combination of circumstances can arise is shown by a case of fatal poisoning described some time ago by Pack *et al.* [P2]. Apart from the typical 'bitter-almond smell', the presence of bitter almonds in the stomach contents of the dead person could be demonstrated microscopically: the conspicuous barrel-shaped cells of the epidermis of the testa (**151**) are a characteristic feature that allows an unequivocal proof of the presence of the almonds.

Two three-year olds were hospitalised after eating several seeds (in one case 10 and in the other a 'handful'; with spontaneous vomiting) in a state of confusion, looking grey, and tending to go into convulsions; sodium thiosulphate as antidote soon made the symptoms of poisoning disappear [K45].

Prunus persica: According to the investigations of Machel and Dorsett [M1] notable amounts of HCN (*ca* 45 mg/100 g fresh weight) can only be detected in seeds freshly removed from their shells. In contrast with earlier indications, cyanogenic glycosides are not present in the pulp.

The seeds of various other cherry species are also rich in amygdalin, e.g. *Prunus padus,* bird cherry, occurring in Europe, *P. serotina,* wild black cherry, and *P. virginiana,* choke cherry, American species which are also planted in Europe. Eating a few fruits of these is probably quite harmless, as long as the seeds are not chewed.

Poisoning with choke cherry seeds, from *P. virginiana* or *P. melanocarpa,* has been reported by Pijoan [P34]. Lewis and Elvin-Lewis [L20] mention *P. serotina* as 'the most dangerous of the eastern cherries' (of North America). Teratogenic effects of *P. serotina* leaves and bark on pregnant sows have been observed by Selby *et al.* [S64].

Finally, it is to be noted that the seeds of fruits which have stones are frequently used to produce a welcome improvement in the aroma of the corresponding alcoholic beverage (cherry brandy; sloe gin). It is possible that the copious enjoyment of such spirits could lead to a combination of alcoholic and (mild) HCN poisoning.

152 Prunus spinosa L.   Blackthorn, Sloe.

Sorbus aucuparia L.   Rowan, Mountain Ash

153 Rowan

Moderate-sized tree, rarely more than 15 m in height, with lax crown. Trunk bark light grey, smooth, glossy, later with longitudinal fissures; winter buds downy. Widespread from the lowlands to beyond the forest limit; soil requirements minimal.

<u>Leaves</u> up to 20 cm long, imparipinnate, with 9–15 oblong-lanceolate sessile leaflets having a serrate or dentate margin; upper surface sparsely, lighter lower surface more strongly, pubescent; autumn colour red.

<u>Flowers</u> white, with receptacle, in many-flowered compound corymbs; V–VII.

<u>Fruits</u> globose pomes formed from 2–5 (mostly 3) carpels, scarlet, usually with 3 oblong pointed reddish pips; VIII–X.

<u>Distribution:</u> Throughout most of Europe; frequently planted along avenues and streets (also in regions at higher altitudes). Often cultivated in North America.

R OWAN fruits are made into jam, jelly, or fruit juice and they have also long played a part in folk medicine as an anti-diarrhoeic, diuretic, emmenagogue, and source of vitamin C. On the other hand, the fresh fruits are considered to be poisonous. From the statistics of the Toxicological Information Centres it is evident that on eating rowan berries only mild symptoms occur, and, compared with the considerable number of calls for information or advice, not necessarily very often [K47; cf. also Tables 1 and 2].

Reviewing the constituents so far found in rowan berries, sorbitol and other saccharides, organic acids and vitamin C (60–110 mg/100 g), tannins, colouring matters, and bitter substances, as well as other ubiquitous substances, cannot be looked upon as poisons. The same is true of the very small amount of amygdalin that occurs in the seeds.

On the other hand, **parasorbic acid,** a characteristic constituent of the berries, is toxic. It is an unsaturated lactone which on hydrolysis gives a 2,4-hexadienoic acid, sorbic acid. The parasorbic acid occurs in the fruits in the form of a glycoside, parasorboside. While sorbic acid is a non-toxic substance and a permitted preservative in foodstuffs, parasorbic acid has local irritant properties, e.g. on the mucosa of the gastro-intestinal tract, that can lead to salivation, vomiting, and gastro-enteritis. Carcinogenic activity is also ascribed to it, which can indeed be demonstrated on subcutaneous injection of large doses but not on oral administration [14]. The toxic action of parasorbic acid is first manifested at high dosage levels: the LD_{50} in mice is

Parasorbic acid   Sorbic acid

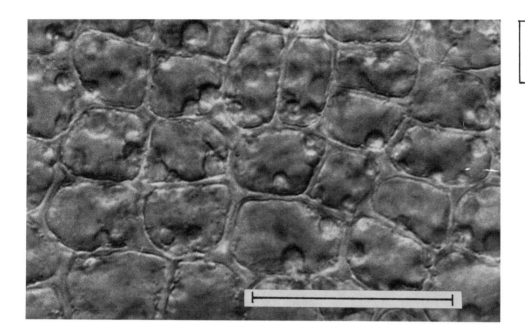

154 Sorbus aucuparia: Epidermis of the pericarp.

750 mg/kg. Since in the pulp of rowan berries there is only 0.02–0.2% [L10], on average 0.04%, of the compound,* it would need about 90 kg (!) of the berries to reach the lethal dose for a live weight of 50 kg. On drying or boiling the fruits, the parasorbic acid, a volatile, oily liquid at room temperature, is largely destroyed or removed.

---

* Diemair and Franzen [D1] found that the parasorbic acid content goes on rising until the fruits are ripe: while the content in the unripe green fruits was 130 mg/100 g dry weight, just before the fruits were fully ripe they had 870 mg/100 g dry weight, corresponding to 200 mg/100 g fresh fruits.

Summarising, it can be said that on eating fresh rowan berries, **mild gastro-intestinal troubles** can occur, which at worst are likely to need only symptomatic treatment.

Microscopical characters of the fruit. The epidermal cells **(154)** of *Sorbus aucuparia* fruits are slightly but irregularly thickened. Stomata are rare; their guard cells bulge and are surrounded by 9–10 subsidiary cells. In the large-sized parenchyma of the pulp, which contains yellow-red chromoplasts and calcium oxalate clusters (*ca* 20 μm), sclereids with thickened, strongly pitted walls occur singly or in groups. For further characters, especially of the testa, see [C27].

The fruits of many other *Sorbus* species (e.g. *S. torminalis,* wild service-tree; *S. aria,* common whitebeam; *S. domestica,* service-tree; and also *S. koehneana* and *S. prattii* (both with white fruits)) are probably usually harmless and at most likely to give rise to slight gastro-intestinal symptoms; some are also described as being edible.

SCROPHULARIACEAE

Digitalis purpurea L.   Foxglove

155 Foxglove

0.4–1.5 m tall biennial herb with a
rosette of leaves in the first year and an
erect unbranched stem in the second
year. Found in open places in forests and
in clear-felling vegetation on sandy loam;
avoids chalk.
<u>Leaves</u> ovate, crenate, lower surface
greyish tomentose; lower leaves
long-petiolate and broad, upper ones
short-petiolate or sessile and narrower.
<u>Flowers</u> in terminal often one-sided
racemes; corolla cylindrical-
campanulate, purple, rarely white,
inside with red spots; VI–VIII.
<u>Fruits</u> ovoid green capsules, bilocular,
dehiscing on two sides, many small seeds.
<u>Distribution:</u> Frequent in western
Europe, absent in the north and south-
east; often planted in gardens.

VARIOUS members of the **Figwort family** are considered to be poisonous because of the presence of aucubin-type iridoids, e.g. *Melampyrum* and *Rhinanthus* species, the seeds of which used to be found as toxic contaminants in bread cereals. However, apart from *Gratiola*, foxglove is the only significantly poisonous genus in the family.

The toxicity of *Gratiola officinalis*, long recognised as a poisonous plant, is not due, as was at one time thought, to the presence of cardiac glycosides (gratiotoxin) but rather to the occurrence of the cucurbitacin glycoside elatericide [M64]. The plant does not appear in the poisoning statistics.

Digitoxin

Because of their cardiotonic glycosides (p.27), the foxglove and the woolly foxglove, *D. lanata*, which originates from south-eastern Europe but is also cultivated, are important medicinal plants. Since these compounds are highly active glycosides with a low therapeutic index, poisoning is quite often observed after medicinal overdosage – according to extensive statistics, between 8 and 20% [L6]; see also the recent review by Kuhlmann [K54].

That the foxglove is encountered as a poisonous plant is due to its popularity as a garden ornamental. Although 2–3 dried leaves is stated to be a lethal dose [M50], serious cases of poisoning are fortunately rare, since firstly the intense bitter taste normally deters people from consuming large amounts of plant material and secondly after taking *Digitalis* spontaneous

vomiting usually takes place, so that absorption of large amounts of glycosides is prevented.

These protective mechanisms do not always work, as is evident from two recently described cases of poisoning. In both cases, elderly people, not knowing anything about the plant, had prepared a tea from foxglove leaves. While an elderly married couple died [C22; L16], an 85-year old man survived, even though after being admitted to hospital he was found to have a serum digitoxin value of more than 50 ng/ml [D9].

'*Throughout his life the man had generally avoided medical care and relied on home remedies. His wife had regularly concocted herbal teas from leaves found in their backyard without problems for many years. However, on the day of admission his wife had felt ill and he himself had picked some leaves from an unfamiliar plant (later identified as* D. purpurea). *He had made a tea with them and had drunk a cup, even although it had an unusually bitter taste.*'

Corrigal *et al.* [C23], as well as Barnikol and Hofmann [B13], have reported on the poisoning of animals with *Digitalis* leaves. In the latter case, 50–100 g of *D. lanata* had accidentally got into some pig mast from a drying installation and had caused the death of five animals. The lethal dose for a 50 kg sucking pig was found to be 4–5 g leaf material.

Symptoms of Digitalis poisoning are in the early stages dizziness and vomiting (which can last for days), followed later by cardiac arrhythmias of various kinds – often changing very rapidly – as well as central symptoms such as disturbances of vision, delirium, or hallucinations.

Treatment. If it has not already occurred spontaneously, vomiting should be elicited; and gastric lavage should be carried out with activated charcoal.

In order to assess the severity of the poisoning, it is important to determine the serum potassium level: >5 mmol/l indicates a dangerous degree of poisoning. With serious cases: cholestyramine (3 × 4 g daily) should be administered to interrupt the enterohepatic circulation of the digitoxin. In addition, secondary elimination of the poison by haemoperfusion, perhaps through selective removal by antibodies adsorbed on charcoal, can be undertaken. When they are injected as Fab fragments, this latter technique also offers the possibility of a specific and effective detoxification [L6].

The further medical treatment for dealing with the cardiac complications (electrode-catheter; atropine; lidocaine or phenytoin, etc.) cannot be dealt with here.

SOLANACEAE

PLANTS of the **Nightshade family** have been of particular interest to man since olden times, as poisonous or medicinal plants (mandrake, deadly nightshade, henbane), as important sources of food (aubergine, potato, tomato), as spices (paprika), or for enjoyment (tobacco, thorn-apple) [H37].

The following brief overview gives the systematic positions of the most important genera together with the pharmacologically significant part of the plant:

I	**Nicandreae:**		*Nicandra* (berries)
II	**Solaneae:**	(a) Lyciinae	*Atropa, Lycium* (berries)
		(b) Hyoscyaminae	*Hyoscyamus, Scopolia* (capsules)
		(c) Solaninae	*Lycopersicon, Physalis, Solanum* (berries)
		(d) Mandragorinae	*Mandragora* (berries)
III	**Datureae:**		*Datura* (capsules)
IV	**Cestreae:**	(a) Cestrinae	*Cestrum* (berries)
		(b) Nicotianinae	*Nicotiana* (capsules)

Major diagnostic features of these mostly herbaceous to woody plants are the arrangement of the conducting tissues in bicollateral vascular bundles in the shoots, greatly differing forms of pubescence [R15], and the wide-spread accumulation of calcium oxalate (often in idioblasts) as single crystals, clusters, or crystal sand.

Toxic constituents. Phytochemically, the Solanaceae are characterised by the occurrence of numerous alkaloids. In the first place, there are the long-known **ester alkaloids of the tropane group.** L-Hyoscyamine is the principal alkaloid in the genera *Atropa, Datura,* and *Hyoscyamus.* During drying of the plant material it is partly converted through racemisation of the acid component into the optically inactive atropine (= DL-hyoscyamine). In the roots of *Mandragora* and the leaves of *Scopolia,* on the other hand, the predominant base is scopolamine.

Both alkaloids have similar parasympatholytic properties (restricting the activity of the salivary, sweat, and bronchial glands; inhibition of gastro-intestinal motility; relaxation of hollow organs such as the gall and urinary bladders and the uterus). Besides these peripheral actions, which in essence are brought about only by the L-forms of the compounds, there are varied effects on the central nervous system. Whereas hyoscyamine in higher doses stimulates the cerebral cortex, scopolamine even in small doses is a motor depressant and at higher doses produces twilight sleep.

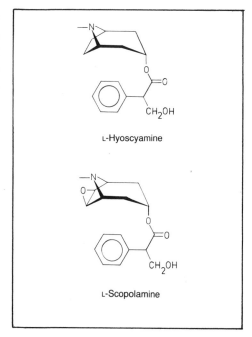

L-Hyoscyamine

L-Scopolamine

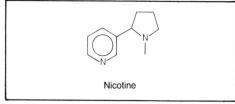

Nicotine

Formation of **alkaloids of the nicotine group** follows part of the same biosynthetic pathway, but their pharmacology is quite different. In the present context, only nicotine is of interest, and in spite of its wide occurrence in the plant kingdom it is only in the leaves of *Nicotiana* species that it accumulates in large quantities (up to 9%). Nicotine acts on the vegetative ganglia initially as a stimulant (increase in blood pressure and gastro-intestinal tone, etc.) and subsequently as a blocker (convulsions, respiratory paralysis). It acts extremely rapidly after being absorbed through the skin, through inhalation, or orally. Taking a concentrated solution can lead to death within a few minutes. Owing to its ready availability in plant protection products (concentrates with up to 90%) and as tobacco products (2–3 cigarettes contain 40–60 mg, the lethal dose for an adult), the alkaloid has often been used to commit suicide. The Hungarian State Institute for Forensic Chemistry in the space of only nine years investigated 300 fatal cases due to nicotine [G27]. It is impossible to estimate the enormous

μ-Solanine

Gluc.
Rham. ⎞Galact.~O⎞

damage arising from the chronic misuse of tobacco and other nicotine-containing luxury products.

Solanines, solanum alkaloids, steroidal alkaloid glycosides, or basic saponins are names under which a group of glycosides has become known whose aglycones (alkamines) belong to the cholestane series (C_{27} steroids). So far, these compounds have been unequivocally detected in the genera *Lycopersicon* and *Solanum*, as well as in *Cestrum parquii*.

Compared with the alkaloid groups already discussed, the toxicity of the solanines is very much less, since when taken by mouth they are only absorbed with difficulty and they are hydrolysed in the gastro-intestinal tract to the less toxic alkamines. On parenteral

Soladulcidine

administration they show effects similar to those exhibited by the cardioactive k-strophanthoside and cause death through paralysis of the central nervous system [N13]. Furthermore, in animal experiments Keeler *et al.* [K17] have been able to demonstrate that, depending on their substituents and configuration, substances of this group have teratogenic activity.

In addition to the accumulation of calcium as oxalate already mentioned, *Solanum* species are able to store considerable quantities of **nitrate** – up to 10% of the dry weight – according to the extent of manuring, the amount of light, and the temperature. Thus, after feeding on potato tops and black nightshade, many fatalities among cattle and sheep could be explained as being due without doubt to nitrate-nitrite poisoning [B23; L22]. On the other hand, the extensive economic damage to the cattle stock of the Argentine can be traced to a quite different toxic principle in *Solanum malacoxylon*. This plant contains a water-soluble steroidal glycoside that is hydrolysed *in vivo* to **1,25-dihydroxycholecalciferol**, a compound having a very much higher biological activity than vitamin D_3. The disease is like D_3-hypervitaminosis and brings about calcification of the heart, liver, and lungs [B14; H27; L30; O8; P45; P46]. Analogous conditions are caused in Florida by *Cestrum diurnum*, day-blooming jessamine, and in the Bavarian Alps by *Trisetum flavescens* (Gramineae), yellow oat-grass [K8; K16; W7].

Atropa bella-donna L.   Deadly Nightshade

156 Deadly Nightshade

0.5–1.5 m tall perennial herb with erect stems and spreading branches.
In clear-cut areas, in sparse forests, at the edges of woods, on nutrient-rich, usually calcareous, loam.
<u>Leaves</u> paired, always one large and one small together, laminae decurrent, petioles short, ovate; greyish green, up to 15 cm long.
<u>Flowers</u> single, pendent, brownish violet (yellow = subsp. *lutea*); VI–VIII.
<u>Fruits</u> glossy black (rarely yellow = subsp. *lutea*) berries seated on a green calyx, with violet juice and numerous black seeds; VII–X.
<u>Distribution:</u> Western to south-eastern Europe, western Asia, and North Africa; rarely planted.

THE sorceresses of Greek mythology – Hecate, Circe – knew well the narcotic, stimulant, and deadly effects of this plant [S57], and Linnaeus gave it the Latin name *Atropa* after the Greek goddess of the underworld, Atropos, who cut the thread of life [W2].

Toxic constituents. All parts of the plant contain a highly active but variable mixture of alkaloids comprising L-hyoscyamine, atropine, and scopolamine (see p.201). The average total tropane alkaloid contents are given in Table 12. But it has to be borne in mind that tetraploid forms, the anthocyanin-free yellow variety, and plants growing on heavy soils and at higher altitudes are richer in alkaloids than other forms [H3; H57]. While scopolamine usually represents a very small proportion of the total alkaloids, rarely exceeding the 1% limit, Heltmann [H38] found up to 30% in the alkaloid mixture present in the leaves of *A. pallidiflora* and *A. acuminata*. Likewise of significance is the fact that while the seeds and unripe fruits contain essentially L-hyoscyamine, in the ripe fruits it is almost exclusively the racemate atropine that occurs and it has only half the activity on the peripheral nervous system.

Table 12. Alkaloid content of various organs of *Atropa bella-donna*.

Plant part	Alkaloid content (%)
Leaves	0.5
Flowers	0.4
Fruits	0.65
Seeds	0.8
Roots	0.85

In the present-day work of the Toxicological Centres, again and again it is the attractive and sweetish but insipid tasting berries that tempt children to eat them and that lead to calls for advice or clinical treatment. On the other hand, poisoning by the leaves and stems is very rare [S107]; in two cases adults had collected them as a wild green vegetable and had boiled and eaten them [J9]. Poisoning with hyoscyamine-containing honey derived from *Atropa* flowers, as observed by Hazslinsky [H29], must no doubt remain an exception. Unlike certain birds – thrushes and pheasants eat the berries without suffering any ill-effects – some mammals and man are very sensitive to atropine.

Symptoms of poisoning. The four most important symptoms after ingesting atropine-containing plant material are: (a) reddening of the face, (b) dryness of the mucous membranes, (c) acceleration of the pulse, and (d) dilatation of the pupils. With therapeutic doses (0.5–2 mg atropine) the effects are limited to the peripheral nervous system. After a 10 mg dose,

symptoms arising from the central nervous system become prominent, e.g. psychomotor disturbances, talkativeness, fits of crying, hallucinations, disturbances of consciousness, and fits of frenzy ('we have seen a boy in his frenzy smash the window of the admissions counter' [K46]). In adults,

50 mg atropine can be dangerous to life and without proper precautions death usually follows within 24 hours as a result of coma and respiratory paralysis. Depending on their age, in children as few as 2–5 berries (in adults 10–20 berries) may be fatal, especially as in man a spontaneous or acquired

b

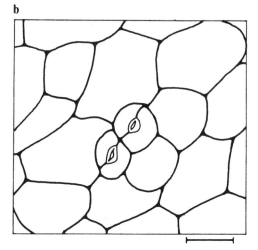

157 **Atropa bella-donna: (a) Epidermis of the pericarp. (b) Epidermis of the pericarp with stomata. (c) Epidermis of the testa.**

a

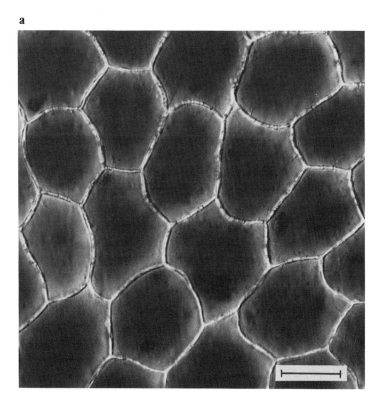

c

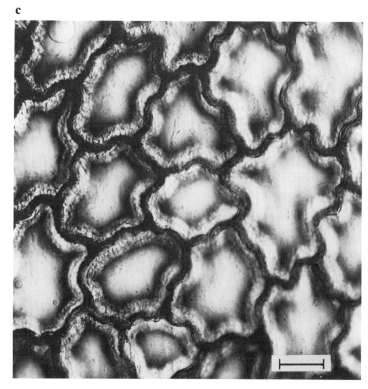

Treatment. (1) Carry out immediate gastric lavage (well-oiled tube) with plenty of water and activated charcoal. Until the doctor arrives, give salt water as emetic (1 tablespoon of salt in a glass of hot water). Apply measures to effect lowering of the temperature, e.g. wrapping in wet cloths, baths, but under no circumstances antipyretics! (2) In the excitation phase diazepam preparations (Valium®, 5 mg) or small (!) doses of short-acting barbiturates give good results [M34]. Theoretically, phenothiazines because of their anticholinergic properties should be less suitable, but in practice moderate doses have also been used with success [G18]. (3) When in a deep coma, in view of the possibility of respiratory paralysis, artificial respiration must be available. **Antidote:** Physostigmine, 1–2 mg i.v., rapidly does away with the peripheral, and also mitigates the central, symptoms of poisoning. In serious cases, if necessary, repeat after 30–60 minutes [K65; M50].

hypersensitivity (delirium and coma even with doses of less than 1 mg) is occasionally observed [M38; M50]. However, in spite of everything, provided medical treatment is instituted in time, the prognosis in cases of atropine poisoning is usually satisfactory.

Besides poisoning from plant material, medicinal poisoning as a result of carelessness or confusion also happens frequently; for example, a 4-year old boy, instead of his nose drops, received atropine eye drops (*ca* 2 × 0.5 ml of a 4% atropine solution in each nostril = 40 mg atropine). Thanks to medical attention his life was saved.

And finally, under special climatic circumstances even therapeutic doses may become a dangerous poison. Blocking the functioning of the sweat glands with atropine makes heat regulation of the body in the tropics impossible, so that death is more likely through overheating and heat stroke than through coma and respiratory paralysis. Thus, Jahnke [J2] encountered several fatal cases in children who had been given a few drops of a 1% solution as eye drops.

Identification of the fruits and their constituents can be carried out in a number of different ways. The specific epithet *bella-donna* is a reminder that in medieval times Italian women valued the mydriatic action of the plant juice as a cosmetic aid. It is precisely this effect that is exploited in carrying out the physiological detection of atropine, up to 50% of which is excreted unchanged in the urine. A few drops of urine or plant juice instilled into the eye of a rabbit bring about maximum dilatation of the pupils. An indirect proof can be obtained via the coumarin glycoside scopolin which accompanies the alkaloids and whose aglycone, scopoletin, fluoresces blue in UV light [V2]. A few drops of the diluted juice of the fruit or of the solution prepared by shaking a few, even whole, seeds with some water fluoresce light blue when irradiated with long-wavelength (365 nm) UV light.

Microscopical characters of the fruit. The pericarp of the deadly nightshade fruit consists of highly pigmented polygonal cells (**157a**) with thin but clearly pitted walls. The cuticle is striated; stomata are relatively rare but are then often present in pairs (**157b**). In the pulp there is only a little crystal sand. The light brown cells of the epidermis of the testa are characterised by ridges on top of the wavy anticlinal walls (**157c**).

Datura stramonium L.   Thorn-apple, Jimsonweed

158 Thorn-apple

0.3–1 m tall herbaceous annual with erect, mostly spreading forked stems. In waste places and other open habitats, along waysides and in gardens on nutrient-rich sandy soils and loam.
<u>Leaves</u> long-petiolate, ovate, jaggedly toothed, dull green; lower ones 20 cm long or more.
<u>Flowers</u> single, erect, tubular, white (subsp. *stramonium*), less often blue (subsp. *tatula*); VI–IX.
<u>Fruits</u> large green capsules, spiny (less often without spines), dehiscing via four valves and containing numerous reniform dark brown (unripe) to black (ripe) seeds with not unpleasant taste; VIII–X.
<u>Distribution:</u> Generally throughout temperate and subtropical regions.

SINCE the 16th century thorn-apple preparations have frequently been used as intoxicants (witches' salves and love potions) and today they still have a certain vogue among more primitive peoples [W2]. Horse dealers knew early on about the sales-promoting effect of this plant: 'Even the most miserable worn-out nag will become as frisky as a thoroughbred when you stick a couple of rolled-up leaves up its rectum.' Medicinally, the dried leaves were long used as a fumigant in bronchial asthma.

Like the deadly nightshade, the thorn-apple contains tropane alkaloids in all parts of the plant. Typical figures for the total alkaloid content of the individual organs are summarised in Table 13. The composition varies quite substantially, according to age and species. Young *Datura* plants are stated to contain mainly scopolamine, in older ones hyoscyamine predominates [H57]. In the flowers of tree species like *D. candida* and *D. suaveolens* the proportion of scopolamine may be as high as 65% [H3].

Table 13. Alkaloid content (calculated on a dry weight basis) of various parts of *Datura stramonium*.

Plant part	Alkaloid content (%)
Leaves	0.38
Flowers	0.61
Shoots	0.16
Fruits	0.66
Pericarp	0.05
Seeds	0.58
Roots	0.23

Even though in 1943 as many as 1524 African soldiers were seen to be intoxicated after enjoying thorn-apple leaves [K16], poisoning with this plant is nevertheless relatively rare because its appearance hardly encourages consumption. In a few cases which have become known to us, confusion or adulteration was involved, e.g. thorn-apple leaves handed over by mistake for nettle tea [V8] or admixed thorn-apple seeds in bread and buckwheat flour [M12; P47]. Liebenow [L23] states that contamination of soyabean meal with (0.01%) *Datura* seed often happens, but cattle and pigs eat meal containing as much as 0.3% without any ill-effects; see also [W34].

There have, however, been frequent poisonings arising from the misuse of particular plant materials for murder and as stimulants. Between 1950 and 1965 the State Chemical Laboratory in Agra, India, alone investigated 2728 fatal cases due to *Datura* species. In this part of the world the seeds are a favourite poison for suicide and murder. Criminals often use extracts of the seeds to stupefy travellers and thus make it easier to carry out robbery and theft in railway carriages [T6].

The readiness with which many young people in all parts of the world experiment toxicologically on themselves is alarming. In the hope of taking a glorious 'trip' like that obtained with LSD, they consume *Datura* flowers, leaves, or seeds, or decoctions of them, or *Datura*-containing medicinal preparations, e.g. Potter's asthma remedy [B4; B12; B21; C2; F3; F7; H12; M7; M31; O2; O12; P49; R11; S43; S53; S61].

Symptoms of poisoning. The peripheral and central symptoms of thorn-apple poisoning are the same as those produced by *Atropa bella-donna*, although acceleration of the pulse and flushing of the face may be absent. Owing to the fact that the scopolamine content may on occasion be higher, under certain circumstances central sedative and hallucinogenic effects may dominate.

'The patient stated that he had had difficulty in negotiating a path through the white lines on the roads with his motor cycle, because they kept jumping about and lashing at his legs' [B26].

'The patient held conversations with a man in a suit whom only he could see, and he felt that he was being followed by black and red, knee-high spiders' [F4].

Such hallucinations occur as a rule 2–4 hours after taking the poison and may continue for several days. The occasionally observed urge to undress and/or look for open water is probably a consequence of the hyperthermia [M34].

'Two 15-year old boys were found by the police wandering naked and delirious through a field. It emerged later that they had eaten 5 or 6 flowers of Datura suaveolens*'* [H5].

'. . . two persons repeatedly swam into a pond in search of red-eyed dolphins' [G18].

Treatment. See *Atropa* (p.205). Sometimes the hallucinations only occur episodically and alternate with phases of somnolence. In these circumstances the patient requires continuous observation and care so that during the periods of acute delirium he cannot injure himself or others.

Because of the characteristic morphology, the identification of the flowers and leaves offers no difficulty. Moreover, the microscopical features are adequately described in the pharmacopoeias and standard works on drug analysis. A further point that may be of use is that after shaking the seeds with water a light green fluorescence may be seen under long-wavelength (365 nm) UV light.

Hyoscyamus niger L.   Henbane

159 Henbane

0.2–0.8 m tall annual or biennial herb with napiform root.
In weed communities along roadsides, on nutrient-rich sandy soils and loam.
<u>Leaves</u> oblong-ovate, sinuate toothed, lower ones petiolate, upper ones amplexicaul.
<u>Flowers</u> with very short pedicels, in dense unilateral spikes, with sticky villous calyx lobes; corolla dirty yellow with violet veins, rarely all yellow, inside at the base dark violet; VI–IX.
<u>Fruits</u> a capsule included in circumsessile calyx and containing up to 200 black seeds (*H. aureus* – yellow; *H. albus* – white); VIII–X.
<u>Distribution:</u> From Scandinavia to southern Europe, northern Africa, northern Asia, northern India.

AS can readily be ascertained from the history and mythology of antiquity, henbane is toxicologically just as potent a herb as the deadly nightshade and thorn-apple. As late as the 17th century, breweries had plantations of the herb in order to be able to strengthen 'weak' beers with extracts of the seeds. The old German name 'Altsitzerkraut' is a reminder that in the country it was occasionally used to help 'useless old people who were just sitting around' into the next world [W2].

Most reports of poisoning with henbane, through confusion with a kind of viper's-grass *(Scorzonera hispanica),* wild parsnip *(Pastinaca sativa),* or with poppy seed, are old. The unpleasant smell and the sticky nature of the plant make it under-standable why man and animals, even without a knowledge of its poisonous properties, usually avoid it. Nevertheless, there is a fatal case on record from Turkey in which children in the absence of fresh greens ate a salad of henbane leaves [K56]. Moreover, there has been no lack of attempts to misuse the flowers of *Hyoscyamus* as a hallucinogenic drug [S7].

The alkaloid content increases in going from the roots (0.08%) via the leaves (0.17%) to the seeds (0.3%). Since the mixture of alkaloids may contain in addition to L-hyoscyamine up to 40% scopolamine, poisoning by henbane, like that due to thorn-apple, is marked in the toxic range by the central sedative activity of this substance.

Because of their size, henbane seeds are most likely to be confused with poppy seed. Unlike those of *Atropa* and *Datura,* they do not exhibit any fluorescence on irradiation with long-wavelength (365 nm) UV light.

Symptoms, treatment, and **antidote:** see *Atropa* (p.205) and *Datura* (p.207).

Lycium barbarum L.   Duke of Argyll's Teaplant, Matrimony Vine

160 Duke of Argyll's Teaplant

1–3 m high shrub with rod-shaped, curving, pendent stems; lower ones mostly with spines.

<u>Leaves</u> cuneate, tapering into the petiole, alternate or in clusters.

<u>Flowers</u> pedicellate, 1–3 in leaf axils, with funnel-shaped tube and five flat corolla lobes; light purple or light violet; VI–IX.

<u>Fruits</u> red, ellipsoid-oblong, pleasantly sweet-tasting, bilocular, several-seeded berries (rarely yellowish); VIII–X.

<u>Distribution:</u> Indigenous to the Near East; planted on poor soils as green cover for steep slopes (waste places, quarries).

THE light red berries of the Duke of Argyll's teaplant have so far been the subject of only a few toxicological enquiries. Its chemical constituents have not yet been sufficiently well characterised – a nitrogen-containing glycoside with parasympatholytic activity is said to be present [H35]. A South African species, *L. ferocissimum,* is also suspected of being poisonous, but its sweet-tasting fruits are at any rate edible.

Treatment. Symptomatic; as far as possible as for *Atropa* (p.205).

Microscopical characters of the fruit. The epidermis of the pericarp is free of stomata. It has thick-walled cells with a granular wax deposit especially on top of the radial walls (**161**).

Surprisingly, the pulp has no calcium oxalate, but in polarised light the numerous carotenoid crystals light up.

161 Lycium barbarum: Epidermis of the pericarp.

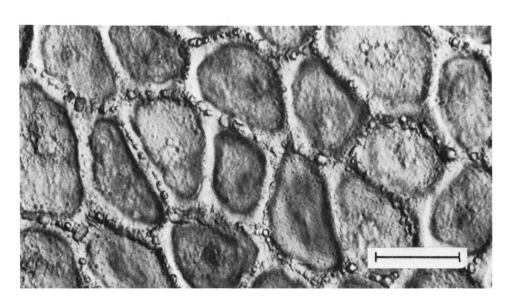

Nicotiana tabacum L.   Tobacco

162 Tobacco

0.75–3 m tall annual with simple or sparsely branched stems, like leaves and calyx, having glandular hairs.
<u>Leaves</u> sessile or short-petiolate; narrow and acuminate; alternate, entire.
<u>Flowers</u> in panicles, with erect trumpet-shaped red corolla tube projecting far beyond the calyx and having a swollen throat; corolla with five acuminate, angular, spreading lobes; VI–IX.
<u>Fruits</u> oblong-ovoid pointed capsules with numerous seeds.
<u>Distribution:</u> Originally from South America; now known only in cultivation.

ALL parts of the plant contain the highly toxic alkaloid nicotine (structure, p.201), partly free and partly combined with acid. The ripe seeds, which until recently were thought not to contain alkaloids, have now also been shown to have small amounts [H35].

In the leaves the alkaloid content varies between 0.5 and 9% of the dry weight; a tobacco from *N. rustica,* used by the Huichol Indians of Mexico on ceremonial occasions to bring about hallucinogenic effects, has been found to contain as much as 18% [S55].

As already pointed out in the introduction to the family, there are three things which make this poison so dangerous:
(1) The high toxicity of nicotine in man. While the lethal dose for an adult is *ca* 40–60 mg, sheep and cattle can tolerate 50 times as much orally without showing any signs of poisoning [K16].
(2) The rapid absorption through skin, lungs, and mucous membranes.

'Thus, for example, the death of a child could be traced to the use of a foul tobacco pipe for blowing bubbles, and the fact that tobacco leaves not only store nicotine but also excrete it via epidermal hairs resulted in the death of

a smuggler – he had wrapped tobacco leaves round his body in order to avoid paying the customs duty' [K 16].

Nicotine solutions are much used as insecticides by gardeners and in commercial undertakings, and the dangers of inhaling such aerosols are particularly great. In the same way, smoking with open wounds in the mouth, e.g. after having a tooth out, can lead to poisoning.

(3) The use of tobacco leaves in the form of cigars and cigarettes or for pipe smoking, chewing, or in snuff. The health risks involved are sufficiently well known. It is not these chronic intoxications, but rather the many cases of ingestion by children dealt with again and again by the Toxicological Information Centres that are our concern here. According to von Mühlendahl and Krienke [M61] it is usually infants between one and three years old who, unnoticed, eat an unquantifiable amount of tobacco from cigarette packets and ashtrays. If the amount of tobacco eaten is small – less than 1 cm of cigarette – or if it has been taken four hours previously without symptoms having appeared, direct removal of the poison by gastric lavage is not necessary. That in the *ca* 3000 cases dealt with by von Mühlendahl and Krienke only 3% of the children showed slight symptoms of poisoning may be due to the slow liberation of nicotine from acid cigarette tobacco. Undoubtedly, much more serious is the ingestion of alkaline tobacco (cigars, snuff) or tobacco suspensions (also when boiling out a pipe).

Symptoms of poisoning. Mild nicotine poisoning gives rise to symptoms such as nausea, dizziness, headache, vomiting, diarrhoea, and tremors of the hands. In cases of serious poisoning

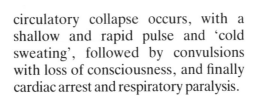

163 *Nicotiana tabacum*: Cells with calcium oxalate sand in the spongy mesophyll.

circulatory collapse occurs, with a shallow and rapid pulse and 'cold sweating', followed by convulsions with loss of consciousness, and finally cardiac arrest and respiratory paralysis.

Treatment. (1) After oral ingestion. Activated charcoal (5–6 teaspoons with water) should be administered, then gastric lavage with 1% potassium permanganate solution.

(2) After percutaneous absorption. Since only a few drops of a concentrated solution are enough to cause serious poisoning, the skin should be washed at once with soap and plenty of water.

In both cases, symptomatic measures for the circulation should be applied. With convulsions, diazepam i.m. or i.v. (Valium® 20 mg), and if respiratory paralysis threatens, intubation and assisted respiration with oxygen, can be given.

Microscopical characters of the leaves. The anatomy of the tobacco leaf has been described in many handbooks

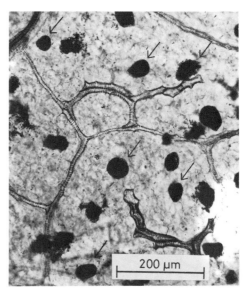

and texts of pharmacognosy, so that it suffices here to illustrate just two of the essential features. On the one hand, even in investigating tobacco remains the numerous cells with calcium oxalate sand in the mesophyll of the leaves (**163**) are a striking feature and, on the other hand, the epidermis has many uniseriate covering and glandular trichomes; part of the latter have a multicellular head filled with a yellow nicotine-containing secretion (**164**).

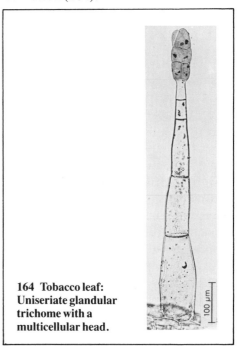

164 Tobacco leaf: Uniseriate glandular trichome with a multicellular head.

Physalis alkekengi L.   Cape-gooseberry, Winter Cherry, Chinese Lantern

165 Cape-gooseberry

0.25–1 m tall perennial herb with blunt-edged, usually branched erect stems. In dry undergrowth, warm riparian woodland, stony hillsides, and vineyards, on nutrient-rich, mostly calcareous clay soils and loam.
<u>Leaves</u> petiolate, mostly paired, acuminate, cordate, entire or incised.
<u>Flowers</u> single, with pubescent pendent pedicels and greenish white corollas; when fruit is ripe, calyx becomes swollen, bell-shaped, enlarged, and red; V–VIII.
<u>Fruits</u> orange-scarlet berries with sour, bitter taste; numerous yellowish white reniform seeds; IX–II.
<u>Distribution:</u> Europe northwards to northern France and central Russia, but doubtfully native in the northern and western parts of this range; often in gardens as an ornamental.

ALTHOUGH the fruits of the Cape-gooseberry (Baccae Alkekengi) were still official in France and Venezuela in 1930 and there are many reports on their curative properties in old books on materia medica, even now there is no certain information on constituents which might be responsible for possible toxic effects – 'leaves and unripe fruits have been suspected of poisoning sheep' [H9; L20].

Völksen [V5] points out that the fruits (only when ripe?) are palatable and have a pleasant acid taste, as long as they do not touch the inner wall of the calyx. Indeed, all parts of the plant, with the exception of the fruit, contain bitter substances, which, via secretory hairs, are easily carried to the pericarp; their chemical nature has only recently been elucidated. They are C_{28} steroids, e.g. physalin A, biogenetically very similar to the withanolides, a group of steroidal lactones from the Solanaceae, of interest, among other things, because of their antimitotic activity [H35; K66].

In the rhizomes of *P. alkekengi* and *P. peruviana* (which has edible, exotic fruits) and in the roots of *Nicandra physaloides,* apple of Peru, pyrrolidine and seco-tropane alkaloids have been detected, but the aerial parts are almost free of them [B16; R19; R20; S108]. As the Swiss Toxicological Information Centre in the course of 118 calls regarding this plant (1973–1977) has not noted any symptoms, it is probable that the ripe fruits, at least, of the Cape-gooseberry can be considered harmless.

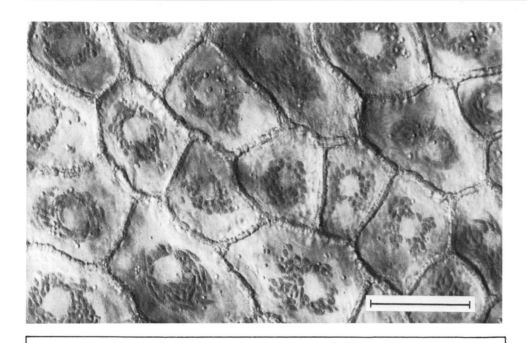

166 Physalis alkekengi: Epidermis of the pericarp.

Microscopical characters of the fruit. The epidermal cells of the pericarp of *P. alkekengi* have beaded and strongly pitted walls and contain numerous chloroplasts which often encircle the nucleus **(166).** Stomata are absent. The pulp has scattered calcium oxalate clusters (*ca* 30 μm) as well as much calcium oxalate sand. The wavy and much thickened walls of the epidermal cells of the testa are distinctly pitted only on the inside periclinal wall.

Solanum L.   Nightshade

THE genus *Solanum* has 1500–2000 species distributed throughout the world and is one of the largest genera of Angiosperms. Many of its species have, in addition to neutral saponins, biogenetically closely related **steroidal glyco-alkaloids** (p.26). In general, it is difficult to give concrete indications regarding the toxicity of individual species or their organs; for not only do widely occurring species tend to form different chemical races, but the content of these *Solanum* alkaloids depends very much on the stage of development of the particular organ concerned.

Generally, it appears that the alkaloid mixtures present in the roots are more complex than those in the aerial parts [H35]. In the fruits of some species, during the ripening process these constituents are metabolised to nitrogen-free compounds, so that ripe berries contain only neutral, scarcely poisonous saponins [S6; T4; W19]. In the tomato *(Lycopersicon lycopersicum)* as well, the steroidal alkaloids disappear as the fruits ripen (it is, of course, well known that the unripe fruits are inedible), but not through conversion to neutral saponins. It is owing to this 'detoxification mechanism' that in Africa and South America, in addition to the aubergine, *S. melongena,* the fruits of other *Solanum* species are valued as foodstuffs. On the other hand, the investigations of Maiti *et al.* [M9] have demonstrated that ripe berries are by no means always free of alkaloids. Of 31 Indian species examined, 23 still contained solanines – in some cases considerable amounts: up to 6.1% of the dry weight.

Symptoms of poisoning. Among the symptoms observed in mild solanine poisoning are: irritation in the neck, headache, exhaustion, vomiting, abdominal pains, severe diarrhoea, and in some cases also fever and circulatory collapse. The symptoms may not occur until 4–19 hours after taking the toxic plant material, and in serious cases nausea and diarrhoea may continue for 3–6 days. In addition, there are distinct neurological disturbances such as hallucinations, apathy, agoraphobia or restlessness, together with convulsions and disturbances of vision.

Treatment. Symptomatic. If vomiting has not started, gastric lavage with the addition of activated charcoal may be instituted. Electrolytes and fluids should be replaced and circulatory stimulants given. If convulsions occur, anticonvulsants such as diazepam may be administered.

Fatal cases of poisoning with *Solanum* alkaloids have rarely been observed, but such cases require very careful diagnosis and confirmation by microbiological, physiological, and microscopical investigations. This is in order to avoid unnecessary surgical and therapeutic intervention, such as removal of the appendix (suspicion of appendicitis), chloramphenicol treatment (suspicion of *Salmonella* infection) [M35; A30], or exchange transfusion (suspicion of botulinism) [A29].

Food poisoning by *Clostridium botulinum* gives rise to similar neurological phenomena but is clearly differentiated by additional symptoms such as constipation, laryngeal paralysis, and loss of voice, while at the same time maintaining full mental alertness. The botulinus toxin inhibits the release of acetylcholine at the synapse, but in solanine poisoning often a reduction in the activity of the non-specific cholinesterase (pseudocholinesterase) in the plasma is measured [M35; P12].

In addition to the microscopical **identification** of plant remains in stomach contents or vomit, it is also possible to detect solanine microchemically by means of the blue colour obtained with a modified Marquis reagent (1% paraldehyde in 90% phosphoric acid) [C18; C19] or in the urine through the red colour produced with selenosulphuric acid [M50].

Solanum dulcamara L.   Bittersweet, Woody Nightshade

167 Bittersweet

0.3–1.8 m tall perennial undershrub with scrambling or prostrate, flexible stems, the lower parts of which become woody and keep through the winter.
In willow and riparian woodland, on river banks and waysides, hedges, and sea shores, mostly on wet and nutrient-rich loam and clay soils.
<u>Leaves</u> petiolate, ovate-oblong to acuminate, upper ones sometimes lobed (with 1–2 lateral leaflets) or hastate.
<u>Flowers</u> in long-pedicellate pendent cymes; corolla 5-partite, recurved at the top, violet, with two green spots at the base; rarely white; VI–VIII.
<u>Fruits</u> scarlet, nodding, many-seeded berries; at first tasting bitter, then sweet; VIII–X.
<u>Distribution:</u> Most of Europe except the extreme north.

THE example of this plant clearly demonstrates that in spite of having an accurate knowledge of its constituents, thus enabling an estimate of its toxicity to be made, a carefully recorded case history is essential. Most of the reports in the older literature are in almost complete contradiction with the experience of the Toxicological Information Centres:

Only 10 berries killed an 11-year old boy [B 50].

A 4½-year old boy died after eating a handful of the red berries of bittersweet [P 39].

In contrast with this, the Berlin Toxicological Centre in the years 1964–1977 recorded 16 cases in which berries of *S. dulcamara* had been ingested and there were mild symptoms such as spontaneous vomiting in only one [K 46].

Thanks to the intensive investigations of various authors [M 24; S 6; S 33; W 19; W 20] there is a wealth of information on the constituents of the individual parts of the plant and also on their variation according to the stage of development.

S. dulcamara is relatively homogeneous morphologically but has three phytochemical races, each distinguished by the occurrence of a different principal alkaloid – soladul-cidine, tomatidenol, and solasodine [S 33]. The berries and vegetative parts of the tomatidenol race appear to be richer in alkaloids than the other two. But for all three races the aerial parts can be arranged in a series with decreasing alkaloid content: green berries > leaves > shoots > ripe berries. The total content of steroidal alkaloids first increases during the growth of the fruit and reaches a maximum when they are fully grown but still unripe – 0.33–0.65% of the dry weight – and then drops sharply just before the fruits become red, so that the ripe berries contain no more than traces of alkaloid. Evidently,

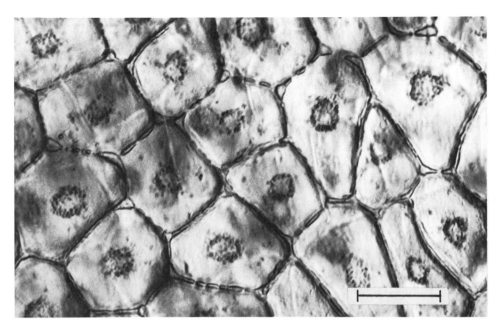

168 **Solanum dulcamara: Epidermis of the pericarp.**

during the ripening process the solanines are metabolised to neutral saponins without the occurrence of glycosidic hydrolysis.

As animal experiments involving pure alkaloids have shown, the toxicity of the solanines depends to a remarkable extent on the degree of gastro-intestinal absorption. After intraperitoneal administration in mice the LD_{50} was found to be 42 mg/kg, but when taken orally, even in doses of 1000 mg/kg, there was no effect [N13]. From observations of other *Solanum* poisonings it has been calculated that in man, who appears to be more sensitive, a toxic dose of solanine is 20–30 mg and a fatal dose <400–500 mg [M50]. Provided the alkaloid content is optimal (unripe berries, alkaloid-richest race) and the maximum fresh weight of an individual berry is 0.4 g, at least 10 berries would have to be eaten before symptoms of poisoning could be expected; a lethal dose would require *ca* 200 berries. Critical assessment of the fatal cases described in the literature reveals that, apart from an exact description of the clinical symptoms, often neither the identity of the plant in question (. . . was found near the house . . .),

nor the nature and amount of the plant material ingested (frequently based only on parental supposition), nor the amount of poison left in the body (subsequent post-mortem and detailed toxicological examinations are exceptions) could be unequivocally determined. Only in one report is there information on most of these points [A4]:

'In August 1948 in England a 9-year old girl died in spite of intensive medical care after being in hospital for 1½ days. The remains of berries were discovered microscopically in the contents of the large intestine. Ca 21 mg alkaloid could be isolated from the liver alone and identified as solanine. The case history showed that the girl was in the habit of eating berries from hedges and from the embankment of a disused railway and that during the previous weeks she had eaten berries on several occasions. Masses of bittersweet (woody nightshade) grew there entangled with blackberries.'

This report gives grounds for thinking that the child must have eaten a considerable amount of the berries over a longish period of time. It is possible, therefore, that because of the accompanying saponins there

was damage to the mucous membrane of the gastro-intestinal tract ('. . . the main feature was an acute inflammation of the mucosa of the stomach and intestines . . .') and hence a considerably increased absorption of the steroidal alkaloids.

Taking into account all the above facts, it seems justified to include bittersweet in the group of poisonous plants that are only likely to give rise to serious symptoms after eating a largish amount of the fruits.

For **symptoms, treatment,** and **detection** of the constituents, see p.214.

Microscopical characters of the fruit. The fruits of *Solanum dulcamara* are very similar to those of *Lycium barbarum* (p.209), but are readily distinguished microscopically. In the epidermis of the pericarp stomata are indeed also absent, but, on the other hand, the walls of the epidermal cells are thinner and distinctly beaded (**168**). In addition, the pulp has cells with calcium oxalate present as crystal sand.

Solanum nigrum L.   Black Nightshade

169 Black Nightshade

0.1–0.8 m tall annual herb with branched, more or less angular stems. In weed communities and cultivated land (vegetable gardens, potato fields, etc.) and along waysides on fresh nutrient-rich clay or sandy loam.

<u>Leaves</u> ovate to broad, triangular to rhombic, acuminate, often sinuate-dentate, almost entire; juicy, remaining dark green on drying.

<u>Flowers</u> short-pedicellate, in umbel-like cymes; corolla deeply 5-partite, white; VI–IX.

<u>Fruits</u> black, rarely yellowish green, glossy, many-seeded berries with peduncles ultimately bending over; mucilaginous acid taste; subsp. *humile* – waxy yellow or greenish berries, subsp. *alatum* – light red berries; VIII–X.

<u>Distribution:</u> Probably originating in southern Europe; now cosmopolitan.

EVEN more than with bittersweet, there are contradictory statements about the toxicity of the black nightshade. As early as the 1st century BC the Greek military doctor Dioscorides pointed out that *S. nigrum* berries could be eaten and at the beginning of this century the plant was cultivated in Mediterranean countries and in America for use in food. Yet, on the other hand, undoubted cases of *S. nigrum* poisoning in man and animals have been observed. An explanation for this is to be found in the fact that the plant has a great tendency to form polyploids and hybrids, so that the concept *S. nigrum* in reality embraces a whole complex of subspecies and forms that morphologically are more or less indistinguishable.

Schreiber [S31] has investigated 22 such entities for *Solanum* alkaloids. Four of them did not at any time contain alkaloids in their leaves, while the remaining 18, depending on their origin, had between 0 and 2.0% based on the dry weight. Generalising, it can be said that here also the alkaloid content of individual plant parts decreases in the order: unripe fruit > leaves > stems > ripe fruit. Schreiber was not able to detect any alkaloids in the ripe berries of any of the entities examined. On the other hand, the green berries of *S. nigrum* normally contain 1.32 ± 0.18% solasodine, based on the dry weight [M23].

Over a period of 14 years the Berlin Poison Control Centre noted [K46] altogether 20 cases of ingestion of *S. nigrum,* and in only two of them were mild symptoms encountered. Thus, after taking a few berries a 2-year old child suffered from nausea, mydriasis, and intense reddening of the head. Of particular interest is the case of poisoning described by Polster [P39]:

A 10-year old girl was brought to our hospital department with the diagnosis: loss of consciousness of unknown

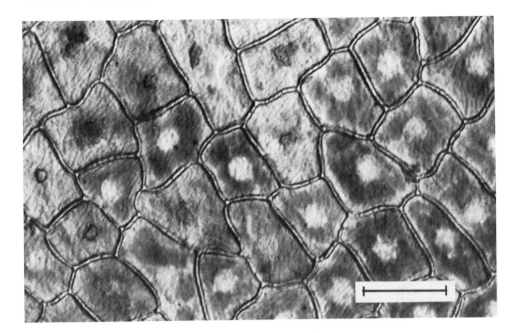

170 Solanum nigrum: Epidermis of the pericarp.

origin. The mother when questioned denied any possibility of poisoning. The child's elder sister later confessed after a serious talking-to by the mother that on the previous day the patient had eaten about 15–20 black berries. The plant when brought in turned out to be black nightshade. However, we were unable to explain the patient's constant changes between a strong desire to sleep and great restlessness. The solution to the puzzle came from the child herself the next day. After eating the berries, she had become nauseated and had felt a severe headache coming on and had therefore taken 4–6 sleeping tablets.

This case is instructive in showing the scepticism and care with which statements made by people accompanying a patient should be judged and how difficult it can be for the doctor involved to diagnose the type of poisoning solely on the basis of the symptoms.

Since this plant is a typical weed of cultivated land, cases of animal poisoning are also regularly observed. Cattle, horses, and pigs, in particular, can become ill when their feed contains a high proportion of black nightshade [C31; L23]. Nevertheless, according to Liebenow [L22] it is not so much the relatively low alkaloid, but rather the high nitrate, content that is responsible for these poisonings.

In this connection it must also be remembered that with the increasing mechanisation of harvesting, processing, and packaging of various kinds of vegetables, parts of this weed can get into food destined for human consumption [B59]. Thus, a case is known to us from Schleswig-Holstein in which kale contained unacceptable amounts of black nightshade.

For **symptoms, treatment,** and **detection** of the constituents, see p.214.

Microscopical characters of the fruit. The berries of the black nightshade have an epidermis (**170**) comprising thin- and smooth-walled cells with fine pitting and faint cuticular striations. Some of the cells contain a red-violet sap (anthocyanins) in which a brightly translucent nucleus can be seen. In the pulp there are scattered calcium oxalate clusters (*ca* 20 μm) as well as much calcium oxalate sand.

Solanum pseudocapsicum L.   Winter, Christmas, or Jerusalem Cherry

171 Christmas Cherry

0.5–1 m tall shrub with glabrous green branches.
<u>Leaves</u> simple, oblong-lanceolate, entire or slightly incised.
<u>Flowers</u> single or in pairs, small, star-shaped, white; VI–VIII.
<u>Fruits</u> 1–2 cm in diameter, globose, pinkish red, shiny berries with numerous white, flattened, reniform seeds (4 mm); IX–X.
<u>Distribution:</u> Various forms are kept as ornamentals and house plants because of the brightly coloured, shiny berries.

WITHIN the genus *Solanum, S. pseudocapsicum,* together with a few other species, e.g. *S. capsicastrum, S. hendersonii, S. seaforthianum,* occupies a special position phytochemically [S32]. Its principal alkaloid, solanocapsine, occurs in all parts of the plant, but it is not present as a glycoside and it has an additional N-atom outside the steroidal skeleton.

As preliminary toxicological studies have shown, the extracts of the individual plant parts are very much less toxic when taken by mouth than when given intraperitoneally. There are, however, no essential differences according to the ripeness of the fruits [M18]. Solanocapsine is stated to calm the heart through a direct effect on the cardiac muscle in which the development of the cardiac impulse is retarded and to cause sinus arrhythmias in toxic concentrations [H3].

Solanocapsine

Because of its attractive fruits, the Christmas cherry is especially fascinating to children, and in a 5-year period the Swiss Toxicological Information Centre [S38] recorded 46 enquiries.

Symptoms of poisoning after eating a few of the berries are reported to be nausea, abdominal pains, dilatation of the pupils, and drowsiness [B50]. No newer data have been seen.

For **treatment,** see p. 214.

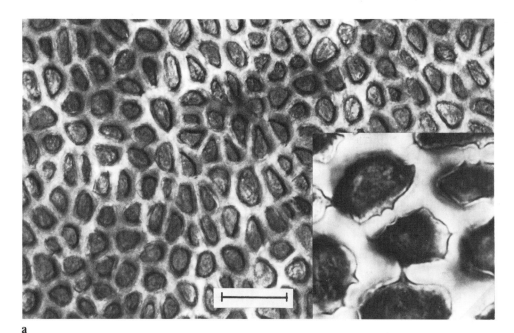

a

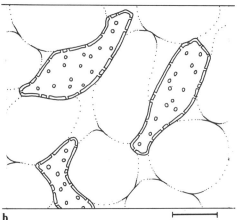

172 **Solanum pseudocapsicum:**
(a) **Epidermis of the pericarp.**
(b) **Sclereid idioblasts in the pulp.**

b

Microscopical characters of the fruit.
The epidermal cells of the pericarp of *S. pseudocapsicum* are small and distinctly thick-walled **(172a).** In surface view, the outlines of the large hypodermal cells show through; stomata are absent. The spongy pulp has a little calcium oxalate sand and numerous sclereid idioblasts with extensively pitted walls **(172b).**

Solanum tuberosum L.   Potato

173 Potato

0.4–1 m tall perennial herb with erect branched stem and underground stolons bearing tubers.
<u>Leaves</u> **interruptedly imparipinnate, with alternating small and large leaflets.**
<u>Flowers</u> **usually in two long-pedunculate cymes; corolla 5-angled, large, reddish white to pale violet; VI–VIII.**
<u>Fruits</u> **globose, greenish yellow, fleshy berries with numerous yellowish white seeds (<300); VIII–IX.**
<u>Distribution:</u> **Originating from South America; now only known in cultivation; at various times, run wild.**

THE potato, together with wheat, rice, and maize, is one of the world's most important foods. And it is a matter of amazement to many people that this food comes from a 'poisonous' plant. But as Table 14 shows, all parts of *S. tuberosum* contain toxic steroidal alkaloids [B23; C32; J20].

The solanines are also present in the potato tuber, but normally in negligible amounts: 7 mg/100 g. Nevertheless, under certain conditions, after incorrect (excessive action of daylight) or overlong storage, the alkaloid content can reach concentrations (35 mg/100 g) which are critical for man. When potatoes sprout and become green, intensive production of alkaloids is initiated, especially in the 'skin' and points of higher metabolic activity, the 'eyes'. It is to be remembered that the biosynthesis of the alkaloids is not necessarily connected with an increase in chlorophyll, so that potatoes which have not changed in colour may also already be toxic [J1]. The way in which such potatoes are prepared greatly affects their palatability. Well peeled and boiled potatoes are very much less dangerous (removal of the solanines with the peelings and in the water used for boiling) than unpeeled baked ones, as the alkaloids are largely heat-stable.

In toxicological practice it is especially after eating the berries and inedible tubers that cases of poisoning have been observed. Poisonings due to the fruits, which are in any case toxic, can be diagnosed quite reliably and rapidly through their morphological and microscopical characters.

Table 14. Alkaloid content (based on the dry weight) of different organs of *Solanum tuberosum*.

Plant part	Alkaloid content (%)
Flowers	0.7
Fruits	1.0
Seeds	0.25
Tops	0.5
Sprouts	0.8–5.0

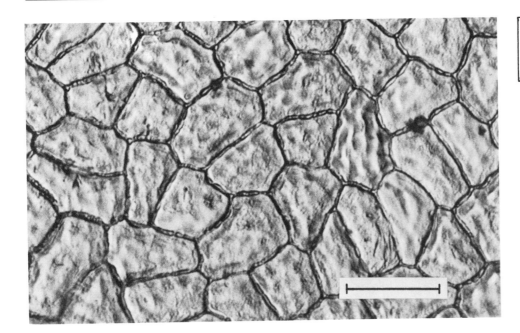

174 Solanum tuberosum: Epidermis of the pericarp.

Extensive investigation is required to recognise a causal relationship between the symptoms of poisoning and the intake of food. McMillan and Thompson [M35] have discussed this problem in connection with a mass poisoning of 78 London school children, because it is often the case that the symptoms arising from food containing potatoes are due not to a too high alkaloid content but rather to a secondary infection with *Salmonella*. But here only the bacteriological examination of blood, serum, vomit, urine, and faeces or food remains can be of help. At the same time, measurements of cholinesterase activity in the plasma and microchemical detection in the urine should be carried out in order to obtain clues as to possible solanine poisoning.

Data on the quantitative estimation of solanine in potatoes and potato products are to be found in [J19; S1; S17]. Although no exact figures are known for the toxic dose in man, it appears that 20–25 mg of the alkaloid is sufficient to elicit symptoms of poisoning [M35; A30].

For **latent period, symptoms, treatment,** and **detection,** see p.214.

Of the cases of poisoning with *S. tuberosum* among farm animals, half can be traced to sprouted potatoes, a third to potato tops, and the rest to spoiled feed or overfeeding. Independent of the solanine content, the feeding of fresh potato tops is always risky because of the not inconsiderable nitrate content [B23]; see also *S. nigrum*.

Microscopical characters of the fruit. The colourless epidermal cells of the potato berry have thin, sometimes beaded walls **(174).** In the large-celled pulp there are innumerable amyloplasts which shine clearly in polarised light. Typical starch grains, like those in potato tubers, occur only very sporadically, however. Calcium oxalate appears to be entirely absent.

Taxus baccata L. Yew

175 Yew

Up to 15 m high evergreen tree, also shrub, with horizontal or downward-pointing branches and oblong-pyramidal or irregular crown. In deciduous and evergreen woods, with a preference for calcareous soils; not in large stands.
<u>Leaves</u> upper side dark green, glossy, lower side light green, matt, shortly mucronate, up to 35 mm long and 2 mm broad; without resin canals, with characteristic walled-in stomata on lower side (177).
<u>Flowers</u> dioecious, male ones in leaf axils of younger twigs and solitary, well separated from each other; III–IV.
<u>Seeds</u> woody, black–brown, surrounded by cup-shaped juicy, mucilaginous and sweet-tasting, scarlet, finely glaucous aril; ripe from VIII.
<u>Distribution:</u> Europe except the east and extreme north; also often planted.

IN antiquity the yew was already known as a tree of death [F24] and it was dedicated to the gods of death. Extracts of yew leaves were used for murder and suicide. Thus, Caesar tells that Catuvolcus, one of the joint kings of the Eburones, chose the freedom of death with *Taxus baccata* rather than face being taken prisoner.

More recently, there have been a number of reports of (successful) suicide attempts with yew leaves [C29; R9; S35]. The amounts taken were 'several tablespoonfuls' and 'a handful'. In one case the toxic properties of the leaves were obviously being tested with a view to their use as an abortifacient [F26].

However, in the work of the Toxicological Information Centres it is not so much the leaves that are significant but rather the seeds which with their attractive aril invite consumption. Beal [B17] gives the data shown in Table 15 (overleaf) for the period of a single year. A similar picture is evident from Ritter [R9]: 343 cases out of 356 took their course without any symptoms and in the rest only mild symptoms of poisoning were noted. Since the toxic principles of the yew are absent from the aril (the only part of the plant in which they are not found), poisoning is not expected as long as the seeds are not chewed or the testa broken in some way. The reviews make it clear that in spite of the large numbers of calls in practice serious cases of poisoning are rare.

Table 15. Ingestion of yew fruits (according to Beal [B 17]).

	Number of cases
Under 5 years old	321
5 Years old and over	25
Unknown age	12
Those under 5 years old who experienced symptoms	6
Those under 5 years old who were hospitalised	2

Toxic constituents. The poisonous substances present in the yew are pseudo-alkaloids known as taxines. They are mixtures with basic properties of polyhydroxyditerpenes (taxinins) esterified with β-dimethylamino-β-phenylpropionic acid and/or acetic acid. A recent review of the chemistry and nomenclature of the taxus alkaloids and other taxane derivatives has been published by Miller [M 36].

Of the other constituents in yew, according to animal experiments carried out by Vohora *et al.* [V 7] the biflavonoids have CNS-depressant, analgesic, and antipyretic activity. Also worth remembering is the cyanogenic-glycoside content of yew leaves. The liberation of hydrocyanic acid, which takes place relatively slowly, does not appear to have any toxicological importance and in any case it certainly has no connection with the 'emission of a gaseous poison' which is supposed to make it dangerous to stand under a yew tree. This assertion, avidly seized upon by the daily press, is so far without any reliable foundation [K 32; K 35].

Symptoms of Taxus poisoning. Starting after about an hour there are nausea, dizziness, abdominal pains, then coma, dilatation of the pupils, reddening of the lips, shallow breathing, and tachycardia. Subsequently, the pulse becomes slower, the blood pressure falls, and death occurs through respiratory paralysis with the heart in diastolic arrest. Owing to its rarity, cases of yew-leaf poisoning may not always be correctly diagnosed.* However, the microscopical identification of yew leaves in the stomach contents or vomit is a sure indication (see **177**).

A severe anaphylactic reaction after ingesting 4–5 *Taxus* leaves is reported by Burke *et al.* [B 55]. The 15-year old patient had previously over a period of several months chewed a yew leaf every day.

The great toxicity of yew leaves and twigs for horses is well known, but other animals are also endangered [B 23; L 23]. In North America, *T. cuspidata,* Japanese yew, whose toxicity is said to be even greater than that of *T. baccata,* has repeatedly been the cause of fatal animal poisonings [A 3; L 33; T 11].

---

* Cf., however, Agatha Christie in *A Pocket Full of Rye:*
Inspector Neele: 'He was poisoned?'
Dr. Bernsdorf: 'Definitely . . . I'd be prepared to make a bet on what the poison was'.
N.: 'Indeed?'
Dr. B.: 'Taxine, my boy. Taxine!'
N.: 'Taxine? Never heard of it.'
Dr. B.: 'I know. Most unusual. . . . Really delightfully unusual! . . . Highly poisonous!'

Treatment. There is no proven treatment for taxine poisoning. Emptying the stomach even hours later makes sense, as the leaves have difficulty in passing through the stomach. Various clinical measures (circulatory stimulants, artificial respiration, cardiac pacemaker) were not able to prevent death in the suicide cases described.

Microscopical characters of the aril and the leaves. The red aril of *Taxus baccata* is characterised by a conspicuous epidermis. It has numerous stomata with distinctly sunken guard cells **(176b)**. The colourless epidermal cells each have several papillae on the external periclinal wall **(176a)**. In the mucilaginous parenchyma lying underneath there are occasional calcium oxalate clusters (*ca* 18 μm).

A remarkable character exhibited by yew leaves is the arrangement of their stomata in rows on the lower surface. The guard cells are again below the level of the epidermis. They are partially lignified and are surrounded by papillose subsidiary cells which form a knobbly ring above the entrance to the stomata **(177)**.

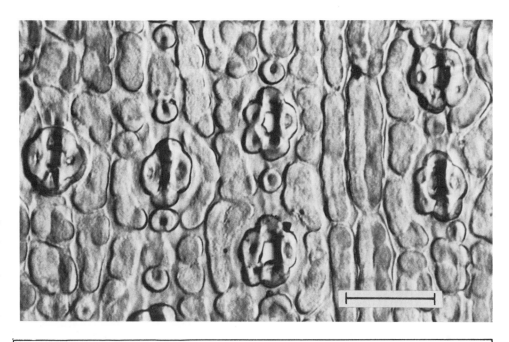

177 Taxus baccata: Epidermis of the leaf.

a

b

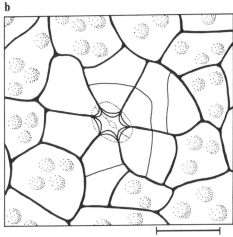

176 Taxus baccata: Aril, showing:
(a) Epidermis. (b) Occasional stomata.

THYMELAEACEAE

Daphne mezereum L.   Mezereon, Spurge Olive

0.5–1.5 m tall, erect, perennial shrub, whose flowers open before the leaves appear.
In beech woods and mixed deciduous forests, on wet, nutrient-rich, usually calcareous loam or weathered-rock soils.
<u>Leaves</u> deciduous, entire, oblanceolate, short-petiolate, clustered at the ends of the branches.
<u>Flowers</u> usually in threes in axils of leaves fallen the previous year; hypanthium tubular or narrowly campanulate; sepals and hypanthium petaloid; colour varying from pink to purple-red, rarely white, strongly scented; III–IV.
<u>Fruits</u> scarlet, drupes with glossy, green, later brown, seed; rarer, yellow fruits (garden form: *D. mezereum* 'Alba'); VIII–IX. *D. laureola*, spurge-laurel, has blue-black and *D. cneorum*, garland flower, brown drupes.
<u>Distribution:</u> Most of Europe except the extreme north, west, and south; often cultivated as a garden plant.

ONE of the first messengers of spring to be seen in gardens and parks is the mezereon. Its former importance as a medicinal and poisonous plant is reflected in the large number of vernacular names given to this decorative shrub in the German-speaking world. Because of the acrid-tasting and skin-irritant substances present, the bark (Cortex Mezerei) and fruits (Fructus Coccognidii) of *Daphne mezereum* – and other *Daphne* species as well – found use as a counter-irritant in gout, rheumatism, and many other ailments. Likewise, in the begging profession the blistering effects of extracts were used to produce wounds in order to arouse pity [N15]. In the last century, because of the therapeutic application of the plant, *Daphne* poisoning was frequent, but nowadays it is mainly children who are at risk through the pleasant-smelling flowers and shiny red berries. While man and animals are prevented from eating large amounts by the sharp taste, there are many observations which show that, after ingesting small pieces of bark, leaf, flower, or fruit, serious toxic symptoms can occur:

'All parts are highly toxic. Two or three fruits may contain enough of the acrid juice to be fatal to a child' [H60].

'. . . doses of a few berries or a few grams of bark being reported fatal to man, dog or horse' [S90].

As little as 3 fruits in a pig and 30 g bark in a horse lead to death [L23].

Nöller [N15] has given a detailed picture of the symptoms of poisoning in a 7-year old boy who, after eating several mezereon flowers, was admitted to the Department of Paediatrics, University of Heidelberg:

After the beginning of the illness (headache and stomach pains) and with an abdominal picture which on its own would not have raised any doubts about a diagnosis of appendicitis, a number of neurologically and psychically striking symptoms developed in the hours that followed. Periods of complete disorientation and very severe motor unrest alternated with periods of complete clarity, with

179 **Flowering mezereon.**

tetanoid fearfulness. Towards evening, signs of meningitis and finally generalised convulsions appeared. Very severe diarrhoea then heralded serious enteritis which only subsided after a week.

Toxic constituents. It is esters with a diterpenoid (daphnane) skeleton which are responsible for these drastic effects. In 1970, almost simultaneously, the toxic principles from the bark, daphnetoxin [S90], and the fruits, mezerein (0.04%) [S13; S14], were isolated and their structures elucidated. Animal experiments showed that mezerein, in addition to its skin-irritant properties, has co-carcinogenic activity

like the chemically related phorbol esters present in many toxic Euphorbiaceae (p.113) [H31]. The resultant interest in these compounds led subsequently to many investigations into their biological activity and the structural features required [F28]. Extensive reviews dealing with the chemistry, distribution, and actions of these substances have been written by Hecker [H31; H32] and by Evans and Soper [E11].

For daphnetoxin Stout *et al.* [S90] determined a LD_{50} in the mouse of *ca* 275 μg/kg, while Schildknecht *et al.* [S13] established the 'mouse-ear inflammation unit' as 0.2 μg mezerein/ear. As regards the quantitative distribution of the skin-irritant substances

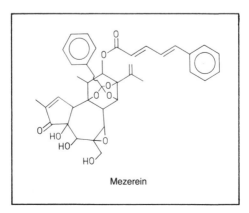

Mezerein

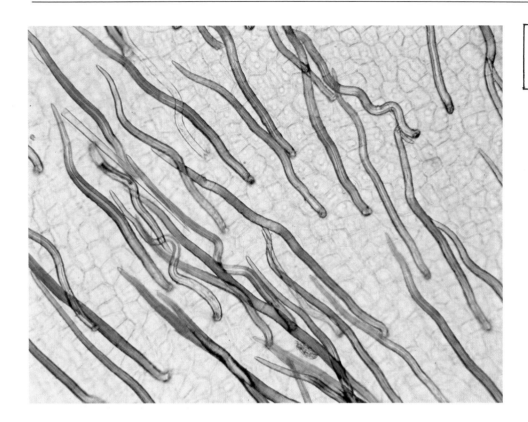

180 Daphne mezereum: Characteristic pubescence of the flowers (photographed in polarised light).

in the different parts of mezereon, there are no precise figures available; but they probably occur in all parts with the exception of the fruit pulp. We have been able to confirm through our own skin tests the statement of Krienke [K 47] that mezerein does not occur in the pulp and that it is the chewed seed that is responsible for the symptoms. On placing fragments of the seed on healthy skin a positive reaction – local reddening – is observed after 4–6 hours. In the following 10 hours the spot treated swells with the formation of pustules and blisters and there is a continual feeling of irritation. The effects slowly disappear in the course of the next two days. A similar test reveals that the pulp (pericarp) has no inflammatory activity.

Treatment. In essence, symptomatic. After ingestion of several berries (especially the chewed seeds) or flowers, direct removal of the poison by gastric lavage can be considered. According to Nöller [N 15], the inflammation of the mucous membranes can be treated with astringents, the neurological and psychical symptoms checked with phenobarbitone (Luminal®), and persistent nausea and salivation can be alleviated by atropine. Moeschlin [M 50] recommends: cooling wrappings, anaesthetising salves, and, internally, calcium gluconate 20 ml i.v.; if necessary, cortisone preparations.

Understandably, the **symptoms** arising from contact between these irritant substances and mucosa are very much more dramatic. Oral poisoning leads within a few hours to a serious condition with severe irritation and a burning sensation in the mouth, swelling of the lips and face, salivation, as well as hoarseness and difficulty in swallowing. There are also severe abdominal pains and headache, numbness, nausea, and bloody diarrhoea. In children, narcotic symptoms and muscular twitching have frequently been seen [N 15].

Microscopical characters of the fruit and the petaloid calyx. The tube of the flowers of *Daphne mezereum* has a dense pubescence, comprising unicellular thick-walled trichomes whose sinuous form is shown in colour in **180.**

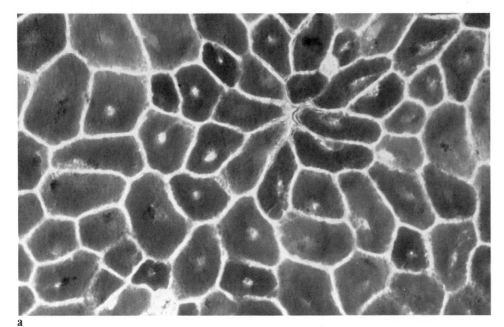

a

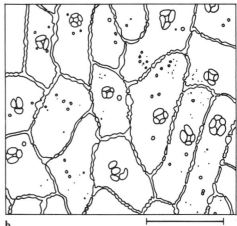

b

181 Daphne mezereum: (a) Epidermis of the pericarp. (b) Testa.

The epidermis of mezereon berries has stomata and occasionally also epidermal idioblasts. It is noteworthy that the guard cells of the stomata are very small and almost semicircular. In contrast with the observations of other authors [B 24; G 30], we find that the epidermis is by no means free of colouring matter **(181a).** The outermost multi-layered part of the testa contains numerous chloroplasts and in the fresh state this gives the single seed of the berry a greenish appearance. The walls of the epidermal cells of the testa are thin and distinctly beaded **(181b).** In the inner part of the testa there is a brown layer of palisade-like stone cells.

VERBENACEAE

Lantana camara L.   Lantana

182 Lantana

0.3–1 m tall herb, erect, with 4-angled stems; in Europe a popular annual summer plant.
<u>Leaves</u> oblong-ovate, tapering, with serrate margin and upper surface reticulately rugose, lower surface often with greyish white pubescence.
<u>Flowers</u> in spicate inflorescences, but crowded into hemispherical heads at ends of branches. Petals mostly orange, during flowering colour changing to yellow, red, or lilac.
<u>Fruits</u> small drupes, with large kernel, first green, becoming blue-black when ripe; IX–X.
<u>Distribution:</u> Originally from tropical America, but now pantropical and partly also in subtropical regions, especially in secondary growth. Other ornamentals are *L. montevidensis* and *L. camara* hybrids formed by crossing with other species such as *L. montevidensis* and *L. urticaefolia*.

WHERE it grows wild, lantana has long been known as a plant poisonous to grazing animals [P8]. Symptoms of *Lantana* poisoning include jaundice, photo-hypersensitivity, and constipation. In dead animals there is accumulation of bile, enlargement of the gall bladder, and renal damage. There is a recent series of papers dealing with the investigation of lantana toxicity in various experimental animals [P7; P9; P10; S49; S50; S109].

Pentacyclic triterpenes, lantadene A and B, have been shown to be the (hepato-)toxic principle. In sheep, 60 mg/kg lantadene A by mouth produces the typical symptoms of *Lantana* poisoning. Lantadene B appears to be less toxic [S40]. The two triterpenes are to be found especially in the leaves [S48]. Non-toxic varieties ('Common Pink', etc.) contain triterpenes with structures different from those of the lantadenes [H14].

Lantadene A

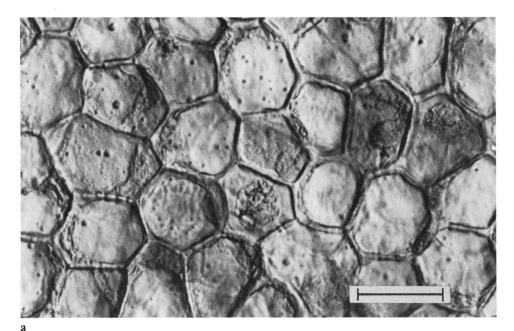

a

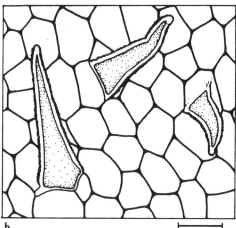

b

183 Lantana camara: (a) Epidermis of the pericarp. (b) Typical trichomes.

The poisoning of children after ingestion of the green fruits (according to Morton [M59] the ripe fruits are eaten in tropical countries) has been repeatedly described.*

Wolfson and Solomons [W31] reported on 17 cases in two years, including one fatal case and three with clinical symptoms which to some extent resembled those of deadly nightshade poisoning, with, for example, dilatation of the pupils. In all the cases, children below six years of age had eaten an undetermined number of unripe fruits; in the case that ended fatally, unlike the other ones, gastric lavage had not been carried out.

There are no recent studies on the toxicity of the unripe fruits and the changes on ripening, or comparisons between animal and human poisoning.

> **Treatment.** Up to three hours after ingesting the unripe fruits, only gastric lavage; for the rest, give corticosteroids, adrenaline, and, if necessary, oxygen [W31].

Microscopical characters of the fruit. The epidermis of the pericarp of *L. camara* consists of polygonal cells with pitted walls which may also show some beading **(183a).** Stomata are present; their guard cells are raised above the level of the (5–6) subsidiary cells. A notable feature of these fruits is the unicellular covering trichomes with a warty surface **(183b)** which occur mainly on those parts of the pericarp that under a handlens appear as silvery-scaly areas standing out from the dark glossy parts.

---

* No cases have as yet been noted in the statistics of the European Toxicological Centres.

Appendix. A note on some British poisonous plants met with in veterinary practice

British poisonous plants are the subject of several fairly recent publications.* Vale and Meredith [V11], drawing on their experience at the Poisons Unit, Guy's Hospital, London, have written a short account of the more important poisonous plants and fungi involved in human intoxication in the United Kingdom. The plants which are most often the subject of enquiries are given in Table 3 on p.16. The authors discuss most of them further and give details of the clinical features and treatment; they have all been dealt with in the foregoing pages of this book.

On the other hand, the accounts by North [N16], published in co-operation with the Pharmaceutical Society of Great Britain, and by Forsyth [F33], published as a reference book of the Ministry of Agriculture, Fisheries and Food, are also particularly concerned with plants responsible for poisoning in animals. It is difficult to say which plant is the most important in affecting farm animals, as it varies from locality to locality and from year to year. However, data on the number of incidents investigated by the Epidemiology Unit, Central Veterinary Laboratories, suggest that in cattle bracken tends to be a more frequent source of poisoning than ragwort and in sheep *Brassica* is probably the chief plant source of poisoning.

The plants listed below are not otherwise mentioned in the present book but are included in these two references as being involved in animal poisoning; the symptoms caused and the active principles (if known) are briefly indicated.

Boraginaceae

Cynoglossum officinale – hound's-tongue: inco-ordination, tympany, rapid pulse, dyspnoea, and diarrhoea; pyrrolizidine alkaloids.

Brassicaceae (Cruciferae)

Brassica oleracea – wild cabbage (kale): haemolytic anaemia, goitre; (+)-S-methyl-L-cysteine sulphoxide and goitrogens of thiouracil or thiocyanate type.

Brassica napus – rape: digestive, respiratory, nervous, and urinary (haemolytic anaemia) syndromes; glucosinolates (S-containing glycosides which decompose enzymatically or in the presence of moisture giving oily organic isothiocyanates (mustard oils)), nitrate, and goitrogens are present in the species.

Sinapis species – white mustard, charlock: acute gastro-enteritis, pain, diarrhoea; glucosinolates.

Raphanus rhaphinistrum – wild radish: gastro-enteritis, liver and kidney disorders; glucosinolates.

Armoracia rusticana – horse-radish; inflammation of stomach or rumen and excitement followed by collapse; glucosinolates yielding, among others, allyl isothiocyanate.

Caryophyllaceae

Saponaria officinalis – soapwort: gastro-enteritis, cardiac and CNS depression; saponins.

Fabaceae

Trifolium hybridum – alsike clover, *Medicago sativa* – lucerne, *Medicago polymorpha* – toothed medick, *Vicia sativa* – common vetch: photosensitisation (trifoliosis).

Hypericaceae

Hypericum species – St. John's-Wort: photosensitisation; hypericin.

Juncaceae

Juncus inflexus – hard rush: gastrointestinal irritation, diarrhoea, nervousness, blindness, then convulsions and death from cerebral haemorrhage.

Lamiaceae (Labiatae)

Glechoma hederacea – ground-ivy: pulmonary oedema, enteritis; volatile oil?

Liliaceae

Hyacinthoides (Endymion) non-scripta – bluebell: abdominal pain, attempted vomiting, weak and slow pulse, lowered temperature, bloody diarrhoea.

Oleaceae

Fraxinus excelsior – ash: acute impaction of the rumen leading to cessation of defaecation and rumination.

Orobanchaceae

Orobanche species – broomrape: gastro-enteritis, diuresis.

Polygonaceae

Fagopyrum esculentum – buckwheat: photosensitisation (fagopyrism).

Scrophulariaceae

Scrophularia auriculata (aquatica) – water figwort: excitement, accelerated respiration, dilated pupils, infrequent and painful urination, diarrhoea, thirst, lack of appetite.

There are other genera with representatives which are known to have caused poisoning in animals in other parts of the world but not in the British Isles. For details, see [N16] and [F33].

---

* See especially: Cooper, M.R. and A.W. Johnson: Poisonous plants in Britain – and their effects on animals and man, pp.330, HMSO, London (1984).

4. Berry-like fruits – a tabular synopsis

In the following synopsis, conspicuous fruits are arranged according to colour (when ripe) and size. In contrast with other fruit keys [M 14], for the individual fruits only details concerning the nature of the pulp, number of stones, arrangement of the fruits on the plant, and the habit of the plant are indicated. This, of course, does not allow the identification of an unknown fruit, but it does narrow down the number of possibilities and further information can be looked for under the plant descriptions in the body of the text. The leaf illustrations on pages 237–267 offer a further aid to identification.

1. Red fruits
1.1 Cherry size
1.1.1 With juicy pulp

No. of stones	Infructescence (No. of fruits)	Plant	Name
One	One to several	Woody	*Cornus mas*
One	Several	Woody	*Aucuba japonica*
Several	One	Herbaceous/woody	*Physalis alkekengi*
Several	One	Woody	*Solanum pseudocapsicum*
Several	One to several	Woody	*Ribes uva-crispa*
Several	Several	Herbaceous	*Actaea rubra*

1.1.2 With mealy pulp

One to several	One to several	Woody	*Crataegus*
Several	Several	Woody	*Sorbus*

1.2 Up to pea size
1.2.1 With juicy pulp

One	One	Woody	*Taxus baccata*
One	Several	Woody	*Daphne mezereum*
One	Several	Woody	*Viburnum opulus*
One	Several	Woody	*Elaeagnus umbellata*
One	Several	Woody	*Hippophae rhamnoides* (yellowish red)
One to several	Several	Woody	*Ribes alpinum*
Several	One	Woody	*Lycium barbarum*
Several	One	Woody	*Solanum pseudocapsicum*
Several	Paired	Woody	*Lonicera xylosteum*
Several	Paired	Woody	*Lonicera tatarica*

1. Red fruits
1.2 Up to pea size
1.2.1 With juicy pulp

Several	One to several	Woody	*Berberis vulgaris*
Several	One to several	Woody	*Rhamnus frangula*
Several	One to several	Climbing	*Bryonia cretica*
Several	One to several	Climbing	*Tamus communis*
Several	Several	Woody	*Ribes rubrum*
Several	Several	Woody	*Solanum dulcamara*
Several	Several	Woody	*Sambucus racemosa*
Several	Several	Climbing	*Lonicera periclymenum*
Several	Several	Herbaceous	*Arum maculatum*
Several	Several	Herbaceous	*Convallaria majalis*

1.2.2 With mealy pulp

One to several	One to several	Woody	*Cotoneaster*
Several	One	Herbaceous	*Asparagus officinalis*
Several	One to several	Woody	*Amelanchier lamarckii*
Several	One to several	Woody	*Ilex aquifolium*
Several	One to several	Woody	*Pyracantha coccinea*
Several	One to several	Woody	*Symphoricarpos orbiculatus*
Several	One to several	Herbaceous/woody	*Gaultheria procumbens*
Several	One to several	Herbaceous/woody	*Vaccinium oxycoccos*
Several	One to several	Herbaceous/woody	*Vaccinium vitis-idaea*
Several	Several	Herbaceous	*Calla palustris*
Several	Several	Herbaceous	*Maianthemum bifolium*
Several	Several	Woody	*Pernettya mucronata*
Several	Several	Woody	*Sorbus aucuparia*
Several	Several	Woody	*Rhus typhina*

2. Blue-black fruits
2.1 Cherry size
2.1.1 With juicy pulp

No. of stones	Infructescence (No. of fruits)	Plant	Name
One	One to several	Woody	*Prunus spinosa*
Several	One	Herbaceous/woody	*Atropa bella-donna*

2.1.2 With mealy pulp

Several	One	Herbaceous	*Nicandra physaloides*
Several	One	Herbaceous	*Paris quadrifolia*
Several	One to several	Woody	*Amelanchier lamarckii*

2.2 Up to pea size
2.2.1 With juicy pulp

One	Several	Woody	*Cornus sanguinea*
One	Several	Woody	*Prunus padus, P. serotina*
One	Several	Woody	*Sarcococca humilis*
One	Several	Woody	*Viburnum lantana, V. rhytidophyllum*
One or two	Several	Woody	*Ligustrum vulgare*
Several	One (double)	Woody	*Lonicera*
Several	One to several	Woody	*Vaccinium*
Several	One to several	Woody	*Rhamnus frangula*
Several	One to several	Woody	*Berberis*
Several	Paired	Woody	*Lonicera ledebourii*
Several	Several	Woody	*Mahonia aquifolium*
Several	Several	Woody	*Rhamnus catharticus*
Several	Several	Woody	*Ribes*
Several	Several	Woody	*Sambucus nigra*
Several	Several	Climbing	*Bryonia alba*
Several	Several	Climbing	*Lonicera henryi*
Several	Several	Herbaceous/woody	*Empetrum nigrum*
Several	Several	Herbaceous/woody	*Phytolacca americana*
Several	Several	Herbaceous	*Actaea spicata*
Several	Several	Herbaceous	*Lantana camara*
Several	Several	Herbaceous	*Sambucus ebulus*
Several	Several	Herbaceous	*Solanum nigrum*

2.2.2. With mealy pulp

One to several	One to several	Woody	*Cotoneaster*
Several	One to several	Herbaceous	*Polygonatum*
Several	Several	Woody	*Juniperus*
Several	Several	Climbing	*Hedera helix*

3. White fruits
3.1 Cherry size
3.1.1 With juicy pulp

No. of stones	Infructescence (No. of fruits)	Plant	Name
Several	Several	Herbaceous	*Actaea pachypoda*

3.1.2 With mealy pulp

One	Several	Herbaceous/woody	*Pachysandra terminalis* (fruit horned)
Several	One to several	Woody	*Symphoricarpos albus*

3.2 Up to pea size
3.2.1 With juicy pulp

One	Several	Woody	*Cornus alba*
One	Several	Epiphytic	*Viscum album* (fruit viscid)
Several	Several	Woody	*Ribes*

3.2.2 With mealy pulp

Several	Several	Woody	*Pernettya mucronata*

4. Yellow fruits
Pyracantha coccinea (var. *lutea*)
Atropa bella-donna (var. *lutea*)
Chaenomeles
Hippophae

5. Green fruits
Solanum tuberosum
Ribes uva-crispa
In addition, the berries of *Solanum nigrum* and *Polygonatum* are more often greenish than black!

While the number of berry-like green fruits is relatively small, many other plants have fruits that are usually green when ripe but whose form is different. They may be capsules as in *Colchicum, Datura,* or *Papaver*, etc., follicles as in *Aconitum* or *Helleborus*, or pods as in *Laburnum, Lupinus,* and other Fabaceae.

5. Compilation of leaf characters

The following pages illustrate the leaves of the plants discussed in the main part of the book (with the exception of a few house plants) arranged according to morphological principles. In the photographic reproduction particular attention has been paid to the presentation of the venation of the lamina (which gave rise to difficulties with some of the thick leathery leaves). The shape and venation of foliaceous leaves can, along with other features, be a genuine help in identifying plants; and with a few exceptions, e.g. *Arum*, they are still on the plant at the time the fruits are ripe. By comparison with the illustrations on the following pages, the suspected identity of a plant can be strengthened or discarded as being improbable.

It must, nevertheless, be remembered that foliaceous leaves, depending on their age and insertion, exhibit considerable variation not only in size but also, according to circumstances, in their shape (heterophylly). Understandably, only a few of the more distinct variations have found a place in the present compilation. Finally, it may be pointed out that very small leaves (<5 cm), whatever their shape, are collected together on p.247.

Cyclamen purpurascens

Arum maculatum var. *maculatum*
(various leaf shapes)

Maianthemum bifolium

Arum maculatum var. *maculatum*
(various leaf shapes)

Hedera helix

Caltha palustris

Calla palustris

Tamus communis

Lonicera henryi

Ilex aquifolium

Cornus sanguinea

Vincetoxicum hirundinaria

Cornus mas

Euonymus europaeus

Cornus sericea

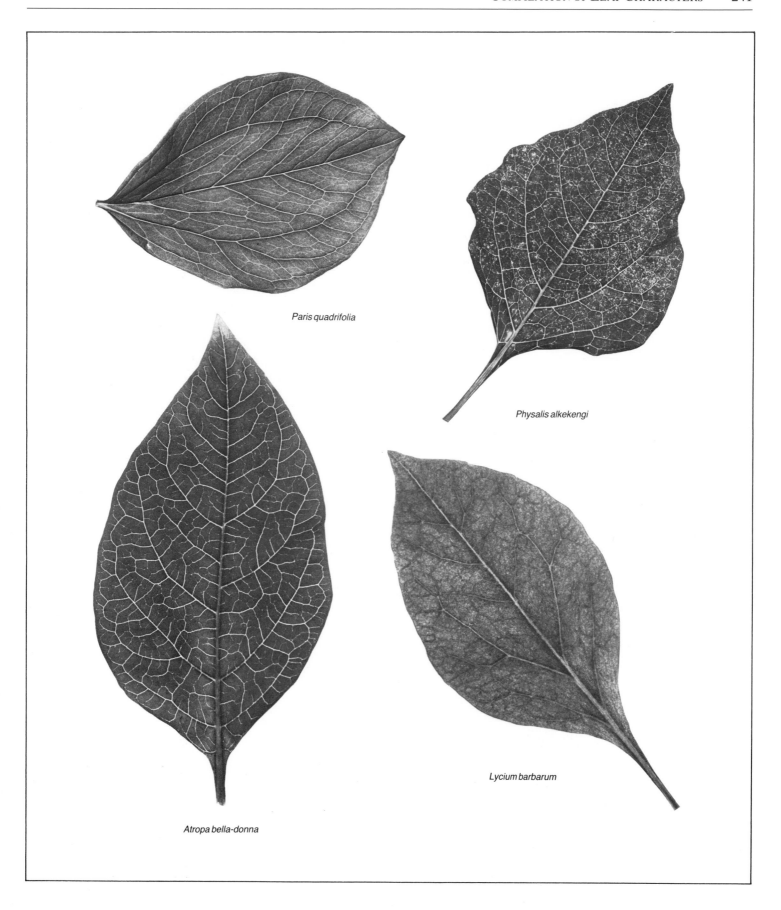

Paris quadrifolia

Physalis alkekengi

Lycium barbarum

Atropa bella-donna

Symphoricarpos albus

Weigela floribunda

Cotoneaster insignis

Cotinus coggygria

Rhamnus frangula

Phytolacca americana

Lonicera caerulea

Lonicera ledebourii

Lonicera periclymenum

Lonicera tatarica

Lonicera caprifolium

Lonicera caprifolium

Lonicera xylosteum

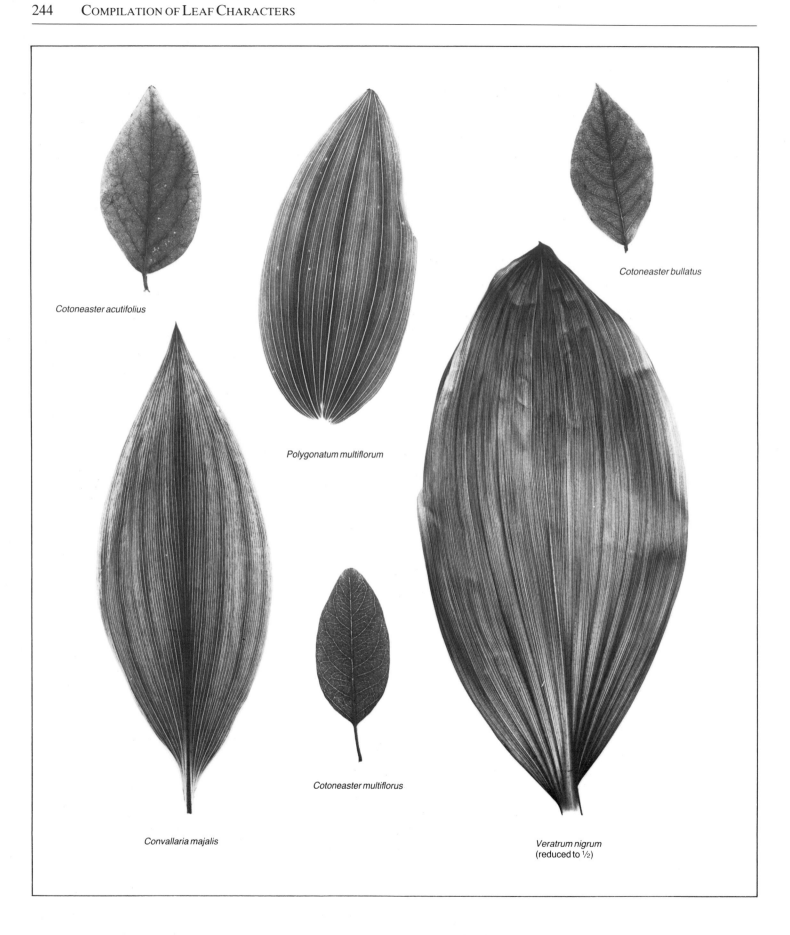

Cotoneaster acutifolius

Polygonatum multiflorum

Cotoneaster bullatus

Cotoneaster multiflorus

Convallaria majalis

Veratrum nigrum
(reduced to ½)

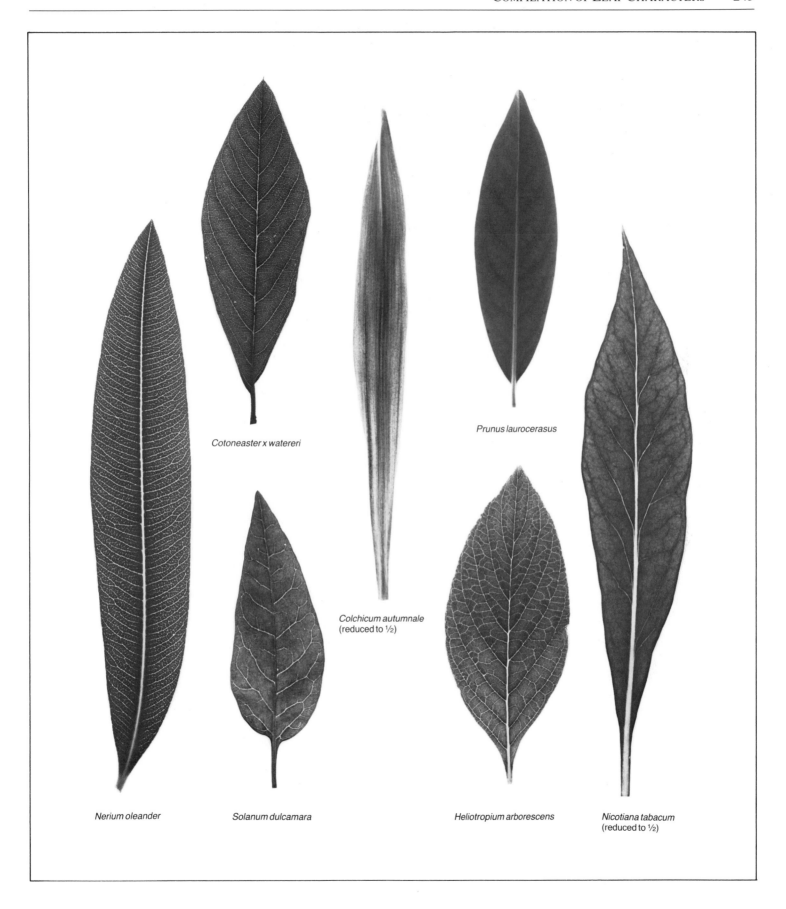

Cotoneaster x watereri

Prunus laurocerasus

Colchicum autumnale
(reduced to ½)

Nerium oleander

Solanum dulcamara

Heliotropium arborescens

Nicotiana tabacum
(reduced to ½)

Rhododendron mollis

Cotoneaster salicifolius

Viscum album

Hippophae rhamnoides

Daphne mezereum

Sarcococca
humilis

Ligustrum vulgare

Lycium barbarum

Elaeagnus umbellata

Catharanthus roseus

Viburnum rhytidophyllum

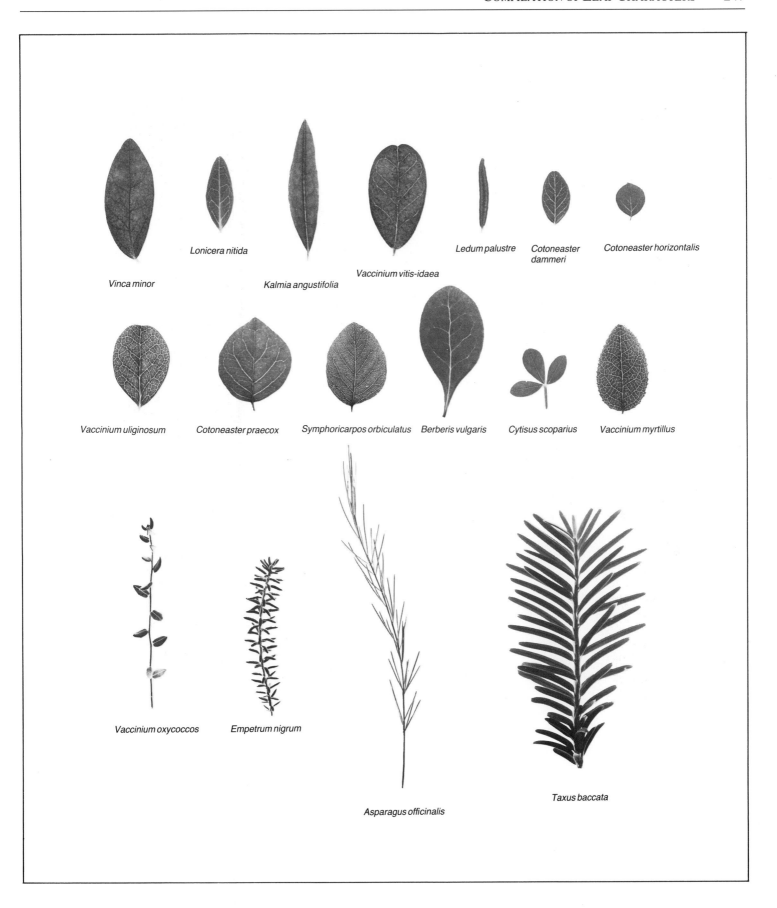

Vinca minor

Lonicera nitida

Kalmia angustifolia

Vaccinium vitis-idaea

Ledum palustre

Cotoneaster dammeri

Cotoneaster horizontalis

Vaccinium uliginosum

Cotoneaster praecox

Symphoricarpos orbiculatus

Berberis vulgaris

Cytisus scoparius

Vaccinium myrtillus

Vaccinium oxycoccos

Empetrum nigrum

Asparagus officinalis

Taxus baccata

Rhamnus catharticus

Amelanchier lamarckii

Viburnum lantana

Sorbus aria

Sorbus intermedia

Digitalis purpurea

Prunus padus

Lactuca virosa
(reduced to ⅔)

Prunus serotina

Prunus laurocerasus

Prunus avium

Chaenomeles japonica

Prunus spinosa

Solanum nigrum

Lantana camara

Symphoricarpos albus

Prunus dulcis

Pyracantha coccinea

Pieris japonica

Gratiola officinalis

Solanum pseudocapsicum

Papaver somniferum
(reduced to ⅔)

Hyoscyamus niger
(reduced to ⅔)

Datura stramonium
(reduced to ⅔)

Ilex aquifolium
(reduced to ⅔)

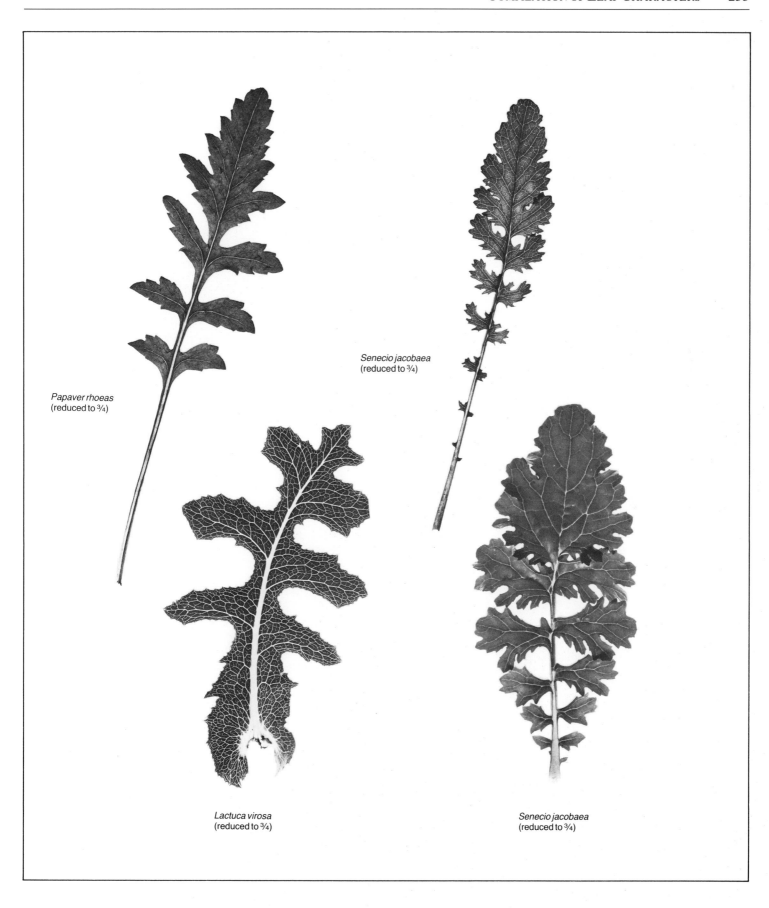

Papaver rhoeas
(reduced to ¾)

Senecio jacobaea
(reduced to ¾)

Lactuca virosa
(reduced to ¾)

Senecio jacobaea
(reduced to ¾)

Bryonia alba

Crataegus monogyna

Hedera helix

Bryonia cretica

Viburnum opulus

Ribes aureum

Ribes niveum

Ribes rubrum

Ribes aureum

Ribes alpinum

Ribes uva-crispa

Ribes sanguineum

Ribes nigrum

Clematis montana
(reduced to ½)

Helleborus niger
(reduced to ½)

Delphinium elatum
(reduced to ½)

Ricinus communis
(reduced to ½)

Corydalis cava

Ranunculus acris

Ranunculus sceleratus

Chelidonium majus

Lupinus polyphyllus
(reduced to ½)

Lupinus luteus
(reduced to ½)

Lupinus angustifolius
(reduced to ½)

Aesculus hippocastanum
(reduced to ½)

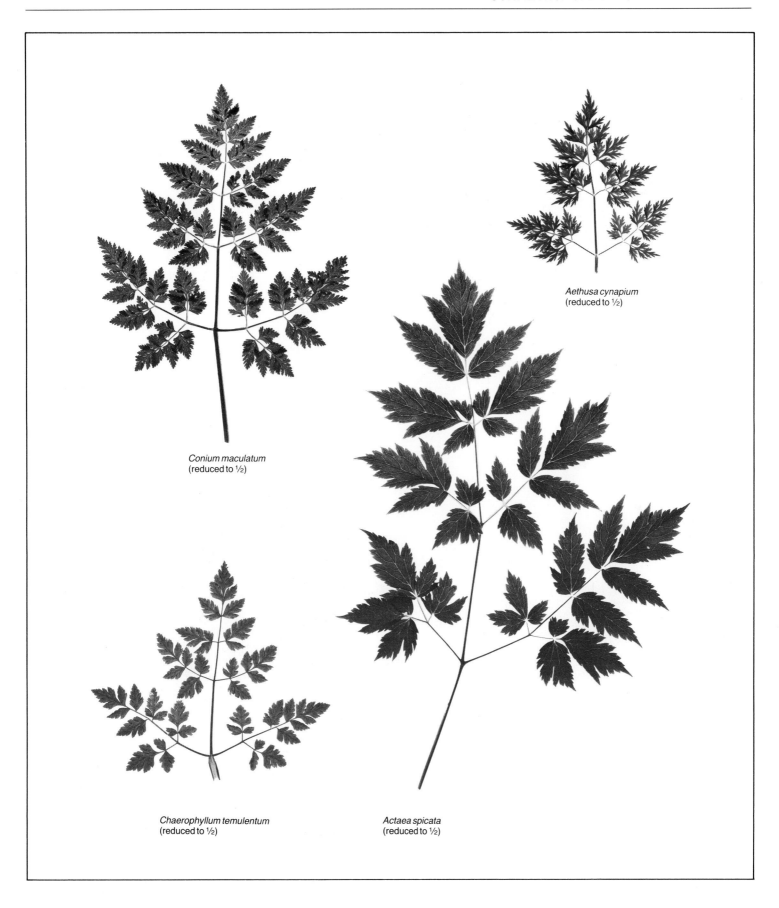

Conium maculatum
(reduced to ½)

Aethusa cynapium
(reduced to ½)

Chaerophyllum temulentum
(reduced to ½)

Actaea spicata
(reduced to ½)

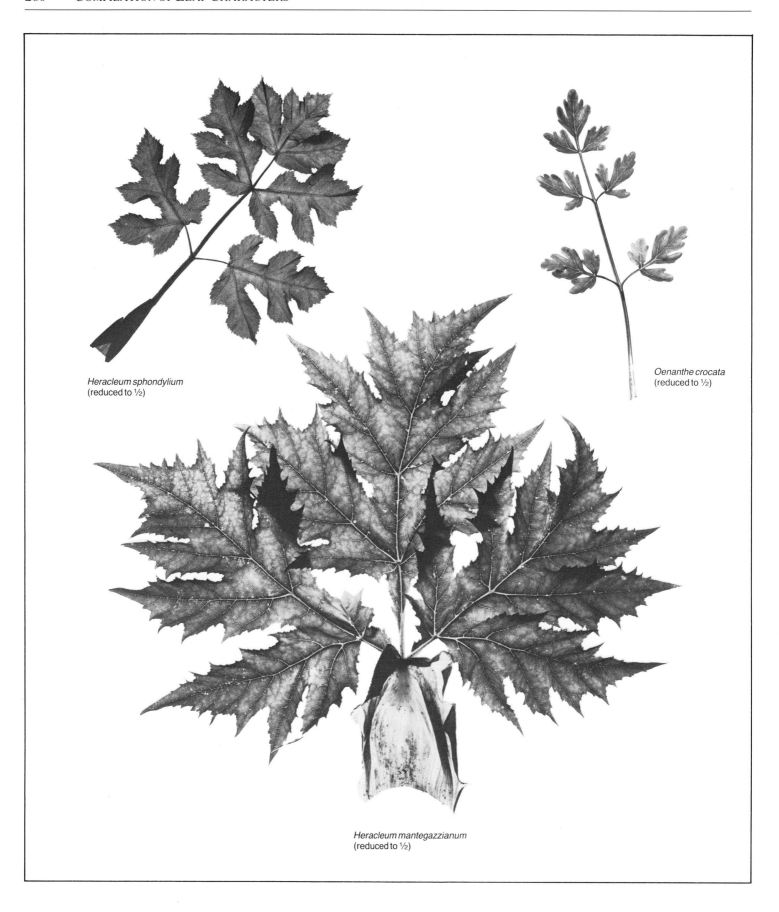

Heracleum sphondylium
(reduced to ½)

Oenanthe crocata
(reduced to ½)

Heracleum mantegazzianum
(reduced to ½)

Ranunculus acris
(reduced to ⅔)

Cicuta virosa
(reduced to ⅔)

Aconitum napellus
(reduced to ⅔)

Adonis vernalis

Pulsatilla vulgaris
(reduced to ⅔)

Aconitum vulparia
(reduced to ⅔)

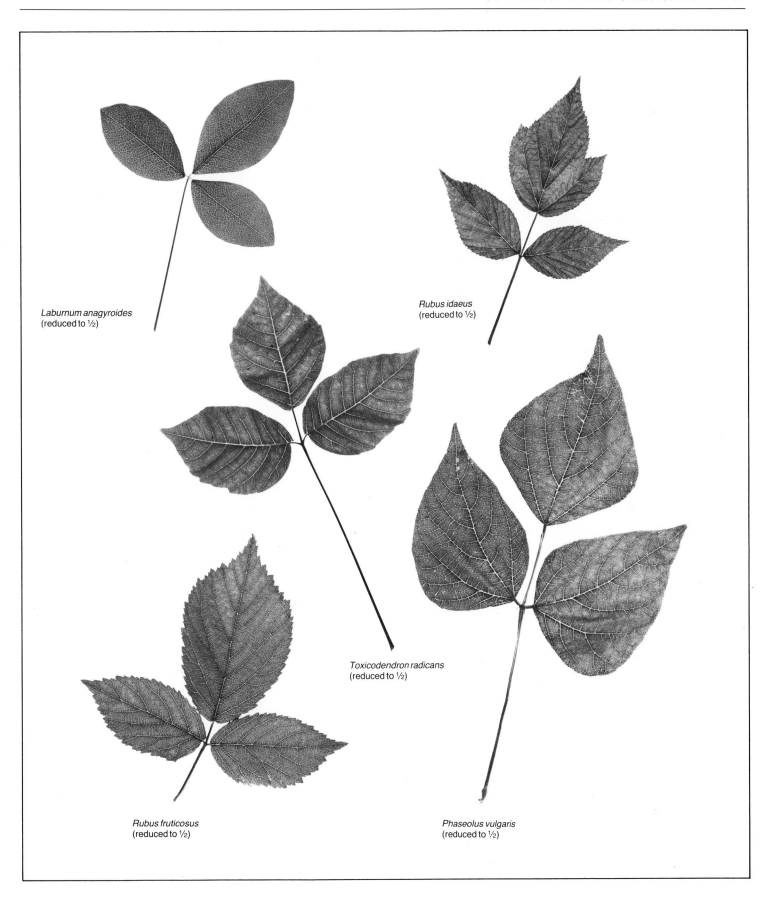

Laburnum anagyroides
(reduced to ½)

Rubus idaeus
(reduced to ½)

Toxicodendron radicans
(reduced to ½)

Rubus fruticosus
(reduced to ½)

Phaseolus vulgaris
(reduced to ½)

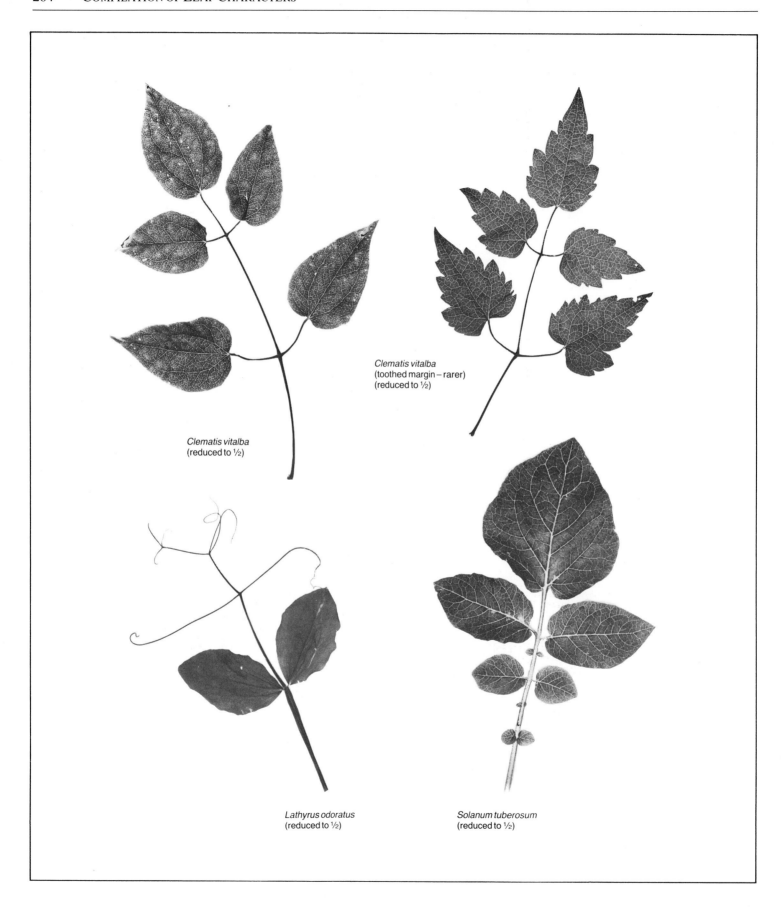

Clematis vitalba
(reduced to ½)

Clematis vitalba
(toothed margin – rarer)
(reduced to ½)

Lathyrus odoratus
(reduced to ½)

Solanum tuberosum
(reduced to ½)

Mahonia aquifolium
(reduced to ½)

Sambucus nigra
(reduced to ½)

Sambucus ebulus
(reduced to ½)

Sambucus racemosa
(reduced to ½)

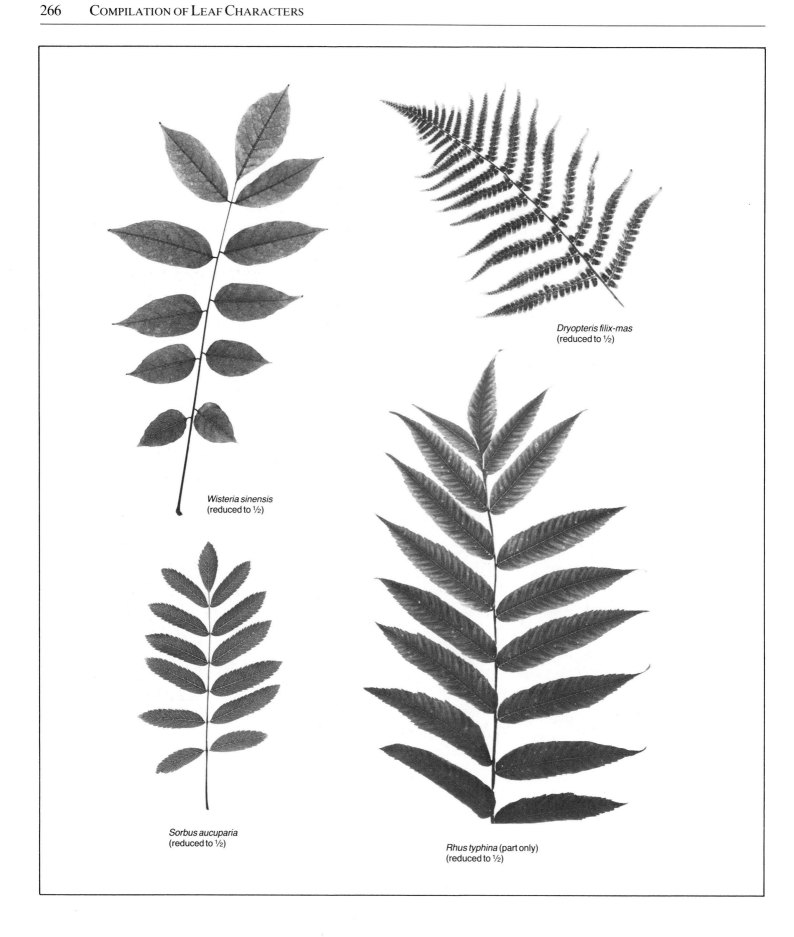

Dryopteris filix-mas
(reduced to ½)

Wisteria sinensis
(reduced to ½)

Sorbus aucuparia
(reduced to ½)

Rhus typhina (part only)
(reduced to ½)

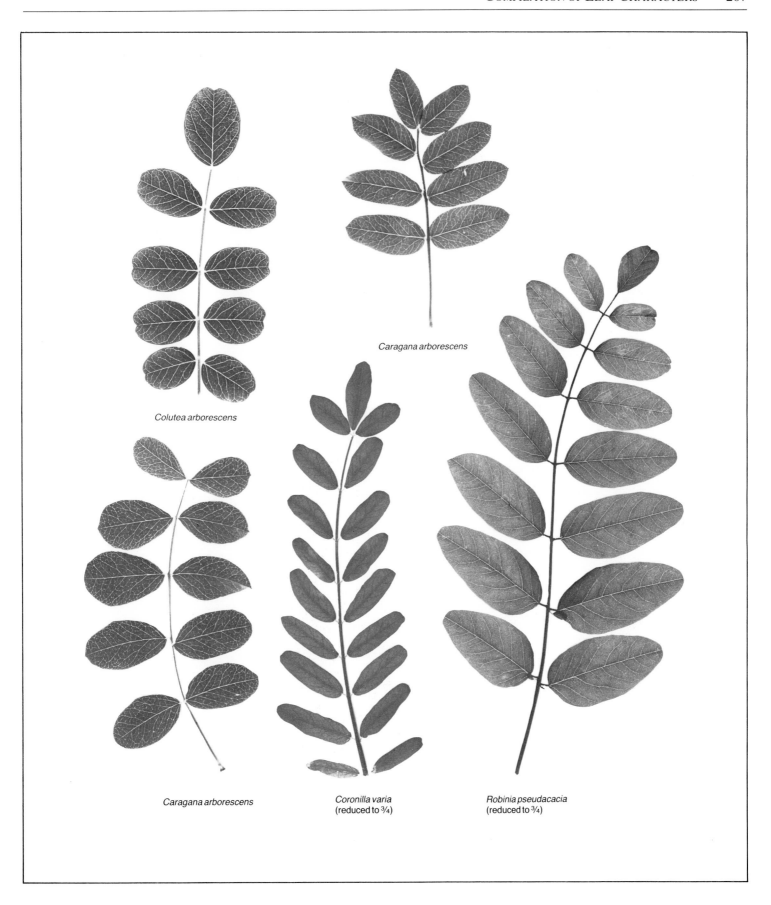

Colutea arborescens

Caragana arborescens

Caragana arborescens

Coronilla varia
(reduced to ¾)

Robinia pseudacacia
(reduced to ¾)

6. Bibliography

[A 1] Abutalybov, M. G., S. M. Aslanov, and E. N. Novruzov: The chemical composition of ripe fruits of the buckthorn growing in the Azerbaijan S. S. R. Rastit. Resurs. *14*, 220–222 (1978). Cited from: Biol.Abstr. *67*, 18 085 (1979).

[A 2] Adler, A. G., P. Walinsky, R. A. Krall, and S. Y. Cho: Death resulting from ipecac syrup poisoning. J. Am. Med. Ass. *243*, 1227–1228 (1980).

[A 3] Alden, C. L., C. J. Fosnaugh, J. B. Smith, and R. Mohan: Japanese yew poisoning of large domestic animals in the midwest. J. Am. Vet. Med. Ass. *170*, 314–316 (1977).

[A 4] Alexander, R. F., G. B. Forbes, and E. S. Hawkins: A fatal case of solanine poisoning. Br. Med. J. *2*, 518 (1948).

[A 5] Altmann, H.: Giftpflanzen – Gifttiere. Die wichtigsten Arten – Erkennen, Giftwirkung, Therapie, BLV, München, Bern, Wien, 144 pp., 1979.

[A 6] Amico, A., L. Stefanizzi, and S. Bruno: Osservazioni morfologiche, estrazione e localizzazione di alcaloidi in *Clivia miniata* Regel. Fitoterapia *50*, 157–165 (1979).

[A 7] Amyot, T. E.: Poisoning by snowberries. Br. Med. J. *1*, 986 (1885).

[A 8] Anderson, T., S. Konracki, D. O. Lyman, and W. E. Parkin: Diarrhea from herbal tea – New York, Pennsylvania. Morbid. Mortal. Weekly Rept *27*, 248–249 (1978).

[A 9] Anet, E. F. L. J., B. Lythgoe, M. H. Silk, and S. Trippett: Oenanthotoxin and cicutoxin. Isolation and structures. J. Chem. Soc. 309–322 (1953).

[A 10] Anger, J.-P., F. Anger, Y. Chauvel, R. L. Girre, N. Curtes, and J.-P. Curtes: Intoxication mortelle par Oenanthe safranée *(Oenanthe crocata)*. Eur. J. Toxicol. *9*, 119–125 (1976).

[A 11] Ansford, A. J. and H. Morris: Fatal oleander poisoning: Med. J. Aust. *1*, 360–361 (1981).

[A 12] Applefeld, J. C. and E. S. Caplan: A case of water hemlock poisoning. J. Am. Coll. Emerg. Phys. *8*, 401–403 (1979).

[A 13] Arai, I., D. L. Dreyer, W. R. Anderson Jr, and G. D. Daves Jr: Neurotoxins of *Karwinskia humboldtiana*. Atropisomerism and diastereomeric oxidation products. J. Org. Chem. *43*, 1253–1254 (1978).

[A 14] Araya, O. S. and E. J. H. Ford: An investigation of the type of photosensitization caused by the ingestion of St. John's Wort *(Hypericum perforatum)* by calves. J. Comp. Pathol. Ther. *91*, 135–141 (1981).

[A 15] D'Arcy, W. G.: Severe contact dermatitis from poinsettia – status of poinsettia as a toxic agent. Arch. Dermatol. *109*, 909–910 (1974).

[A 16] Arlette, J. and J. C. Mitchell: Compositae dermatitis – current aspects. Contact Dermatitis *7*, 129–136 (1981).

[A 17] Aronow, R.: Camphor poisoning. J. Am. Med. Ass. *235*, 1260 (1976).

[A 18] Arzneimittelbrief: Die heutige Therapie der Psoriasis *15* (6), 61–63 (1981).

[A 19] Arzneimittelkommission der Deutschen Apotheker: Warnung vor Arnikatee innerlich. Pharm. Ztg *126*, 2082 (1981).

[A 20] Autenrieth, W. and K. H. Bauer: Die Auffindung der Gifte und stark wirkenden Arzneistoffe – zum Gebrauch in chemischen Laboratorien, 6th revised ed., T. Steinkopf, Dresden, Leipzig, 343 pp., 1943.

[A 21] Ayres Jr, S. and S. Ayres: Philodendron as a cause of contact dermatitis. Arch. Dermatol. *78*, 330–333 (1958).

[A 22] Adawadkar, P. D. and M. A. El Sohly: Isolation, purification and antimicrobial activity of anacardic acids from *Ginkgo biloba* fruits. Fitoterapia *52*, 129–135 (1981).

[A 23] Anderson, L. A. and J. D. Phillipson: Mistletoe – the magic herb. Pharm. J. *229*, 437–439 (1982).

[A 24] Arditti, J. and E. Rodriguez: Dieffenbachia: uses, abuses, and toxic constituents: a review. J. Ethnopharmacol. *5*, 293–302 (1982).

[A 25] Anonymous (Nachrichten): Gesundheitsschädigung durch Holzöl. Pharm. Ztg *82*, 725 (1937).

[A 26] Anonymous (Wichtige Mitteilungen): Warnung vor der Abgabe von Colchicin. Dtsch. Apoth. Ztg *120*, 523 (1980).

[A 27] Anonymous: Tod durch 'O-Tee'. Pharm. Ztg *125*, 1307 (1980).

[A 28] Anonymous: Which antidote for cyanide? Lancet *2*, 1167 (1977). Med. Monatschr. Pharm. *2*, 286 (1979).

[A 29] Anonymous: Solanine poisoning. Br. Med. J. *2*, 1458–1459 (1979).

[A 30] Anonymous: Potato poisoning. Lancet *2*, 681 (1979).

[B 1] Baar, A. van: Dieffenbachia: houdt den dief . . . niet. Ned. Tijdschr. Geneesk. *119*, 1187–1188 (1975).

[B 2] Baer, H.: The poisonous Anacardiaceae. In: Kinghorn, A. D. (ed.), Toxic plants, pp. 161–170, 1979.

[B 3] Balansard, J. and P. Flandrin: Heterosides of the leaves of the holly tree *(Ilex aquifolium)*. Med. Trop. (Madrid) *6*, 203–205 (1946). Cited from: Chem. Abstr. *45*, 7307 (1951).

[B 4] Ballantyne, A., P. Lippiett, and J. Park: Herbal cigarettes for kicks. Br. Med. J. *2*, 1539–1540 (1976).

[B 5] Banach, K.: Ostre zatrucia antrazwiazkami spowodowane spozyciem owoców szaklaku pospolitego (Acute poisoning with anthracene compounds caused by ingestion of fruits of buckthorn). Wiad. Lek. *33*, 405–408 (1980).

[B 6] Bandmann, H. J. and W. Dohn: Das Lorbeeröl als nicht seltene Ursache allergischer Kontaktekzeme. Münch. Med. Wochenschr. *102*, 680 (1960).

[B 7] Baranyai, A.: Personal communication (1980).

[B 8] Barbieri, L., A. Gasperi-Campani, M. Derenzine, C. M. Betts, and F. Stirpe: Selective lesions of acinar pancreatic cells in rats poisoned with abrin. Virchow's Arch. B. Zellpathol. *30*, 15–24 (1979).

[B 9] Barker, B. E., P. Farnes, and P. H. La Marche: Peripheral blood plasmacytosis following systemic exposure to *Phytolacca americana* (pokeweed). Pediatrics *38*, 490–493 (1966).

[B 10] Barnes, B. A.: The pharmacology and toxicology of certain species of Dieffenbachia. Master's thesis, University of Florida, Gainesville, pp. 1–47 (1953).

[B 11] Barnes, B. A. and L. E. Fox: Poisoning with Dieffenbachia. J. Hist. Med. Allied Sci. *10*, 173–181 (1955).

[B 12] Barnett, A. H., F. W. Jones, and E. R. Williams: Acute poisoning with Potter's asthma remedy. Br. Med. J. *2*, 1635 (1977).

[B 13] Barnikol, H. and W. Hofmann: Digitalisvergiftung beim Schwein. Tierärztl. Umsch. *28*, 612–616 (1973).

[B 14] Barros, S. de, E. Tabone, M. dos Santos, M. Andujar, and J.-A. Grimaud: Histopathological and ultrastructural alterations in the aorta in experimental *Solanum malacoxylon* poisoning. Virchow's Arch. B. Cell Pathol. *35*, 169–176 (1981).

[B 15] Bartel, J. and H. U. Gerber: Ein Beitrag zur Vergiftung mit Wasserschierling *(Cicuta virosa* L.) bei Kindern. Kinderärztl. Prax. *30*, 543–547 (1962).

[B 16] Basey, K. and J. G. Woolley: Alkaloids of *Physalis alkekengi*. Phytochemistry *12*, 2557 (1973).

[B 17] Beal, J. L.: Poisonous properties of Taxus. Taxus Symposium, Wooster, Ohio, October 1975.

[B 18] Becker, L. E. and G. B. Skipworth: Ginkgo-tree dermatitis, stomatitis, and proctitis. J. Am. Med. Ass. *231*, 1162–1163 (1975).

[B 19] Beetz, D., H. J. Cramer, and H. C. Mehlhorn: Zur Häufigkeit der epidermalen Allergie gegenüber Kamille in kamillenhaltigen Arzneimitteln und Kosmetika, Dermatol. Monatschr. *157*, 505–510 (1971).

[B 20] Beijersbergen, J. C. M.: Allergische Reaktionen durch Kontakt mit Blumenzwiebeln? Münch. Med. Wochenschr. *117*, 698 (1975).

[B 21] Belton, P. A. and D. O. Gibbons: Datura intoxication in West Cornwall. Br. Med. J. *1*, 585–586 (1979).

[B 22] Benner, M. H. and H. J. Lee: Anaphylactic reaction to chamomile tea. J. Allergy Clin. Immunol. *52*, 307–308 (1973).

[B 23] Bentz, H.: Nutztiervergiftungen. Erkennung und Verhütung, G. Fischer, Jena, 361 pp., 1969.

[B 24] Berger, F.: Handbuch der Drogenkunde – Erkennung, Wertbestimmung und Anwendung, W. Maudrich, Wien, 7 vols., 1949–1967.

[B 25] Berndt, H.: Vergiftungen durch *Cicuta virosa* L., Wasserschierling. Pharmazie *2*, 521–523 (1947).

[B 26] Bethel, R. G. H. Abuse of asthma cigarettes. Br. Med. J. *2*, 959 (1978).

[B 27] Bickoff, E. M., S. C. Witt, and B. E. Knuckles: Studies on the chemical and biological properties of coumestrol and related compounds. Tech. Bull. Agric. Res. Service, U.S. Dept Agric. no. *1408* (1969).

[B 28] Bildzeitung: Giftketten jetzt auch im Bundesgebiet, 31.5.1972.

[B 29] Billington, D., H. Osmundsen, and H. S. A. Sherratt: The biochemical basis of Jamaican akee poisoning. New Engl. J. Med. *295*, 1482 (1976).

[B 30] Birecka, H., M. W. Frohlich, L. Hull, and M. J. Chaskes: Pyrrolizidine alkaloids of *Heliotropium* from Mexico and adjacent U.S.A. Phytochemistry *19*, 421–426 (1980).

[B 31] Birk, Y.: Saponins. In: Liener, I.E. (ed.), Toxic constituents of plant foodstuffs, pp. 169–210 (1969). Cf. Birk, Y. and I. Peri: Saponins. In: Liener, I. E. (ed.), Toxic constituents of plant foodstuffs, 2nd ed., pp. 161–182 (1980).

[B 32] Bismarck, R. and W. Floehr: Über Bingelkrautvergiftungen in einer weidenden Kuhherde. Dtsch. Tierärztl. Wochenschr. *81*, 433–434 (1974).

[B 33] Black, O.F.: Calcium oxalate in the dasheen. Am. J. Bot. *5*, 447–451 (1918).

[B 34] Bleumink, E., H. M. G. Doeglas, A. H. Klokke, and J. P. Nater: Allergic contact dermatitis to garlic. Br. J. Dermatol. *87*, 6–9 (1972).

[B 35] Bleumink, E., J. C. Mitchell, T. A. Geissman, and G. H. N. Towers: Contact hypersensitivity to sesquiterpene lactones in chrysanthemum dermatitis. Contact Dermatitis *2*, 81–88 (1976).

[B 36] Bohlmann, F.: Acetylenic compounds in the Umbelliferae. In: Heywood, V. H. (ed.), The biology and chemistry of the Umbelliferae, Academic Press, London, pp. 279–291, 1971.

[B 37] Bohlmann, F.: Neues über die Chemie der Compositen. Naturwissenschaften *67*, 588–594 (1980).

[B 38] Bohnic, P.: Contribution to the knowledge of the chemism of holly *(Ilex aquifolium)*. Farm. Vestn. (Ljubljana) *10*, 57–58 (1959).

[B 39] Bolton, J. F.: Rhododendron poisoning. Vet. Rec. *67*, 138–139 (1955).

[B 40] Bors, G., I. Popa, A. Voicu, and I. S. Radian: Beiträge zum Studium der Vergiftungen mit *Nerium oleander* L. Pharmazie *26*, 764–766 (1971).

[B 41] Braico, K. T., J. R. Humbert, K. L. Terplan, and J. M. Lehotay: Laetrile intoxication. New Engl. J. Med. *300*, 238–240 (1979).

[B 42] Brauchli, J., J. Lüthy, U. Zweifel, and C. H. Schlatter: Pyrrolizidine alkaloids in *Symphytum officinale* L. and their dermal absorption in rats. Experientia *37*, 667 (1981).

[B 43] Braun, E.: Anatomische Untersuchungen über die Blätter einiger pharmazeutisch interessanter Polypodiaceen. Arch. Pharm. *273*, 201–222 (1935).

[B 44] Braun, H.: Heilpflanzen-Lexikon für Ärzte und Apotheker. Anwendung, Wirkung, Toxikologie, 4th ed, G. Fischer, Stuttgart, New York, 302 pp., 1981.

[B 45] Brodersen, H.-P., W.-D. Schreiner, H. J. Pfänder, and D. Frohne: Dieffenbachia – eine schön(e) giftige Zierpflanze, Dtsch. Apoth. Ztg *119*, 1617–1620 (1979).

[B 46] Brogger, J. N.: Renal failure from Philodendron. Mod. Vet. Pract. *51*, 46 (1970).

[B 47] Browinska-Szmalowa, Z.: Die Verteilung der Alkaloide in den keimenden Samen von *Chelidonium majus* L. Biul. Inst. Rośl. Leczn. *3*, 132 (1957). Cited from: Dtsch. Apoth. Ztg *100*, 398 (1960).

[B 48] Brücher, H.: Tropische Nutzpflanzen, Springer, Berlin, Heidelberg, New York, 529 pp., 1977.

[B 49] Brugsch. H. G.: Toxic hazards: the castor bean. New Engl. J. Med. *262*, 1039–1040 (1960).

[B 50] Brugsch, H. and O. R. Klimmer: Vergiftungen im Kindesalter, 2nd ed., F. Enke, Stuttgart, 438 pp., 1966.

[B 51] Budzikiewicz, H., A. Römer, and K. Taraz: 4-Desoxyevonin, ein neues Alkaloid aus *Evonymus europaea* L. Z. Naturforsch. *27b*, 800–805 (1972).

[B 52] Budzikiewicz, H., and H. Thomas: p-Cumaroxy-ursolsäure, ein neuer Inhaltsstoff von *Ilex aquifolium* L. Z. Naturforsch. *35b*, 230–231 (1980).

[B 53] Bundesanzeiger no. 67, dated 10.4.1975: Bekanntmachung einer Liste giftiger Pflanzenarten (Publication of a list of poisonous plant species). Printed in: Dtsch. Apoth. Ztg *115*, 647–650 (1975).

[B 54] Burbach, J. P. E.: De blaartrekkende werking van boterbloemen. Ned. Tijdschr. Geneesk. *107*, 1128–1130 (1963).

[B 55] Burke, M. J., D. Siegel, and B. Davidow: Consequence of yew *(Taxus)* needle ingestion. N.Y. State J. Med. *79*, 1576–1577 (1979).

[B 56] Bylka, W. and Z. Kowalewski: Flavonoid compounds of *Symphoricarpos albus* (Caprifoliaceae). Herba Polon. *26* (1), 11–20 (1980). Cited from: Biol. Abstr. *71*, 68 581 (1981).

[B 57] Bailleul, F., A. M. Leveau, and M. Durand: Nouvel iridoïde des fruits de *Lonicera alpigena*. J. Nat. Prod. *44*, 573–575 (1981).

[B 58] Bramley, A. and R. Goulding: Laburnum 'poisoning'. Br. Med. J. *2*, 1220–1221 (1981).

[B 59] Brain, K. R. and T. D. Turner: Toxic fruits in frozen peas. J. Ass. Publ. Anal. *9*, 100–101 (1971).

[B 60] Bean, W. J.: Trees and shrubs hardy in the British Isles, 8th ed. revised, Sir George Taylor (general ed.), D. L. Clarke (chief ed.), John Murray, London, 4 vols., 1981.

[B 61] Bishay, D. W., Z. Kowalewski, and J. D. Phillipson: Peptide and tetrahydro-isoquinoline alkaloids from *Euonymus europaeus*. Phytochemistry *12*, 693–698 (1973).

[C 1] Caldwell, M. E. and W. R. Brewer: Possible hazards of eating bracken fern. New Engl. J. Med. *303*, 164 (1980).

[C 2] Callahan, R., F. Piccola, K. Gensheimer, W. E. Parkin, J. Prusakowski, G. Scheiber, and S. Henry: Plant poisonings – New Jersey. Morbid. Mortal. Weekly Rept *30*, 65-67 (1981).

[C 3] Calnan, C. D.: Petty spurge *(Euphorbia peplus* L.). Contact Dermatitis *1*, 128 (1975).

[C 4] Camm, E. H., H. W. Buck, and J. C. Mitchell: Phytophotodermatitis from *Heracleum mantegazzianum*. Contact Dermatitis *2*, 68–72 (1976).

[C 5] Caplan, Y. H., K. G. Orloff, and B. C. Thompson: A fatal overdose with colchicine. J. Anal. Toxicol. *4*, 153–155 (1980).

[C 6] Carey, F. M., J. J. Lewis, J. L. MacGregor, and M. Martin-Smith: Pharmacological and chemical observations on some toxic nectars. J. Pharm. Pharmacol. *11*, 269T–274T (1959).

[C 7] Carlton, B. E., E. Tufts, and D. E. Girard: Water hemlock poisoning complicated by rhabdomyolysis and renal failure. Clin. Toxicol. *14*, 87–92 (1979).

[C 8] Casterline, C. L.: Allergy to chamomile tea. J. Am. Med. Ass. *244*, 330–331 (1980).

[C 9] Chamberlain, T. J.: Licorice poisoning, pseudoaldosteronism, and heart failure. J. Am. Med. Ass. *213*, 1343 (1970).

[C 10] Chaudhuri, R. K. and O. Sticher: A new class of monoterpene alkaloid glycosides from *Lonicera xylosteum*. Planta Med. *39*, 217 (1980).

[C 11] Chauliaguet, J., A. Hébert, and F. Heim: Sur les principes actifs de quelques Aroïdées. Compt. Rend. Acad. Sci., Paris *124*, 1368 (1897).

[C 12] Chavant, L., H. Combier, and J. Cros: *Symphoricarpos racemosus* (Michaux). Recherches phytochimiques et étude de la toxicité du fruit. Plant. Méd. Phytothér. *9*, 267–272 (1975).

[C 13] Cherian, S., W. T. Smith Jr, and L. Stoltz: Soluble proteins of Dieffenbachia. Trans. Ky Acad. Sci. *37*, 16–19 (1967).

[C 14] Chiarlo, B., E. Cajelli, and G. Piazzai: Sui costituenti delle drupe di *Sambucus ebulus*. I. Pigmenti antocianici e acidi fenolici. Fitoterapia *49*, 99–101 (1978).

[C 15] Chiarlo, B., P. Ambrosetti, and A. Bolla: The constituents of the drupes of *Sambucus ebulus*. II. Fatty acids, sterols, aliphatic and triterpenic alcohols. Chromatographia *12*, 494–495 (1979).

[C 16] Chin, K. C. and T. J. Beattie: Laburnum poisoning. Lancet *1*, 1299 (1979).

[C 17] Chung, S. G., B. Z. Ahn, and P. Pachaly: Inhaltsstoffe von *Andromeda polifolia*. Planta Med. *38*, 269–270 (1980).

[C 18] Clarke, E. G. C. and M. Williams: Microchemical tests for the identification of alkaloids. J. Pharm. Pharmacol. *7*, 255–262 (1955).

[C 19] Clarke, E. G. C.: Identification of solanine. Nature *181*, 1152–1153 (1958).

[C 20] Comotti, R.: Recherches sur la localisation des alcaloïdes des Amaryllidacées. Thèse, Université de Paris, 1910. Cited from: [J 8].

[C 21] Conn, E. E.: Cyanogenesis, the production of hydrogen cyanide by plants. In: Keeler *et al.* (eds.), Effects of poisonous plants on livestock, pp. 301–310, 1978.

[C 22] Cooper, L., G. Grunenfelder, and J. Blackmon: Poisoning associated with herbal teas – Arizona, Washington. Morbid. Mortal. Weekly Rept *26*, 257–259 (1977).

[C 23] Corrigall, W., R. R. Moody, and J. C. Forbes: Foxglove *(Digitalis purpurea)* poisoning in farmed red deer *(Cervus elaphus)*. Vet. Rec. *102*, 119–122 (1978).

[C 24] Cortesi, R.: A propos du Tamier commun. Pharm. Acta Helv. *12*, 1–6 (1937).

[C 25] Costanza, D. J. and W. V. Hoversten: Accidental ingestion of water hemlock. Calif. Med. *119*, 78–82 (1973).

[C 26] Cronin, E. H. and D. B. Nielsen: Tall larkspur and cattle on high mountain ranges. In: Keeler *et al.* (eds.), Effects of poisonous plants on livestock, pp. 521–534, 1978.

[C 27] Czaja, A. T.: Mikroskopische Untersuchung von Obst und Obsterzeugnissen. In: Schormüller, J. (general ed.), Handbuch der Lebensmittelchemie, Springer, Berlin, Heidelberg, New York, vol. V/2, pp. 259–310, 1968.

[C 28] Czech. K.: Preface to: Späth, G.: Vergiftungen und akute Arzneimittelüberdosierungen, G. Witzstrock, Baden-Baden, 1978.

[C 29] Czerwek, H. and W. Fischer: Tödlicher Vergiftungsfall mit *Taxus baccata* – Versuche zum Nachweis der Taxusalkaloide aus Leichenorganen. Arch. Toxicol. *18*, 88–92 (1960).

[C 30] Castillo, B. del, A. G. de Marina, and M. P. Martinez-Honduvilla: Fluorimetric determination of oenanthotoxin. Ital. J. Biochem. *29*, 233–237 (1980).

[C 31] Carey, J. C.: Black nightshade poisoning in swine. N. Am. Vet. *36*, 446 (1955).

[C 32] Coxon, D. T.: The glycoalkaloid content of potato berries. J. Sci. Food Agric. *32*, 412–414 (1981).

[C 33] Chittenden, F. J. (ed.): The Royal Horticultural Society Dictionary of Gardening, Clarendon Press, Oxford, 4 vols. and Supplement, 1950.

[C 34] Clarke, M. L., D. G. Harvey, and D. J. Humphreys: Veterinary toxicology, 2nd ed., Baillière Tindall, London, 328 pp., 1981.

[C 35] Clapham, A.R., T. G. Tutin, and E. F. Warburg: Excursion flora of the British Isles, 3rd ed., Cambridge University Press, Cambridge, London, New York, New Rochelle, Melbourne, Sydney, 499 pp., 1981. Flora of the British Isles, 2nd ed., Cambridge University Press, Cambridge, 1269 pp., 1962.

[D 1] Dabija, G., C. Domilexcu, and S. Nemteanu: Über die Giftigkeit des Aronstabs *(Arum maculatum)* für Tiere. Arch. Vet. *4*, 157–168 (1968).

[D 2] Dähncke, R. M. and S. Dähncke: Beerenkompass, Gräfe und Unzer, München, 79 pp., 1977.

[D 3] Danos, B.: Personal communication (newspaper report in Népszabadság dated 26.5.1981).

[D 4] David, A. and D. K. Vallance: Bitter principles of Cucurbitaceae. J. Pharm. Pharmacol. *7*, 295–296 (1955).

[D 5] Davis, J. H.: *Abrus precatorius* (rosary pea), the most common lethal plant poison. J. Fla med. Ass. *65*, 189–191 (1978).

[D 6] Deinzer, M. L., P. A. Thomson, D. M. Burgett, and D. L. Isaacson: Pyrrolizidine alkaloids: their occurrence in honey from tansy ragwort *(Senecio jacobaea* L.). Science *195*, 497–499 (1977).

[D 7] Dickie, C. W., M. H. Hamann, W. D. Carroll, and F. H. Chow: Oxalate *(Rumex venosus)* poisoning in cattle. J. Am. Vet. Med. Ass. *173*, 73–74 (1978).

[D 8] Dickinson, J. O., M. P. Cooke, R. R. King, and P. A. Mohamed: Milk transfer of pyrrolizidine alkaloids in cattle. J. Am. Vet. Med. Ass. *169*, 1192–1196 (1976).

[D 9] Dickstein, E. S. and F. W. Kunkel: Foxglove tea poisoning. Am. J. Med. *69*, 167–169 (1980).

[D 10] Diemair, W. and K. Franzen: Über das Vorkommen der Parasorbinsäure und der Sorbinsäure. Z. Lebensmittelunters. *109*, 373–378 (1959).

[D 11] Dirksen, G., P. Plank, U. Simon, T. Hänichen, P. Daniel, and A. Speiss: Über eine enzootische Kalzinose beim Rind. VII. Nachweis der kalzinogenen Wirkung von Goldhafer *(Trisetum flavescens* L.P.B.) beim Wiederkäuer. Dtsch. Tierärztl. Wochenschr. *81*, 1–5 (1974).

[D 12] Dixon, P. M., E. A. McPherson, A. C. Rowland, and W. MacLennan: Acorn poisoning in cattle. Vet. Rec. *104*, 284–285 (1979).

[D 13] Dominguez, X.A., J. G. Garcia, M. de Lourdes Maffey, J. G. Mares and C. Romboldt: Chemical study of the latex, stems, bracts and flowers of 'Christmas Flower' *(Euphorbia pulcherrima)*. J. Pharm. Sci. *56*, 1184–1185 (1967).

[D 14] MacDonald, E. J. and M. M. Airaksinen: Some pharmacological properties of the oil from *Ledum palustre* and some of its substituents in mice. Abstracts of the 20th Meeting of the Gesellschaft für Arzneipflanzenforschung, Helsinki, July 1972, p.33.

[D 15] Dore, W. D.: Crystalline raphides in the toxic houseplant Dieffenbachia. J. Am. Med. Ass. *185*, 1045 (1963).

[D 16] Dorling, P. R., C. R. Huxtable, and P. Vogel: Lysosomal storage in *Swainsona* spp. toxicosis: an induced mannosidosis. Neuropathol. & Appl. Neurobiol. *4*, 285–296 (1978).

[D 17] Dorsey, C.: Philodendron dermatitis. Calif. Med. *88*, 329–330 (1958).

[D 18] Doskotch, R. W., M. Y. Malik, and J. L. Beal: Cucurbitacin B, the cytotoxic principle of *Begonia tuberhybrida* var. *alba*. J. Nat. Prod. (Lloydia) *32*, 115–122 (1969).

[D 19] Drach, G. and W. H. Maloney: Toxicity of the common houseplant Dieffenbachia. J. Am. Med. Ass. *184*, 1047–1048 (1963).

[D 20] Drever, J. C. and J. A. A. Hunter: Hazards of giant hogweed. Br. Med. J. *3*, 109 (1970).

[D 21] Druckrey, H.: Tödliche medizinale Aconitin-Vergiftung. Samml. Vergiftungsfällen *13*, 21–26 (1943/44).

[D 22] Dubois, J. M. and M. F. Schneider: Block of Na-current and intra-membrane charge movement in myelinated nerve fibres poisoned with a vegetable toxin. Nature *289*, 685–688 (1981).

[D 23] Duisberg, H.: Honig und Kunsthonig. In: Schormüller, J. (general ed.), Handbuch der Lebensmittelchemie, Springer, Berlin, Heidelberg, New York, vol. V/1, pp. 491–559, 1967.

[D 24] Duke, J. A.: A handbook of legumes of world economic importance, Plenum, New York, 345 pp., 1981.

[D 25] Dupuis, G.: Studies on poison ivy: in vitro lymphocyte transformation by urushiol-protein conjugates. Br. J. Dermatol. *101*, 617–624 (1979).

[D 26] Dyson, D. A. and A. E. Wrathall: Congenital deformities in pigs possibly associated with exposure to hemlock *(Conium maculatum)*. Vet. Rec. *100*, 241–242 (1977).

[D 27] Duncan, C. S.: Oak leaf poisoning in two horses. Cornell Vet. *51*, 159–162 (1961).

[D 28] Dony, J. G., F. H. Perring, and C. M. Rob: English names of wild flowers. A list recommended by the Botanical Society of the British Isles, reprint with corrections, The Botanical Society of the British Isles, 121 pp., 1980.

[E 1] Eckardt, F.: Über Vergiftungen im Säuglingsalter. Kinderärztl. Prax. *20*, 488–492 (1952).

[E 2] Edgar, J. T. and I. M. Thin: Plant poisoning involving male fern. Vet. Rec. *82*, 33-34 (1968).

[E 3] Editor: Toxic reactions to plant products sold in health food stores. Med. Lett. *21*, 29–31 (1979).

[E 4] Edmonds, L. D., L. A. Selby, and A. A. Case: Poisoning and congenital malformations associated with consumption of poison hemlock by sows. J. Am. Vet. Med. Ass. *160*, 1319–1324 (1972).

[E 5] Egerer, I.: Augenaffektion durch den Saft der Zierpflanze Dieffenbachia. Klin. Monatsbl. Augenheilk. *170*, 128–130 (1977).

[E 6] Eiselt, M. G. and R. Schröder: Laubgehölze, 4th ed., J. Neumann-Neudamm, Melsungen, Basel, Wien, 670 pp., 1976.

[E 7] Engel, S. and K. Horn: Phytodermatosen durch *Dictamnus alba, Sanicula europaea* und *Phyllodendron consanguineum*. Dermatol. Monatschr. *158*, 22–27 (1972).

[E 8] Evans, I. A., B. Widdop, R. S. Jones, G. D. Barber, H. Leach, D. L. Jones, and R. Mainwaring-Burton: The possible human hazard of the naturally occurring bracken carcinogen. Biochem. J. *124*, 28p-29p (1971).

[E 9] Evans, I. A., R. S. Jones, and R. Mainwaring-Burton: Passage of bracken fern toxicity into milk. Nature *237*, 107–108 (1972).

[E 10] Evans, W. C., B. Widdop, and J. D. J. Harding: Experimental poisoning by bracken rhizomes in pigs. Vet. Rec. *90*, 471–475 (1972).

[E 11] Evans, F. J. and C. J. Soper: The tigliane, daphnane and ingenane diterpenes, their chemistry, distribution and biological activities. A review. J. Nat. Prod. (Lloydia) *41*, 193–233 (1978).

[E 12] Evans, F. J. and R. J. Schmidt: Plants and plant products that induce contact dermatitis. Planta Med. *38*, 289–316 (1980).

[E 13] Everist, S. L.: Effect of land use on plant poisoning of livestock in Australia. In: Keeler *et al.* (eds.), Effects of poisonous plants on livestock, pp. 47–56, 1978.

[E 14] McEwan, T.: Organo-fluorine compounds in plants. In: Keeler *et al.* (eds.), Effects of poisonous plants on livestock, pp. 147–158, 1978.

[E 15] McEwan, T.: Poisoning of chickens and ducks by pyrrolizidine alkaloids of *Heliotropium europaeum*. Aust. Vet. J. *55*, 601–602 (1979).

[E 16] Ewart, W. B., S. W. Rabkin, and P. A. Mitenko: Poisoning by cantharides. Can. Med. Ass. J. *118*, 1199 (1978).

[E 17] Everett, T. H. (ed.): The New York Botanical Garden Illustrated Encyclopedia of Horticulture, Garland Publishing, New York, London, 10 vols., 1980–1982.

[F 1] Fairbairn, J. W. and L. D. Kapoor: The laticiferous vessels of *Papaver somniferum* L. Planta Med. *8*, 49–61 (1960).

[F 2] Faivre, M. and C. Barral: La toxicité d'une plante ornementale – Un cas d'intoxication par *Dieffenbachia picta*. Nouv. Presse Méd. *3*, 1313–1314 (1974).

[F 3] Fama, P. G.: Datura poisoning. N. Z. Med. J. *85*, 108 (1977).

[F 4] Fama, P. G.: Datura poisoning. N. Z. Med. J. *90*, 399 (1979).

[F 5] Fawcett, N. P.: Pediatric facets of poisonous plants. J. Fla Med. Ass. *65*, 199–204 (1978).

[F 6] Fazekas, I. G.: Tödliche Oxalat-(Kleesalz-) Vergiftung, mit besonderer Berücksichtigung der histologischen Veränderungen. Arch. Toxicol. *17*, 179–182 (1958).

[F 7] Fensbo, C. and C. Harbeck: Datura stramonium anvendt som urtete. Ugeskr. Laeg *141*, 1150–1151 (1979).

[F 8] Fisher. A.A.: Contact photodermatitis. In: Fisher, A.A., Contact dermatitis, 2nd ed., Lea & Febiger, Philadelphia, 1973.

[F 9] Fisher, A. A.: Dermatitis due to plants and spices. In: Fisher, A.A., Contact dermatitis, 2nd ed., Lea & Febiger, Philadelphia, 1973.

[F 10] Fisher, H. H.: Origin and uses of ipecac. Econ. Bot. *27*, 231–234 (1973).

[F 11] Fitschen, J.: Gehölz-Flora, 6th ed., Quelle & Meyer, Heidelberg, 396 pp., 1977.

[F 12] Flotow, E.: Vergiftungen bei Kindern. Pharm. Zentralh. *90*, 361–364 (1951).

[F 13] Fochtman, F. W., J. E. Manno, C. L. Winck, and J. A. Cooper: Toxicity of the genus Dieffenbachia. Toxicol. Appl. Pharmacol. *15*, 38–45 (1969).

[F 14] Forrester, R. M.: 'Have you eaten laburnum?' Lancet *1*, 1073 (1979).

[F 15] Forth, W., D. Henschler, and W. Rummel: Allgemeine und spezielle Pharmakologie und Toxikologie, 3rd ed., B. I. Wissenschaftsverlag, Mannheim, Wien, Zürich, 1981.

[F 16] Fox, D. W., M. C. Hart, P. S. Bergeson, P. B. Jarrett, A. E. Stillman, and R. J. Huxtable: Pyrrolizidine (Senecio) intoxication mimicking Reye syndrome. J. Pediatr. *93*, 980–982 (1978).

[F 17] Francis, H.: Man against the giant hogweed. Lancet *2*, 269 (1970).

[F 18] Frank, A.: Auffallende Purpura bei artifiziellem Abort. Dtsch. Med. Wochenschr. *86*, 1618–1620 (1961).

[F 19] Franke, W.: Nutzpflanzenkunde, 2nd ed., G. Thieme, Stuttgart, New York, 470 pp., 1981.

[F 20] Frankenberg, L.: Enzyme therapy in cyanide poisoning: effect of rhodanase and sulfur compounds. Arch. Toxicol. *45*, 315–323 (1980).

[F 21] Frankfurter Rundschau dated 24.7.1973.

[F 22] Frey-Wyssling, A.: Crystallography of the two hydrates of crystalline calcium oxalate in plants. Am. J. Bot. *68*, 130–141 (1981).

[F 23] Friedrich, H. and E. Krüger: Über toxische Crassulaceen und Untersuchungen an Bryophyllum–Arten. Dtsch. Apoth Ztg *108*, 1273–1281 (1968).

[F 24] Friese, W.: Beitrag zur Kenntnis der Eibe (*Taxus baccata* L.). Pharm. Zentralh. *90*, 259–262, 289-291 (1951).

[F 25] Fröhlich, J.: Blausäurevergiftungen. Med. Monatschr. Pharm. *3*, 79–81 (1980).

[F 26] Frohne, D. and O. Pribilla: Tödliche Vergiftung mit *Taxus baccata*. Arch. Toxicol. *21*, 150–162 (1965).

[F 27] Frohne, D. and H. J. Pfänder: Giftige Doldengewächse. Dtsch. Apoth. Ztg *121*, 2269–2275 (1981).

[F 28] Fürstenberger, G. and E. Hecker: Zum Wirkungsmechanismus cocarcinogener Pflanzeninhaltsstoffe. Planta Med. *22*, 241–266 (1972).

[F 29] Fiddes, F. S.: Poisoning by aconitine. Br. Med. J. *2*, 779–780 (1958).

[F 30] Fahr. E.: Psoralene: Photobiologische und dermatologische Wirkungen. Pharm. Ztg *127*, 163–170 (1982).

[F 31] McFarland III, M. F. and J. McFarland: Accidental ingestion of podophyllum. Clin. Toxicol. *18*, 973–978 (1981).

[F 32] Franz, H., P. Ziska, and A. Kindt: Isolation and properties of 3 lectins from mistletoe (*Viscum album*). Biochem. J. *195*, 481–484 (1981).

[F 33] Forsyth, A.A.: British poisonous plants, 2nd ed. with additions, Reference book 161, Ministry of Agriculture, Fisheries and Food, Her Majesty's Stationery Office, London, 131 pp., 1968 (1980).

[F 34] Fitter, F., A. Fitter, and M. Blamey: The wild flowers of Britain and northern Europe, 3rd ed., Collins, London, 336 pp., 1978.

[G 1] Gaetani, G. F., C. Mareni, E. Salvidio, S. Galiano, T. Meloni, and P. Arese: Favism: erythrocyte metabolism during haemolysis and reticulocytosis. Br. J. Haematol. *43*, 39–48 (1979).

[G 2] Galitzer, St. J. and F. W. Oehme: Studies of the comparative toxicity of *Kochia scoparia* (L.) Schrad. (fireweed). Toxicol. Lett. *3*, 43–49 (1979).

[G 3] Gans, O.: Über die Dermatitis durch *Achillea millefolium*. Dtsch. Med. Wochenschr. *55*, 1213–1215 (1929).

[G 4] Gasperi-Campani, A., L. Barbieri, E. Lorenzoni, L. Montanaro, S. Sperti, E. Bonetti, and F. Stirpe: Modeccin, the toxin of *Adenia digitata*. Biochem. J. *174*, 491–496 (1978).

[G 5] Gassner, G.: Mikroskopische Untersuchung pflanzlicher Lebensmittel, G. Fischer, Stuttgart, 395 pp., 1973.

[G 6] McGee, J. O' D., R. S. Patrick, C. B. Wood, and L. H. Blumgart: A case of veno-occlusive disease of the liver in Britain associated with herbal tea consumption. J. Clin. Pathol. 29, 788–794 (1976).

[G 7] Geidel, K.: Klinische Beobachtung und tierexperimentelle Untersuchungen über die Wirkung von Saft der Euphorbia lathyris (Springwolfsmilch) am Auge. Klin. Monatsbl. Augenheilk. 141, 374–379 (1962).

[G 8] Gellin, G. A., C. R. Wolf, and T. H. Milby: Poison ivy, poison oak, and poison sumac – common causes of occupational dermatitis. Arch. Environ. Health 22, 280–286 (1971).

[G 9] Genest, K., A. Lavalle, and E. Nera: Comparative acute toxicity of Abrus precatorius and Ormosia seeds in animals. Arzneimittel-Forsch. 21, 888–889 (1971).

[G 10] Gessner, O.: Tödliche Vergiftung durch Früchte des Ligusterstrauches (Ligustrum vulgare L.) bei einem 5jährigen Kinde. Samml. Vergiftungsfällen (Arch. Toxikol.) 13, 1–2 (1943/44).

[G 11] Gessner, O.: Gift- und Arzneipflanzen von Mitteleuropa, 3rd ed., revised by G. Orzechowsky, C. Winter, Heidelberg, 582 pp., 1974.

[G 12] Gildemeister, E. and F. Hoffmann: Die ätherischen Öle, Akademie-Verlag, Berlin, vols. 6 and 7, 1961.

[G 13] Giusti, G. V. and E. Moneta: Ein Fall von Abtreibung durch Petersilienabsud und Naphthalin, Arch. Kriminol. 152, 161–164 (1973).

[G 14] Godeau, R. P., Y. Pelissier, and I. Fouraste: Constituents of Viburnum tinus: 3. Anthocyanic compounds and flavonic compounds of the fruit. Plant. Méd. Phytothér. 13, 37–40 (1979). Cited from: Biol. Abstr. 69, 33 076 (1980).

[G 15] Goetz, U.: Krebsmittel Laetrile – wirkungslose 'Wunderdroge'. Die Zeit, no. 22, dated 22.5.1981.

[G 16] Goldman, L., R. H. Preston, and H. R. Muegel: Dermatitis venenata from English ivy (Hedera helix). Arch. Dermatol. 74, 311–312 (1956).

[G 17] Gopinath, C. and E. J. H. Ford: The effect of ragwort (Senecio jacobaea) on the liver of the domestic fowl (Gallus domesticus): a histopathological and enzyme histochemical study. Br. Poult. Sci. 18, 137-141 (1977).

[G 18] Gowdy, J. M.: Stramonium intoxication – review of symptomatology in 212 cases. J. Am. Med. Ass. 221, 585–587 (1972).

[G 19] Greer, M. J.: Plant poisoning in cats. Mod. Vet. Pract. 42, 62 (1961).

[G 20] MacGregor, J. T.: Mutagenic activity of hymenovin, a sesquiterpene lactone from western bitterweed. Food & Cosmet. Toxicol. 15, 225–227 (1977).

[G 21] Greiner, H.: Wurmfarnvergiftung. Samml. Vergiftungsfällen (Arch. Toxikol.) 14, 124–125 (1952/54).

[G 22] Griebel, C.: Tanninlösung als Mikroreagenz auf Alkaloidmekonate. Pharm. Ztg 85, 116–118 (1949).

[G 23] Griebel, C.: Verwechslung von Tabaksamen (Nicotiana rustica L.) mit Mohn. Z. Lebensmittelunters. u. -Forsch. 90, 109–112 (1950).

[G 24] Griebel, C.: Zur Mikroskopie der Heidelbeerfrüchte. Z. Lebensmittel-unters. u. -Forsch. 92, 331–337 (1951).

[G 25] Gross, M., H. Baer, and H. M. Fales: Urushiols of poisonous Anacardiaceae. Phytochemistry 14, 2263–2266 (1975).

[G 26] Grundy, H. F. and F. Howarth: Pharmacological studies on hemlock water dropwort. Pharmacol. 11, 225–230 (1956).

[G 27] Grusz-Harday, E.: Tödliche Nikotinvergiftungen. Arch. Toxicol. 23, 35–41 (1967).

[G 28] Gunby, P.: Plant known for centuries still causes problems today. J. Am. Med. Ass. 241, 2246–2247 (1979).

[G 29] Gunby, P.: Keep away from that 'tree', folks! J. Am. Med. Ass. 244, 2596 (1980).

[G 30] Guse, P.: Zur Mikroskopie gesundheitsschädlicher Früchte verschiedener botanischer Artzugehörigkeit. Dissertation, Hamburg, 1977.

[G 31] Gustine, D. L., J. S. Shenk, B. G. Moyer, and R. F. Barnes: Isolation of β-nitropropionic acid from crownvetch. Agron. J. 66, 636–639 (1974).

[G 32] Gustine, D. L., B. G. Moyer, P. J. Wangsness, and J. S. Shenk: Ruminal metabolism of 3-nitropropanoyl-D-glucopyranoses from crownvetch. J. Anim. Sci. 44, 1107–1111 (1977).

[G 33] Gustine, J., L. Gobble, and R. F. Barnes: Relationship between β-nitropropionic acid content of crownvetch and toxicity in nonruminant animals. J. Anim. Sci. 42, 616–621 (1976).

[H 1] Haas, H. T. A. and W. Poethke: Vergiftung durch Alkaloide von Veratrum album in Baldriantinktur. Samml. Vergiftungsfällen (Arch. Toxikol.) 13, 3–8 (1943/44).

[H 2] Hänsel, R., M. Kartarahardja, J. T. Huang, and F. Bohlmann: Sesquiterpenlacton-β-D-glucopyranoside sowie ein neues Eudesmanolid aus Taraxacum officinale. Phytochemistry 19, 857–861 (1980).

[H 3] Hagers Handbuch der Pharmazeutischen Praxis, 4th ed., List, P.H. and L. Hörhammer (eds.), Springer, Berlin, Heidelberg, New York, 8 vols., 1967–1980.

[H 4] Haidvogl, M., G. Fritsch, and H. M. Grubbauer: Vergiftung durch rohe Gartenbohnen (Phaseolus vulgaris und Phaseolus coccineus) im Kindesalter. Pädiat. Pädol. 14, 293–296 (1979).

[H 5] Hall, R. C. W., M. K. Popkin, and L. E. Michenry: Angel's trumpet psychosis: a central nervous system – anticholinergic syndrome. Am. J. Psychiat. 134, 312–314 (1977).

[H 6] Hall, I. H., K. H. Lee, C. O. Starnes, Y. Sumida, R. Y. Wu, T. G. Waddell, J. W. Cochran, and K. G. Gerhart: Anti-inflammatory activity of sesquiterpene lactones and related compounds. J. Pharm. Sci. 68, 537–542 (1979).

[H 7] Haller, B. and W. Bruder: Vergleichende rasterelektronenmikroskopische Untersuchungen von Blattfragmenten im Dienst der Kriminaltechnik. Arch. Kriminol. 163, 105–111 (1979); 164, 45–50 (1979); 165, 148–152 (1980).

[H 8] Hammersen, G.: Vergiftungen im Kindesalter. Med. Monatschr. Pharm. 3, 161–167 (1980).

[H 9] Hardin, J. W. and J. M. Arena: Human poisoning from native and cultivated plants, Duke University Press, Durham, North Carolina, 194 pp., 1974.

[H 10] Harr, J. R. and O. H. Muth: Selenium poisoning in domestic animals and its relationship to man. Clin. Toxicol. 5, 175–186 (1972).

[H 11] Harris, J. H.: Dermatitis of the eyelids due to Philodendron (scandens cardatum) plants. Arch. Dermatol. 45, 1066–1068 (1942).

[H 12] Harrison, E. A. and D. H. Morgan: Abuse of herbal cigarettes containing stramonium. Br. Med. J. 2, 1195 (1976).

[H 13] Hart, M.: Hazards to health. Jequirity-bean poisoning. New Engl. J. Med. 268, 885–886 (1963).

[H 14] Hart, N. K., J. A. Lamberton, A. A. Sioumis, H. Suares, and A. A. Seawright: Triterpenes of toxic and non-toxic taxa of Lantana camara. Experientia 32, 412–413 (1976).

[H 15] Hartley, W. J.: A comparative study of darling pea (Swainsona spp.) poisoning in Australia with locoweed (Astragalus and Oxytropis spp.) poisoning in North America. In: Keeler et al. (eds.), Effects of poisonous plants on livestock, pp. 363–369, 1978.

[H 16] Hartmann, K.: Augenschädigung durch den Saft der Euphorbia peplus (Wolfsmilch). Klin. Monatsbl. Augenheilk. 104, 324–326 (1940).

[H 17] Hauschild, F.: Pharmakologie und Grundlagen der Toxikologie, 3rd ed., G. Thieme, Leipzig, 1162 pp., 1961.

[H 18] Hausen, B. M.: On the occurrence of the contact allergen primin and other quinonoid compounds in species of the family of Primulaceae. Arch. Dermatol. Res. 261, 311–321 (1978).

[H 19] Hausen, B. M.: Arnikaallergie. Hautarzt 31, 10–17 (1980).

[H 20] Hausen, B. M.: Woods injurious to human health, Walter de Gruyter, Berlin, New York, 189 pp., 1981.

[H 21] Hausen, B. M. and K. H. Schulz: Chrysanthemum-Allergie. Berufsdermatosen 21, 199–214 (1973).

[H 22] Hausen, B. M., K. H. Schulz, O. Jarchow, K. H. Klaska, and H. Schmalle: A first allergenic sesquiterpene lactone from Chrysanthemum indicum L.: Arteglasin A. Naturwissenschaften 62, 585–586 (1975).

[H 23] Hausen, B. M. and K. H. Schulz: Occupational contact dermatitis due to croton (*Codiaeum variegatum* [L.] A. Juss. var. *pictum* [Lodd.] Muell. Arg.). Sensitization by plants of the Euphorbiaceae. Contact Dermatitis *3*, 289–292 (1977).

[H 24] Hausen, B. M., H.-D. Herrmann, and G. Willuhn: The sensitizing capacity of Compositae plants. Contact Dermatitis *4*, 3–10 (1978).

[H 25] Hausen, B. M. and K. H. Schulz: Chrysanthemum allergy. III. Identification of the allergens. Arch. Dermatol. Res. *255*, 111–121 (1978).

[H 26] Hausen, B. M. and K. H. Schulz: Allergische Kontaktdermatitis durch Löwenzahn (*Taraxacum officinale* Wiggers). Dermatosen *26*, 198 (1978).

[H 27] Haussler, M. R., R. H. Wassermann, T. A. McCain, M. Peterlik, K. M. Bursac, and M. R. Hughes: 1,25-Dihydroxyvitamin D_3 glycoside: identification of a calcinogenic principle of *Solanum malacoxylon*. Life Sci. *18*, 1049–1056 (1976).

[H 28] Hawkes, J. G., R. N. Lester, and A. D. Skelding (eds.): The biology and taxonomy of the Solanaceae, Academic Press, London, New York, 738 pp., 1979.

[H 29] Hazslinsky, B.: Poisonous honey from deadly nightshade. Z. Bienenforsch. *3*, 93–96 (1956). Cited from: Chem. Abstr. *50*, 14891 (1956).

[H 30] Hecker, E. and R. Schmidt: Phorbol esters, the irritants and cocarcinogens of *Croton tiglium* L. Fortschr. Chem. Org. Naturst. *31*, 377–467 (1974).

[H 31] Hecker, E.: Chemische Carcinogene pflanzlicher Herkunft. Dtsch. Apoth. Ztg *111*, 2002 (1971).

[H 32] Hecker, E.: Structure-activity relationships in diterpene esters irritant and cocarcinogenic to mouse skin. In: Slaga, T. J., A. Siwak, and R. K. Boutwell (eds.), Carcinogenesis, Raven Press, New York, vol. 2, pp. 11–48, 1978.

[H 33] Hegarty, M. P.: Toxic amino acids of plant origin. In: Keeler *et al.* (eds.), Effects of poisonous plants on livestock, pp. 575–585, 1978.

[H 34] Hegi, G.: Illustrierte Flora von Mitteleuropa, 3rd ed., C. Hanser, München, 6 vols., 1966–.

[H 35] Hegnauer, R.: Chemotaxonomie der Pflanzen, Birkhäuser, Basel, Stuttgart, 6 vols., 1962–.

[H 36] Heijst, A. N. P. van, S. A. Pikaar, and R. G. van Kesteren: Dieffenbachia van pijlgif tot kamerplant. Ned. Tijdschr. Geneesk. *121*, 1996–1999 (1977).

[H 37] Heiser Jr, C. B.: Nightshades – the paradoxical plants, W. H. Freeman, San Francisco, 200 pp., 1969.

[H 38] Heltmann, H.: Morphological and phytochemical studies in *Atropa* species. Planta Med. *36*, 230–231 (1979).

[H 39] Hembree, J. A., C. J. Chang, J. L. McLaughlin, G. Peck, and J. M. Cassady: Potential antitumor agents: a cytotoxic cardenolide from *Coronilla varia*. J. Nat. Prod. *42*, 293–298 (1979).

[H 40] Henderson, J. A., E. V. Evans, and R. A. McIntosh: The antithiamine action of Equisetum. J. Am. Vet. Med. Ass. *120*, 375–378 (1952).

[H 41] Hermkes, L.: Eine seltene Vergiftung mit den Früchten des Spindelbaums (Pfaffenhütchen). Münch. Med. Wochenschr. *88*, 1011–1012 (1941).

[H 42] Herrmann, H.-D., G. Willuhn, and B. M. Hausen: Helenalinmethacrylate, a new pseudoguianolide from the flowers of *Arnica montana* L. and the sensitizing capacity of their sesquiterpene lactones. Planta Med. *34*, 299–304 (1978).

[H 43] Herweijer, C. H. and L. F. den Houter: Poisoning due to fat hen *(Chenopodium album)* in sheep. Neth. J. Vet. Sci. *4*, 52–54 (1971).

[H 44] Herz, W.: Sesquiterpene lactones from livestock poisons. In: Keeler *et al.* (eds.), Effects of poisonous plants on livestock, pp. 487–497, 1978.

[H 45] Heyndrickx, A., V. Coulier, and J. Ureel: An acute fatal poisoning of a child due to the anthelmintic aspidinolfilicin (Filmaron). J. Pharm. Belg. *21*, 387–396 (1966).

[H 46] Heywood, V. H., J. B. Harborne, and B. L. Turner (eds.): The biology and chemistry of the Compositae, Academic Press, London, New York, 1189 pp., 1977.

[H 47] Hikino, H., Y. Ohizumi, C. Konno, K. Hashimoto, and H. Wakasa: Subchronic toxicity of ericaceous toxins and Rhododendron leaves. Chem. Pharm. Bull. *27*, 874–879 (1979).

[H 48] Hirono, I., M. Haga, M. Fujii, S. Matsuura, M. Nakayama, T. Furuya, M. Hikichi, and H. Takanashi: Induction of hepatic tumors in rats by senkirkine and symphytine. J. Natn. Cancer Inst. *63*, 469–472 (1979).

[H 49] Hjorth, N., J. Roed-Petersen, and K. Thomsen: Airborne contact dermatitis from Compositae oleoresins simulating photodermatitis. Br. J. Dermatol. *95*, 613–620 (1976).

[H 50] Hörhammer, L., H. Wagner, and H. Reinhardt: Neue Methoden im pharmakognostischen Unterricht. II. Mitt. Chromatographische Unterscheidung handelsüblicher Viburnum-Drogen. Dtsch. Apoth. Ztg *105*, 1371–1373 (1965).

[H 51] Holstein, E.: Schädigung durch Oxalsäure und Kleesalz bei Einwirkung auf die Haut. Arch. Toxicol. *19*, 1–4 (1961).

[H 52] Holttum, R. E.: Plant life in Malaya, Longmans, London, 254 pp., 1973.

[H 53] Holz, W. and W. Richter: Über den Alkaloidgehalt im Duwock (*Equisetum palustre* L.). Angew. Bot. *34*, 28–32 (1960).

[H 54] Holzach, O. and H. Flück: Untersuchungen über die Alkaloide und Hautreizstoffe von *Tamus communis* L. Pharm. Acta Helv. *26*, 349–352 (1951).

[H 55] Hooper, P. T. and W. A. Scanlan: *Crotalaria retusa* poisoning of pigs and poultry. Aust. Vet. J. *53*, 109–114 (1977).

[H 56] Hooper, P. T. and K. B. Locke: Swainsona poisoning in the Northern Territory. Aust. Vet. J. *55*, 249 (1979).

[H 57] Hoppe, H. A.: Drogenkunde, 8th ed., Walter de Gruyter, Berlin, New York, vol. 1, 1311 pp., 1975.

[H 58] Horák, F. and O. Horáková: Zur Frage des Vorkommens von herzwirksamen Glykosiden in der wohlriechenden Weisswurz *Polygonatum odoratum* (Mill.) Druce (*P. officinale* All.). Pharmazie *14*, 487 (1959).

[H 59] Hotovy, R.: *Fagus sylvatica* L., Rotbuche. Pharmazie *3*, 513–523 (1948).

[H 60] Howard, R. A., G. P. de Wolf Jr, and G. H. Pride: Living with poisonous plants. Arnoldia *34* (2), 41–96 (1974).

[H 61] Humbert, J. R., J. H. Tress, E. J. Meyer, and K. Braico: Fatal cyanide poisoning: accidental ingestion of amygdalin. J. Am. Med. Ass. *238*, 482 (1977).

[H 62] Hummel, K.: Mikroskopische Untersuchung der ölliefernden Früchte und Samen. In: Schormüller, J. (general ed.), Handbuch der Lebensmittelchemie, Springer, Berlin, Heidelberg, New York, vol. IV, pp. 356–401 (1969).

[H 63] Humphreys, D. J.: A review of recent trends in animal poisoning. Br. Vet. J. *134*, 128–145 (1978).

[H 64] Husemann, C. and H. H. Bracker: Der (giftige) Sumpfschachtelhalm *Equisetum palustre*, ein Standorts- und Bewirtschaftungsproblem. Z. Kulturtech. *1*, 129–143 (1960).

[H 65] Hutchinson, T.W.S.: Onions as a cause of Heinz body anaemia and death in cattle. Can. Vet. J. *18*, 358–360 (1977).

[H 66] Huxtable, R. J.: Herbal teas and toxins: novel aspects of pyrrolizidine poisoning in the United States. Perspect. Biol. Med. *24*, 1–14 (1980).

[H 67] Huxtable, R. J., A. Stillman, and D. Ciaramitaro: Characterization of alkaloids involved in human Senecio (pyrrolizidine) poisoning. Proc. West. Pharmacol. Soc. *20*, 455–459 (1977).

[H 68] Huxtable, R. J., D. Ciaramitaro, and D. Eisenstein: The effect of a pyrrolizidine alkaloid, monocrotaline, and a pyrrole, dehydroretronecine, on the biochemical functions of the pulmonary endothelium. Mol. Pharmacol. *14*, 1189–1203 (1978).

[H 69] Hohnholz, J. H. and R. Schmid: Maniok. Bedeutung für Wirtschaft und Ernährung in Südostasien. Naturwiss. Rundsch. *35*, 95–102 (1982).

[H 70] Habs, H.: Kreuzkraut *Senecio nemorensis* ssp. *fuchsii*. Karzinogene und mutagene Wirkung des Alkaloidextraktes einer in der Phytotherapie gebräuchlichen Droge. Dtsch. Apoth. Ztg *122*, 799–804 (1982).

[H 71] Harvey, D. J.: Examination of the diphenylpropanoids of nutmeg as their trimethylsilyl, triethylsilyl and tri-*n*-propylsilyl derivatives using combined gas chromatography and mass spectrometry. J. Chromatog. *110*, 91–102 (1975).

[H 72] Hruby, K., K. Lenz, and J. Krausler: Vergiftungen mit *Veratrum album* (weisser Germer). Wien. Klin. Wochenschr. *93*, 517–519 (1981).

[I 1] Ieven, M., J. Totté, D. vanden Berghe, and A. J. Vlietinck: Antiviral activity of some Amaryllidaceae alkaloids. Planta Med. *33*, 284 (1978).

[I 2] Ieven, M., D. A. vanden Berghe, and A. J. Vlietinck: Inhibition of polio virus by lycorine, a plant alkaloid. Planta Med. *36*, 254–255 (1979).

[I 3] Inouye, H. and T. Nishioka: Über die Monoterpenglucoside und verwandte Naturstoffe – XIX. Über die Struktur des Nüzhenids, eines bitter schmeckenden Glucosids aus *Ligustrum lucidum* sowie *Ligustrum japonicum*. Tetrahedron *28*, 4231–4237 (1972).

[I 4] I.A.R.C. Monographs on the evaluation of carcinogenic risk of chemicals to man, vol. 10, Parasorbic acid, pp. 199–204 (1976).

[I 5] Ivie, G. W., D. A. Witzel, and D. D. Rushing: Toxicity and milk bittering properties of tenulin, the major sesquiterpene lactone constituent of *Helenium amarum* (bitter sneezeweed). J. Agric. Food Chem. *23*, 845–849 (1975).

[I 6] Ivie, G. W., D. A. Witzel, W. Herz, R. Kannan, J. O. Norman, D. D. Rushing, J. H. Johnson, L. D. Rowe, and J. A. Veech: Hymenovin. Major toxic constituent of western bitterweed (*Hymenoxis odorata* DC.). J. Agric. Food Chem. *23*, 841–845 (1975).

[I 7] Ivie, G. W.: Toxicological significance of plant furocoumarins. In: Keeler *et al.* (eds.), Effects of poisonous plants on livestock, pp. 475–485, 1978.

[J 1] Jadhay, S. J.: Formation and control of chlorophyll and glycoalkaloids in tubers of *Solanum tuberosum* L. and evaluation of glycoalkaloid toxicity. Adv. Food Res. *21*, 307–354 (1975).

[J 2] Jahnke, W.: Atropinvergiftungen im heissen Klima. Arch. Toxicol. *16*, 243–247 (1957).

[J 3] James, L. F.: Oxalate toxicosis. Clin. Toxicol. *5*, 231–243 (1972).

[J 4] James, L. F.: Oxalate poisoning in livestock. In: Keeler *et al.* (eds.), Effects of poisonous plants on livestock, pp. 139–145, 1978.

[J 5] James, L. F., W. J. Hartley, M. C. Williams, and K. R. van Kampen: Field and experimental studies in cattle and sheep poisoned by nitro-bearing Astragalus or their toxins. Am. J. Vet. Res. *41*, 377–382 (1980).

[J 6] Janeczko, Z.: The structure of the sugar moiety of steroidal saponosides isolated from the roots of *Polygonatum multiflorum* L. Planta Med. *36*, 266 (1979).

[J 7] Jaretzky, R. and E. Risse: Über die Abführwirkung des Bingelkrautes. Arch. Pharm. *280*, 125–131 (1942).

[J 8] Jaspersen–Schib, R.: Toxische Amaryl-lidaceen. Pharm. Acta Helv. *45*, 424–433 (1970).

[J 9] Jaspersen–Schib, R.: Pflanzenvergiftungen während 10 Jahren. Schweiz. Apoth. Ztg *114*, 265–267 (1976).

[J 10] Jaspersen–Schib, R.: Exotische Halsketten aus toxischen Samen und Früchten. Schweiz. Apoth. Ztg *114*, 391–393 (1976).

[J 11] Jeghers, H. and R. Murphy: Practical aspects of oxalate metabolism. New Engl. J. Med. *233*, 208–215, 238–246 (1945).

[J 12] Jensen, S. R. and B. J. Nielsen: Cyanogenic glucosides in *Sambucus nigra* L. Acta Chem. Scand. *27*, 2661–2662 (1973).

[J 13] Jesser, H.: Belladonnawurzel anstatt Attichwurzel. Pharm. Zentralh. *66*, 337 (1925).

[J 14] Johnston, C. T. and J. K. Routledge: Suspected *Helleborus viridis* poisoning of cattle. Vet. Rec. *89*, 202 (1971).

[J 15] Jones, R. T., G. R. Drummond, and R. O. Chatham: *Heliotropium europaeum* poisoning of pigs. Aust. Vet. J. *57*, 396 (1981).

[J 16] Jurenitsch, J., M. Pöhm, and G. Weilguny: Cytisin und N-Methylcytisin in Zellkulturen von *Laburnum anagyroides* Med. Pharmazie *36*, 370–373 (1981).

[J 17] Jans, B.P.: Untersuchungen am Milchsaft des Schöllkrautes (*Chelidonium majus* L.). Ber. Schweiz. Bot. Ges. *83*, 306–344 (1973).

[J 18] Jaeckle, K. and F. R. Freemon: Pokeweed (*Phytolacca americana*) poisoning. South Med. J. *74*, 639–640 (1981).

[J 19] Jellema, R., E. T. Elema, and T. M. Malingré: Fluorodensitometric determination of potato (*Solanum tuberosum*) glyco-alkaloids on thin-layer chromatograms. J. Chromat. *210*, 121–129 (1981).

[J 20] Jones, P.G. and G. R. Fenwick: The glyco-alkaloid content of some edible solanaceous fruits and potato products. J. Sci. Food Agric. *32*, 419–421 (1981).

[K 1] Kaladas, P. M. and R. D. Poretz: Purification and properties of a mitogenic lectin from *Wisteria floribunda* seeds. Biochemistry *18*, 4806–4812 (1979).

[K 2] Kalbfleisch, H. H.: Perorale Aconitin-Vergiftungen (Verwechslung von Meer-rettichwurzeln mit Eisenhutwurzeln). Samml. Vergiftungsfällen (Arch. Toxikol.) *13*, 17–20 (1943/44).

[K 3] Kaminsky–Kröger, C.: Die Heidelbeere, *Vaccinium myrtillus* L. (III). Pharmazie *6*, 603–613 (1951).

[K 4] Kang, S. S. and W. S. Woo: Triterpenes from the berries of *Phytolacca americana*. J. Nat. Prod. *43*, 510–513 (1980).

[K 5] Kanngiesser, F.: Über die Giftigkeit einiger Beeren. Ber. Dtsch. Pharm. Ges. *25*, 326–327 (1915).

[K 6] Kanngiesser, F.: Über die Giftigkeit der Aronsbeeren (*Arum maculatum*). Z. Med. Beamte *29*, 595–597 (1916).

[K 7] Karrer, P. and C. H. Eugster: Über ein Alkaloid aus *Equisetum palustre*. Helv. Chim. Acta *31*, 1062–1066 (1948).

[K 8] Kasali, O.B., L. Krook, W. G. Pond, and R. H. Wassermann: *Cestrum diurnum* intoxication in normal and hyperparathyroid pigs. Cornell Vet. *67*, 190–221 (1977).

[K 9] Kasim, M. and H. Lange: Zur toxikologisch-chemischen, Aufklärung von Vergiftungen bei Wiederkäuern durch Herbstzeitlose (Verfahren zur Colchizinbestimmung). Arch. Exp. Veterinärmed. *27*, 601–603 (1973).

[K 10] Kaszás, T. and G. Papp: Ricinussamen-Vergiftung von Schulkindern. Arch. Toxicol. *18*, 145–150 (1960).

[K 11] Kauss, H.: Plant lectins (phytohem-agglutinins). Progr. Bot. *38*, 58–70 (1976).

[K 12] Kating, H. and W. Wissner: Untersuchungen über herzwirksame Glykoside bei den europäischen und kleinasiatischen Arten der Gattung *Helleborus*. Pharm. Ztg *119*, 1985–1994 (1974).

[K 13] Kawazu, K.: Isolation of vibsanines A, B, C, D, E and F from *Viburnum odoratissimum*. Agric. & Biol. Chem. (Japan) *44*, 1367–1372 (1980). Cited from: Biol. Abstr. *71*, 12 708 (1981).

[K 14] Kaznelson, I. B., W. L. Besser, I. T. Ionow, M. P. Gorjatschin, I. I. Iofin, and N. A. Tschartorizhskij: Vergiftungen mit den Samen der Rizinuspflanze (klinisch-experimentelle Beobachtungen). Sowjetskaja Medizina *2*, 131 (1960). Cited from: Ärztl. Prax. *12*, 2582 (1960).

[K 15] Keeler, R. F. and L. D. Balls: Teratogenic effects in cattle of *Conium maculatum* and Conium alkaloids and analogs. Clin. Toxicol. *12*, 49–64 (1978).

[K 16] Keeler, R. F.: Toxins and teratogens of the Solanaceae and Liliaceae. In: Kinghorn, A. D. (ed.), Toxic plants, pp. 59–82, 1979.

[K 17] Keeler, R. F., K. R. van Kampen, and L. F. James (eds.): Effects of poisonous plants on livestock, Academic Press, New York, San Francisco, London, 600 pp., 1978.

[K 18] Kelly, R. W., R. J. M. Hay, and G. H. Shackell: Formononetin content of grasslands pawera red clover (*Trifolium pratense*) and its estrogenic activity to sheep. N. Z. J. Exp. Agric. *7*, 131–134 (1979).

[K 19] Kenten, R. H.: The partial purification and properties of a thiaminase from bracken (*Pteridium aquilinum* (L.) Kuhn). Biochem. J. *67*, 25–33 (1957).

[K 20] Ketel, W. G. van: Occupational contact dermatitis due to *Codiaeum variegatum* and possibly to *Aeschynanthus pulcher*. Dermatosen in Beruf und Umwelt *27*, 141–142 (1979).

[K 21] Kieler Nachrichten: Dekorativ, aber gefährlich (*Heracleum mantegazzianum*), no. 152, dated 4.7.1981.

[K 22] Kim, H. L.: Toxicity of sesquiterpene lactones. Res. Commun. Chem. Pathol. Pharmacol. *28*, 189–192 (1980).

[K 23] Kinamore, P. A., R. W. Jaeger, F. J. de Castro, and K. O. Peck: Abrus and Ricinus ingestion: Management of three cases. Clin. Toxicol. *17*, 401–405 (1980).

[K 24] King, W. D.: Syrup of Ipecac: a drug review. Clin. Toxicol. *17*, 353–358 (1980).

[K 25] Kinghorn, A. D. and F. J. Evans: A biological screen of selected species of the genus *Euphorbia* for skin irritant effects. Planta Med. *28*, 325–335 (1975).

[K 26] Kinghorn, A. D. (ed.): Toxic plants, Columbia University Press, New York, 195 pp., 1979.

[K 27] Kinghorn, A. D.: Cocarcinogenic irritant Euphorbiaceae. In: Kinghorn, A. D. (ed.), Toxic plants, pp. 137–159, 1979.

[K 28] Kingsbury, J. M.: The problem of poisonous plants. In: Kinghorn, A. D. (ed.), Toxic plants, pp. 1–6, 1979.

[K 29] Kingsbury, J. M.: Poisonous plants of the United States and Canada, Prentice-Hall, Englewood Cliffs, New Jersey, 626 pp., 1964.

[K 30] Klaschka, F., W. Grimm, and H.-U. Beiersdorff: Tulpen-Kontaktekzem als Berufsdermatose. Hautarzt *15*, 317–321 (1964).

[K 31] Klásek, A., T. Reichstein, and F. Šantavý: Die Pyrrolizidin-Alkaloide aus *Senecio alpinus* (L.) Scop., *S. subalpinus* Koch und *S. incanus* L. subsp. *carniolicus* (Willd.) Br.-Bl. Helv. Chim. Acta *51*, 1088 (1968).

[K 32] Kleine Mitteilung: Sind Eiben wirklich gefährlich und giftig? Z. Angew. Phytother. 149, IV/1981.

[K 33] Klöver, E. and H. Wenderoth: Die Blausäurevergiftung durch bittere Mandeln in psychologischer und therapeutischer Sicht. Med. Klin. *60*, 213–216 (1965).

[K 34] Knight, B.: Ricin – a potent homicidal poison. Br. Med. J. *1*, 350–351 (1979).

[K 35] Koch, W.: Giftige Gasausscheidungen von Eibenbäumen? Münch. Med. Wochenschr. *112*, 1398 (1970).

[K 36] Konopa, J., J. M. Woynarowski, and M. Lewandowska-Gumieniak: Isolation of viscotoxins: cytotoxic basic polypeptides from *Viscum album*. Hoppe-Seyler's Z. Physiol. Chem. *361*, 1525–1534 (1980).

[K 37] Koopmann, H.: Tödliche Schöllkraut-Vergiftung *(Chelidonium majus)*. Samml. Vergiftungsfällen (Arch. Toxikol.) *8*, 93–98 (1937).

[K 38] Korninger, H. C. and K. Lenz: Vergiftungen im Kindesalter. Wien. Klin. Wochenschr. *90*, 1–7 (1978).

[K 39] Kósa, F. and E. Virágos-Kis: Tod eines dreijährigen Kindes nach dem Genuss von unreifen Mohnkapseln. Zacchia *5*, 604–610 (1969).

[K 40] Koster, M. and G. K. David: Reversible severe hypertension due to licorice ingestion. New Engl. J. Med. *278*, 1381–1383 (1968).

[K 41] Kraus, Lj. and D. Dupakova: Der derzeitige Stand der Bewertung von Arbutindrogen. Pharmazie *19*, 41–45 (1964).

[K 42] Krauze, S. and W. Dziedzianowicz: Untersuchungen über die Giftigkeit von Buchensamen *(Fagus silvatica* L.). Nahrung *3*, 213–227 (1959).

[K 43] Kreitmair, H.: *Chelidonium majus* L. – das Schöllkraut. Pharmazie *5*, 85–88 (1950).

[K 44] Krienke, E. G. and A. Zaminer: Pflanzenvergiftungen auf Kinderspielplätzen. Öffentl. Gesundheitswesen *35*, 458–474 (1973).

[K 45] Krienke, E. G.: Akzidentelle Vergiftungen durch Pflanzen aus der Sicht einer Giftinformationszentrale. Internist *17*, 399–410 (1976).

[K 46] Krienke, E. G. and K. E. von Mühlendahl: Akzidentelle Vergiftungen durch Pflanzen. Notfallmedizin *4*, 486–495, 552–559, 619–627 (1978).

[K 47] Krienke, E. G. and K. E. von Mühlendahl: Vergiftungen im Kindesalter, F. Enke, Stuttgart, 273 pp., 1980.

[K 48] Kroeber, L.: Das neuzeitliche Kräuterbuch, 2nd ed., Hippokrates-Marquardt, Stuttgart, vol. 3, Giftpflanzen, 476 pp., 1949.

[K 49] Krook, G.: Occupational dermatitis from *Lactuca sativa* (lettuce) and *Cichorium* (endive). Contact Dermatitis *3*, 27–36, (1977).

[K 50] Krüssmann, G.: Handbuch der Laubgehölze, 2nd ed., P. Parey, Berlin, Hamburg, 3 vols., 1976–1978.

[K 51] Krumrey, G.: Zum Problem 'Riesenschierling'. Schule u. Beratung 10/80, III-2 (1980).

[K 52] Kuballa, B. and R. Anton: Choix d'une méthode pharmacologique pour l'étude des principes toxiques de Dieffenbachia. Plant. Méd. Phytothér. *11*, 58–70 (1977).

[K 53] Kuballa, B., A. A. J. Lugnier, and R. Anton: Phlogogen constituents of Dieffenbachia. Planta Med. *39*, 250–251 (1980).

[K 54] Kuhlmann, J.: Herzglykoside. II. Digitalisintoxikation. Dtsch. Apoth. Ztg *121*, 2291–2298 (1981).

[K 55] Kühn, L. and S. Pfeifer: Die Gattung *Papaver* und ihre Alkaloide. Pharmazie *18*, 819–843 (1963).

[K 56] Kürkçüoğlu, M.: Henbane *(Hyoscyamus niger)* poisonings in the vicinity of Erzurum. Turk. J. Pediat. *12*, 48–56 (1970).

[K 57] Kurokawa, T., M. Tsuda, and Y. Sugino: Purification and characterization of a lectin from *Wisteria floribunda* seeds. J. Biol. Chem. *251*, 5686–5693 (1976).

[K 58] Kwasniewski, V.: Die Gerbsäure-Mikroreaktionen der mekonsauren Alkaloide des Opiums und der chelidonsauren Schöllkrautalkaloide, ihre Unterscheidungs- und Anwendungsmöglichkeiten. Arch. Pharm. *285*, 445–448 (1952).

[K 59] Kwasniewski, V.: Über einen neuen Mikronachweis der Alkaloidchelidonate des Schöllkrauts. Pharm. Ztg *88*, 49–50 (1952).

[K 60] Kwasniewski, V.: Das Vorkommen von Saponinen bei den Papaveraceen. Dtsch. Apoth. Ztg *113*, 1889–1890 (1973).

[K 61] Köppel, C., J. Tenczer, U. Tönnesmann, T. Schirop, and K. Ibe: Acute poisoning with pine oil – metabolism of monoterpenes. Arch. Toxicol. *49*, 73–78 (1981).

[K 62] Kakrani, A. L., C. S. Rajput, S. K. Khandare, and V. E. Redkar: Yellow oleander seed poisoning with cardiotoxicity. Indian Heart J. *33*, 31–33 (1981).

[K 63] Kuballa, B., A. A. J. Lugnier, and R. Anton: Study of *Dieffenbachia exotica* induced edema in mouse and rat hindpaw: respective role of oxalate needles and trypsin-like protease. Toxicol. Appl. Pharmacol. *58*, 444–451 (1981).

[K 64] Kelleway, R. A. and L. Geovjian: Acute bracken fern poisoning in a 14-month-old horse. Vet. Med. Small Anim. Clin. *73*, 295–296 (1978).

[K 65] Kuschinsky, G.: Indikation von Physostigmin. Intern. Prax. *21*, 492 (1981).

[K 66] Kirson, I. and E. Glotter: Recent developments in naturally occurring ergostane-type steroids. A review. J. Nat. Prod. *44*, 633–647 (1981).

[K 67] Kalbhen, D. A.: A contribution to the chemistry and pharmacology of nutmeg *(Myristica fragrans)*. Angew. Chem. (Internat. Ed.) *10*, 370–374 (1971).

[L 1] Ladeira, A. M., S. O. Andrade, and P. Sawaya: Studies on *Dieffenbachia picta* Schott: toxic effects in guinea pigs. Toxicol. Appl. Pharmacol. *34*, 363–373 (1975).

[L 2] Lampe, K. F.: Systemic plant poisoning in children. Pediatrics *54*, 347–351 (1974).

[L 3] Lampe, K. F.: Changes in therapy in Abrus and Ricinus poisoning suggested by recent studies in their mechanism of toxicity. Clin. Toxicol. *9*, 21 (1976).

[L 4] Lamson, P. D.: On the pharmacological action of helenalin, the active principle of *Helenium autumnale*. J. Pharmacol. Exp. Ther. *4*, 471–489 (1913).

[L 5] Langhammer, L., K. Blaszkiewitz, and I. Kotzorek: Nachweis einer toxischen Verfälschung von Herba Equiseti. Dtsch. Apoth. Ztg *112*, 1749–1751 (1972).

[L 6] Larbig, D., U. Raff, P. Wernet, R. Haasis, and C. Schwarzenberg: Therapie der Digitalisintoxikation mit spezifischen Antikörpern. In: Okonek et al. (eds.), Humantoxikologie, G. Fischer, Stuttgart, New York, 1979.

[L 7] Lavie, D. and E. Glotter: The cucurbitanes, a group of tetracyclic triterpenes. Fortschr. Chem. Org. Naturst. *29*, 307–362 (1971).

[L 8] O'Leary, S. B.: Poisoning in man from eating poisonous plants. Arch. Environ. Health *9*, 216–242 (1964).

[L 9] Letcher, R. M. and K. M. Wong: Structure and synthesis of the phenanthrenes TaI and TaV from *Tamus communis*. J. Chem. Soc. Perkin Trans. I, 739–742 (1978).

[L 10] Letzig, E. and W. Handschack: Vergleichende Untersuchungen über einige Inhaltsstoffe bitterer und süsser Ebereschenfrüchte während des Reifens. Nahrung *7*, 591–605 (1963).

[L 11] Leunis, J.: Synopsis der Pflanzenkunde, Hahn'sche Buchhandlung, Hannover, vol. 2, Specialle Botanik, 1885.

[L 12] Leveau, A. M., M. Durand, and R. R. Paris: Sur la toxicité des fruits de divers *Lonicera* (Caprifoliacées). Plant. Méd. Phytothér. *11*, 94–105 (1977).

[L 13] Leveau, A. M., M. Durand, and R. R. Paris: Sur la toxicité des fruits de *l'Aucuba japonica* (Cornacées). Plant. Méd. Phytothér. *13*, 199–204 (1979).

[L 14] Lewin, L.: Die Gifte in der Weltgeschichte, J. Springer, Berlin, 536 pp., 1920.

[L 15] Lewin, L.: Gifte und Vergiftungen (= 4th ed. of Lehrbuch der Toxikologie), G. Stilke, Berlin, 1929.

[L 16] Lewis, W. H.: Reporting adverse reactions to herbal ingestants. J. Am. Med. Ass. *240*, 109–110 (1978).

[L 17] Lewis, W. H.: Snowberry *(Symphoricarpos)* poisoning in children. J. Am. Med. Ass. *242*, 2663 (1979).

[L 18] Lewis, W. H.: Poisonous plants of the central United States (Book review). Econ. Bot. *35*, 299 (1981).

[L 19] Lewis, W. H. and P. R. Smith: Poke root herbal tea poisoning. J. Am. Med. Ass. *242*, 2759–2760 (1979).

[L 20] Lewis, W. H. and M. P. F. Elvin-Lewis: Medical botany – plants affecting man's health, J. Wiley, New York, London, Sydney, Toronto, 515 pp., 1977.

[L 21] Leyland, A.: Laburnum *(Cytisus laburnum)* poisoning in two dogs. Vet. Rec. *109*, 287, (1981).

[L 22] Liebenow, H.: *Solanum nigrum* and other weeds as nitrate-containing plants – their nitrate content. Wiss. Z. Humboldt-Univ. Berlin, Math.-Naturwiss. Reihe *19*, 73–80 (1970).

[L 23] Liebenow, H. and K. Liebenow: Giftpflanzen. Ein 'Vademekum für Tierärzte, Humanmediziner, Biologen und Landwirte', 2nd ed., F. Enke, Stuttgart, 248 pp., 1981.

[L 24] Liener, J. E.: Phytohemagglutinins (Phytolectins). Ann. Rev. Pl. Physiol. *27*, 291–319 (1976).

[L 25] Liener, J. E.: Significance for humans of biologically active factors in soybeans and other food legumes. J. Am. Oil Chem. Soc. *56*, 121–129 (1979).

[L 26] Lim, K. H.: External eye allergy from sap of *Dieffenbachia picta*. Singapore Med. J. *18*, 176–177 (1977).

[L 27] Lin, J. Y., M. J. Hou, and Y. C. Chen: Isolation of toxic and nontoxic lectins from the bitter pear melon *Momordica charantia* L. Toxicon *16*, 653–660 (1978).

[L 28] Lindner, E.: Toxikologie der Nahrungsmittel, 2nd ed., G. Thieme, Stuttgart, 200 pp., 1979.

[L 29] Lingelsheim, A. V.: Pharmakognostische Studien, insbesondere über Drogen des 6. Deutschen Arzneibuchs. Arch. Pharm. *266*, 218–231 (1928).

[L 30] Liskova-Kiar, M. and L. Proschek: Influence of partially purified extracts of *Solanum malacoxylon* on bone resorption in organ culture. Calcif. Tissue Res. *26*, 39–46 (1978).

[L 31] Lockey, S. D. and L. Dunkelberger: Anaphylaxis from an Indian necklace. J. Am. Med. Ass. *206*, 2900–2901 (1968).

[L 32] Loeffelhardt, W., B. Kopp, and W. Kubelka: Intracellular distribution of cardiac glycosides in leaves of *Convallaria majalis*. Phytochemistry *18*, 1289–1292 (1979).

[L 33] Lowe, J. E., H. F. Hintz, H. F. Schryver, and J. M. Kingsbury: *Taxus cuspidata* (Japanese yew) poisoning in horses. Cornell Vet. *60*, 36–39 (1970).

[L 34] Lüthy, J., U. Zweifel, and C. Schlatter: Pyrrolizidin-Alkaloide in Huflattich *(Tussilago farfara* L.) verschiedener Herkunft. Mitt. Geb. Lebensmittelunters. u. Hyg. *71*, 73–80 (1980).

[L 35] Lüthy, J., U. Zweifel, B. Karlhuber, and C. Schlatter: Pyrrolizidine alkaloids of *Senecio alpinus* and their detection in foodstuffs. J. Agric. Food Chem. *29*, 302–305 (1981).

[L 36] Lutomski, J.: Chemie und therapeutische Verwendung von Süssholz (*Glycyrrhiza glabra* L.). Pharm. Unser. Zeit *12*, 49–54 (1983).

[M 1] Machel, A. R. and C. I. Dorsett: Cyanide analyses of peaches. Econ. Bot. *24*, 51–52 (1970).

[M 2] Macleod, N. S. M., A. Greig, J. M. Bonn, and K. W. Angus: Poisoning in cattle associated with *Dryopteris filix-mas* and *D. borreri*. Vet. Rec. *102*, 239–240 (1978).

[M 3] Madaus, G.: Lehrbuch der biologischen Heilmittel, G. Thieme, Leipzig, vol. 1, 1938.

[M 4] Madaus, G. and F. Koch: Tierexperimentelle Studien zur Frage der medikamentösen Sterilisierung durch *Caladium seguinum (Dieffenbachia seguine)*. Z. Gesamte Exp. Med. *109*, 68 (1941).

[M 5] Mager, P. P., A. Seese, and K. Takeya: Structure-toxicity relationship applied to grayanotoxins. Pharmazie *36*, 381–382 (1981).

[M 6] Mahe, M., J. van den Driessche, and L. Girre: A propos de l'activité pharmacologique de quelques plantes indigènes sur le système nerveux. Plant. Méd. Phytothér. *12*, 248–258 (1978).

[M 7] Mahler, D. A.: The jimson-weed high, J. Am. Med. Ass. *231*, 138 (1975).

[M 8] Maitai, C. K.: The toxicity of the plant *Catha edulis* in rats. Toxicon *15*, 363–366 (1977).

[M 9] Maiti, P. C., S. Mookherjea, R. Mathew, and S. S. Dan: Studies on Indian *Solanum* I. Alkaloid content and detection of solasodine. Econ. Bot. *33*, 75–77 (1979).

[M 10] Majak, W. and R. J. Bose: Nitropropanylglucopyranoses in *Coronilla varia*. Phytochemistry *15*, 415–417 (1976).

[M 11] Malizia, E., L. Sarcinelli, and G. Andreucci: Ricinus poisoning: a familiar epidemy. Acta Pharmacol. Toxicol. *41*, Suppl. 1, 351–361 (1977).

[M 12] Malorny, G.: Stechapfelsamenvergiftungen nach Genuss von Buchweizenmehlzubereitungen. Samml. Vergiftungsfällen (Arch. Toxikol.) *14*, 181–184 (1952/54).

[M 13] Mancini, S. D. and J. M. Edwards: Cytotoxic principles from the sap of *Kalmia latifolia*. J. Nat. Prod. (Lloydia) *42*, 483–488 (1979).

[M 14] Mandel, W.: Merkmalskatalog zur raschen Erkennung wildwachsender Früchte für klinisch-toxikologische Zwecke, Dissertation, München, 1974.

[M 15] Manno, B. R. and J. E. Manno: Toxicology of ipecac: a review. Clin. Toxicol. *10*, 221–242 (1977).

[M 16] Manno, J. E., F. W. Fochtman, C. L. Winek, and S. P. Shanor: Toxicity of plants of the genus *Dieffenbachia*. Toxicol. Appl. Pharmacol. *10*, 405–406 (1967).

[M 17] der Marderosian, A.: Poisonous plants in and around the home. Am. J. Pharm. Educ. *30*, 115–140 (1966).

[M 18] der Marderosian, A., F. B. Giller, and F. C. Roja Jr: Phytochemical and toxicological screening of household ornamental plants potentially toxic to humans. J. Toxicol. & Environ. Health *1*, 939–953 (1976).

[M 19] der Marderosian, A. and F. C. Roja Jr: Literature review and household ornamental plants potentially toxic to humans. In: Kinghorn, A. D. (ed.), Toxic plants, pp. 103–135 (1979).

[M 20] Maretić, Z., F. E. Russel, and J. Ladavac: Tulip bulb poisoning. Period. Biol. *80*, 141–143 (1978).

[M 21] Maretić, Z.: Poisoning by castor beans *(Ricinus communis)*. Arh. Hig. Rada Toksikol. *31*, 251–257 (1980). Cited from: Biol. Abstr. *71*, 84712 (1981).

[M 22] Martinek, A.: Ranunculosid als Inhaltsstoff der getrockneten Blätter, Stengel und Blüten von *Helleborus niger*. Planta Med. *26*, 218–224 (1974).

[M 23] Máthé Jr, I., H. van Mai, and I. Máthé Sr: Variation in the solasodine production in stands of various stages of development of *Solanum nigrum* L. during the vegetation period. Planta Med. *36*, 237–238 (1979).

[M 24] Máthé Jr, I. and I. Máthé Sr: Variation in alkaloids in *Solanum dulcamara* L. In: Hawkes *et al.* (eds.), The biology and taxonomy of the Solanaceae, pp. 211–222, 1979.

[M 25] Mathes, G.: Personal communication, 1980.

[M 26] Mattocks, A. R.: Recent studies on mechanisms of cytotoxic action of pyrrolizidine alkaloids. In: Keeler *et al.* (eds.), Effects of poisonous plants on livestock, pp. 177–187, 1978.

[M 27] Mayer, C., W. Trueb, J. Wilson, and C. H. Eugster: Konstitution der Dihydropalustraminsäure und Bemerkungen zur Struktur des Palustrins. Helv. Chim. Acta *51*, 661–668 (1968).

[M 28] Mebs, D.: Kath. Naturwiss. Rundsch. *34*, 19–21 (1981).

[M 29] Medsger, O. P.: Edible wild plants, Collier MacMillan, London, 323 pp., 1974.

[M 30] Mehra, P. N. and T. C. Mittal: Significance of internal secretory glands in relation to filicin. Planta Med. *9*, 189–199 (1961).

[M 31] Mendelson, G.: Treatment of hallucinogenic-plant toxicity. Ann. Intern. Med. *85*, 126 (1976).

[M 32] Merfort, I.: Lipophile Inhaltsstoffe der Blätter und Früchte von *Symphoricarpos albus* (L.) Blake, Dissertation, Düsseldorf, 1980.

[M 33] Mezger, O. and W. Heess: Herbstzeitlosensamen-Giftmordversuch. Samml. Vergiftungsfällen (Arch. Toxikol.) *3*, 47–48 (1932).

[M 34] Mikolich, J. R., G. W. Paulson, and C. J. Cross: Acute anticholinergic syndrome due to jimson seed ingestion – clinical and laboratory observation in six cases. Ann. Intern. Med. *83*, 321–325 (1975).

[M 35] McMillan, M. and J. C. Thompson: An outbreak of suspected solanine poisoning in schoolboys. Quart. J. Med. *48*, 227–243 (1979).

[M 36] Miller, R. W.: A brief survey of Taxus alkaloids and other taxane derivatives. J. Nat. Prod. *43*, 425–437 (1980).

[M 37] Miller, J. M. and E. E. Conn: Metabolism of hydrogen cyanide by higher plants. Plant Physiol. *65*, 1199–1202 (1980).

[M 38] Minors, E. H.: Five cases of belladonna poisoning. Br. Med. J. *2*, 518–519 (1948).

[M 39] Miranda, C. L., P. R. Cheeke, J. A. Schmitz, and D. R. Buhler: Toxicity of *Senecio jacobaea* (tansy ragwort) in rats. Toxicol. Appl. Pharmacol. *56*, 432–442 (1980).

[M 40] Miranda, C. L., P. R. Cheeke, and D. R. Buhler: Effect of pyrrolizidine alkaloids from tansy ragwort *(Senecio jacobaea)* on hepatic drug-matabolizing enzymes in male rats. Biochem. Pharmacol. *29*, 2645–2649 (1980).

[M 41] Misra, S. B. and S. N. Dixit: Antifungal principle of *Ranunculus sceleratus*. Econ. Bot. *34*, 362–367 (1980).

[M 42] Mitchell, J. and A. Rook: Botanical dermatology – plants and plant products injurious to the skin, Greengrass, Vancouver, 787 pp., 1979.

[M 43] Mitchell, M. I. and P. A. Routledge: Hemlock water dropwort poisoning – a review. Clin. Toxicol. *12*, 417–426 (1978).

[M 44] Mitchell, J. C. and G. Dupuis: Allergic contact dermatitis from sesquiterpenoids of the Compositae family of plants. Br. J. Dermatol. *84*, 139–150 (1971).

[M 45] Mitchell, J. C.: Allergic contact dermatitis from *Hedera helix* and *Brassaia actinophylla*. Contact Dermatitis *7*, 158–159 (1981).

[M 46] Mitchell, R. G.: Laburnum poisoning in children. Report on ten cases. Lancet *2*, 57–58 (1951).

[M 47] Mobacken, H.: Allergic plant dermatitis from *Scindapsus aureus*. Contact Dermatitis *1*, 60–61 (1975).

[M 48] Moeller, J. and C. Griebel: Mikroskopie der Nahrungs- und Genussmittel aus dem Pflanzenreiche, 3rd ed., J. Springer, Berlin, 529 pp., 1928.

[M 49] Moertel, C. G.: A trial of laetrile now. New Engl. J. Med. *298*, 218–219 (1978).

[M 50] Moeschlin, S.: Klinik und Therapie der Vergiftungen, 6th ed., G. Thieme, Stuttgart, New York, 640 pp., 1980.

[M 51] Moffat, A. C.: Forensic pharmacognosy – poisoning with plants. J. Forens. Sci. Soc. *20*, 103–109 (1980).

[M 52] Mohabbat, O., M. Shafiq Younos, A. A. Merzad, R. N. Srivastava, G. G. Sediq, and G. N. Aram: An outbreak of hepatic veno-occlusive disease in north-western Afghanistan. Lancet *2*, 269–271 (1976).

[M 53] Moore, R. H. S.: Poisoning by old man's beard *(Clematis vitalba)*? Vet. Rec. *89*, 569–570 (1971).

[M 54] O'Moore, L.B.: *Arum maculatum* poisoning in cattle. Irish Vet. J. *9*, 146–147 (1955).

[M 55] Morfitt, J. M.: Laburnum poisoning. Lancet *1*, 1195 (1979).

[M 56] Mořkovský, O. and J. Kučera: A mass poisoning by seeds of *Laburnum anagyroides* in children in a kindergarten. Česk. Pediat. *35*, 284–285 (1980).

[M 57] Morse, D. L., L. Boros, and P. A. Findley: More on cyanide poisoning from laetrile. New Engl. J. Med. *301*, 892 (1979).

[M 58] Morton, J. F.: Folk-remedy plants and esophageal cancer in Coro, Venezuela. Morris Arbor. Bull. *26*, 24–31 (1975).

[M 59] Morton, J. F.: Ornamental plants with poisonous properties II. Proc. Fla State Hort. Soc. *75*, 484–491 (1962).

[M 60] Mothes, K.: Zur Geschichte unserer Kenntnisse über die Alkaloide. Pharmazie *36*, 199–209 (1981).

[M 61] Mühlendahl, K. E. von and E. G. Krienke: Vergiftungen im Kindesalter Nikotin-(Zigaretten-)Vergiftungen. Pädiat. Prax. *21*, 291–293 (1979).

[M 62] Müller, A. H.: Über Vergiftung mit Besenginster. Dtsch. Med. Wochenschr. *76*, 1027 (1951).

[M 63] Müller-Stoll, W. R.: Die Wurzelstöcke des Adlerfarns, *Pteridium aquilinum* (L.) Kuhn, und ihre Verwertung als Nahrungs- und Futtermittel. Pharmazie *4*, 122–137 (1949).

[M 64] Müller, A. and M. Wichtl: Zur Frage der Herzwirksamkeit des Gnadenkrauts *(Gratiola officinalis* L.). Pharm. Ztg *124*, 1761–1766 (1979).

[M 65] Munro, I. C.: Naturally occurring toxicants in foods and their significance. Clin. Toxicol. *9*, 647–663 (1976).

[M 66] Mutter, L.: Poisoning by western water hemlock. Can. J. Public Health *67*, 386 (1976).

[M 67] Morton, J. F.: Brazilian pepper – its impact on people, animals and the environment. Econ. Bot. *32*, 353–359 (1978).

[M 68] Mitchell, A.: A field guide to the trees of Britain and Northern Europe, 2nd ed., Collins, London, 416 pp., 1978.

[N 1] Nagaratnam, N., D. P. K. DeSilva, and N. DeSilva: Colchicine poisoning following ingestion of *Gloriosa superba* tubers. Trop. Geogr. Med. *25*, 15–17 (1973).

[N 2] Nahrstedt, A.: Cyanogenese in *Cotoneaster*-Arten. Phytochemistry *12*, 1539–1542 (1973).

[N 3] Nahrstedt, A.: Potentiell carcinogene Inhaltsstoffe höhere Pflanzen. Pharm. Unser. Zeit *6*, 150–157 (1977).

[N 4] Nahrstedt, A.: Mandelsäurenitrilglykoside in der Krebstherapie. Dtsch. Apoth. Ztg *118*, 1105–1107 (1978).

[N 5] Nestler, A.: Die hautreizende Wirkung des roten Hartriegels und der Kornelkische. Umschau *41*, 860–861 (1913).

[N 6] Nestler, A.: Die hautreizende Wirkung der einheimischen Wolfsmilcharten. Pharm. Zentralh. *67* (11), 161–164 (1926).

[N 7] Neugebauer, W.: Lathyrismus. Arch. Toxicol. *19*, 215–223 (1961).

[N 8] Neugebauer, W.: Akute Kaliumoxalatvergiftung (Kleesalzvergiftung). Arch. Toxicol. *19*, 275–277 (1962).

[N 9] Neururer, H., M. Wichtl, and U. Creuzburg: Untersuchungen zur Frage einer chemischen Bekämpfung des Sumpfschachtelhalmes *(Equisetum palustre* L.) und deren Auswirkung auf die Fütterung. Pflanzenschutzberichte *22*, 115–124 (1959).

[N 10] Nghia, N.V., L. Bezanger-Beauquesne, and M. Torck: Recherches sur la caractérisation des flavonoïdes. Plant. Méd. Phytothér. *5*, 177–187 (1971).

[N 11] Nielsen, H.: Giftpflanzen. 148 europäische Arten. Bestimmung – Wirkung – Geschichte, Kosmos Franckh, Stuttgart, 141 pp., 1979.

[N 12] Nikonow, G. K. and S. A. Syrkina-Krugljak: Chemische Untersuchung der aktiven Prinzipien von *Actaea spicata* L. Pharm. Zentralh. *103*, 601 (1964).

[N 13] Nishie, K., M. R. Gumbmann, and A. C. Keyl: Pharmacology of solanine. Toxicol. Appl. Pharmacol. *19*, 81–92 (1971).

[N 14] Niyogi, S. K.: Elevation of enzyme levels in serum due to *Abrus precatorius* (jequirity bean) poisoning. Toxicon *15*, 577–580 (1977).

[N 15] Nöller, H. G.: Eine Seidelbastintoxikation beim Kinde. Monatschr. Kinderheilk. *103*, 327–330 (1955).

[N 16] North, P.: Poisonous plants and fungi in colour, Blandford Press, London, 161 pp., 1967.

[O 1] Ober, W. B.: Did Socrates die of hemlock poisoning? N. Y. State J. Med. *77*, 254–258 (1977).

[O 2] Oberda, G. M.: Jimson weed. J. Am. Med. Ass. *232*, 597 (1975).

[O 3] Occhini, P. and C. T. Rizzini: Ação toxica de duas sp. de *Dieffenbachia*. Rev. Bras. Med. *15*, 10 (1958).

[O 4] Odefey: Personal communication, 1981.

[O 5] Odenthal, K.-P., W. Molls, and G. Vogel: Alkaloide aus *Corydalis solida* und deren pharmakologische Wirkungen im Vergleich zu Bulbocapnin. Planta Med. *42*, 115 (1981).

[O 6] Oehme, F. W.: The hazard of plant toxicities to the human population. In: Keeler *et al.* (eds.), Effects of poisonous plants on livestock, pp. 67–80, 1978.

[O 7] Oehme, F. W.: Veterinary toxicology: the epidemiology of poisonings in domestic animals. Clin. Toxicol. *10*, 1–21 (1977).

[O 8] Okada, K. A., B. J. Carillo, and M. Tilley: *Solanum malacoxylon* Sendtner: a toxic plant in Argentina. Econ. Bot. *31*, 225–236 (1977).

[O 9] Okonek, S., C. J. Schuster, R. Bork, B. Zöller, P. Main, G. Alzen, K. Diether, L. S. Weilemann, and T. Erdmann: Vergiftungen – Giftinformation 1977, Ärztebl. Rheinl.-Pfalz *31*(12) (1978).

[O 10] Okonek, S., G. Fülgraff, and R. Frey: Humantoxikologie. Akute Vergiftungen – Giftinformation, G. Fischer, Stuttgart, New York, 202 pp., 1979.

[O 11] Okuda, T., T. Yoshida, S. Koike, and N. Toh: New diterpene esters from *Aleurites fordii* fruits. Phytochemistry *14*, 509–515 (1975).

[O 12] Olie, J. P., C. Gay, P. Lebeau, and P. Deniker: Intoxication volontaire au *Datura* à partir d'un médicament anti-asthmatique. Nouv. Presse Méd. *10*, 429 (1981).

[O 13] Olsen, J. D.: Rat bioassay for estimating toxicity of plant material from larkspur (*Delphinium* sp.). Am. J. Vet Res. *38*, 277–279 (1977).

[O 14] Olsen, J. D.: Larkspur toxicosis: a review of current research. In: Keeler *et al.* (eds.), Effects of poisonous plants on livestock, pp. 535–543, 1978.

[O 15] Olsen, J. D.: Tall larkspur poisoning in cattle and sheep. J. Am. Vet. Med. Ass. *173*, 762–765 (1978).

[O 16] Olsnes, S. and A. Pihl: Abrin and ricin – two toxic lectins. Trends Biochem. Sci. *3*, 7–10 (1978).

[O 17] Opp, M.: Beautiful but dangerous. Med. World News *18*(10), 38–43 (1977).

[O 18] Ortega, J. A. and J. E. Creek: Acute cyanide poisoning following administration of laetrile enemas. J. Pediat. *93*, 1059 (1978).

[O 19] Oshio, H., M. Tsukui, and T. Matsuoka: Isolation of l-ephedrine from 'Pinelliae Tuber'. Chem. Pharm. Bull. *26*, 2096–2097 (1978).

[O 20] Osisiogu, I. U., J. O. Uzo, and E. N. Ugochukwu: The irritant effects of cocoyams. Planta Med. *26*, 166–169 (1974).

[P 1] Pachaly, P.: Terpenoide toxischer Ericaceen Europas. Dtsch. Apoth. Ztg *120*, 429 (1980) and Pharm. Ztg *125*, 480–481 (1980).

[P 2] Pack, W. K., H. W. Raudonat, and K. Schmidt: Über eine tödliche Blausäurevergiftung nach dem Genuss bitterer Mandeln *(Prunus amygdalus)*. Z. Rechtsmed. *70*, 53–54 (1972).

[P 3] Panciera, R. J.: Oak poisoning in cattle. In: Keeler *et al.* (eds.), Effects of poisonous

plants on livestock, pp. 499–506, 1978.

[P 4] Panossian, A. G., G. M. Avetissian, M. N. Nikishchenko, V. H. Mnatsakanian, G. V. Gasparian, S. H. Pashinian, G. S. Vartanian, and K. G. Karaguezian: Biologically active substances from *Bryonia alba*. Planta Med. *39*, 254 (1980).

[P 5] Pass, D.: Poisoning of chickens and ducks by pyrrolizidine alkaloids of *Heliotropium europaeum*. Aust. Vet. J. *55*, 602 (1979).

[P 6] Pass, D. A., G. G. Hogg, R. G. Russell, J. A. Edgar, I. M. Tence, and L. Rikard-Bell: Poisoning of chickens and ducks by pyrrolizidine alkaloids of *Heliotropium europaeum*. Aust. Vet. J. *55*, 284–288 (1979).

[P 7] Pass, M. A. and T. Heath: Gallbladder paralysis in sheep during lantana poisoning. J. Comp. Pathol. *87*, 301–306 (1977).

[P 8] Pass, M. A., A. A. Seawright, T. J. Heath, and R. T. Gemmell: Lantana poisoning: a cholestatic disease of cattle and sheep. In: Keeler *et al.* (eds.), Effects of poisonous plants on livestock, pp. 229–237, 1978.

[P 9] Pass, M. A., R. T. Gemmell, and T. J. Heath: Effect of lantana on the ultrastructure of the liver of sheep. Toxicol. Appl. Pharmacol. *43*, 589–596 (1978).

[P 10] Pass, M. A., L. Findlay, M. W. Pugh, and A. A. Seawright: Toxicity of reduced lantadene A in the rat. Toxicol. Appl. Pharmacol. *51*, 515–521 (1979).

[P 11] Patel, S. and J. Wiggins: Eucalyptus oil poisoning. Arch. Dis. Childh. *55*, 405–406 (1980).

[P 12] Patil, B. C., R. P. Sharma, D. K. Salunkhe, and K. Salunkhe: Evaluation of solanine toxicity. Food & Cosmet. Toxicol. *10*, 395–398 (1972).

[P 13] Pelletier, S. W. and N. V. Mody: Developments in the chemistry of diterpenoid alkaloids. J. Nat. Prod. *43*, 41–71 (1980).

[P 14] Petcu, P.: Beiträge zur Phytochemie von *Berberis dielsiana*. Planta Med. *16*, 421–425 (1968).

[P 15] Petcu, P.: Untersuchung der im Klausenburger Botanischen Garten akklimatisierten *Berberis hakodate* Hort. Arch. Pharm. *296*, 753–757 (1963).

[P 16] Petcu, P.: Studien über *Berberis serrata* Koehne. Pharmazie *19*, 53–55 (1964).

[P 17] Petcu, P.: Der Gehalt an Alkaloiden und Vitamin C in *Berberis guimpelii*. Planta Med. *13*, 178–181 (1965).

[P 18] Petcu, P.: Phytochemische Untersuchungen an *Berberis hauniensis* Zab. Arch. Pharm. *298*, 73–77 (1965).

[P 19] Petcu, P.: Phytochemische Untersuchungen an *Berberis virescens* Hook. Pharmazie *21*, 54–56 (1966).

[P 20] Petcu, P. and T. Goina: Neue Methoden zur Extrahierung der Alkaloide aus *Berberis vulgaris*. Planta Med. *18*, 372–375 (1970).

[P 21] Petkov, V., P. Manolov and K. Paparkova: Screening pharmacologique du *Sambucus ebulus* L. Plant. Méd. Phytothér. *13*, 134–138 (1979).

[P 22] Pfänder, H. J. and D. Frohne: Identifizierung und Charakterisierung einiger

giftverdächtiger roter Früchte. Dtsch. Apoth. Ztg *120*, 2052–2056 (1980).

[P 23] Pfeifer, S. and I. Mann: Über Alkaloide der Gattung *Papaver*. Pharmazie *20*, 643–649 (1965).

[P 24] Phelan, W. J.: Camphor poisoning, over-the-counter dangers. Clin. Toxicol. *9*, 26 (1976).

[P 25] McPherson, A.: Pokeweed and other lymphocyte mitogens. In: Kinghorn, A. D. (ed.), Toxic plants, pp. 83–87, 1979.

[P 26] McPherson, A.: Pokeweed lectins. In: Kinghorn, A.D. (ed.), Toxic plants, pp. 87–89, 1979.

[P 27] McPherson, A.: Abrus lectin and abrin. In: Kinghorn, A.D. (ed.), Toxic plants, pp. 92–100, 1979.

[P 28] McPherson, A. and S. Hoover: Purification of mitogenic proteins from *Hura crepitans* and *Robinia pseudacacia*. Biochem. Biophys. Res. Commun. *89*, 713–720 (1979). Cited from: Biol. Abstr. *69*, 5592 (1980).

[P 29] Philadelphy, A.: Eine bullöse Hauterkrankung durch *Achillea millefolium*. Wien. Klin. Wochenschr. *41*, 88–89 (1928).

[P 30] Phillips, R.: Wild flowers of Britain, Pan Books, London, 192 pp., 1978.

[P 31] Phillipson, J. D. and C. Melville: An investigation of the alkaloids of some British species of *Equisetum*. J. Pharm. Pharmacol. *12*, 506–508 (1960).

[P 32] Pierce, K. R., J. R. Joyce, R. B. England, and L. P. Jones: Acute hemolytic anemia caused by wild onion poisoning in horses. J. Am. Vet. Med. Ass. *160*, 323–327 (1972).

[P 33] Pierce, J. H.: Encephalitis signs from Philodendron leaf. Mod. Vet. Pract. *51*, 42 (1970).

[P 34] Pijoan, M.: Cyanide poisoning from choke cherry seed. Am. J. Med. Sci. *204*, 550–553 (1942).

[P 35] Pingel, I.: Giftpflanzen aus Erlanger Kinderspielplätzen und öffentlichen Anlagen, Dissertation, Erlangen, 1980.

[P 36] Plowman, T.: Folk uses of New World aroids. Econ. Bot. *23*, 97–122 (1969).

[P 37] Pohlenz, J., J. Lüthy, H. P. Minder, and A. Bivetti: Enzootische Leberzirrhose beim Rind, verursacht durch Pyrrolizidinalkaloide nach Aufnahme von *Senecio alpinus* (Alpenkreuzkraut). Schweiz. Arch. Tierheilk. *122*, 183–193 (1980).

[P 38] Pohlmann, J.: The cucurbitacins in *Bryonia alba* and *Bryonia dioica*. Phytochemistry *14*, 1587–1589 (1975).

[P 39] Polster, H.: Zwei Fälle von Nachtschattenvergiftung. Kinderärztl. Prax. *21*, 208–211 (1953).

[P 40] Ponsinet, G. and G. Ourisson: Études chimiotaxonomiques dans la famille des Euphorbiacées. 3. Répartition des triterpènes dans le latex d'*Euphorbia*. Phytochemistry *7*, 89–98 (1968).

[P 41] Pora, E., E. Pop, D. Roska, and A. Radu: Der Einfluss der Wirtspflanze auf den Gehalt an hypotensiven und herzwirksamen Prinzipien der Mistel (*Viscum album* L.). Pharmazie *12*, 528–538 (1957).

[P 42] Praxiskurier: Täglich drei Vergiftungen durch Pflanzen. No. 32/33, dated 6.8.1980.

[P 43] Preininger, V., P. Vrublovsky, and V. Stastny: Alkaloidvorkommen in Mohnsamen (*Papaver somniferum* L.). Pharmazie *20*, 439–441 (1965).

[P 44] Preussmann. R.: Carcinogene Pflanzeninhaltsstoffe. Planta Med. *22*, 217–228 (1972).

[P 45] Puche, R. C., H. Faienza, J. L. Valenti, G. Juster, G. Osmetti, K. Hayase, and J. A. Dristas: On the nature of arterial and lung calcifications induced in cattle by *Solanum glaucophyllum*. Calcif. Tissue Res. *26*, 61–64 (1978).

[P 46] Puche, R. C., A. M. Masoni, D. A. Alloatti, and E. Roveri: The antirachitic activity of *Solanum glaucophyllum* leaves. Planta Med. *40*, 378–381 (1980).

[P 47] Pulewka, P.: Die Aufklärung einer ungewöhnlichen, durch *Datura stramonium* in Brotmehl hervorgerufenen Massenvergiftung. Klin. Wochenschr. *27*, 672–674 (1949).

[P 48] Pulewka, P., M. Bühler, and B. Klumpp: Sekundenverschluss der Bronchien durch Reizgifte. Arzneimittel-Forsch. *10*, 953–955 (1960).

[P 49] Pöschke, H.-J.: Gift-Tee schon an 300 Kunden im Bundesgebiet ausgeliefert. Westfäl. Rundsch., dated 16.3.1982.

[P 50] Petričić, J. and G. Stanić: Flavonoids, saponins, tannins, and arbutin as constituents of leaves of *Viburnum tinus, V. opulus*, and *V. lantana*. Acta Pharm. Jugosl. *30*, 97–101 (1980).

[P 51] Pausanias: Description of Greece, Book X, xxxviii, 7. Translated by W. H. S. Jones, Loeb Classical Library, Heinemann, London, Harvard University Press, Cambridge, Mass., vol. 4, pp. 594–597, 1935.

[R 1] Rainer, O.: Zur Vergiftung mit rohen, grünen Bohnen (Phasinvergiftung). Med. Klinik *57*, 270–272 (1962).

[R 2] Ramstad, E.: Eine neue charakteristische mikrochemische Reaktion zum Nachweis von Schöllkraut. Pharm. Acta Helv. *16*, 15–21, 40–43 (1941).

[R 3] Rehm, S.: Die Bitterstoffe der Cucurbitaceen. Ergebn. Biol. *22*, 108–136 (1960).

[R 4] Reisch, J.: Vorkommen und biologische Wirkung des Acetylens und seiner Derivate. Pharmazie *20*, 271–275 (1965).

[R 5] Renz, J. and A. von Wartburg: Zur Chemie und Pharmakologie der Podophyllum-Glukoside und ihrer derivate. I. Mitt. Arzneimittel-Forsch. *11*, 327–333 (1961); II. Mitt. ibid. *11*, 459–469 (1961).

[R 6] Richards, H. G. H. and A. Stephens: A fatal case of laburnum seed poisoning. Med. Sci. Law *10*, 260–266 (1970).

[R 7] Riede, B.: Augenverletzung mit dem Saft der Pflanze 'Dieffenbachia seguine'. Dtsch. Gesundheitswesen *26*, 73–76 (1971).

[R 8] Ripperger, H.: Isolation and structure of cucurbitacin from *Bryonia dioica*. Tetrahedron *32*, 1567–1570 (1976).

[R 9] Ritter, S.: Personal communication, 1981.

[R 10] Roberg, M.: Über das Vorkommen und die Verteilung von Saponinen in Kräuterdrogen. Arch. Pharm. *275*, 84–103 (1937).

[R 11] Robert, G. and U. Menichini: Intossicazione voluttuaria da stramonio. Minerva Med. *69*, 763–767 (1978).

[R 12] Robson, P.: Water hemlock poisoning. Lancet *2*, 1274–1275 (1965).

[R 13] Rockoff, A. S.: Camphor dangers. Pediatrics *60*, 778 (1977).

[R 14] Rodriguez, E., G. H. N. Towers, and J. C. Mitchell: Biological activities of sesquiterpene lactones. Phytochemistry *15*, 1573–1580 (1976).

[R 15] Roe, K. E.: Terminology of hairs in the genus *Solanum*. Taxon *20*, 501–508 (1971).

[R 16] Röder, E.: Alkaloidinhaltsstoffe einiger Senecioarten. Cited from: Dtsch. Apoth. Ztg *120*, 469 (1980).

[R 17] Roggenkämper, P.: Keratopathie, hervorgerufen durch Pflanzensaft. Klin. Monatsbl. Augenheilk. *164*, 421–423 (1974).

[R 18] Romano, E., V. Russo, A. Gullo, and S. Valenti: Intossicazione da cicuta. Minerva Anestesiol. *44*, 45–48 (1978).

[R 19] Romeike, A.: Hygrin, das Hauptalkaloid in Nicandra-Warzeln. Naturwissenschaften *52*, 619 (1965).

[R 20] Romeike, A.: Über das Vorkommen von Hygrin in Wurzeln von *Nicandra physaloides* (L.) Gaertn. Pharmazie *20*, 738–739 (1965).

[R 21] Rook, A.: Plant dermatitis, the significance of variety-species sensitization. Br. J. Dermatol. *73*, 283–287 (1961).

[R 22] Rook, A. and H. T. H. Wilson: Primula dermatitis. Br. Med. J. *1*, 220–222 (1965).

[R 23] Rosenboom, H.: Gift vom Spielplatz. Stern no. 32, pp. 96–98, 1981.

[R 24] Roshchina, V. V., V. P. Solomatkin, and V. D. Roshchina: Cicutoxin as an inhibitor of electron transport in photosynthesis. Fiziologiya Rast. *27*, 704–709 (1980). Cited from: Biol. Abstr. *72*, 12 707 (1981).

[R 25] Rossiiskii, D. M.: Rhododendron as a cardiovascular remedy. Farmakol. Toksikol. *17*(4), 33–34 (1954). Cited from: Chem. Abstr. *48*, 14 125 (1954).

[R 26] Rost, E. and E. Gilg: Der Giftsumach, *Rhus toxicodendron* L., und seine Giftwirkungen. Ber. Dtsch. Pharm. Ges. *22*, 297–358 (1912).

[R 27] Rubino, M. J. and F. Davidoff: Cyanide poisoning from apricot seeds. J. Am. Med. Ass. *241*, 359 (1979).

[R 28] Runyon, R.: Toxicity of fresh poinsettia (*Euphorbia pulcherrima*) to Sprague-Dawley rats. Clin. Toxicol. *16*, 167–173 (1980).

[R 29] Rugman, F., J. Meecham, and J. Edmondson: *Mercurialis perennis* (dog's mercury) poisoning: a case of mistaken identity. Br. Med. J. *287*, 1924 (1983).

[S 1] Sachse, J. and F. Bachmann: Über die Alkaloidbestimmung in *Solanum tuberosum* L. Z. Lebensmittelunters. u. -Forsch. *141*, 262–274 (1969).

[S 2] Sakai, W. S., M. Hanson, and R. C. Jones: Raphides with barbs and grooves in *Xanthosoma sagittifolium* (Araceae). Science *178*, 314-315 (1972).

[S 3] Sakai, W. S. and M. Hanson: Mature raphid and raphid idioblast structure in plants of the edible Aroid genera *Colocasia, Alocasia* and *Xanthosoma*. Ann. Bot. *38*, 739–748 (1974).

[S 4] Samuelsson, G.: Toxische Proteine in Pflanzen der Loranthaceae, Planta Med. *13*, 453–456 (1965).

[S 5] Samuelsson, G., L. Borsub, A. L. Jayawardene, L. Falk, and S. Ziemilis: Screening of plants of the families Loranthaceae and Viscaceae for toxic proteins. Acta Pharm. Suec. *18*, 179–184 (1981).

[S 6] Sander, H.: Über *Solanum dulcamara* L. – Abbau von Spirosolanoglykosiden in reifenden Früchten. Planta Med. *11*, 23–36 (1963).

[S 7] Sands, J. M. and R. Sands: Henbane chewing. Med. J. Aust. *2*, 55–58 (1976).

[S 8] Sandusky, G. E., C. J. Fosnaught, J. B. Smith, and R. Mohan: Oak poisoning of cattle in Ohio. J. Am. Vet. Med. Ass. *171*, 627–629 (1977).

[S 9] Sayre, J. W. and S. Kaymakgalan: Cyanide poisoning from apricot seeds among children in Central Turkey. New Engl. J. Med. *270*, 1113–1115 (1964).

[S 10] Schantz, M. von: Über die Zusammensetzung des ätherischen Öles von *Ledum palustre* L. Abstracts of the 20th Meeting of the Gesellschaft für Arzneipflanzenforschung, Helsinki, July 1972.

[S 11] Scheel, B.: Gefahr am Spielplatzrand. Lübeck. Nachr. dated 23.8.1981.

[S 12] Scheerer, G.: *Sambucus racemosa* L., der Traubenholunder. Pharmazie *2*, 519–521 (1947).

[S 13] Schildknecht, H., G. Edelmann, and R. Maurer: Zur Chemie des Mezereins, des entzündlichen und cocarcinogenen Giftes aus dem Seidelbast *Daphne mezereum*. Chemikerzeitung *94*, 347–355 (1970).

[S 14] Schildknecht, H. and R. Maurer: Die Struktur des Mezereins aus der Frucht des Seidelbasts *Daphne mezereum*. Chemikerzeitung *94*, 849 (1970).

[S 15] Schier, W.: Drogenverfälschungen – ein (leider) aktuelles Thema. Dtsch. Apoth. Ztg *121*, 323–329 (1981).

[S 16] Schilcher, H.: Zyanidvergiftung durch Leinsamen? Dtsch. Ärztebl. *76*, 955–956 (1979).

[S 17] Schilling, J. and M. Zobel: Eine papierchromatographische Methode zur Solaninbestimmung in Kartoffeln und Kartoffelprodukten. Pharmazie *21*, 103–105 (1966).

[S 18] Schimmer, O., R. Beck, and U. Dietz: Phototoxizität und Photomutagenität von Furocumarinen und Furocumarindrogen bei *Chlamydomonas reinhardii*. Planta Med. *40*, 68–76 (1980).

[S 19] Schimmer, O.: Die mutagene und cancerogene Potenz von Furocumarinen. Pharm. Unser. Zeit *10*, 18–28 (1981).

[S 20] Schindler, H.: Über Acetylandromedol (Andromedotoxin) in verschiedenen Ericaceen, insbesondere in Rhododendron, und seine annähernde Bestimmung. Planta Med. *10*, 232–237 (1962).

[S 21] Schlemmer, F.: DAPI – Tätigkeitsbericht für das Jahr 1965. Dtsch. Apoth. Ztg *106*, 1463–1469 (1966).

[S 22] Schmaltz, D., M. Dateschidse, E. Hötzsch, and W. Jaensch: Untersuchungen über einige deutsche Arzneipflanzen *(Chelidonium majus)*. Hippokrates (5), 104–108 (1940).

[S 23] Schmidt, G.: Zur Frage des Nachweises und der Ausscheidung von Spartein – Tödliche Sparteinvergiftung bei einem Kleinkind. Arch. Toxicol. *19*, 244–253 (1961).

[S 24] Schmidt, H. and P. Ølholm-Larsen: Allergic contact dermatitis from croton *(Codiaeum)*. Contact Dermatitis *3*, 100 (1977).

[S 25] Schmutz, J. and T. Reichstein: Convallosid, ein stark herzwirksames Glykosid aus Semen Convallariae majalis L. Pharm. Acta Helv. *22*, 359–372 (1947).

[S 26] Schneider, G.: Pflanzliche Lectine. Pharm. Heute *2* (5/6, 7) (1977) (Supplement to Dtsch. Apoth. Ztg).

[S 27] Schneider, E.: Von der Teufelsmilch zum Antitumorwirkstoff. Dtsch. Apoth. Ztg *119*, 1436–1439 (1979).

[S 28] Schoeb, T. R. and R. J. Panciera: Blister beetle poisoning in horses. J. Am. Vet. Med. Ass. *173*, 75–77 (1978).

[S 29] Schoenemann, H.: Vergiftung mit Tee aus Arnikablüten. Münch. Med. Wochenschr. *85*, 787–788 (1938).

[S 30] Scholz, C., R. Hänsel, and C. Hille: Quantitative Dünnschichtchromatographie der Chelidonium-Hauptalkaloide. Pharm. Ztg *121*, 1571–1574 (1976).

[S 31] Schreiber, K.: Über das Vorkommen von Solasodinglykosiden in *Solanum nigrum* L. und ihre industrielle Verwertung. Planta Med. *6*, 435–439 (1958).

[S 32] Schreiber, K.: The steroid alkaloids of Solanum. In: Hawkes *et al.* (eds.), The biology and taxonomy of the Solanaceae, pp. 193–202, 1979.

[S 33] Schreiber, K. and H. Rönsch: Die Steroidalkaloide und -sapogenine chemisch unterschiedlicher Sippen von *Solanum dulcamara* L. Arch. Pharm. *298*, 285–293 (1965).

[S 34] Schreiber, W.: Jimson seed intoxication: recognition and therapy. Milit. Med. *144*, 329–332 (1979).

[S 35] Schulte, T.: Tödliche Vergiftungen mit Eibennadeln *(Taxus baccata)*. Arch. Toxicol. *34*, 153–158 (1975).

[S 36] Schulz, V.: Zyanidvergiftung. Dtsch. Ärztebl. *75*, 2757–2758 (1978).

[S 37] Schurno, A.: Beobachtung einer Vergiftung durch Beeren der tatarischen Heckenkirsche. Kinderärztl. Prax. *26*, 357–360 (1958).

[S 38] Schweizerisches Toxikologisches Informationszentrum, Zürich, Jahresberichte 1973–1979.

[S 39] Seaman, J. T.: Pyrrolizidine alkaloid poisoning of horses. Aust. Vet. J. *54*, 150 (1978).

[S 40] Seawright, A.A. and J. Hrdlicka: The oral toxicity for sheep of triterpene acids isolated from *Lantana camara*. Aust. Vet. J. *53*, 230 (1977).

[S 41] Seeliger, J.: Über eine seltene Vergiftung mit weisser Nieswurz. Arch. Toxicol. *16*, 16–18 (1956/57).

[S 42] Segelman, A. B., F. P. Segelman, J. Karliner, and R. D. Sofia: Sassafras and herb tea. J. Am. Med. Ass. *236*, 477 (1976).

[S 43] Seigler, D. S.: Plants of the northeastern United States that produce cyanogenic compounds. Econ. Bot. *30*, 395–407 (1976).

[S 44] Seigler, D. S.: The naturally occurring cyanogenic glycosides. Progr. Phytochem. *4*, 83–120 (1977).

[S 45] Seigler, D. S. and J. F. Pereira: Modernized preparation of cassave in the Llanos Orientales of Venezuela. Econ. Bot. *35*, 356–362 (1981).

[S 46] Selby, L. A., R. W. Menges, E. C. Houser, R. E. Flatt, and A. A. Case: Outbreak of swine malformations associated with the wild black cherry, *Prunus serotina*. Arch. Environ. Health *22*, 496–501 (1971).

[S 47] Sharma, S. C., O. P. Sati, and R. Chand: Constituents of the fruits of *Asparagus racemosus* Willd. Pharmazie *36*, 709 (1981).

[S 48] Sharma, O. P., H. P. S. Makkar, R. N. Pal, and S. S. Negi: Lantadene A content and toxicity of the lantana plant *(Lantana camara)* to guinea pigs. Toxicon *18*, 485–488 (1980).

[S 49] Sharma, O. P., H. P. S. Makkar, R. K. Dawra, and S. S. Negi: Hepatic and renal toxicity of lantana in the guinea pig. Toxicol. Lett. *7*, 347–351 (1981).

[S 50] Sharma, O. P., H. P. S. Makkar, R. N. Pal, and S. S. Negi: Fragility of erythrocytes in animals affected by lantana poisoning. Clin. Toxicol. *18*, 25–35 (1981).

[S 51] Shaw, D. and J. Pearn: Oleander poisoning. Med. J. Aust. *2*, 267–269 (1979).

[S 52] Sherratt, H. S. A. and S. S. Al-Bassam: Glycine in ackee poisoning. Lancet *2*, 1243 (1976).

[S 53] Shervette III, R. E., M. Schydlower, R. M. Lampe, and R. G. Fearnow: Jimson 'loco' weed abuse in adolescents. Pediatrics *63*, 520–523 (1979).

[S 54] Shutt, D. A.: The effects of plant oestrogens on animal reproduction. Endeavour *35*, 110–113 (1976).

[S 55] Siegel, R. K., P. R. Collings, and J. L. Diaz: On the use of *Tagetes lucida* and *Nicotiana rustica* as a Huichol smoking mixture: the Aztec 'yahutli' with suggestive hallucinogenic effects. Econ. Bot. *31*, 16–23 (1977).

[S 56] Siegel, R. K.: Herbal intoxication – psychoactive effects from herbal cigarettes, tea and capsules. J. Am. Med. Ass. *236*, 473–476 (1976).

[S 57] Siegers, C.-P.: I. Vergiftungen durch Pflanzen. Z. Allg. Med. *54*, 1151–1158 (1978); II. Vergiftungen durch Pilze. Ibid.

54, 1190–1195 (1978).

[S 58] Slater, G. E., B. H. Rumack, and R. G. Peterson: Podophyllin poisoning. Systemic toxicity following cutaneous application. Obstet. Gynecol. *52*, 94–96 (1978).

[S 59] Slob, A., B. Jekel, and B. de Jong: On the occurrence of tuliposides in the Liliiflorae. Phytochemistry *14*, 1997–2005 (1975).

[S 60] Slob, A. and H. Q. Varekamp: Tuliposide contents of tulip *(Tulipa)* species and cultivars during the flowering stage. Proc. K. Ned. Akad. Wetensch., ser. C *80*, 201–211 (1977).

[S 61] Smidt, N. and L. Bieder: Datura intoxication. N. Z. Med. J. *87*, 61–62 (1978).

[S 62] Smith, L. W. and C. C. J. Culvenor: Plant sources of hepatotoxic pyrrolizidine alkaloids. J. Nat. Prod. *44*, 129–152 (1981).

[S 63] Smith, M. C.: Japanese pieris poisoning in the goat. J. Am. Vet. Med. Ass. *173*, 78–79 (1978).

[S 64] Smith, M. C.: Fetal mummification in a goat due to Japanese pieris *(Pieris japonica)* poisoning. Cornell Vet. *69*, 85-87 (1979).

[S 65] Smith, R. P. and D. M. Smith: Acute ipecac poisoning. New Engl. J. Med. *265*, 523–525 (1961).

[S 66] Smolenski, S. J., A. D. Kinghorn, and M. F. Balandrin: Toxic constituents of legume forage plants. Econ. Bot. *35*, 321–355 (1981).

[S 67] Solereder, H.: Beiträge zur Anatomie der Araceen. Beih. Bot. Centralbl., Abt. I, *36*, 60–77 (1919).

[S 68] Speer, J. D., W. O. Robertson, and L. R. Schultz: Ipecacuanha poisoning. Another fatal case. Lancet *1*, 475–477 (1963).

[S 69] Spevak, Lj. and M. Soć: Dva slucaja trovanja cajem od oleanderovog lisca (Two cases of poisoning with the tea from oleander leaves). Arh. Hig. Rada Toksikol. *26*, 147–150 (1975).

[S 70] Spoerke, D. G. and A. R. Temple: Dermatitis after exposure to a garden plant *(Euphorbia myrsinites)*. Am. J. Dis. Childh. *133*, 28–29 (1979).

[S 71] Spoerke, D. G. and S. E. Spoerke: Three cases of *Zigadenus* (death camas) poisoning. Vet. Hum. Toxicol. *21*, 346–347 (1979).

[S 72] Sprecher, E.: Vergiftung durch Eicheln? Dtsch. Med. Wochenschr. *104*, 1470 (1979).

[S 73] Stahl, E. and U. Kaltenbach: Die basischen Inhaltsstoffe des Aronstabes *(Arum maculatum* L.). Arch. Pharm. *298*, 599–604 (1965).

[S 74] Stahl, E.: Strychnin in indischen und afrikanischen Schmuckketten. Pharm. Ztg *117*, 1107–1111 (1972).

[S 75] Stahl, E.: Vergiftungen mit Rizinus-Samen – eine aktuelle Warnung. Dtsch. Apoth. Ztg *117*, 465–467 (1977).

[S 76] Stahl, N., A. Weinberger, D. Benjamin, and J. Pinkhas: Case report – Fatal colchicine poisoning in a boy with familial Mediterranean fever. Am. J. Med. Sci. *278*, 77–81 (1979).

[S 77] Stallbaumer, M.: Onion poisoning in a dog. Vet. Rec. *108*, 523–524 (1981).

[S 78] Starreveld, E. and C. E. Hope: Cicutoxin poisoning (water hemlock). Neurology 25, 730–734 (1975).

[S 79] Steel, E. G., D. A. Witzel, and A. Blanks: Acquired coagulation factor X activity deficiency connected with *Hymenoxys odorata* DC. (Compositae), bitterweed poisoning in sheep. Am. J. Vet. Res. 37, 1383–1386 (1976).

[S 80] Stein, Z. L. G.: Pokeweed-induced gastroenteritis. Am. J. Hosp. Pharm. 36, 1303 (1979).

[S 81] Steiner, M. and E. S. von Kamienski: Der papierchromatographische Nachweis primärer, sekundärer und tertiärer Alkylamine in Pflanzen. Naturwissenschaften 40, 483 (1953).

[S 82] Stermirtz, F. R. and G. S. Yost: Analysis and characterization of nitro compounds from *Astragalus* species. In: Keeler *et al.* (eds.), Effects of poisonous plants on livestock, pp. 371–378, 1978.

[S 83] Steyn, D. G.: The toxicity of bitter-tasting cucurbitaceous vegetables (vegetable marrow, watermelons, etc.) for man. S. Afr. Med. J. 24, 713–715 (1950).

[S 84] Stillman, A. E., R. Huxtable, P. Consroe, P. Kohnen, and S. Smith: Hepatic veno-occlusive disease due to pyrrolizidine *(Senecio)* poisoning in Arizona. Gastroenterology 73, 349–352 (1977).

[S 85] Stirpe, F., R. F. Legg, L. J. Onyon, P. Ziska, and H. Franz: Inhibition of protein synthesis by a toxic lectin from *Viscum album* L. (mistletoe). Biochem. J. 190, 843–845 (1980).

[S 86] Stoewsand, G. S., J. L. Anderson, and R. C. Lamb: Cyanide content of apricot kernels. J. Food Sci. 40, 1107 (1975).

[S 87] Stöber, M., H.-P. Ziegler, and K. von Benten: Beitrag zur Eichelvergiftung des Rhindes – Krankheitsfälle im Herbst 1973. Dtsch. Tierärztl. Wochenschr. 81, 155–161 (1974).

[S 88] Stone, R. P. and W. J. Collins: *Euphorbia pulcherrima:* toxicity to rats. Toxicon 9, 301–302 (1971).

[S 89] Stout, G. H., B. M. Malofsky, and V. F. Stout: Phytolaccagenin: a light atom X-ray structure proof using chemical information. J. Am. Chem. Soc. 86, 957–958 (1964).

[S 90] Stout, G. H., W. G. Balkenhol, M. Poling, and G. L. Hickernell: The isolation and structure of daphnetoxin, the poisonous principle of *Daphne* species. J. Am. Chem. Soc. 92, 1070–1071 (1970).

[S 91] Stowe, C. M., G. Fangmann, and D. Trampel: Schefflera toxicosis in a dog. J. Am. Vet. Med. Ass. 167, 74 (1975).

[S 92] Straub, W.: Kontaktdermatitis nach Tragen neuer Hüte. Münch. Med. Wochenschr. 94, 598–599 (1952).

[S 93] Streicher, E.: Akutes Nierenversagen und Ikterus nach einer Vergiftung mit Rhabarberblättern. Dtsch. Med. Wochenschr. 89, 2379–2381 (1964).

[S 94] Strel'nikova, E. E.: Qualitative and quantitative determination of alkaloids in *Empetrum nigrum.* Uch. Zap., Kemerov. Gos. Pedagog. Inst. (10), 66–68 (1969). Cited from: Chem. Abstr. 75, 85 153 (1971).

[S 95] Stuart, B. P., R. J. Cole, and H. S. Grosser: Cocklebur (*Xanthium strumarium* L. var. *strumarium*) intoxication in swine: review and redefinition of the toxic principle. Vet. Pathol. 18, 368–383 (1981).

[S 96] Sullivan, J. B., B. H. Rumack, H. Thomas, R. G. Peterson, and P. Bryson: Pennyroyal oil poisoning and hepatotoxicity. J. Am. Med. Ass. 242, 2873–2874 (1979).

[S 97] O'Sullivan, B. M. and J. A. Goodwin: An outbreak of *Swainsona* poisoning in horses. Aust. Vet. J. 53, 446–447 (1977).

[S 98] Sunell, L. A. and P. L. Healey: Distribution of calcium oxalate crystal idioblasts in corms of taro *(Colocasia esculenta).* Am. J. Bot. 66, 1029–1032 (1979).

[S 99] Suzuki, M.: Studies on the irritating substance of *Pinellia ternata* Breitenbach (Araceae). Arzneimittel-Forsch. 19, 1307–1309 (1969).

[S 100] Swart, F. W. J.: Vergiftiging van geiten door hondspeterselie. Tijdschr. Diergeneesk. 100, 989–990 (1975).

[S 101] Swinscow, D.: Accidental poisoning of young children. Arch. Dis. Childh. 28, 26–29 (1953).

[S 102] Szaufer, M., Z. Kowalewski, and J. D. Phillipson: Chelidonine from *Symphoricarpos albus.* Phytochemistry 17, 1446–1447 (1978).

[S 103] Szendrei, K., I. Novak, M. Bathory, E. Minker, M. Koltai, J. Reisch, and G. Buzas: Kondensierte Aromaten als Inhaltsstoffe des Rhizoms von *Tamus communis.* Pharmazie 23, 211–212 (1968).

[S 104] Stahl, E.: Rosa Pfeffer, ein gefährliches exotisches Gewürz? Dtsch. Apoth. Ztg 122, 337–340 (1982).

[S 105] Sakakibara, J., N. Shirai, and T. Kaiya: Diterpene glycosides from *Pieris japonica.* Phytochemistry 20, 1744–1745 (1981).

[S 106] Stengl, P., H. Wiedenfeld, and E. Röder: Lebertoxische Pyrrolizidinalkaloide in Symphytum-Präparaten. Dtsch. Apoth. Ztg 122, 851–855 (1982).

[S 107] Scholz, H., S. Kascha, and H. Zingerle: Atropin-Vergiftung durch 'Gesundheitstee'. Fortschr. Med. 98, 1525–1526 (1980).

[S 108] Sahai, M. and A. B. Ray: Secotropane alkaloids of *Physalis peruviana.* J. Org. Chem. 45, 3265–3268 (1980).

[S 109] Sharma, O. P., H. P. S. Makkar, R. K. Dawra, and S. S. Negi: A review of the toxicity of *Lantana camara* (Linn.) in animals. Clin. Toxicol. 18, 1077–1094 (1981).

[S 110] Šantavý, F.: Papaveraceae alkaloids. In: Manske, R. H. F. (ed.), The alkaloids. Chemistry and physiology, Academic Press, New York, London, vol. 12, pp. 333–454, 1970; ibid., vol. 17, pp. 385–544, 1979.

[S 111] Sherry, C. J., L. E. Ray, and R. E. Herron: The pharmacological effects of a ligroin extract of nutmeg *(Myristica fragrans).* J. Ethnopharmacol. 6, 61–66 (1982).

[T 1] Tafelkruyer, J. and W. G. van Ketel: Sensitivity to *Codiaeum variegatum.* Contact Dermatitis 2, 288–296 (1976).

[T 2] Tandon, B. N., H. D. Tandon, R. K. Tandon, M. Narndranathan, and Y. K. Yoshi: An epidemic of veno-occlusive disease of liver in Central India. Lancet 2, 271–272 (1976).

[T 3] Tattje, D. H. E. and R. Bos: Composition of essential oil of *Ledum palustre.* Planta Med. 41, 303–307 (1981).

[T 4] Telek, L., H. Delpin, and E. Cabanillas: *Solanum mammosum* as a source of solasodine in the lowland tropics. Econ. Bot. 31, 120–128 (1977).

[T 5] Teuscher, E.: Pharmazeutische Biologie, F. Vieweg, Braunschweig/Wiesbaden, 549 pp., 1979.

[T 6] Tewari, S. N.: Forensisch-toxikologische Isolierung, Identifizierung und Mikrobestimmung von Datura-Alkaloiden mit Hilfe der Papierchromatographie. Arch. Kriminol. 140, 61–71 (1967).

[T 7] Tewari, S. N.: Zur Isolierung und Identifizierung der Glykoside von *Cerbera thevetia* (gelbem Oleander) in gerichtsmedizinischem Sektionsmaterial. Arch. Kriminol. 141, 149–156 (1968).

[T 8] Thieme, H. and H.-J. Winkler: Die Phenolglykoside der Ericaceen. Pharmazie 26, 235–243 (1971).

[T 9] Thomas, H. and H. Budzikiewicz: Ilex-Lacton, ein Bisnormonoterpen neuartiger Struktur aus *Ilex aquifolium.* Phytochemistry 19, 1866–1868 (1980).

[T 10] Thomas, H. and H. Budzikiewicz: Inhaltsstoffe der Früchte von *Ilex aquifolium* L. Z. Pflanzenphysiol. 99, 271–276 (1980).

[T 11] Thomson, G. W. and I. K. Barker: Japanese yew *(Taxus cuspidata)* poisoning in cattle. Can. Vet. J. 19, 320–321 (1978).

[T 12] Tidwell, R. H., J. L. Beal, D. G. Patel, A. Tye, and P. N. Patil: A study of the cyanogenic content and toxicity of the fruit of selected species of *Cotoneaster.* Econ. Bot. 24, 47–50 (1970).

[T 13] Tittel, G., H. Hink, and H. Wagner: Quantitative Bestimmung der Pyrrolizidinalkaloide in Symphyti Radix durch HPLC. Planta Med. 37, 1–8 (1979).

[T 14] Tolokneva, A. Z.: Cardiac action of various *Rhododendron* species. Farmakol. Toksikol. 19(1), 39–43 (1956), Cited from: Chem. Abstr. 50, 11 616 (1956).

[T 15] Towers, G. H. N.: Contact hypersensitivity and photodermatitis evoked by Compositae. In: Kinghorn, A. D. (ed.), Toxic plants, pp. 171–183, 1979.

[T 16] Towers, G. H. N.: Photosensitizers from plants and their photodynamic action. Progr. Phytochem. 6, 183–202 (1980).

[T 17] Towers, G. H. N., E. A. Graham, I. D. Spenser, and Z. Abramowski: Phototoxic furanoquinolines of the Rutaceae. Planta Med. 41, 136–142 (1981).

[T 18] Trestrail, J. H. and M. E. Spartz: Castor and camphorated oil confusion and its toxic results. Clin. Toxicol. 9, 30 (1976).

[T 19] Trunzler, G.: Ein weiterer Beitrag zur Pharmakologie und Toxikologie des Andromedotoxins, einer neuen blutdrucksenkenden Substanz im pflanzlichen Antihypertonicum Rauwoplant®. Aus unserer Arbeit. Mitt. Forsch. Prax. *2*(10), 1–8 (1958).

[T 20] Tschiapke, L., G. Balansard, and P. Bernard: Chemical and toxicological study of *Anchomanes difformis*. Planta Med. *36*, 257–258 (1979); Herba Hung. *19*(1), 55–63 (1980).

[T 21] Turdiev, I.: Poisoning of pigs by *Psoralea drupacea* seeds. Svinovodstvo (U.S.S.R.) *4*, 35 (1974).

[T 22] Tyler, V. E., L. R. Brady, and J. E. Robbers: Pharmacognosy, 8th ed., Lea & Febiger, Philadelphia, 520 pp., 1981.

[T 23] Thorp, F. and G. S. Garshfield: Onion poisoning in horses. J. Am. Vet. Med. Ass. *94*, 52–53 (1939).

[U 1] Uchida, T., M. Yamaizumi, E. Mekada, Y. Okada, M. Tsuda, T. Kurokawa, and Y. Sugino: Reconstitution of hybrid toxin from fragment A of diphtheria toxin and a subunit of *Wistaria floribunda* lectin. J. Biol. Chem. *253*, 6307–6310 (1978).

[U 2] Unger, W.: Radix Belladonnae und Radix Sambuci Ebuli. Arch. Pharm. *263*, 606–611 (1925).

[U 3] Unterhalt, B.: Toxische Aminosäuren und Proteine in Pflanzen. Dtsch. Apoth. Ztg *120*, 1093–1096 (1980).

[U 4] Urban, G.: Pfaffenhütchen-Vergiftung. Samml. Vergiftungsfällen (Arch. Toxikol.) *13*, 27–32 (1943/44).

[V 1] Vallance, W. B.: Pennyroyal poisoning. A fatal case. Lancet *2*, 850–851 (1955).

[V 2] Váradi, J.: Die Identifizierung von Belladonna-Blättern und -Tinktur auf Grund der Fluoreszenz der Chrysatropasäure. Gyógyszerészet *3*, 251 (1959). Cited from: Pharm. Zentralh. *100*, 176 (1961).

[V 3] Verspyck Mijnssen, G. A. W.: Pathogenesis and causative agent of 'tulip finger'. Br. J. Dermatol. *81*, 737–745 (1969).

[V 4] Vlad, L., A. Munta, and I. G. Crisan: Digitalis-ähnliche kardiotonische Wirkung der Extrakte von Viburnum-Arten. Planta Med. *31*, 228–231 (1977).

[V 5] Völksen, W.: Zur Kenntnis der Inhaltsstoffe und arzneilichen Verwendung einiger Physalisarten – *Ph. alkekengi, Ph. franchetii, Ph. peruviana* u.a. Dtsch. Apoth. Ztg *117*, 1199–1203 (1977).

[V 6] Vogel, S. N., T. R. Sultan, and R. P. ten Eyck: Cyanide poisoning. Clin. Toxicol. *18*, 367–383 (1981).

[V 7] Vohora, S. B., I. Kumar, S. A. Shah, and M. S. Y. Khan: Effects of biflavonoids of *Taxus baccata* on the central nervous system. Indian J. Med. Res. *71*, 815–820 (1980).

[V 8] Vollmer, H. and M. Roberg: Vergiftung durch Stechapfelblätter. Samml. Vergiftungsfällen (Arch. Toxikol.) *13*, 189–196 (1943/44).

[V 9] Vincieri, F. F., S. A. Coran, and M. Bambagiotti: Composition of the *Oenanthe aquatica* essential oil. Planta Med. *20*, 101–112 (1976).

[V 10] Vincieri, F. F., S. A. Coran, V. Gianellini, and M. Bambagiotti: Isolation and structural elucidation of *Oenanthe aquatica* (L.) fruit C_{15}-polyacetylene hydrocarbons. Chem. Ber. *114*, 468–476 (1981).

[V 11] Vale, J. A. and T. J. Meredith: In: Vale, J. A. and T. J. Meredith (eds.), Poisoning. Diagnosis and treatment, Update Books, London, Dordrecht, Boston, chapters 1, 2, and 30 (pp. 1–8, 9–12, and 193–201), 1981.

[V 12] Vogt, D. D.: Absinthium: a nineteenth-century drug of abuse. J. Ethnopharmacol. *4*, 337–342 (1981).

[W 1] Wagner, H.-J.: 3 Todesfälle durch Intoxikation (Invertseife) oder durch anaphylaktischen Schock (Rosskastanienextrakt). Arch. Toxicol. *21*, 83–88 (1965).

[W 2] Wagner, H.: Rauschgift-Drogen, Springer, Berlin, Heidelberg, New York, 142 pp., 1969.

[W 3] Wagner, H., U. Neidhardt, and G. Tittel: DC- und HPLC-Analyse der Pyrrolizidin-N-oxid-Alkaloide von Symphyti Radix. Planta Med. *41*, 232–239 (1981).

[W 4] Waldschmidt-Leitz, E. and L. Keller: Über Ricin: Reinigung und Differenzierung der Wirkungen. Hoppe-Seyler's Z. Physiol. Chem. *350*, 503–509 (1969).

[W 5] Walter, W. G.: Dieffenbachia toxicity. J. Am. Med. Ass. *201*, 140–141 (1967).

[W 6] Walter, W. G. and P. N. Khanna: Chemistry of the Aroids. I. *Dieffenbachia seguine, amoena* and *picta*. Econ. Bot. *26*, 364–372 (1972).

[W 7] Wasserman, R. H.: The nature and mechanism of action of the calcinogenic principle of *Solanum malacoxylon* and *Cestrum diurnum*, and a comment on *Triseteum flavescens*. In: Keeler *et al.* (eds.), Effects of poisonous plants on livestock, pp. 545–553, 1978.

[W 8] Wattendorf, J.: Gefährliche Schönheiten: Aronstabgewächse im Zimmer. Bull. Ass. Am. Jard. Bot. Fribourg *13*(19), 1–3 (1980).

[W 9] Waud, R. A.: A Digitalis-like action of extracts made from holly. J. Pharmacol. Exp. Ther. *45*, 279 (1932).

[W 10] Weber, U.: Über zwei als Heilpflanzen benutzte Araceen: die ostasiatische *Pinellia ternata* (Thunb.) Breitenb. und das einheimische *Arum maculatum*. Süddtsch. Apoth. Ztg *82*, 295–297, 303–304 (1942).

[W 11] Wehmer, C.: Die Pflanzenstoffe, 2nd ed., G. Fischer, Jena, 2 vols. + supplement vol., 1511 + 244 pp., 1929–1935.

[W 12] Weil, A. T.: Nutmeg as a narcotic. Econ. Bot. *19*, 194–217 (1965).

[W 13] Weimark, G. and E. Nilsson: Phototoxicity in *Heracleum sphondylium*. Planta Med. *38*, 97–111 (1980).

[W 14] White, J. W. and M. L. Riethof: The composition of honey. III. Detection of acetylandromedol in toxic honeys. Arch. Biochem. Biophys. *79*, 165–167 (1959).

[W 15] Williams, M. C., F. R. Stermitz, and R. D. Thomas: Nitro compounds in *Astragalus* species. Phytochemistry *14*, 2306–2308 (1975).

[W 16] Williams, M. C. and R. C. Barneby: The occurrence of nitro-toxins in Old World and South American *Astragalus* (Fabaceae). Brittonia *29*, 327–331 (1977).

[W 18] Williams, M. C., L. F. James, and B. O. Bond: Emory milkvetch (*Astragalus emoryanus* var. *emoryanus*) poisoning in chicks, sheep, and cattle. Am. J. Vet. Res. *40*, 403–406 (1979).

[W 19] Willuhn, G.: Untersuchungen zur chemischen Differenzierung bei *Solanum dulcamara* L. – Der Steroidgehalt in Früchten verschiedener Entwicklungsstadien der Tomatidenol- und Soladulcidin-Sippe. Planta Med. *15*, 58–73 (1967).

[W 20] Willuhn, G.: Untersuchungen zur chemischen Differenzierung bei *Solanum dulcamara* L. – Der Steroidgehalt in Früchten der Solasodin-Sippe. Planta Med. *16*, 462–466 (1968).

[W 21] Willuhn, G.: Neue Ergebnisse der Arnikaforschung. Pharm. Unser. Zeit *10*, 1–7 (1981).

[W 22] Winek, C. L., J. Butala, S. P. Shanor, and F. W. Fochtman: Toxicology of poinsettia. Clin. Toxicol. *13*, 27–45 (1978).

[W 23] Wirth, W. and C. Gloxhuber: Toxikologie – für Ärzte, Naturwissenschaftler und Apotheker, 3rd ed., G. Thieme, Stuttgart, New York, 414 pp., 1981.

[W 24] Wissner, W. and H. Kating: Botanische und phytochemische Untersuchungen an den europäischen und kleinasiatischen Arten der Guttung *Helleborus*. Planta Med. *26*, 128–143, 228–249, 364–374 (1974).

[W 25] Wissner, W. and H. Kating: Untersuchungen über die Hellebrinführung der unterirdischen Organe von Helleborus-Arten. Planta Med. *20*, 344–349 (1971).

[W 26] Withers, L. M., F. R. Cole, and R. B. Nelson: Water-hemlock poisoning. New Engl. J. Med. *281*, 566 (1969).

[W 27] Witzel, D. A., L. P. Jones, and G. W. Ivie: Pathology of subacute bitterweed (*Hymenoxys odorata*) poisoning in sheep. Vet. Pathol. *14*, 73–78 (1977).

[W 28] Witzel, D. A., G. W. Ivie, and J. W. Dollahite: Mammalian toxicity of helenalin, the toxic principle of *Helenium microcephalum* DC. (smallhead sneezeweed). Am. J. Vet. Res. *37*, 859–861 (1976).

[W 29] Wöhlbier, W. and S. Beckmann: Über die Inhaltsstoffe des Sumpfschachtelhalms (*Equisetum palustre*). Chem. Ber. *83*, 310–314 (1950).

[W 30] Wolff, K.: Psoriasis und PUVA. Dtsch. Med. Wochenschr. *104*, 1543–1546 (1979).

[W 31] Wolfson, S. L. and T. W. G. Solomons: Poisoning by fruit of *Lantana camara*. Am. J. Dis. Childh. *107*, 173–176 (1964).

[W 32] Woo, W. S. and S. S. Kang: Triterpenes from the berries of *Phytolacca americana*. J. Nat. Prod. *43*, 510–513 (1980).

[W 33] Woynarowski, J. M. and J. Konopa: Interaction between DNA and viscotoxin: cytotoxic basic polypeptides from *Viscum album*. Hoppe-Seyler's Z. Physiol. Chem. *361*, 1535–1546 (1980).

[W 34] Worthington, T. R., E. P. Nelson, and M. J. Bryant: Toxicity of thornapple (*Datura stramonium* L.) seeds to the pig. Vet. Rec. *108*, 208–211 (1981).

[Y 1] Yeoh, H. H. and Y. Y. Oh: Cyanide content of cassava *(Manihot esculenta)*. Malays. Agric. J. *52*, 24–28 (1979).

[Y 2] Yoshihira, K., M. Fukuoka, M. Kuroyanagi, S. Natori, M. Umeda, T. Morohoshi, M. Enomoto, and M. Saito: Chemical and toxicological studies on bracken fern, *Pteridium aquilinum* var. *latinusculum*. I. Introduction, extraction and fractionation of constituents, and toxicological studies including carcinogenicity tests. Chem. Pharm. Bull. *26*, 2346–2364 (1978).

[Z 1] Zipf, K.: Vergiftungen durch Rauschbeeren. Samml. Vergiftungsfällen (Arch. Toxikol.) *13*, 139–140 (1943/44).

[Z 2] Zymalkowski, F.: Toxine und Triterpene aus *Rhododendron ponticum*. Dtsch. Apoth. Ztg *109*, 1571 (1969).

[Z 3] Zymalkowski, F., P. Pachaly, and S. auf dem Keller: Die Bestimmung von Acetylandromedol (Grayanotoxin I) in Extrakten von *Rhododendron ponticum*. Planta Med. *17*, 8–13 (1969).

7. Index

Note: English plant names which have been taken from the list of recommended names published by the Botanical Society of the British Isles are distinguished by an asterisk. See the translator's note on p.9.

Page numbers in **bold face** refer to main entries. Those in *italics* refer to pages on which there are figures or, in the case of chemical substances, structures.